From Chapter 1, "By Way of Introduction":

"The orientation of this book is strongly biased in two directions; it is scientific, and it is psychological. A scientific study of language, as opposed to a speculative discussion, begins with direct observations of communicating individuals and searches for the relation of these observations to the existing body of scientific knowledge. There exist many speculations of a literary or philosophical nature that are interesting and stimulate the imagination; unless these speculations lead to scientific observations and generalizations, they are not discussed here. Rejecting opinions in favor of facts helps to reduce this vast topic to manageable proportions. The psychological bias restricts the discussion to the effects of language on the behavior of the individual. Psychology is the science of behavior. Our present interest is not in language as one of the social graces, but as a kind of cooperative human behavior."

GEORGE A. MILLER is Professor of Psychology at Harvard University.

Language and Communication

George A. Miller

McGraw-Hill Book Company, Inc.
New York
Toronto
London

LANGUAGE AND COMMUNICATION

First published as a McGraw-Hill Paperback in 1963.

42001

PREFACE

This manuscript was begun in the summer of 1946, when the author first tried to select a text for an undergraduate course entitled The Psychology of Speech and Communication. No text could be found. The choice was between assigning six or seven different books or no book at all. This annoyance provided a stimulus. Now, five years and two mimeographed versions later, the response to this stimulus has been completed. The outcome is a book aimed at upper-class undergraduate or graduate courses in the psychology of communication.

Communication, if it is anything at all, is a social event. The spread of information through a group of people is one of the most important social events that can occur. When one tries to assemble the facts about this important social event, however, the data come from all fields of science. The diversity of sources has made the job an exacting one. One is never certain that something of vital importance is not hiding in an obscure transaction of a mathematical, philological, phonetic, sociological, anthropological, philosophical, or engineering society. The author does not want to suggest that he has either read all this literature or evaluated it correctly. This text is not an encyclopedia of linguistics. There are a lot of facts here, but certainly not all of them.

The purpose was to pull together in one book the more important approaches to the study of communicative behavior. In an introductory and necessarily superficial way the book tries to suggest the breadth of the spectrum of linguistic studies. These various approaches are discussed in terms that make sense to a modern psychologist.

The bias is behavioristic—not fanatically behavioristic, but certainly tainted by a preference. There does not seem to be a more scientific kind of bias, or, if there is, it turns out to be behaviorism after all. The careful reader will discover occasional subjective lapses. Undoubtedly in these instances, a scientific approach is possible, but the author was unable to find one or think of one. The argument nonetheless goes as far down the behavioristic path as one can clearly see the way. It is necessary to be explicit about this behavioristic bias, for there is much talk in the pages that follow about patterns and organizations. Psychological interest in patterning is traditionally subjective, but not necessarily so. Discussion of the patterning of symbols and the influences of context run through the manuscript like clotheslines on which the variegated laundry of language and communication is hung out to dry. It is not pleasant to think that these clotheslines must be made from the sand of subjectivity.

It is a pleasant chore to recall help received from others. Professor C. T. Morgan deserves the reader's gratitude for his corrections of many obscurities and some downright mistakes. Professor S. S. Stevens' dogged persistence as an editor and critic made it possible to avoid some of the stylistic hazards an author can put in the reader's way. Doctor J. G. Beebe-Center has taken some of the arguments seriously enough to answer them with criticism and encouragement. Doctor D. A. Ramsdell has never tired of contending that language is even more complicated than this book pretends to find it. Doctor M. R. Rosenzweig gave valuable criticisms of the first draft, Doctor R. L. Solomon made numerous improvements in Chap. 9, and Professor B. F. Skinner was kind enough to read Chap. 8. Doctors F. C. Frick, E. B. Newman, and J. C. R. Licklider scuttled many of the author's thoughtless thoughts before they could become embarrassing in less congenial gatherings. Professor Roman Jakobson helped to reduce the number of linguistic blunders, and Doctor Yehoshua Bar-Hillel provided similar advice on several points of logic. The most valued critics, however, have been the undergraduates whose examination papers were faithful mirrors of their teacher's inadequacies. Against all these friendly critics is balanced the one person who was never critical, who typed four versions of the manuscript and mimeographed two, and who had persistent faith that the job was worth doing. Students and colleagues were helpful, but without the unwavering interest and industry of Katherine James Miller, the job would not have been done.

Some of the writing was done while the author held a position in the Psycho-Acoustic Laboratory. Good use was made of the laboratory's secretarial, drafting, and photographic facilities. Consequently, this book appears as PNR-100 from the Psycho-Acoustic Laboratory, Harvard University, under contract with the United States Navy, Office of Naval Research (Contract N5ori-76, Project NR142-201), and reproduction for any purpose of the United States government is permitted.

Acknowledgments

For the quotations used at the beginnings of chapters, the author wishes to make grateful acknowledgment to the following sources: Houghton Mifflin Company, for the quotation in Chap. 4, from G. K. Zipf, *The Psycho-biology of Language*, 1935, p. 17; George Allen & Unwin, Ltd., for the quotation in Chap. 5, from Bertrand Russell, *Introduction to Mathematical Philosophy*, 1919, p. 55; The Macmillan Company, for the quotation in Chap. 9, from Sigmund Freud, *Psychopathology of Everyday Life*, 1914; Anderson & Ritchie, for the quotation in Chap. 10, from Aldous Huxley, *Words and Their Meanings*, 1940, pp. 8–9. Oxford University Press and Mrs. A. N. Whitehead, for the quotation in Chap. 11, from A. N. Whitehead, *An Introduction to Mathematics*,

1939, pp. 59, 61; Prentice-Hall, for the quotation in Chap. 12, from C. W. Morris, *Signs, Language and Behavior*, 1946, p. 214.

For permission to quote and reproduce figures, the author makes grateful acknowledgment to the following: American Institute of Physics; *American Journal of Psychology;* American Psychological Association; Anderson & Ritchie; *Ann. Otol. etc., St. Louis;* Beacon House; *Bell System Technical Journal;* Bell Telephone Laboratories; Bureau of Publications, Teachers College, Columbia University; Cambridge University Press; *Character and Personality;* Columbia University Press; The Commonwealth Fund; Duke University Press; *Genetic Psychology Monographs;* Harper & Brothers; Harvard University Press; William Heinemann, Publishers; Henry Holt and Company; Houghton Mifflin Company; *Journal of the Acoustical Society of America; Journal of Applied Psychology; Journal of Educational Psychology; Journal of Experimental Psychology; Journal of General Psychology; Journal of Psychology; Journal of Speech and Hearing Disorders;* The Journal Press; *Language Monographs;* H. and L. Lieber; Linguistic Society of America; The Macmillan Company; C. K. Ogden; Oxford University Press; *The Physical Review;* Prentice-Hall; *Psychological Monographs; Quarterly Journal of Experimental Psychology; Sociometry;* University of Chicago Press; University of Minnesota Press; University of Pittsburgh Press; D. Van Nostrand; Warwick and York, Inc., Publishers; John Wiley & Sons, Inc.

GEORGE A. MILLER

CAMBRIDGE, MASS.
July, 1951

PREFACE TO REVISED EDITION

I have taken advantage of this re-issue of the book to make several minor corrections in the text. In general, however, I have not attempted to introduce new material or to soften the behavioristic bias that characterized the original text.

GEORGE A. MILLER

CAMBRIDGE, MASS.
January, 1963

CONTENTS

FOREWORD TO THE TEACHER

Since few courses in language and communication are currently offered in departments of psychology, a few words of advice may prove helpful to psychologists who contemplate introducing such a course.

The first point concerns the order in which the subject matter is introduced. Some experimentation has led to the conclusion that there are two satisfactory orders. One is to begin with the molar, social phenomena of communication and then to proceed by more and more detailed analysis to the molecular facts of perception and phonetics. This order has the advantage of catching the student's interest initially and of keeping fairly good morale. The second possible order is exactly the reverse of the first and is the order adopted in this book. Proceeding from the detailed to the general, from the dull to the interesting, costs something in student enthusiasm. There are two reasons for paying the price. The first is that for most students language is a magical and subjective affair. It is not easy for the beginner to think scientifically, objectively, about language and communication. If a course of this sort is to have any permanent effect upon the student, it will probably be in the replacement of this magical attitude by a more scientific and reasonable one. The best way to introduce this kind of thinking is in terms of phonetics, perception, and statistics. Then when the more highly personalized functions of language are introduced, there is far less resistance to a continuation of this attitude.

The second reason for beginning at the molecular level is that we know better what we are talking about. The percentage of speculation is much lower for the discussion of phonetics than it is for the discussion of propaganda. As a consequence of this better factual support, it is possible to outline certain basic concepts about communication in a relatively compelling way. Once these concepts are established as valid in the regions where the evidence is well known, it is then much easier to generalize them for regions where the evidence is yet to be gathered. Thus the detailed study of the mechanical parts of communication can provide a firm foundation for the interpretation of more ambiguous subjects. The opposite approach, unfortunately, provides only the most ephemeral basis for the perceptual and phonetic studies and encourages students to waste too much time resisting ideas they cannot fully understand.

There is also a certain historical justification for beginning with phonetics and perception. Our knowledge of language and communication has grown in that order. Studies of the social aspects of communication are recent innovations, whereas the perceptual processes have been of interest since the earliest psychological inquiries.

With a little effort the student can be helped over this initial barrier. Demonstrations are most valuable. Some demonstrations that have proved simple and instructive are: (1) recording breathing during speech and during quiet, (2) displaying speech waves on a cathode-ray oscilloscope, (3) administering some standard audiometric test, (4) constructing passages at different orders of approximation to English by having members of the class add successive words. Many other demonstrations are possible, depending upon the facilities available to the instructor. The effects of filtering, masking, or otherwise distorting phonographically recorded speech always provide an interesting period if the electronic gadgetry is at hand. In addition to demonstrations, the standard devices of motion pictures and slides are also useful.

In later sections of the course there are numerous verbal learning experiments that make interesting demonstrations. Few instructors will want to miss the chance of demonstrating the distortions of testimony or the natural growth of rumor, for these have considerable appeal to most students. If the projection lantern can be equipped with a reasonably good camera shutter, tachistoscopic demonstrations can be introduced.

With all the devices of visual education, however, there are still sections of the course that students will not understand until they have actually worked with the materials themselves. The simple distinction between types and tokens is usually difficult until the student has actually counted words in a passage and computed some simple type-token ratios. This is conveniently done in the form of a homework problem. Other assignments that have proved valuable are: (1) translating from phonetic notation into ordinary English, (2) computing the readability of three or four short passages, (3) outlining procedures for teaching certain specific words to a young child, (4) collecting rumors and the relevant data about them.

The book can be divided into two parts, the first including Chaps. 1 through 5, and the second including Chaps. 6 through 12. Courses for students with backgrounds in linguistics and in the engineering sciences should emphasize the first part. Courses for students in psychology and sociology should emphasize the second part. It is not advisable, however, to delete the first five chapters, for they develop several ideas about amount of information and redundancy that are used in the last seven chapters. In general, terms are defined explicitly the first time they are introduced, and not thereafter.

Most teachers will find that they are able to lecture far beyond the content of the text in several of the chapters, but few will be able to do so for every chapter. The discussion of the mathematical theory of information is apt to require work by teacher and student alike. This theory should be studied in the original form in the book by Shannon and Weaver, *The Mathematical Theory of Communication*. Chapters by Licklider and Miller in S. S. Stevens' *Hand-*

book of Experimental Psychology may also prove useful. Although this theory has many implications for psychology, it is relatively new and unfamiliar. In graduate seminars these references are suitable for student reports. A good background for lectures on acoustic phonetics can be obtained from the well-illustrated book by Potter, Kopp, and Green, *Visible Speech*, and Bloch and Trager, in their *Outline of Linguistic Analysis*, provide an excellent orientation toward physiological phonetics. On the perception of speech the final section of Fletcher, *Speech and Hearing*, though now somewhat out of date, is still the best thing available. Armed with these references, the lecturer need have little fear of misinforming his students on these relatively technical subjects.

The subject of language and communication is at least as broad as the subject of psychology itself. In many respects, therefore, a course in the psychology of communication resembles an introductory course in general psychology. The principal difference is that the examples are drawn from human verbal behavior. With this specialization and with somewhat more sophisticated students it is possible to go into more detail, but anyone who has offered a broad introductory course in psychology will have little difficulty preparing lectures on language and communication.

Chapter 1

BY WAY OF INTRODUCTION

> "When *I* use a word," Humpty Dumpty said in rather a scornful tone, "it means just what I choose it to mean—neither more nor less."
>
> "The question is," said Alice, "whether you *can* make words mean so many different things."
>
> "The question is," said Humpty Dumpty, "which is to be master—that's all."
>
> —Lewis Carroll

The object of this book is to summarize for students of psychology the results of scientific studies of language and communication. These studies have been made by men of widely differing backgrounds and interests and for diverse and often unrelated purposes. Communication is so pervasively important in all walks of life that every branch of the social sciences is concerned with it, studies it, and adds to the general fund of knowledge about it. The beginning student is often overwhelmed by the variety of forms that the study of communication can assume and finds it quite difficult to reconcile one with another or to develop any well-rounded evaluation of the subject as a whole. He needs an introductory orientation to this heterogeneous field of knowledge. It is this need which the following pages are designed to satisfy.

The orientation of this book is strongly biased in two directions; it is *scientific*, and it is *psychological*. A scientific study of language, as opposed to a speculative discussion, begins with direct observations of communicating individuals and searches for the relation of these observations to the existing body of scientific knowledge. There exist many speculations of a literary or philosophical nature that are interesting and stimulate the imagination; unless these speculations lead to scientific observations and generalizations, they are not discussed here. Rejecting opinions in favor of facts helps to reduce this vast topic to manageable proportions. The psychological bias restricts the discussion to the effects of language on the behavior of the individual. Psychology is the science of behavior. Our present interest is not in language as one of the social graces, but as a kind of cooperative human behavior.

In some respects the scientific study of communication resembles the task of soaring off the ground with a tug at your own bootstraps. Science is, in one sense of the term, the set of symbols that scientists use to communicate their knowledge to other scientists. These symbols are published in journals and books and tables, and the symbols of one generation are studied by the scientists of the next. A science of communication, like all other science, must consist of such a set of scientific symbols. The peculiar aspect of a science of communication is that its scientific symbols refer to other symbols. It uses language to talk about language, and it is somewhat puzzling that new symbols about old symbols could clarify the problem in any way.

The ordinary language of every day's sociabilities becomes the object discussed in another language of science. It is as if we used microscopes to study microscopes or yardsticks to study yardsticks. A similar dilemma confronted the pioneer psychologists who set out to understand the human mind. Their only weapon was the human mind itself, and they were forced to ask themselves, Can the mind comprehend itself? The student of language must ask himself a similar question. Can we advance our knowledge of the use of symbols by the use of symbols? Or, more bluntly, is a science of communication possible?

Such a bootstrap undertaking requires a new attitude toward language. To the student who begins the study of verbal behavior for the first time language is a personal, almost magical thing bound up inextricably with his private thoughts and feelings and ideas. Before he can begin a scientific study of speech and communication, he must learn to take a detached, *formal* attitude toward it. In the formal attitude the personal, meaningful aspects of verbal behavior are often ignored, and the symbols are seen as simple patterns of muscular twitches, or agitations of the air molecules, or patterns of squiggles on the page. The scientific study of language begins with this formal impersonal attitude toward these twitches, agitations, and squiggles.

The formal attitude toward communication is an important first step. A scientist can consider that his own verbal behavior is not under scientific scrutiny; he uses it to talk about the verbal behavior of other people. It is often easier to be objective about what other people are doing than about what we ourselves are doing. A scientist can forget that his friend across the room is saying something. He looks at the movements of the mouth and face as a kind of artistic dance. He listens to the melody rather than the words. He asks himself, Does the pitch glide up or down at the pauses, does every grouping of sounds follow the same pattern? Does the talker use more verbs than adjectives? Why does he select that particular pattern of symbols instead of some other? What does his speech reveal about him as a speaker? What is his effect upon the other listeners? After a little practice the scientist is able to look at verbal behavior as impersonally as he regards a falling stone or a whirring motor. Then he is ready to begin the formal, scientific study of verbal behavior.

WHY BEHAVIOR?

An interesting theory of the origin of language in the human race holds that speech movements imitate gestures normally made with the arms and head. Suppose, for instance, a primitive man wanted to make a beckoning gesture, but it was dark, or his hands were full, or his companion was not looking. In this crisis he got the idea of making a gesture with his tongue at the same time his throat made a noise. The friend interpreted the sound as phonation modified by a beckoning tongue movement and came running. Presumably.

Whether or not this theory is correct we shall probably never know. It does serve to illustrate a behavioral approach to the problem of communication. To think of speech as audible movement and comparable to movements of the arms and legs is to think of speech as vocal behavior. Viewed in this way, speech is not essentially different from acts of other types. Its apparent uniqueness rests upon its importance to man, the talking animal. Speech accomplishes the same sort of result that other behaviors could, only more expeditiously.

Many people who have not considered carefully the psychologist's problems have been puzzled that he is reluctant to use mentalistic terms like 'experience,' 'consciousness,' 'ideas,' etc., unless he can relate them to observable behavior. The reason is simple enough. Science is a public affair, but personal experiences are personal. To enter the domain of science, personal experiences must be made accessible, observable, public. Unless the personal experience is reflected by the person's behavior in some public way, it cannot be studied. If a psychologist wished to study your dreams, for example, you would have to convert them into vocal behavior. Then he could study your vocalizations. But he cannot study the dream itself.

One of the psychologist's great methodological difficulties is how he can make the events he wishes to study publicly observable, countable, measurable.

It is significant to note that the device most often used for conversion from private to public is verbal behavior. Thus speech is a crucial problem for psychology. None of his other activities gives the same sort of insight into another person as does his verbal behavior. Since men spend so many of their waking hours generating and responding to words, and since speech is such a typically human mode of adjustment, no general theory of psychology will be adequate if it does not take account of verbal behavior.

This is no simple task. The psychologist has usually found it easier to think clearly about nonverbal behavior, and he has accumulated information about knee jerks, stomach contractions, salivating dogs, etc., and has attempted to bring some order into this mass of behavioral observations. By assuming a formal attitude toward verbal behavior we hope to be able to treat it within the broad framework of the psychologist's generalizations.

How One Thing Signifies Another

Begin with some basic, perhaps self-evident, concepts. It is natural to distinguish an organism from its environment. We say the organism is designed by evolution to convert food and water into tissues and work and to reproduce. To accomplish these functions in an ever-changing world, the state of the organism and the state of the environment must be able to mold and direct the organism's behavior. The necessary information is supplied by means of specialized cells called receptors and neurons. Because of these cells the central nervous system is affected indirectly by the changes going on in and around the organism.

Such statements are widely accepted and would not concern us here but for an implication they hold for the study of speech and language. Intermediate between the stimulating situation and the response to it is always the activity of receptor cells and sensory nerves. As far as the brain is concerned the activity of the sensory nerves stands for, or represents, the stimuli. The representation is adequate for most behavioral adaptations; it is nonetheless a highly schematic and inaccurate picture of the world. Thus physics tells us the thing we perceive to be a table is mostly open space and is held together by fields of force in a way entirely foreign to our general knowledge of tables.

It is common to begin a discussion of communication by pointing out that words are *signs* that conveniently replace the objects or ideas they represent. It would be misleading to imply, however, that this representative character of words distinguishes them sharply from all other stimuli to which we respond. The word 'chair' is clearly not the chair itself, but a symbol for the chair. Similarly, the light reflected from the object is not the chair itself. In either case the response is made to something that represents the chair. The something may be light rays reflected from the chair, or it may be sound waves arbitrarily associated with the chair. But it is not the chair.

In short, listeners respond to spoken words in the same way they respond to other energies that impinge upon their receptor organs.

As they affect the organism's behavior, stimuli do not present themselves in random, unorganized ways. We do not respond to the chair as if its right arm belonged to the table nearby and the seat were an especially thick portion of the carpet. The chair hangs together as a unit, separated from the table unit beside it and the carpet unit beneath it. It is an important psychological problem to discover the conditions under which stimuli are responded to as stable configurations. The problem is basic to verbal behavior; without such organization we could achieve no agreement as to the objects our words represent.

These remarks, which hold for stimuli in general, also apply to the verbal stimuli that affect us. Words do not present themselves in random, unorganized ways. Sentences hold together as units, and the component parts complement and modify one another according to their patterning. Words are not distinguished from other stimuli on the basis of configuration, for we impose organization on all the stimuli to which we respond.

Words cannot be distinguished from other stimuli on the basis of their representative role or their organization into patterns. What, then, is the distinguishing mark of a verbal stimulus? One possible distinction is that words have an *arbitrary* significance. Words signify only what we have learned that they signify. The fact that we say 'chair' and not '*Stuhl*' is a matter of social coincidence. In contrast, the association between the light rays reflected from a chair and the chair itself is not arbitrary. Verbal signs that are organized into linguistic systems are usually called verbal *symbols*.

The arbitrary nature of a verbal stimulus is clear when we consider the role of learning. In general we learn to repeat those acts which are rewarded. If bumping into a chair is never rewarded, we soon stop behaving that way and start walking around it. In such cases the nature of the physical situation ensures that our responses develop in a certain way. Our response to the word 'chair,' however, develops differently. In order that we learn to respond correctly to the word 'chair,' *it is necessary for another organism to intervene and reward us each time we respond correctly*. Since the intervening organism can reward a range of possible responses, the choice of the sound pattern 'chair' is quite arbitrary.

The first encounter with a foreign language usually leaves the visitor surprised at the perversity of the foreigners. Why would anybody use an improbable name like '*Pferd*' for something that is clearly a horse? The arbitrariness of names is usually easier to accept, however, than the arbitrariness of grammatical structure. Why would anybody wait till the end of a sentence to give the verbs? It is hard to abandon the feeling that the unfamiliar is absurd and illogical. It is part of the formal attitude toward language to see that one name or one grammatical rule can be just as good as another. The important thing is that everyone agrees to the name or rule, whatever it is.

Once a society has adopted a set of symbols and rules for combining them, the conventions are no longer arbitrary. If everyone agrees to call a horse a horse, then we are no longer free to call horses by any symbol that occurs to us. Selecting new words arbitrarily isolates us from the rest of the language community. The arbitrary decision was made centuries ago, and many people abide by it. The point is that other decisions might have been made.

We have said that we must study behavior, that verbalization is a special and important kind of behavior, that behavior must be guided by stimulation, and that the association between stimulation and action may be quite arbitrary. A general introduction would not be complete, however, if it did not stress the importance of order, of pattern, in verbal behavior.

Speech sounds do not occur as isolated bits. They are interwoven in elaborate designs. It is instructive to imagine a language that makes no use of the pattern of its individual sounds. 'Ah' might stand for 'How do you do' and 'ee' for 'Please help me,' and so on. There would be very few things such a language could talk about, for men can make and distinguish less than 100 different speech sounds. If we produce only some 50 different sounds and we want to use them to talk about millions of different things, we must use combinations of sounds. If, for example, we use all the possible pairs of 50 sounds, we can make 2500 different statements. If 2500 statements are not enough, we can go on to use patterns of three or four or even a thousand sounds. There are many more patterns than there are individual sounds. The ability to use such patterns, however, is uniquely human.

A language is of little value if its elements cannot be arranged and rearranged in a variety of sequences. We must know, for example, how a child learns the word 'bear' and the word 'eats,' but we must also study how the child learns to distinguish 'the bear eats' from 'eats the bear' from 'bear the eats.' To step on a man's toe and then to apologize is not the same as to apologize first and then step on his toe. The order of events is often more significant than the events themselves.

As soon as we begin to consider all the possible patterns of speech elements, we discover that the vast majority of these possible patterns is never used. Some patterns sound too much alike, some patterns are too hard to pronounce, some are prohibited by grammar or by common sense. Our choice of symbol sequences for the purposes of communication is restricted by rules. The job is to discover what the rules are and what advantages or disadvantages they create.

THE IDEALIZED COMMUNICATION SYSTEM

Communication means that information is passed from one place to another. Whenever communication occurs, we say that the component parts involved in the transfer of information comprise a communication system. Although the specific character of these parts changes from one system to another, there are general functions that the components must perform if the communication is to succeed. By abstracting these necessary functions that every communication system must perform it is possible to describe a sort of idealized communication system in very general terms.

Every communication must have a *source* and a *destination* for the information that is transferred, and these must be distinct in space or time. Between the source and the destination there must be some link that spans the intervening space or time, and this link is called a communication *channel*. In order that the information can pass over the channel, it is necessary to operate on it in such a way that it is suitable for transmission, and the component that performs this operation is a *transmitter*. At the destination there must be a *receiver* that converts the transmitted information into its original form. These five components—source, transmitter, channel, receiver, and destination—comprise the idealized communication system. In one form or another these five components are present in every kind of communication.

In most communication systems the source of the information is a human being. From his past experience and present needs and perceptions this source has information to pass along to others. The transmitter discussed most thoroughly in the following pages is the human speech machinery. This machinery operates upon the information and changes it into a pattern of sound waves that is carried through the air. The channel of principal interest to us will be the air medium that connects the talker's speech machinery with the listener's ears. The ear is a receiver that operates upon the acoustic waves to convert them into nervous activity at their destination, the nervous system of the listener. This particular system is called the vocal communication system.

Many other examples of communication systems can be described. When a person writes himself a note on his memorandum pad, the writer at one time is the source, the process of writing is the transmitter, the permanence of the pad is the channel that spans intervening time, the reader's eyes are the receiver, and the same person at a later time is the destination. A telegraph system is a simple example: the source supplies a sequence of letters that is converted by the transmitter into dots, dashes, and spaces, the receiver reconverts the signal into letters, and the message is passed along to its destination.

The operation of the transmitter is often referred to as *encoding*. The code is the pattern of energies that can travel over the connecting link. The receiver reverses the operation of the transmitter and reconverts the coded message into a more usable form. Thus the operation of the receiver is referred to as *decoding*. We usually think of codes in terms of secrets and international intrigue, but here we shall speak of codes in a much more general sense. Any system of symbols that, by prior agreement between the source and destination, is used to represent and convey information will be called a code. Thus, in the sense we use the word here, the French language is one code and the German language another. Spoken English is the code that will interest us primarily, but similar considerations apply for all codes.

One additional factor must be considered before the idealized communication system is complete. This factor concerns the possibility of error. Mistakes may occur in encoding or decoding the messages or may be introduced while the signal is in transit over the channel. If the people communicating are unfamiliar with the code, or if they are unable to distinguish the differences among the symbols, errors become likely. If there is a disturbance in the channel that changes the individual symbols or permutes their order, errors in communication result. It is sometimes convenient to lump all these sources of error together under a single name, *noise*. When we say that a communication system is noisy, we mean that there is a good chance for error to occur. If the chance of error is very great, we say that the noise level is high. If errors are very unlikely, we say the noise level is low.

The higher the noise level in a communication system, the more difficult it is to get reliable information over that system. In most communication systems, therefore, some provisions are made to combat the deleterious effects of noise. Just what the countermeasures are depends upon what kinds of errors are most likely.

THE IMPORTANCE OF STATISTICS

Statistics is the branch of mathematics that describes how things are *on the average*. The idea of statistics is that a single observation may not be reliable, and that if the observation is repeated many times the result may not always be the same. In such cases it is necessary to talk about the likelihood rather than the certainty that some particular event will occur.

The importance of statistics for the study of language is often overlooked. It is sometimes assumed that a science must make accurate predictions of exactly what is going to happen. This ideal is sometimes approached, for example, by the astronomer who can predict years in advance the exact minute an eclipse will begin. Such accuracy cannot be hoped for in a science of communication. The very nature of communication makes it clear that it is a variable, statistical kind of process. If we could predict in advance exactly what a talker was going to say, then he would not need to say it. The very fact that communication occurs implies that the accuracy of predictions of communicative behavior is limited. If verbal behavior were not highly variable, it would be useless.

Once the idea is accepted that communicative behavior is necessarily variable, the importance of statistics for the study of language becomes obvious. Communicative behavior is neither completely predictable nor completely unpredictable; it is in an intermediate position where it is possible only to say that, *on the average*, certain things will happen. Statistics is the language of averages, and so is the proper language for a science of communication.

It is a consequence of this intrinsic variability that scientific statements about verbal behavior are only probably true, true on the average. This variability complicates an already complex study and makes it difficult to evaluate the relative effects of the many variables that influence verbal behavior. It is possible to understand the general nature of statistical relations without any extensive knowledge of statistical methods; although the statistical machinery is suppressed in the following pages, the statistical concepts are indispensable.

These introductory remarks can be summarized as follows: The orientation toward communication assumed in this book is scientific and psychological. Certain basic assumptions about communication can be listed: (1) Scientific psychology is concerned with the analysis of behavior, and the use of mentalistic concepts should whenever possible be related to and justified in terms of behavioral evidence.   (2) Verbal symbols differ from other stimuli in that they are organized into a linguistic system and are learned through the intervention of other people.   (3) The component elements of the stream of verbalization change significance according to the context in which they occur, and it is essential to consider the patterns they form as well as the elements themselves.   (4) All communication systems include, in one form or other, five components: the source of information, the transmitter to encode the information into communicable form, the channel that conveys the coded information through space or time, the receiver to decode the message, and the destination of the information.   The various possibilities for errors introduce noise into the system.   (5) In order to serve its purpose, communicative behavior is necessarily variable and so must be discussed in statistical terms. These assumptions are elaborated, related, and supported with factual evidence in the following chapters.

Chapter 2

THE PHONETIC APPROACH

Language is a poor thing. You fill your lungs with wind and shake a little slit in your throat, and make mouths, and that shakes the air; and the air shakes a pair of little drums in my head—a very complicated arrangement, with lots of bones behind—and my brain seizes your meaning in the rough. What a round-about way, and what a waste of time!

—Du Maurier

Communication takes place when there is information at one place or person and we want to get it to another place or another person. The first step in getting it there is to encode the information in a set of symbols. The definition of a 'code' is quite broad. It may consist of spoken sounds, of written squiggles, the motions of a flagman's arms, the clatter of a telegraph key, the gestures of a deaf-mute, or whatever other set of symbols is convenient. The coded message travels the intervening space and is decoded by the person who receives it.

Our analysis of communication begins with the most important encoding procedure of all—human vocalization. Other ways of encoding information could be studied instead, but certainly speech is the first learned and most widely used. In many respects speech is the basic coding procedure. Some linguists reserve the term 'language' exclusively for the code of vocal symbols; writing, gestures, Braille, etc., are also codes that can be used for communication but are not dignified by the title of languages. In this narrow sense of the term, we begin our analysis of communicative behavior with the study of language.

Encoding information into the sounds of the human voice is a kind of behavior and, like all behavior, is limited by the nature of the bodily machinery that must do the work. The first task, therefore, is to examine this machinery. Then the acoustic product, the speech sounds themselves, are discussed, and the communicative aspects of these sounds are considered. The scientific study of this process is called *phonetics*. Physiological or motor phonetics deals with the manner in which the sounds are produced, and acoustic phonetics is concerned with the physical analysis of the sound waves of speech.

To produce sound a physical system must include a source of energy and a vibrating body. Usually resonators are added to provide characteristic quality to the sound. In the speech mechanism the source of energy is the breath stream, which causes the vocal folds to vibrate. The discussion of physiological phonetics begins with this source of energy.

RESPIRATORY FUNCTIONS DURING SPEECH

Speech is sometimes called an 'overlaid' function. The activity of breathing serves to supply oxygen for the body. Vocalization is a sort of biological afterthought, a secondary function laid over the more basic process of breathing.

Breathing is accomplished by changing the size of the chest cavity. When the cavity is increased in volume, the air pressure in the lungs is slightly decreased, and the outside air flows into this region of lower pressure. Expiration merely reverses the process by increasing the internal pressure.

Passive expiration is accomplished by the relaxation of the muscles of inspiration. When the muscles relax, the weight of the ribs and the elasticity of the lung tissues force air out of the lungs and return the cavity to its former position. *Active* expiration uses the muscles that make up the walls of the abdominal cavity. When these muscles contract, the viscera are forced inward and the floor of the chest cavity is forced upward. Muscles of expiration in the chest cooperate with the abdominal muscles and act to lower the rib cage.

The maximum capacity of the lungs varies widely among individuals, but 5000 cubic centimeters (about 0.2 cubic feet) is a fair average for men. Only some 4000 cc of the maximum capacity can be inhaled and exhaled in a single respiratory cycle, and this volume is referred to as the *vital capacity*. During average breathing the lungs hold about 2500 cc of air, and approximately 500 cc passes in and out of the lungs in each cycle. This value of 500 cc, called *tidal air*, is an average. Some men may normally inhale as much as 1500 cc with each breath. The vital capacity can be estimated from the sitting height, the weight, and the surface area of the body, but measurements of chest expansion bear little relation to vital capacity (Dreyer, 1919; West, 1920).*

There are many ways to obtain continuous records of respiratory activity. Figure 1 shows some samples obtained by recording changes in the circumference of the chest during singing, talking, and quiet. Other methods use a stomach balloon to indicate the pressure on the viscera, or collect and measure the breath in a gas mask, or enclose the entire body in a tank to record changes in body volume. It is even possible to employ x-rays (Bloomer and Shohara, 1941). X-rays are particularly valuable because they make it possible to see the synchronous movements of all the various parts of the respiratory system.

A useful index obtained from these records is the *I-fraction*. The time during which air is taken in is called I, and the total duration of the respiratory cycle (in and out together) is D. The I-fraction is defined as the ratio of I to D. The I-fraction averages between 0.40 and 0.45 during quiet breathing

---

* References to the literature are given alphabetically by author in the bibliography at the back of the book.

but drops to about 0.16 during speech (Fossler, 1930). Only one-sixth of our time is spent taking air in when we talk; the rest of the time we are slowly letting it out. During singing the *I*-fraction is even smaller.

Figure 1 illustrates how song, speech, and silence differ from each other. Varying lengths of phrases make breathing during speech less regular than quiet breathing. When we talk or sing, the inspiratory movement occurs quickly between phrases, and the expiratory movement is slow and irregular. The rate of expiration of air in medium loud singing varies from 40 to 200 cc per second, the lower values holding for trained singers.

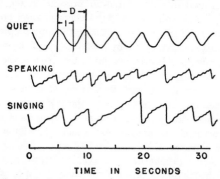

FIG. 1. Kymograph record of changes in chest girth during singing, speaking, and quiet breathing. The downward deflection represents inspiration, the upward deflection expiration. *D* is the duration of a complete respiratory cycle; *I* is the inspiratory portion of the cycle.

As we get ready to talk, air is drawn into the chest, which is momentarily poised in a slightly inflated position. As speech begins, the abdominal muscles contract slightly in advance of the first syllable. The contraction forces the viscera against the floor of the chest cavity and provides a firm support for the action of the chest muscles. Muscles between the ribs then contract in quick strokes that force air upward through the vocal organs during each syllable. The abdominal muscles continue to contract in a slow controlled movement, and as a breath phrase ends, the large muscles of inspiration quickly inflate the lungs for the next phrase. A careful examination of the records in Fig. 1 discloses short individual pulses imposed upon the slow expiratory movements. These breath pulses have been shown to correspond to the successive syllables of the spoken words (Stetson, 1928).

Many voice teachers feel that a large vital capacity is important for a good voice. The facts do not support this idea. The quality and strength of the voice, even the ability to control the strength, show no correlation with the amount of air the person can take into his lungs. There is even a little evidence that people with a small vital capacity have better vocal quality than do people with a large capacity (Idol, 1936).

PHONATION AND RESONANCE

Animals with lungs have a handy source of sound in the valve that protects the air tract. This valve is called the *larynx*. In the lungfish—the first animal able to break away from the purely aquatic mode of life—the larynx is very primitive, a simple sphincter muscle with no cartilaginous framework. All reptiles, birds, and mammals, however, have a fairly rigid scaffolding of cartilage to which the muscles of the larynx are attached. Most mammals have rather simple *vocal folds* that consist of a bundle of muscle fibers covered by a layer of mucous membrane. When man's ancestors began climbing about in trees, however, they found they had to use their forelimbs independently. To provide a firm support for the actions of the arms, it is necessary to lock air into the chest cavity. These animals developed a more elaborate double valve, and when they vocalize, it is the lower half of this valve that provides the voice. This highly evolved larynx gives man greater flexibility in speech and song than can be achieved with the simpler larynx of most four-footed animals (Negus, 1929).

Phonation. In man the larynx sits at the top end of a windpipe about 12 centimeters long and 2 centimeters in diameter. In mammals the larynx is always located close behind the tongue. Since most animals need and have long, powerful jaws, the larynx is usually rather far forward. In the course of man's evolution, however, the jaw became smaller and moved backward, and the larynx was also forced backward. The same course of development can be observed during the lifetime of any individual, until in the adult the larynx is opposite the fourth vertebra. The anterior prominence of the larynx—the Adam's apple— is easily located just under the chin. The structure of the larynx is sketched in Fig. 2.

Small muscles attached to laryn- geal cartilages cause them to move

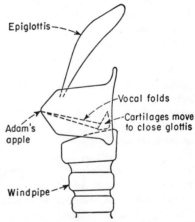

FIG. 2. Outline sketch of the cartilages of the larynx, as seen from the left side.

together and to rotate so as to bring the two vocal folds together. During quiet breathing these muscles are relaxed, and from above the two folds form a V-shaped opening—the *glottis*—for the passage of air. This opening averages about 1.8 cm in length for men, 1.2 cm for women.

To make a noise the vocal folds move together and close the glottis. Pressure builds up below the valve as the muscles of expiration contract. With sufficient pressure, the vocal folds are forced apart briefly, and a puff of air escapes. The folds then close together again until the pressure once more builds up to force them apart. This opening and closing goes on 100 or 200 times each second, and the successive puffs of air provide the sound that is our voice. This process is called *phonation.*

The exact mode of vibration of the vocal folds is complex and a matter of some controversy. Stroboscopic observations and high-speed motion pictures indicate that the movement is elliptical, but the phase of this motion varies at different points along the folds (P. Moore, 1938; Farnsworth, 1940). The lateral movement is greater than the vertical movement.

Many phoneticians have experimented with models of the larynx. One of the most successful models is made by placing two rubber cushions, filled with air, over the end of an air hose (Carhart, 1942). Although the models can be easily observed and measured, it is a dubious procedure to generalize too freely from the models to the human speech organs. It is quite clear, however, that the folds, both in models and in man, vibrate at several frequencies simultaneously and so produce a very rich and complex note.

A steady note, however, is of little value for communication. In order to carry messages the note must be turned on and off, or changed in pitch, etc. It is the changes in this sound that make it possible for speech to convey information. The three principal aspects of the laryngeal tone that can change are (1) the rate at which puffs of air are produced, (2) the size of the puffs, and (3) the richness or complexity of the vibrations.

The rate at which the folds vibrate can be changed either by increasing the tension on the vocal folds or by increasing the subglottal air pressure. In either case the rate of vibration tends to increase, and thus the pitch of the voice is raised. Communication in the English language does not rely to any great extent upon pitch changes in speech. It is principally the intensity (size of the puffs) and the quality (complexity of the vibrations) that vary as we talk. The intensity is increased by increasing the subglottal air pressure. The complexity is changed by modifying the size and shape of the throat and mouth cavities above the larynx.

Resonance. Adjustments of the sizes and openings of the throat, nose, and mouth produce the different sounds of English speech. The effect of these cavities upon the quality of the sound that passes through them is called *resonance.* The simplest way to think of resonance is in terms of a pendulum. If you give a pendulum a single push and allow it to swing freely, it moves back and forth—vibrates—at a rate determined by its length. In other words, a pendulum has a *natural period.* As the swinging continues, it decreases in amplitude because of friction, and the rate at which the swinging decreases is called the *damping.* If the pendulum reaches a position of rest in a short time, it is highly damped, and if it takes a long time to stop swinging, it has a low damping factor.

Suppose we strike the pendulum a series of blows. The number of blows per second is called the *frequency* of the activating force. If the time between blows corresponds to the natural period of the pendulum, the swing may become quite large. The child who pumps on the garden swing is applying this same principle—he pumps in synchrony with the movement of the swing and builds up a large amplitude of vibration. What happens if we apply the blows at some other rate? Under these conditions the pendulum swings as we strike it, thus exhibiting forced vibrations, but the successive blows do not reinforce the motion and may even stop it. *Resonance is that special case of forced vibration where the natural frequency of the system corresponds to the frequency of activation.*

Now think what happens to the pendulum when it is struck a sharp, sudden blow. It shivers and shakes and vibrates in a number of different ways. If we want it to swing smoothly, we must apply a gentler push, starting lightly and building up in force. The ideal sort of push is called *sinusoidal.*

If we apply several different frequencies, the system will resonate only to those frequencies that correspond rather closely with the natural period of the vibrating system. A frequency of activation that does not correspond to the natural period may have some effect. How much, depends upon the sharpness of the resonance. Some systems resonate to a wide range of frequencies, while others more sharply tuned give little response unless the frequency of the driving force coincides closely with the natural frequency of the system.

In general, systems that are sharply resonant have little damping, and systems that are not sharply resonant have high damping. A pendulum swinging in air is an example of a highly resonant system; it takes a long time for the motion to stop after the force is withdrawn. A pendulum hung in water, however, would be much less resonant, would respond more uniformly to forces applied at different frequencies, and would approach a state of rest quickly once we stopped beating on it.

The Vocal Resonators. The relevance of these facts to the production of speech sounds is quite direct. The vocal folds open and close during phonation to provide short puffs of air. These air puffs are the periodic force. They contain a fundamental frequency and a multitude of harmonics. The vibrating system that they act upon consists of the air in the throat, the nose, and the mouth. These volumes of air have natural frequencies determined by the sizes of the cavities and the sizes of the openings between them. Some of the harmonics strike at the resonant frequencies of the cavities, and in this case they are reinforced. The harmonics that do not coincide with the system's resonant points are considerably diminished in amplitude.

The importance of air cavities in phonation can be readily demonstrated by cupping the hands around the mouth. This provides an additional resonant cavity that reinforces some components of the voice and attenuates others. The quality that results may seem quite foreign to the normal voice. The throat, nose, and mouth modify in a similar way the quality of the sound coming from the larynx. These cavities act as open-tube resonators; their natural frequency is lowest when their volumes are largest and their apertures are smallest.

When the shapes of the vocal resonators change, their natural periods change. Consequently, different harmonics are reinforced in the different sounds. It is this change in which harmonics are reinforced by resonance that makes the major difference between 'boot' and 'beet.'

The voice cavities are highly damped, and when the larynx stops producing air puffs, the cavities stop vibrating rather promptly. The fundamental frequency of a man's voice is usually about 125 cycles per second. If there are 125 puffs of air every second, the successive puffs are spaced at intervals of 0.008 sec. During this time the amplitude of vibration in the cavities decays to about one-fifth its initial value.

The nasal cavity is the least important of the three major resonators. Its shape is relatively fixed. The only change we can make in it is to open or close the passage between the nose and the throat. This is done by moving the velum (the soft back part of the roof of the mouth). English talkers with a lazy velum leave this door to the nasal cavity hanging open most of the time, so have an unpleasant nasal resonance in all their sounds.

The mouth and throat are capable of large variations in size and shape. Together they comprise a double resonator. The mathematical theory of such systems has been worked out (Crandall, 1927; Dunn, 1950) and physical constants for all the different speech sounds can be stated, but this is a complex physical problem.

To summarize briefly: The larynx provides a sound compounded of many frequencies of vibration. The head cavities resonate to some of these frequencies and not to others. By changing the shape and size of these cavities we change the resonant frequencies, and the sounds that leave our mouths have different proportions of the various harmonics. The quality of the vowels depends upon which harmonics are reinforced.

PHONETICS AND PHONEMICS

The different speech sounds that comprise a language are formed by adjusting the shape of the path from the larynx out through the mouth. This process of adjustment is called *articulation*. To articulate means literally to join together. In speech the lips, tongue, teeth, and palate (roof of the mouth) move together to interrupt or constrict the breath stream. These organs are called the *articulators*. The rapid and intricate movement of these articulators is one of the most complex skills we possess.

The student should supplement the following description of these movements with a small mirror and a flashlight to illuminate the back of the mouth.

Careful inspection of the speech organs is necessary to appreciate the complexity of the process of articulating.

A *palatograph* provides a somewhat more elaborate method of observing articulatory movements (Moses, 1940). The roof of the mouth is coated with a powder that rubs off whenever it is touched by the tongue. The sound is then produced and the articulatory movements are inferred from an examination of the disturbances of the coating. The palatograph has, generally, supported the contention that no single articulatory position is uniquely associated with any particular speech sound. The shape of the palate, the associated sounds, the position of the head, and the rate of articulation are known to change the positions and areas of contact on the palatograph. Some experimenters have combined the palatograph with x-ray pictures and with records of breathing activity (G. O. Russell, 1928).

Articulation. There are five chief *types of articulation*. (1) *Plosives*, or *stops*. The breath stream is completely stopped by closing the passage. The 'p' in 'pop' and the 'g' in 'gag' are examples. (2) *Fricatives*, or *spirants*. A narrow slit or groove is formed for the air to pass through. Examples are the 'th' in 'thin' and 'sh' in 'shin.' (3) *Laterals*. The middle line of the mouth is stopped, but an air passage is left around one or both sides. The 'l' in 'let' is a lateral. (4) *Trills*. The air current is used to make one of the articulators vibrate rapidly. There are no good examples in English, but a trilled 'r' is common in European languages. (5) *Vowels*. The passage is left relatively unobstructed. Vowels are usually contrasted with consonants; plosives, fricatives, laterals, and trills are all consonants.

Some of the articulators can move about; others must remain relatively fixed. This difference provides a useful distinction between mobile articulators and fixed articulators. The mobile articulators are (1) the lower lip and jaw, (2) the tip of the tongue, (3) the front of the tongue, (4) the back of the tongue, and (5) the vocal folds. The fixed articulators are (1) the upper lip, (2) the upper teeth, (3) the gum ridge, (4) the hard palate, (5) the soft palate (velum), and (6) the glottis. If every mobile articulator could move to every fixed articulator, there would be 30 different combinations that could occur. This is obviously impossible. The lower lip cannot move back to articulate with the velum. In actuality, only eight of the 30 possibilities occur. These eight combinations are given names in Table 1; they are referred to as the *positions of articulation*. A more complete classification might add the uvula and the pharynx to the list of fixed articulators; uvular and pharyngeal sounds occur in many languages.

The highest speed at which various articulatory movements can be made has been carefully measured. Subjects were asked to repeat simple syllables in rhythmic groups. 'Tat, tat, tat, *tat*,' for instance, was used to measure the speed of articulatory movements made with the tip of the tongue. In one study (Hudgins and Stetson, 1937) the results showed that 8.2 syllables

TABLE 1. POSITIONS OF ARTICULATION

Fixed articulators	Mobile articulators			
	Lower lip (labial)	Tip of tongue (apical)	Front of tongue (frontal)	Back of tongue (dorsal)	Vocal folds (glottal)
Upper lip.........	Bilabial				
Upper teeth.......	Labiodental	Dental			
Gum ridge.........	....	Alveolar			
Hard palate.......	....	Cacuminal	Palatal		
Soft palate.......	....	....	....	Velar	
Glottis...........	....	....	....	....	Glottal

per second could be produced with the tip of the tongue, 7.3 per second with the jaw, 7.1 with the back of the tongue, 6.7 with the velum, and 6.7 with the lower lip. Muscles of the face and lips, which are innervated by the facial nerve, move very slowly (Kaiser, 1934). In order to say 'bab, bab, bab, *bab*' as rapidly as possible we use the jaw muscles in addition to the lip muscles. The jaw, innervated by the trigeminal nerve, is capable of more rapid movements than the lips and, of course, carries the lips along with it. The tongue, innervated by the hypoglossal nerve, is clearly the most mobile articulator.

The Phonetic Classification. Now the job is to provide a classification of all the speech sounds that can occur. This classification is based upon observations of the speech organs and their articulations. For each speech coordination we want to have a separate name and a separate symbol; these phonetic symbols can then be used as an alphabet to transcribe speech. The first step in this classification is the distinction between consonants and vowels.

The basic criteria for vowel classes are (1) the part of the tongue that acts as an articulator, (2) the height to which the tongue is raised, and (3) the position of the lips. The part of the tongue that is used is classified as front, middle, or back. Usually seven different heights of the tongue are distinguished. The lips may be either rounded or unrounded. This gives 3 parts $\times$ 7 heights $\times$ 2 lip positions = 42 classes of vowels. Each of the 42 has a different printed symbol to represent it. The skilled phonetician knows and distinguishes all of these vowels. In addition he may use further criteria to draw still finer distinctions. For example, any vowel can be produced with the velum raised to close the entrance to the back of the nasal cavity or with the velum lowered and the entrance open. Vowels produced with the velum raised are oral vowels; those produced with the velum lowered are nasal vowels. Adding this criterion gives 84 different vowel sounds. Further distinctions can be made by specifying the position of the tip of the tongue, the degree of tension in the muscles, and occurrence or nonoccurrence of phonation during the vowel (*e.g.*, the 'h' in 'he' and 'hoe' are sometimes called voiceless vowels).

Consonant sounds are conveniently classified according to (1) the four types and (2) the eight positions of articulation. To the four fundamental types listed above it is useful to add a fifth, the nasalized stops, or *nasals* (*e.g.*, the final sounds in 'rum,' 'run,' and 'rung'). In these sounds the air pressure built up by blocking the air passage is partly released through the nose. Nasalization is not, properly speaking, a type of articulation; it is a modification that can be added to any of the more basic types by simply opening the passage to the nasal resonator. Speaking loosely, however, we have five types of articulation, which with eight positions makes 40 alternative consonants. Of these only 36 are important; no trill can be articulated by the front of the tongue, and no nasal, lateral, or trill can be produced by the vocal folds.

In addition to these basic criteria, the phonetician also has several other criteria for specifying more subtle distinctions among consonants. The most important of these is the presence or absence of phonation during the production of the sound. For example, the English words 'pip' and 'bib' differ in that 'b' is accompanied by phonation while 'p' is not. Since any phone can be either *voiced* or *voiceless*, this increases the number of consonants distinguished to 72.

It is also possible to consider what the other mobile articulators are doing at the same time. The initial phones in 'cost' and 'crew' are both voiceless velar plosives; the back of the tongue presses against the velum to stop the air stream. But while the back of the tongue is occupied in this way, the front of the mouth is behaving quite differently for these two words. The concurrent activity of these other articulators is often called *coarticulation*. Coarticulation provides numerous possible distinctions among consonants.

The degree of constriction can also be specified to provide further distinctions among the fricative consonants. The way the pressure is released can be used to distinguish numerous plosive consonants.

These physiological classifications of the speech coordinations can be as complete as we like. It is, of course, not desirable to provide a different symbol for every different speech coordination. There are an indefinite number of more or less noticeably different phones. The same talker speaking the same words twice cannot make every sound in the second utterance absolutely identical with every sound in the first. The classification and the phonetic symbols represent *categories* of sound, which are usually called *phones*. With a crude, or broad, classification very different sounds may be put in the same category and represented by the same phonetic symbol. With a fine, or narrow, classification the sounds that are brought together in any one category are all quite similar, though not necessarily indistinguishable.

So much for phones in isolation. The phonetic description is not yet complete, however. It is also necessary to record variations in the length, the loudness, and the pitch of the phones, both for vowels and consonants. In many languages these features of the speech (often called *prosodic* features) form essential distinctions, and they must be classified with just as much care as the individual phonetic segments.

The Phonemic Classification. The phonetician who masters these distinctions and learns one of the several alphabets of phonetic symbols is able to transcribe any language he hears. His knowledge of the structure and function of the speaking machinery enables him to analyze and describe the formation of foreign speech so precisely and simply that he or any other phonetician can produce the speech correctly.

The linguist who undertakes to analyze and learn some hitherto unrecorded language must begin with a phonetic transcription of what he hears. If he has no familiarity with the language, he must record every subtle distinction he is able to detect; he does not know which of these distinctions have functional significance for the people who speak the language. As he becomes familiar with the language, however, he will find that some of these distinctions are irrelevant and can be neglected. This process of preserving only the essential distinctions results eventually in an alphabet of *phonemic symbols*. Phonetic symbols are indicated by placing them inside brackets; phonemic symbols are inside slanted lines.

To make the distinction between phonetic and phonemic symbols more concrete, imagine that we face the following job: We are studying a native tribe that speaks a language never heard before. We want to develop a system of symbols for writing that language. We would like a system designed to have one symbol for every phoneme and one phoneme for every symbol. That is to say, we want to avoid the discrepancies between spelling and pronunciation that are so notorious in English. How would we go about this task?

Since we know nothing about the language, we could begin with a phonetic transcription. We observe the positions and movements of the articulators with great care and write them down with phonetic symbols. This phonetic transcription, based upon the positions and movements of the articulators, ignores the particular conventions of this particular language. It carries along too much excess baggage. The phonetic analysis makes fine distinctions that may not have symbolic value. What we want are the phonemic constants of the language. The phonemes must be analyzed out of a mass of irrelevant phonetic distinctions. The problem, therefore, is to find rules to reduce the phonetic transcription to the basic phonemes that make a difference to the natives who speak the language.

How can we decide that a certain phonetic distinction is irrelevant in this particular language? To find a familiar example, consider the English language for a moment. In English the 'p' in the word 'pin' does not have the same phonetic characteristics as the 'p' in the word 'spin.' The first is aspirated; the second is unaspirated. Since these are two different phonetic events, why do we not use two different symbols to represent them? We do have two different symbols in phonetic transcription. In phonemic transcription, however, this distinction is considered irrelevant, and both sounds are represented by the single written symbol /p/. The question is, How do we know that this particular phonetic distinction is irrelevant in English?

We cannot generalize from one language to another. Just because the distinction between aspirated and unaspirated sounds is irrelevant in English, we cannot assume that it will also be irrelevant in the native language that we are studying. Suppose, for example, that both the aspirated [p'] and the unaspirated [p⁼] occur in the native language. We record a great many occurrences of both of these phones. Then we look at all our records to see whether or not the two ever appeared in the same phonetic environments. Suppose that we find in our records a case where [p'i] occurred and another where [p⁼i] occurred at the beginning of words or phrases; we also find cases where both [p'u] and [p⁼u] occurred, etc. In short, we find several instances where these two sounds appeared *in the same phonetic environments* and where the words so formed symbolized different things. We must conclude that the distinction is not irrelevant for this language. If [p'i] signifies 'tree' and [p⁼i] signifies 'canoe,' the difference must be carried by the presence or absence of aspiration; since the accompanying vowels are identical, the consonant must indicate the difference. This is the *distributional* approach to phonemics.

In English the aspirated and the unaspirated varieties of /p/ never occur in identical environments. There are always other differences around them somewhere. Since these other differences can serve to convey the information, the distinction between [p'] and [p⁼] is irrelevant in English.

The crucial point, therefore, is to discover whether or not the phones appear in the same environment. If they are sometimes preceded and followed by identical phonemes, the distinction is essential. If they are never preceded and followed by identical phonemes, the distinction is irrelevant.

A technique for analyzing the phonetic transcription of a language to discover its basic phonemes can be outlined in five steps (Bloch and Trager, 1942):

1. The first step is to alphabetize all the speech units that have been phonetically transcribed. These units may be words, or phrases, etc. This operation brings together all the units that begin with the same phone or with phonetically similar phones. *If two initial phones that are phonetically similar (but not identical) never occur in front of the same phonemes, there is no need to distinguish between them.* They can be grouped together in the same phoneme.

This rule for forming phonemes is basic to distributional analysis. Consider an example. Imagine that the language we are studying (not English) uses the phonetically similar sounds [p] and [b] at the beginning of words. Suppose that [p] occurs only before [i] and that [b] occurs only before [u] and that neither occurs before any other phonemes. There are four possible combinations that could occur: [pi], [pu], [bi], and [bu]. Of these four the language uses only two: [pi] and [bu]. If we used the same phonemic symbol, say /b/, for both of them, it would cause no confusion in this language. Phonetic combinations with which confusion could occur are not used. So these two phones, [p] and [b], could form a single phoneme in this imaginary language.

This first step produces a list of initial phonemes. Each phoneme is defined by the phones that are brought together to form it.

2. We repeat this operation for all other positions in the speech units. The speech units are alphabetized according to the second phone, then the third, etc. For each position we get a list of phonemes defined by the phones that occur in that position.

3. Next we compare and combine the lists for all the different positions and so construct a master list of phonemes. Further reduction in the number of phonemic symbols is possible at this point. *If two phonetically similar (but*

not identical) phones never occur in exactly the same position, they are classed together as the same phoneme. The reasoning is, as before, that they can be combined because the language does not contain any sequences that are identical except for these phones.

Another way of stating this rule is to say that we do not need to distinguish phonemes if the distinction is always carried also by the surrounding phonemes. In English we do not make a separate phoneme for the laterally released [t^L]. It occurs only medially between a vowel and [l] ('atlas') or medially between [r], [l], or [n] and [l] ('artless,' 'faultless,' 'gently'). Laterally released [t^L] always occurs in these positions and never occurs anywhere else. Other sounds similar to [t^L] occur elsewhere but never in these positions. Therefore [t^L] is included in the English phoneme /t/. By discovering such *complementary distributions* among the lists of phonemes for different positions, the number of phonemes in the master list is reduced.

4. Once the inventory of phonemes is complete, we must consider the prosodic features of the language. Variations of duration, loudness, and pitch play a secondary role in English, but in some languages these prosodic features are quite important. Thus the same phonemes may mean one thing with one pitch and duration but something altogether different with another pitch or duration. Consequently, the recorded durations, loudnesses, and pitches must be classified in much the same way as the phonetic symbols were classified into phonemes.

For example, a rising pitch at the end of a sentence in English indicates that the speaker is asking a question. In written English we designate this inflection by a question mark. By analyzing the phonetic records in this way we obtain the characteristic durations, accents, and intonations of the language.

5. Finally, we attempt to specify the characteristic groupings of phonemes in the language. In English, for example, only six consonants occur before /l/ at the beginning of a word: 'play,' 'clay,' 'blame,' 'glade,' 'flame,' and 'slay.' The consonants that occur after an initial /s/ are those in 'spill,' 'still,' 'skill,' 'sphere,' 'sthenic,' 'smile,' 'slay,' 'swim,' and 'snow.' Many possible sequences fail to appear, *e.g.*, initial /tl/ or /sr/. An exhaustive catalogue of such sequences of phonemes amounts to a description of the *phonemic structure* of the language. In what follows we shall have much to say about the importance of these sequential aspects of language.

English Phonemes. When we say that English talkers use not more than 14 or 15 different vowels, we are simply observing that there are not more than 14 or 15 different vowel phonemes that English listeners must differentiate. (Some linguists say English has as few as 7 vowel phonemes.) The English phonemes that are usually distinguished are arranged in Fig. 3 according to the part of the tongue used and the height of that part in the mouth. Each symbol in Fig. 3 represents a phoneme. Key words explain the values of the symbols. Combinations of these phonemes are used as *diphthongs*. The most important diphthongs in English are:

/eɪ/	in	l*a*te	/oʊ/	in	s*oa*p
/aɪ/	in	d*i*ne	/aʊ/	in	h*ow*
/ju/	in	*you*	/ɔɪ/	in	b*oi*l

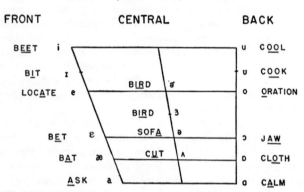

FIG. 3. Chart of the English vowel phonemes, arranged according to the part of the tongue and the height of the tongue during articulation of the vowels. /a/ is not ordinarily heard as a separate phoneme but is often encountered in stage and Eastern speech. /ɜ/ is used in Southern speech; the general American pronunciation is /ɚ/.

One untrained in the ways of phonetics usually regards these diphthongs as simple vowels like all the others.

In Table 2 the consonant phonemes of English are listed according to type and place of articulation. Where English contrasts the voiced and voiceless forms of the same consonant, the table lists the voiceless form first. Key words explain the values of the symbols. The consonants represented by /b/, /p/, /m/, and /w/, for example, are all bilabial sounds because they are produced with the lips. They are all formed in the same articulatory position. But they differ in the manner of articulation: /p/ and /b/ differ because /b/ is accompanied by phonation, while /p/ is not; /b/ and /m/ are formed in the same place and both are voiced, but they differ because the /b/ is formed with the passage to the nasal cavity closed, and /m/ is formed with the passage open. These differences can be read from the labels of the rows and columns in Table 2. (These differences can also be represented in terms of binary *distinctive features*, such as nasal vs. oral, voiced vs. voiceless, stop vs. continuant, etc. Cf. Jakobson, 1949.)

The use of this phonetic symbolism can be illustrated by examples. Words like /fonetɪks/ ('phonetics') come out fairly well, but /dʒʌdʒ/ ('judge') and /tʃaɪld/ ('child') require some study. Here is an old Chinese proverb:/ɪt ɪz tu leɪt tu rɪpɛər ə likɪŋ boʊt hwɛn wʌn ɪz ɪn ðə mɪdl əv ðə rɪvə/

Table 2. Classification of English Consonants

Type of articulation	Position of articulation							
	Bilabial	Labiodental	Dental	Alveolar	Cacuminal	Palatal	Velar	Glottal
Plosives	p (*p*ie) b (*b*y)			t (*t*o) d (*d*o)			k (*k*ey) g (*g*o)	ʔ
Nasals	m (*m*e)			n (*n*o)			ŋ (si*ng*)	(None)
Fricatives	w (*w*e)	f (*f*ine) v (*v*ine)	θ (*th*in) ð (*th*en)	s (*s*ip) z (*z*ip) r (*r*ip)		ʃ (*sh*e) ʒ (a*z*ure) j (*y*es)		h (*h*e)
Laterals				l (*l*ip)		(None)		(None)
Trills								(None)

The vocal machinery does not produce phonemes the way a typewriter prints letters. The shapes of the resonating cavities change in a continuous sort of movement, with articulatory thrusts modified by the positions assumed for preceding and following sounds. All this activity is closely coordinated with the activity in the larynx and the control of the breath stream. When we say that the information we communicate is coded into a sequence of phonemes, we are deliberately neglecting these complex dependencies among the successive sounds. In fact, however, these dependencies control to a large extent our choice of successive symbols. Not all the possible sequences of phonemes are used. Some phonemes are very difficult to produce immediately after certain other phonemes. For example, we seldom put more than three or four consonants in a row. Consonants and vowels tend to alternate because the vowel gives the articulators time to get ready for the next consonant. We must know which sound sequences occur before we can give a description of the language. And it is important to note that speech sounds are grouped together to form phonemes only after we have inspected the sequence of sounds preceding and following.

Communication about millions of things by means of a handful of different phonemes is possible only if we can arrange the phonemes into many different sequences. Not all of the theoretically possible patterns are possible in practice. The speech mechanism moves easily and naturally in some directions, and these are the patterns we tend to use most often. Difficult sequences like /kgnpb/ do not occur. Coordinations of the speech mechanism govern not only the particular sounds we produce but also the patterns of sounds we use.

ACOUSTIC ANALYSIS OF SPEECH

What is propagated when a speech sound travels through the air? Not the air particles themselves, for the molecules that leave the talker's mouth are not the same ones that move the listener's eardrum. It is the disturbance that is propagated. The air molecules simply move back and forth around their resting position. The local movements of the air molecules as a sound wave passes through them create an alternating sequence of condensations— molecules crowded together—and rarefactions—molecules widely separated. As the vibrating body pushes in one direction, the molecules on that side are crowded together and the air pressure is momentarily increased. When the vibrating body swings back in the other direction, the molecules are pulled apart and there is a partial vacuum. It is the condensations and rarefactions that travel through the air as a sound wave and move a listener's eardrum. These waves of sound are the subject matter studied by that branch of physics known as *acoustics*.

The Measurement of Sound. Acoustical and electrical devices—microphones, amplifiers, and oscilloscopes—can respond to changes in the air pressure, convert this mechanical energy into electrical energy, and display the changes in a graph that shows the pressure as a function of time. Such a graph reveals the sound wave in complete detail and enables us to see exactly what the pressure is at any instant in time. The pictures are complex and reveal the presence of many harmonics. In order to understand these complicated sound vibrations, it is necessary to know something about the simplest kind of periodic motion, the kind that physicists refer to as simple harmonic motion.

Imagine a man who has hold of one of the strings on a Maypole and who is running around and around the pole at a constant speed and at a constant distance from the pole. There are three things to know in order to specify this behavior: (1) how long the string is, or how large the circular path that he is traveling; (2) how fast he is running, or how many times he circles the pole every minute; (3) his angular direction from the pole at a given instant in time. The first of these is called the *amplitude*, the second is called the *frequency*, and the third is called the *phase*.

Imagine now a source of light to one side of the runner and a wall on the other side. The runner's shadow falls on the wall, and as he circles the pole, his shadow moves back and forth. This situation is illustrated in Fig. 4. The shadow moves back and forth periodically on the wall in simple harmonic motion. The shadow's motion is the same as the simplest motion of a vibrating body.

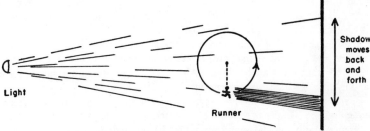

FIG. 4. How simple harmonic motion is produced by the projection of uniform circular motion. As the runner circles the pole at a constant speed, the motion of his shadow corresponds to the simplest motion of a vibrating body.

The next step is to think of the wall behind the runner as moving at a steady rate up into the air. If the wall is covered with photographic materials that retain a record of the shadow's position, the shadow will trace out a sinuous, undulating path on the moving wall. The path will look like Fig. 5, and it is called a *sine wave*. Like the circular motion that generates it, the sine wave has three characteristics: (1) its *amplitude*, or how far it is displaced from zero; (2) its *frequency*, or the number of repetitions of the wave in a unit of time; (3) its *phase*, or the point in the cycle at any instant of time. Each one of these three characteristics can be measured and represented by a number, and so three numbers will completely describe any sine wave.

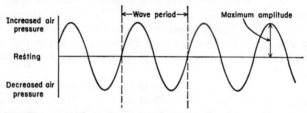

FIG. 5. The sine wave, with amplitude plotted as a function of time. The wave period is the length of time necessary for a complete cycle; frequency is the reciprocal of the period.

The sine wave describes the simplest sort of sound that we can produce. A tuning fork, for example, vibrates sinusoidally when it is struck and pushes the air molecules together and pulls them apart in this simple fashion. A pendulum swings in this manner but does it slowly enough so that we can follow each swing back and forth with our eyes.

A complete alternation from zero through increased pressure and back to zero, on through the decreased pressure and back to zero, corresponds to one complete revolution of the runner about the Maypole. For this reason a complete revolution is called one *cycle*, and the frequency of vibration is measured in terms of the number of *cycles per second*. It is convenient to abbreviate this by *cps*. Under optimal conditions the human ear can detect the presence of acoustic vibrations up to about 20,000 cps.

The maximum amplitude represents the maximum increase or decrease in air pressure that the sound wave produces, and corresponds to the radius of the circle that the runner follows. Air pressure is measured in dynes of force acting upon a surface of a given area, and so we measure amplitude in terms of *dynes per square centimeter*. It is convenient to abbreviate this expression to *dynes/cm²*. Under optimal conditions the human ear is able to detect the presence of a sinusoidal sound wave that has an average amplitude as small as 0.0001 dyne/cm².

Complex Sounds and Their Spectra. Next we consider the situation when several frequencies of vibration occur together. To describe this more intricate kind of motion, it is useful to know what the spectrum of the sound is. The word spectrum is borrowed from optics. Newton discovered, in his famous experiment with prisms, that white light is really composed of many colored lights. When we analyze such a compound light into the various colors that make it up, we measure the spectrum of the light. The situation is so similar in acoustics that the term was taken over to describe the analysis of a complex sound into its various component tones.

Imagine once more the runner and the Maypole. Suppose there was a second runner, faster than the first, who regarded the first runner as his Maypole and ran in circles around him. If we project, as before, the shadow of the second runner, the wave form that the shadow traces on the moving wall will be more complex, because it will depend upon the combined movements of both runners. This complex wave form will not be sinusoidal, but note that it can be analyzed into two components that are sinusoidal.

We can proceed in this fashion to add as many runners as we like, each circling one and being circled by another. If we add enough of these sinusoidal components together, we can make the wave form as complicated as we please. The important thing is that it is always possible, theoretically, to analyze the compounded wave into a set of individual sine waves. In other words, the simple sine wave is the building block we use to construct more complicated kinds of waves.

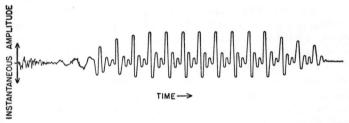

FIG. 6. A complex wave, with amplitude plotted as a function of time, of the sort produced by the human voice.

Most of the sounds we hear every day are generated by bodies that vibrate in this complicated way. In Fig. 6 a plot is drawn showing the sound pressure as a function of time for a complex vibration like the human voice. Such a plot shows the *wave form* of a sound. The problem is to analyze this complex wave form. There are several frequencies of vibration going on together in such a complex wave form, and each component has its own amplitude and its own phase. The statement of the frequency, amplitude, and phase of all the component sine waves that add to give the complex wave form is called the *spectrum* of the complex sound.

There is a simple relation among the frequencies of the sine waves that make up the compound wave. In a musical tone, for example, the high frequencies are simple multiples of the lowest, or *fundamental*, frequency. If the fundamental or, as it is often called, the *first harmonic*, is 200 cps, the second harmonic is 400 cps, and the third harmonic 600 cps, etc. If f is the fundamental frequency, the harmonics fall at $2f$, $3f$, $4f$, etc. To describe a complex wave completely, we need to give only one number for the frequency of the fundamental and two numbers (the amplitude and phase) for every one of the harmonics. Since the frequencies of the harmonics are simple multiples of the fundamental frequency, we do not need to give a number for the frequency of each one of them.

It is a simple matter to calculate how many numbers are needed to specify completely the wave form of a complex vibration. Suppose the first harmonic is 200 cps and that the highest component in the sound is at 10,000 cps. The harmonics must be spaced 200 cycles apart, and so there can be only 10,000/200 of them, or 50 harmonics. Now for each of these harmonics it is necessary to specify the amplitude and the phase. Therefore, 50 amplitude numbers plus 50 phase numbers specify this particular wave completely. In more general terms, let the width of the range of frequencies that can occur be W, and let the spacing between the successive harmonics be F, the frequency of the fundamental. Then there can be W/F harmonics in this range of frequencies. Since the fundamental frequency is the reciprocal of the time it takes for one complete vibration, $F = 1/T$. When this equivalence is substituted into the preceding expression, it is possible to say that there are TW harmonics produced in a band of frequencies W cycles wide by a complex tone with a fundamental period T. Now for each one of these TW harmonics it is necessary to specify its amplitude and its phase. Thus the complex wave is specified completely by $2TW$ numbers.

It is easy to see how a lot of sine waves can add together to form a complicated wave. It is not so easy to see that *any* periodic wave can be analyzed into a lot of sine waves. But this is exactly what we do. Whatever the pattern of vibration may be, it is possible to analyze it into component sine waves. It may take an infinite number of sine waves to do it, but the analysis is theoretically possible. The mathematical procedure for doing this is *Fourier analysis*.

To perform the Fourier analysis—actually to draw the curve, determine the fundamental frequency and the amplitudes and phases of all the components—is a tedious job. Fortunately, however, we can get very much the same information by using the principle of resonance. We have seen that some systems are tuned to respond maximally to some frequencies of the applied force and scarcely at all to other frequencies. Suppose we take a complex sound, like the human voice, and pass it through such a resonant system. If the voice contains components that have the same frequency as the resonant system, these components will be passed and will appear at the output of the resonant system. Since the system is insensitive to other frequencies, these will be reduced in amplitude.

Resonant systems that serve this purpose are called *filters*. A microphone converts the sound into electricity. Then resonant electrical networks filter out the several components in the complex wave. By measuring the amount of energy that passes through each one of a large set of filters we can measure the relative amplitudes of the components at any frequency of vibration.

Decibels. Next it is necessary to know how to state the magnitude of the sound pressure for each component. Sound pressures are usually expressed as ratios. This procedure requires us to say that a given sound pressure is so-and-so many times more or less than some other sound pressure. Physicists have agreed to use 0.0002 dyne/cm² as the standard reference pressure and to express all other sound pressures by their ratio to this reference level. Instead of saying that we have a sound pressure of 2 dynes/cm², we express it as a multiple of 0.0002, thus: 2/0.0002 = 10,000 = 10⁴.

The wide range of intensities involved in speech makes it inconvenient to write the pressure ratios in full. Instead, a shorthand procedure is used; we take the number 10 and write the proper exponent after it. Thus a ratio of 100,000,000 can be written conveniently as 10⁸. This trick of writing 10 to the appropriate power saves time in writing and is easier to read at a glance. In this form, however, the 10 does not say anything—it is always the same. So we just write the exponent and take the 10 for granted. This procedure of dealing with the exponents is called the logarithm. 'Log to the base 10 of y' means the exponent to which 10 would have to be raised to equal y.

The logarithm of the ratio of the energy in the wave to some reference level is called a *bel*. This unit is inconveniently large and is usually divided into 10 parts, called *decibels*. Decibels are the units used to describe the amplitude of a sound wave. The mathematical expression for decibels, when we know the energy ratio, is

$$\text{db} = 10 \log \frac{e_x}{e_0},$$

where e_x is the sound energy we want to state and e_0 is the reference energy. In practice, however, we seldom measure the sound energy directly. Instead we measure the sound pressure. Energy is proportional to pressure squared, and so we can write instead

$$\text{db} = 10 \log \left(\frac{p_x}{p_0}\right)^2 = 20 \log \frac{p_x}{p_0}.$$

In words, the sound pressure in decibels equals 20 times the logarithm of the ratio between the sound pressure in dynes per square centimeter and the reference level of 0.0002 dyne/cm².

When first encountered, these logarithmic units of measurement may seem unnecessarily complicated. Some approximate measurements of familiar sounds can serve to provide a general orientation toward the decibel unit. The faintest detectable sound is about −5 db, 5 db below the reference level of 0.0002 dyne/cm². A very low whisper at 5 feet from the talker's lips averages about 20 db. The general level of background noise in a well-designed radiobroadcasting studio is between 25 and 30 db. The audience noise in a motion-picture theater is about 45 db. Noise in a large store runs around 60 db, and the average factory noise is about 75 db. The noise in a subway station when an express train passes through is about 100 db. The point at which sounds cause pain to the listener is about 140 db. The report of a 12-inch cannon, at 12 ft in front of and below the muzzle, is about 230 db.

Speech Power. *Speech power* is the rate at which speech energy is expended. Power is measured in watts. The average acoustic power radiated by a talker during conversational speech, when the average is taken over a long period of time and includes the pauses between the phrases, is about ten-millionths of a watt (10 microwatts). If we ignore the pauses and consider only the time the talker talks, the value becomes about 15 microwatts. The acoustic power radiated by the average talker in a large auditorium is about 25 to 50 microwatts; 15 million such talkers would be required to produce a single horsepower of acoustic energy. Even when we talk as loudly as possible, the average power radiated acoustically is only about 0.001 watt, or 1000 microwatts. At the other end of the scale, the faintest voice we can manage without whispering is 0.1 microwatt, and a whisper may radiate as little as 0.001 microwatt (Fletcher, 1929). If we convert into decibels, the difference between the loudest shout and the faintest whisper is 10 log (1000/0.001) = 10 log 1,000,000 = 10 log 10^6 = 60 db.

When the acoustic power is averaged over very short periods of time—0.01 sec, for example—the rise and fall of the average power during the course of a syllable can be plotted. As you might suspect, vowels radiate the most power and consonants are relatively weak. If we measure the maximum power produced during the course of the different sounds, we obtain the values shown in Table 3 (Sacia and Beck, 1926). These measurements were made for conversational speech, and so the average includes both accented and unaccented occurrences of the sounds. Several consonants have been omitted from this analysis; their power was insufficient for measurement.

TABLE 3. CONVERSATIONAL VALUES OF AVERAGE
POWER OF SPEECH SOUNDS IN MICROWATTS

(Sacia and Beck, 1926)

Vowels		Diphthongs		Semi-vowels		Consonants	
u	13	oʊ	22	l	0.33	d	0.08
ɔ	47	aɪ	20	ŋ	0.35	t	0.14
ɑ	34			n	2.11	k	0.34
æ	9			m	1.85	v	0.03
ɛ	17					f	0.08
ɪ	9					dʒ	0.47
i	12					tʃ	1.44
ɚ	10					ʃ	1.83
ʌ	15					z	0.72
						s	0.94

In an open field, where no sound can bounce back off a wall, it is possible to make an accurate measurement of the sound pressure generated by a conversational level of speech. If the measuring microphone is placed 18 in. directly in front of the talker's lips, conversational speech registers about 76 db above the standard reference pressure of 0.0002 dyne/cm².

The Spectrum of Speech. Over-all measures of speech intensity do not reveal how the energy is distributed among the component frequencies. A more detailed picture is given in Fig. 7. The tone produced by the vibrations of the vocal folds is schematized by the spectrum at the top. Each component frequency in the laryngeal tone is represented by a vertical line; the height of the line indicates the intensity of the component. The tone then passes through the resonating cavities of the throat and mouth. These cavities respond at some frequencies more than at others; this fact is indicated by the middle curve. The two peaks in this curve indicate two resonant frequencies. These peaks are sometimes called the vowel *formants*. The result of passing the laryngeal tone through the vocal tract is indicated in the spectrum at the bottom of Fig. 7. Some of the components have been weakened relative to the others, and the tone now has its characteristic vowel quality. Note that the formants are independent of the fundamental frequency of the voice. Another laryngeal tone of higher fundamental frequency could pass through the same vocal resonances and have the same vowel quality; it would simply sound higher in pitch.

Since the formants change as the talker advances from one speech sound to the next, the distribution of energy also changes from moment to moment. There are two ways of presenting speech spectra: (1) the spectrum as measured over periods of time short

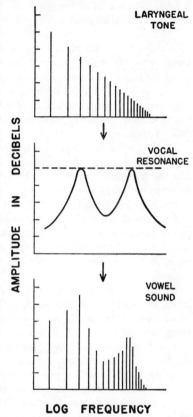

FIG. 7. Effects upon the spectrum of the laryngeal tone produced by the resonances of the vocal tract.

enough that the differences in spectrum for the different speech sounds can be detected, or (2) the spectrum as measured over a long period of time, with all sounds represented together in a single average spectrum.

The Short-term Spectrum. The simplest technique for analyzing speech is to use filters. We collect a battery of filters that resonate to different ranges of frequencies. The first filter might respond to all vibrations from 20 to

500 cps, the next from 500 to 1000 cps, the third from 1000 to 1500 cps, etc. At the output of each of the filters is some kind of metering device that registers the amount of energy in the frequency range of each filter. The cleverest method of doing this is to let the output of each filter control the intensity of a light. When a lot of energy passes through one of the filters, the light connected to that filter glows brightly.

The lights are then arranged side by side in order according to the center frequencies of the filters, and light-sensitive paper is drawn past them at a steady rate. Thus the passage of time is indicated by the horizontal distance along the paper. Frequency is displayed in the vertical direction, with high frequencies at the top and low frequencies at the bottom. The amplitude is shown by the degree of darkening of the light-sensitive paper. Such a device combines time, frequency, and amplitude in a single record. This record is called a *spectrogram.*

The device just described is essentially that developed by the Bell Telephone Laboratories to make life easier for the deaf (Potter, Kopp, and Green, 1947). The machine converts the acoustic pattern into a pattern of lights, and the deafened individual who learns to read the visual record can listen, as it were, to others and to himself.

A sample of this *visible speech* is shown in Fig. 8. The filters used for this record were very narrow (only 45 cycles wide), and each harmonic of the voice shows up as a horizontal bar. Notice the difference between the shishing /s/ sound in the first and last words and the vowels with their discrete, evenly spaced components.

The records for vowels in Fig. 9 were made with broader filters (300 cycles wide), and some of the fine detail of Fig. 8 has disappeared in Fig. 9. The wider filter emphasizes the vocal resonances. The major shifts in the speech energy are quite clear. The dark bars indicate the position of the formants. The acoustic analysis shows plainly that different frequency regions are emphasized in the different vowels.

Speech is a continuous process; speech movements are modified by the movements that precede and follow them. This fact is shown clearly by the acoustic analysis. In Fig. 10 the sentence 'I can see it' is shown in two ways. First the spectrograms of sounds as they appear when spoken separately are simply pasted together. Then the same sounds are produced together in the connected sentence. The differences occur during the period between phonemes when the speech equipment must travel from one position to the next. The vowel in the word 'can,' for example, appears as a steady glide from the /k/ to the /n/.

Some sounds are influenced more than others by the coarticulation of the associated sounds. The most susceptible in English are the consonants /k/, /g/, /h/, /ŋ/, /l/, and /r/. Figure 11 illustrates the different patterns that can be obtained for the consonant /k/ when it precedes different vowels.

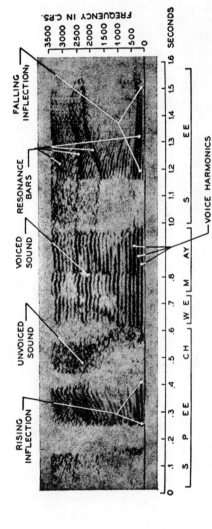

FIG. 8. Sound spectrogram of the words 'Speech we may see,' using a narrow-band analyzing filter to reveal the individual harmonics. *(From Potter, Kopp, and Green, 1947, courtesy of Bell Telephone Laboratories and D. Van Nostrand Company, Inc., publishers.)*

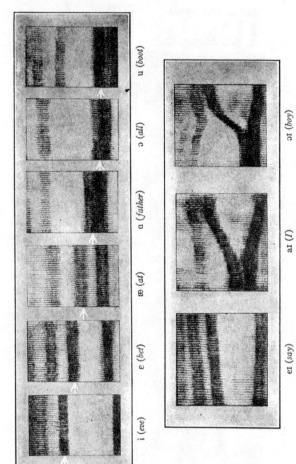

FIG. 9. Dark bars indicate the formants of the different vowel sounds. Note the shift in the formants during the diphthongs. (*From Potter, Kopp, and Green, 1947, courtesy of Bell Telephone Laboratories and D. Van Nostrand Company, Inc., publishers.*)

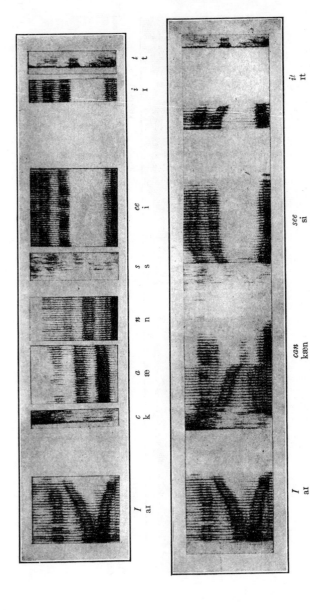

FIG. 10. The influence of adjacent sounds in the flow of speech, as shown by the spectrogram of the words 'I can see it.' In the upper strip the sounds are shown as they appear when spoken separately. Below the sounds are combined and spoken as a single sentence. (*From Potter, Kopp, and Green, 1947, courtesy of Bell Telephone Laboratories and D. Van Nostrand Company, Inc., publishers.*)

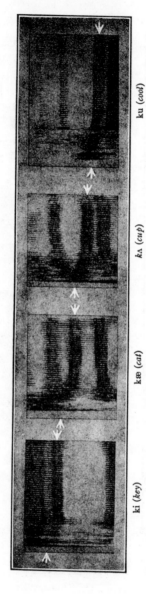

ki (key)   kæ (cat)   kʌ (cup)   ku (cool)

Fig. 11. Effects of coarticulation of different vowels upon the spectrogram of the consonant phoneme /k/. (*From Potter, Kopp, and Green, 1947, courtesy of Bell Telephone Laboratories and D. Van Nostrand Company, Inc., publishers.*)

These particular consonants are produced in the back of the mouth and thus are more affected by the positions of the vocal cavities than are the consonants produced in the front of the mouth.

The resonance bars in the same sounds as pronounced by different people are quite similar. The pitch of the voice, whether soprano or bass, has little effect upon the relative positions of the formants or upon the characteristic durations of the different sounds.

The preceding section presented a classification of the vowels based upon the position of the tongue, front or back, high or low, when the vowel is produced (Fig. 3). A very similar classification can be obtained from the acoustic evidence. In Fig. 8 the two lowest resonance bars show the most marked differences among the vowels. Suppose we now read off the frequencies of these two important resonances and plot them on a graph. The center frequency of the lowest resonance is plotted on the horizontal coordinate of the graph, and the second resonance is plotted on the vertical coordinate. The plot is drawn in Fig. 12, and the circles indicate average positions of the different vowels (Potter and Peterson, 1948; Joos, 1948). The dotted line encloses the area in which most vowels fall.

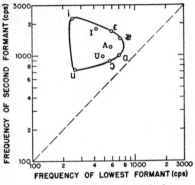

FIG. 12. The center frequencies of the first two formants for the sustained English vowels are plotted to show the characteristic differences. Compare this acoustic analysis with the physiological classification shown in Fig. 3. (*After Potter and Peterson*, 1948.)

Every point within this area designates a slightly different sound. Occasionally a vowel will be produced outside the area, but the large majority of vowels fall inside.

When this acoustic vowel area is compared with the classification in Fig. 3, we note that the front vowels are at the top and the back vowels at the bottom. The two classifications are almost identical.

Figure 13 summarizes the physiological and acoustical description for three vowel sounds, [i], [ɔ], and [u]. From x-ray pictures (after G. O. Russell, 1928) the approximate position of the vocal organs can be sketched. As the tongue moves into its various positions, the relative sizes of the throat and mouth cavities are changed. For simplification the vocal tract can be regarded as a series of cylindrical sections placed end to end; sound passing through such a series of cylinders is filtered in the same way the laryngeal tone is filtered by the resonating cavities of the vocal tract (Dunn, 1950). The acoustic output of these systems, when they are activated by the laryngeal tone, is described by the spectra on the right in Fig. 13; sound intensity is plotted against the frequency. The relative positions of the first three formants are indicated approximately.

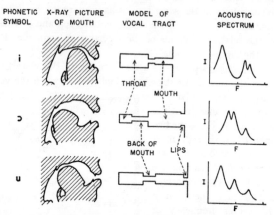

FIG. 13. Summary figure showing the phonetic symbols, the positions of the speech organs, the sizes of the resonating cavities, and the resulting acoustic spectra. (*After Dunn*, 1950.)

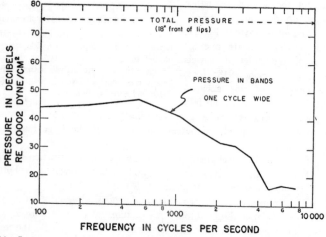

FIG. 14. Long-term acoustic spectrum of male voices. (*After Rudmose et al.*, 1948.)

The Long-term Spectrum. So much for the short-term spectrum of speech. What does the long-term, or average, spectrum look like if we throw all the speech sounds into a single measurement? The answer is shown in Fig. 14 (Rudmose *et al.*, 1948). Male voices, speaking at a loud conversational level, were picked up by a microphone 18 in. in front of the lips and analyzed by a set of band-pass filters. In this graph no account is taken of the differences among the speech sounds, and the short-term variations are completely lost. Figure 14 tells us that most of the speech energy is, on the average, in the frequency range below 1000 cps but that the presence of speech pressure can be detected up to frequencies of 8000 cps or more.

The Vocalization of Information

The purpose of these intricate adjustments of the vocal tract is to produce a variety of alternative sounds so that different sounds can assume different symbolic values. Unless a variety of alternative sounds or alternative patterns of sounds is available, no information can be communicated. This simple observation has profound implications, for it enables us to state more exactly what we mean by the word 'information.'

In these and the following pages 'information' is used to refer to *the occurrence of one out of a set of alternative discriminative stimuli.* A discriminative stimulus is a stimulus that is arbitrarily, symbolically, associated with some thing (or state, or event, or property) and that enables the stimulated organism to discriminate this thing from other things. The *content of the information* concerns the particular discriminative stimulus that does occur. The *amount of the information* concerns the range of possible alternatives that could occur.

Amount of Information. The amount of information increases as a function of the number of alternatives. If only two alternative stimuli can possibly occur (*e.g.*, the 'dit' and 'dah' of radiotelegraphic code), the occurrence of one or the other carries relatively little information. But if there are 10,000 alternatives possible (*e.g.*, the ideograms of Chinese), the occurrence of one out of this large set carries considerable information. The stimulus itself, the actual physical event that occurs, could be identical in two different situations; yet when it is one of two possibilities it is less informative than when it is one of 10,000 possibilities. The amount of information a stimulus conveys cannot be determined from an examination of that stimulus alone; the amount of information depends upon the number of things that could have happened instead but didn't.

This concept of information must not be confused with the popular usage of the term 'meaning.' The English language may be meaningless to a Frenchman, but it still encodes a certain amount of information. Our definition does not say that the listener must be able to decode the message. The amount of information is the measure of a talker's freedom of choice when he selects a message. It is a measure, not of a particular message, but of a total situation.

It turns out to be mathematically convenient *to define the amount of information as the logarithm of the number of alternatives* (Shannon, 1948). According to this definition the occurrence of 1 out of 10 possible alternatives carries only half the amount of information that is carried by the occurrence of 1 out of 100 alternatives and only a third as much as by the occurrence of 1 out of 1000 alternatives. Figure 15 is a graph of the relation between the number of alternatives and the logarithmic measure of the amount of information.

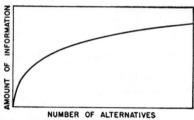

FIG. 15. The amount of information per symbol is plotted as a logarithmic function of the number of alternative symbols.

This definition of the amount of information is used throughout the remainder of this book. The alternatives we must consider may be alternative sine waves, or alternative spectra, or alternative phonemes, or alternative syllables, or alternative words, etc. In every case the amount of information is defined as the logarithm of the number of possible alternatives. We shall, therefore, return to the problem of estimating the number of alternative speech units again and again in the pages that follow.

Information in a Sound Wave. Now this definition will be used to obtain a quantitative measure of the amount of information that can be encoded in a speech wave. For the moment we shall not be concerned with whether a listener could actually understand the information or would act in accordance with it; we shall deal first with the full range of conceivable possibilities.

To estimate the amount of information, it is necessary to estimate somehow the number of different, alternative sound waves that can occur. The totality of different sound waves must include, along with all the speech sounds, all the sounds of music, all the bells, noises, whistles, etc., that can ever be produced. The task is not as formidable as it sounds, for all we need to use are the concepts of frequency and intensity and spectra introduced already.

First it is necessary to decide how long a time the sound wave lasts. Obviously, if there is an unlimited amount of time, there can be an unlimited number of different sound waves. To make matters perfectly definite, take the interval of time as 1 sec.

How many different sound waves that last 1 sec could there be? In order to answer this question, we consider what happens when we apply Fourier analysis to a wave form 1 sec long. The most complicated case possible is the one that has all the harmonics of the lowest possible fundamental frequency. In this example the fundamental cannot be any lower than 1 cps because this is the assumed duration of the message.

If we had chosen the duration of the message as 0.1 sec, the fundamental frequency would be 10 cps. If we had chosen the duration as 10 sec, the fundamental frequency would be 0.1 cps. In general, the lowest possible fundamental frequency in the Fourier analysis is given by $1/T$, where T is the duration of the signal that is analyzed. Since all the harmonics must be multiples of this fundamental period, T also determines the frequency of every sine-wave component analyzed out of the complex wave.

Since we are considering the most complicated case imaginable, all harmonics of 1 cps must be present. There are components at 2 cps, at 3 cps, at 4 cps, etc. In the preceding section we saw that the upper limit of the speech spectrum—the frequency of the highest component—is about 10,000 cps. If we take 10,000 cps as a convenient value, therefore, we can have 10,000 harmonics in the most complicated speech wave of 1 sec duration.

For every one of these 10,000 component frequencies we must state, in order to describe it completely, both the amplitude and the phase. In other words, we must write down two numbers, one for amplitude and one for phase, for every harmonic. Two numbers for each of 10,000 components is 20,000 numbers. This 1-sec interval of speech can, therefore, be described completely by these 20,000 numbers. The general rule is that if T is the duration of the signal in seconds and W is the width in cycles per second of the band of frequencies contained in the signal, $2TW$ numbers are required to describe the most complicated case. For the case considered here this formula yields $2 \times 1 \times 10,000 = 20,000$ numbers.

To describe the set of 10,000 harmonics, we must state the amplitude and phase of the component at 1 cps, then the amplitude and phase of the component at 2 cps, then the amplitude and phase of the component at 3 cps, etc., for all the harmonics in the wave. The amplitude of the 1-cps component might be 0.1 dyne/cm² and its phase angle 30°, the 2-cps component might be 0.0071 dyne/cm² and 186°22′, and so we should proceed through the list of 10,000 harmonics until we had the set of 20,000 numbers.

Consider now the question of how many alternative sets of 20,000 values there can be. We have a set of $2TW = 20,000$ numbers, and every one of these numbers can assume a range of different values. Every time one of these 20,000 numbers changes by even a slight amount, we have a new set of numbers and thus a different speech wave and a new and different spectrum. How many alternative waves are possible depends upon how many different sets of values these 20,000 numbers can assume.

Infinite Number of Alternative Values. Take first the case when no restrictions are imposed. Any one of these 20,000 numbers can assume any one of an infinite set of values. In this case there is an infinite number of possible alternatives, and we must conclude that a 1-sec message can contain an infinite amount of information.

In any practical situation, however, the 20,000 amplitudes and phases cannot assume any one of an infinite number of values. This would require the receiver to distinguish infinitesimal differences in amplitude and phase as representing different messages. Even the slightest disturbance or distortion completely changes the message. There are, therefore, practical considerations that force the 20,000 numbers to assume discriminably different values, and there is not an infinite number of discriminable values within the finite amplitude of the speech.

Two Alternative Values. Now take the case where the numbers are restricted to certain specific values. To impose a severe restriction, suppose that the 20,000 numbers are limited to one or the other of two possible values. The first number can have either one of these alternative values, and so can the second number. The first two numbers together, however, can form any one of four alternative pairs. Call the two alternative numbers A and B. If the first number is A, the second can be A or B; if the first is B, the second can be A or B. The four alternative pairs are AA, AB; BA, and BB. When we add the third number there become eight possible triplets: AAA, AAB; ABA, ABB; BAA, BAB; BBA, and BBB. If the message were described by four numbers there would be 16 alternatives, and if by five numbers there would be 32 alternatives, etc.

The general rule is that, if there are n numbers in the list and if any of the numbers can assume any one of a alternative values, there can be a^n different alternative sets of numbers. In our particular example we chose a to be 2 and n to be 20,000. The 20,000 numbers can take either one of the two possible values, and so there are $2^{20,000}$ alternative messages possible. According to the definition of amount of information, information is proportional to the logarithm of the number of alternatives. Thus we have $\log 2^{20,000}$, or 20,000 $\log 2$, as the measure of the amount of information.

The General Case. The question has been answered for two specific instances, and all that remains is to state the answer in general terms. Let T be the duration of the message, let W be the width of the band of frequencies, let S be the maximum amplitude of the signal, and let N be the size of a discriminable difference in amplitude.

The number of alternative values that the amplitude can assume will be $(S + N)/N$, the total range divided by the size of the discriminable difference. For example, if the value of S is 100 and the smallest difference that can be reliably used is 2, then there are only $(100 + 2)/2$, or 51, discriminably different values that the amplitude can assume. Since there are $2TW$ of these amplitudes* to be assigned and each one can assume any of $(S + N)/N$ values, there are $[(S + N)/N]^{2TW}$ different alternative signals. Every possible speech spectrum is included in this set of $[(S + N)/N]^{2TW}$ spectra, along with

---

* There is a mathematical relation that enables us to express the amplitude and phase of a single component in terms of two amplitudes, one for a sine and one for a cosine wave. In either case, however, two numbers are required for every component.

billions of other spectra that would never be associated with the sounds of speech.

Since we have defined information as the logarithm of the number of alternative possibilities, the final form of the solution is

$$\text{Amount of information} = \log\left(\frac{S+N}{N}\right)^{2TW} = 2TW \log\frac{S+N}{N}.$$

Or, in words: *The amount of information in a speech wave is proportional to the duration of the speech, to the range of frequency components involved, and to the logarithm of the number of discriminable steps in amplitude.* In order to increase the amount of information we must talk longer, or increase the range of frequencies in the speech spectrum, or make use of finer distinctions in intensity.

It is clear that a large number of different speech waves could be generated in the course of a few minutes. If all of the small differences among these waves could be discriminated reliably by the listener, a staggering amount of information could be transferred in this short period of time. It is equally clear, however, that all of the potential distinctions are not used in ordinary vocal communication. Most of the spectra considered above cannot be generated by the speech mechanism. Speech waves that are very different in detail are judged to be the same by the listener, and we cannot use these detailed differences to signify different things. The number of alternatives that is actually used is far less than the number of alternatives that some ideal machine might be able to distinguish.

Out of all the billions of different spectra that could conceivably be used for communication, the English language selects and uses no more than 50 phonemes. (If prosodic features of stress are ignored, 30 phonemes might be a realistic estimate for English.) With only 50 alternatives the amount of information encoded in the occurrence of a single phoneme is log 50, or something less than 6 log 2. Compared with the amount of information that sound waves might convey, the amount actually conveyed by phonemes is quite small. These particular 50 sounds are easy to produce and are enough different from one another so that we can learn to distinguish them accurately. In addition to the limit imposed by the talker's inability to produce all the conceivable sounds, a further limit on the number of different phonemes is imposed by the listener's inability to hear minute differences in the sounds. In order to understand the listener's capacity to discriminate among different sounds, we proceed in the next chapter to examine the process of hearing.

DISCUSSION QUESTIONS

1. How would we need to change our present system of spelling in order to use a typewriter that wrote at the sound of the voice?

2. In military communication microphones are sometimes strapped to a talker's throat in order to free his hands for other work. What kind of speech could be heard over such a throat microphone?

3. How could we use visible speech equipment to aid in the correction of speech disorders?

4. Speech sounds affect the person who makes them in much the same way they affect the person who listens to them. Are there other stimuli we could generate that would have this advantage?

5. Is there any evidence in the visible speech records to support the notion that the syllable is an important unit for the analysis of speech movements?

6. The Bell Telephone Laboratories have built a device that synthesizes a fairly good imitation of human speech. How does it work?

SELECTED REFERENCES

BLOCH, B., and G. L. TRAGER. *Outline of Linguistic Analysis.* Baltimore: Linguistic Society of America, Waverly Press, 1942. At that time an excellent introduction to phonetics and phonemics. Surveys techniques used by linguists for working with native speakers to arrive at a complete description of a language.

CURRY, R. O. *Mechanism of the Human Voice.* New York: Longmans, 1940. A concise review of a large body of experimental results.

FLETCHER, HARVEY. *Speech and Hearing.* New York: Van Nostrand, 1929. This book, which summarizes the research of the Bell Telephone Laboratories prior to 1929, has become a classic reference in the field of telephonic communication.

GRAY, G. W., and C. M. WISE. *The Bases of Speech* (Rev. Ed.). New York: Harper, 1946. Chapters II–V of this general text provide supplementary reading for the present chapter.

POTTER, RALPH K., G. A. KOPP, and H. C. GREEN. *Visible Speech.* New York: Van Nostrand, 1947. Presents the basic technical and phonetic principles of visible speech, with procedures to be used in teaching people to read these patterns.

SHANNON, C. E., and W. WEAVER. *The Mathematical Theory of Communication.* Urbana: University of Illinois Press, 1949. Students with mathematical training can extend their knowledge of information theory by reading Shannon's work. Students without such training will find Weaver's popularization readable.

WOOD, ALEXANDER. *Acoustics.* New York: Interscience, 1941. A readable book in acoustics for the student who wants to push his information in this area beyond the scanty glimpse provided in this chapter.

Chapter 3

THE PERCEPTION OF SPEECH

Nature has given to men one tongue, but two ears, that we may hear from others twice as much as we speak.

—EPICTETUS

Vocal communication requires a listener to discriminate among vocal sounds, and the amount of information he can extract from the sounds depends upon the acuity of his discrimination. His ability to distinguish different sounds is good but not perfect. There are many subtle differences a listener cannot detect. Some sounds are too faint, some vibrations are too rapid, some differences are too small to be heard. These limits beyond which men cannot hear are called *thresholds*.

THE LIMITS OF HEARING

What is the slightest sound a human ear can detect? The answer to this question depends on a long list of 'if's,' 'and's,' and 'but's.' Before we can answer it, we must enumerate some of the conditions under which the measurement is made. First it is necessary to assume that the listener's location is perfectly quiet except for the sound we want him to hear. The sound should be a simple sine wave with a single frequency of vibration, for if the sound is complex and contains several component frequencies, we shall not know which component the listener hears. A sound with but a single frequency component is called a *pure tone*. The tone should go on and off intermittently and should stay on at least half a second, for if a tone is very brief, it is hard to hear. The listener should face the source of sound so that it falls equally on both ears, for both ears together are more sensitive than one alone. The sound pressure is measured in the absence of the listener; the calibrating microphone is placed where the listener's head is going to be. The frequency of the tone should be fixed somewhere between 2000 and 4000 cps; the threshold of detectability varies markedly with frequency, but the ear is most sensitive in this range. The listener is young and has no impairment of hearing. When all of these conditions are satisfied, a listener is able to detect a tone of about 0.0001 dyne/cm². In terms of the amplitude of movement, the eardrum moves about 0.000000001 cm! If the ear were much more sensitive, it would begin to report the random movements of the air molecules.

The Audible Area. A curve representing the *threshold of hearing* for tones of different frequencies (Sivian and White, 1933) is shown at the bottom of Fig. 16. (It is sometimes called the threshold of *detectability*, or of *audibility*.) The curve shows, for example, that a tone of 100 cps must have an intensity of at least 30 db (above 0.0002 dyne/cm²) before its presence can be detected. If it is less intense, it is inaudible. A tone of 1000 cps can be heard at 0 db intensity, and a tone of 10,000 cps can be detected at 10 db intensity.

This threshold curve sets the lower limit of the audible area. Only tones that fall above the threshold of detectability can be used for communication.

At the other end of the intensity scale the ear imposes another limit upon the range of usable intensities. If a tone becomes too intense, it causes pain and people refuse to listen. As the intensity of the tone is increased, most normal subjects say that it becomes uncomfortably loud at about 110 db. If the intensity is raised still further, they report that it begins to tickle their ears at about 133 db. If the intensity is increased still further, subjects report a sharp pain at about 140 db (Silverman, 1947).

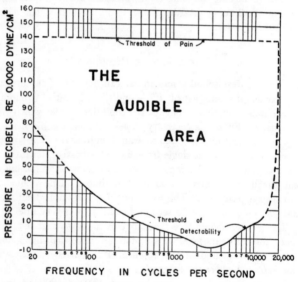

FIG. 16. The range of frequencies and intensities that can be heard by a normal human subject.

Unlike the threshold of detectability, these *tolerance thresholds* do not change significantly for different frequencies. The tolerable limit is about the same for all frequencies. The limit may change, however, with repeated exposures. The listener seems to toughen up as he becomes accustomed to loud sounds.

After some experience with loud sounds the average listener does not report that he is uncomfortable until the level reaches about 123 db.

Ordinarily we do not attempt to use such intense sounds for communication. But sometimes the noise is so great—in boiler factories, engine rooms, etc.—that we are forced to shout directly into the listener's ear. Even this may not be effective in the most intense noises.

The *threshold of pain* is shown in Fig. 16 at 140 db. The area on the graph below 140 db and above the threshold of detectability comprises the set of frequencies and intensities that is available for vocal communication. These tones comprise the *audible area*.

Acuity for Differences. Any acoustic information a listener receives must be carried by combinations of tones (spectra) that fall inside the audible area. A great variety of tonal combinations can be produced in this area, but if different combinations are to have different symbolic values, they must be recognizably different sounds. Thus it is necessary to know not only the boundaries of the auditory area but also the limits of differentiation within these boundaries. How different must two tones be in order that an average listener can recognize them as different?

In what ways can two sounds differ? Two pure tones can differ in frequency, in amplitude, and in phase. Complex sounds have several components and each one of the components in one sound can differ in frequency, amplitude, and phase from each one of the components in another sound. Since there are so many billions of different complex sounds, it is virtually impossible to study all of them. Consequently, most of our information about the discriminative acuity of man's hearing has been obtained for pure tones.

For frequencies below 1000 cps the just noticeable difference in the frequency of two pure tones is about 3 cycles. Above 1000 cps the number of cycles that a tone must change in order to sound noticeably different is proportional to the frequency of the tone; as the frequency of the tone increases, the size of the just noticeable difference increases proportionately (Shower and Biddulph, 1931). Somewhat larger differences in frequency are necessary if the tone is less than 50 db above the threshold of hearing.

The threshold for differences in intensity is, for most pure tones, about 0.3 db (Riesz, 1928). For very low and very high frequency tones and for faint tones it is necessary to make a somewhat larger change in intensity if the change is to be detected.

Differences in the phases of two tones can be detected, and this information is useful for locating the source of a sound in space. Phase differences do not seem to play an important role in the perception of speech, however, and so we need not consider them here.

The Number of Distinguishable Tones. These data obtained for pure tones give us the following general topography for the interior of the auditory area. From the lowest to the highest frequency there are about 1600 distinguishably different frequencies. From the lowest to the highest intensity there are about 350 distinguishably different intensities. It has been estimated (Stevens and Davis, 1938) that the auditory area can be divided into about 340,000 tones in such a way that every one of these 340,000 tones is detectably different from all the others. Most of these tones are clustered in the middle of the auditory area where acuity for differences is greatest. In order to be discriminably different the tones must be spaced farther apart at low or high frequencies and at low intensities.

Does the fact that we can discriminate among 340,000 pure tones mean that we could have a language of 340,000 different tonal symbols? The answer is obviously in the negative. These differences can be detected only if the tones are sounded one after the other. In communication the two tones may be separated by many other tones, and when one appears, it is very difficult to recognize it as different from its closest neighbors. To draw an analogy, we may be able to tell twins apart when they stand side by side, but if we meet one of them alone on the street, we are not able to decide which one he is. It is easier to detect a difference than to make a positive identification in the absence of the other similar stimuli.

The fact is, therefore, that a listener cannot identify absolutely any one of 340,000 pure tones. How many tones he might recognize for the purposes of practical communication is a matter for speculation. No experimental evidence is available. The important thing to note, however, is how these 340,000 distinguishable tones are distributed through the audible area. The ear is most sensitive to differences among tones when the tones are 50 db above the threshold of hearing and in the range of frequencies between 500 and 4000 cps. Since a listener can discriminate tones most easily in this portion of the audible area, it follows logically that this portion has the largest capacity for handling information—a larger number of alternative messages can be distinguished in this portion than in any other portion of the audible area. Thus we can say what range of frequencies and intensities offers the greatest possibilities for vocal communication, although we cannot say exactly how many alternative messages might be possible with a pure-tone communication system.

In looking at the audible area in Fig. 16, therefore, we see now that the thresholds are the limits between no information and some information. Within the bounds of the area, however, we can think of regions near the threshold as capable of handling some information while the center of the area handles most information.

The Number of Distinguishable Spectra. The discrimination of pure tones does not give a complete answer, however. Vocal communication relies not upon pure tones, but upon many tones heard simultaneously. We must ask, therefore, how many different spectra a listener might distinguish. How many alternative combinations of the distinguishable tones are there?

This question can be approached crudely in the following way: There are about 300 alternative amplitudes (a) that any one of about 1600 distinguishable frequencies (n) might assume. The number of spectra composed of 1600 components, where each component can assume any one of 300 values, is a^n, or 300^{1600}, a truly astronomical number. It is much longer than this sentence that says it is too long to waste paper by writing it out. Obviously there are not 300^{1600} distinguishable speech sounds. The question is, Why not?

Consider a single one of this tremendous number of different acoustic symbols. Let this be the one that has all of the 1600 different frequencies present and every one of them at an amplitude of 50 db. Then we could generate a different acoustic symbol by changing the amplitude of one of the 1600 components by 0.3 db, a just noticeable increment in that one component. This difference between the two spectra is too small to be reliably distinguished in any practical situation, although the individual components are recognizably different when heard alone.

What factors limit us so that we are not free to use all of the 300^{1600} combinations? An obvious factor is that the intensity of the speech changes according to the distance between the talker and the listener. If an acoustic symbol began with 1600 components all at 50 db, by the time it reached a listener some yards away all of the components might have dropped to 10 db. A listener at one distance would hear one symbol, and a listener at another distance would hear a different symbol. Consequently, all the sounds that have the same pattern of amplitudes, and that differ only in the general level at which the pattern occurs, must be classed together as a single symbol. A pattern of amplitudes at 90 db is obviously louder than the same pattern at 40 db, but we cannot take advantage of this discrimination for the purposes of communication.

The fact that listeners are often at a distance means that most of the sounds reach them at relatively low intensities. Only in very noisy situations do we generate speech at levels anywhere near the threshold of discomfort. Because the speaker's output power is limited and because loud sounds are unpleasant for the listener, the practical upper limit is probably around 100 db.

Another practical consideration that limits the number of usable spectra is the relatively high pitch of the human voice. We do not generate 1600 properly spaced harmonics. On a sustained vowel, for example, the fundamental frequency for a male voice is about 125 cps. Harmonics are multiples of the fundamental, and so we have component tones at 125, 250, 375, 500, 625, etc. For a particular speech sound the voice gives about 80, rather than 1600, tones to use in different combinations of intensities.

Furthermore, slight differences of frequency have little communicative value because the language is used by sopranos and basses alike. Thus the particular frequencies that are involved are less important than the pattern of amplitudes these frequencies assume. We cannot produce one speech symbol by a pattern of amplitudes imposed upon the harmonics of 125 cps and a different symbol by the same pattern imposed upon the harmonics of 120 cps. The frequency difference would be perceptible, but the distinction would be useless for designating different things.

The vocal resonators cannot control the intensity of each component independently. They are too broadly tuned to respond to a single component frequency. If the harmonic at 1000 cps is reinforced by the resonators, then the harmonics at 875 and 1125 cps are also reinforced. It is also necessary to remember that the listener must make an absolute identification, not just perceive that a change has occurred. And it is well known that the perception of one tone is influenced by the occurrence of another tone at the same time.

Even with fairly generous allowances for these practical limits, it is obvious that there are far more acoustically distinguishable vocal patterns than we ever attempt to use for informative purposes. Or, to express the same idea somewhat differently, there is a lot more information in the acoustic pressure waves than the listener needs. Vocal communication does not begin to approach the theoretical limits that our knowledge of the limits of hearing would lead us to expect. We can only conclude, therefore, that the system contains a large safety factor—that fine discriminations (and thus more rapid communication) are sacrificed to obtain greater dependability.

Take a simple numerical example. Compare a language that uses two sounds with a language that uses eight sounds. In order to label each of eight different objects with one of eight different names, the two-sound language must use sequences of three sounds in a row. The eight-sound language can label each of the same eight objects with a single sound. Clearly the two-sound language is slower, because it must use three sounds for every one that the eight-sound language uses. But the two-sound language is also more dependable, because its two sounds can be easily distinguished. With the eight-sound language the listener is forced to make finer distinctions and is more apt to confuse the different sounds.

The number of alternative speech sounds is limited, therefore, in the interest of dependability. The ear could draw finer distinctions, but the greater the demands we make upon discrimination the more the process is subject to errors. We cannot conclude that dependability is the sole reason our spoken language sacrifices speed—most of us cannot absorb, remember, and use information at the rate at which human speech normally provides it. These higher mental processes take time, and a more rapid flow of information to the listener would not be much more efficient than the present rate. More on this topic later.

The Effects of Masking

One of the important limitations on the way we can combine tones into symbolic patterns is the interference that one tone produces in the discrimina tion of a second tone. We began this discussion by placing a listener in a perfectly quiet room and giving him pure tones. Now we want to take him out into the noise of the world and have him listen to complex sounds.

The ability to hear two sounds at once is one of the most useful properties of the human ear. This ability—taken for granted in the preceding discussion—allows us to respond selectively to certain components in the total acoustic pattern and to ignore others, to hear a friend's voice in spite of a background of noise, to follow the theme and still hear the obbligato. The eye has no such ability. Put a red and a yellow light together, and they lose their separate identities in an orange compound. But put an 800-cycle tone together with a 1200-cycle tone, and we hear two tones, not one halfway between.

Remarkable as this ability is, it is not infallible. Put the two tones close together in frequency, and they will *beat;* a beating pair of tones sounds like a single tone that is waxing and waning in intensity. Or make one tone fainter than the other, and the fainter tone may become inaudible although it is still above its normal threshold in the quiet.

The selective mechanism is studied in its simplest form when two pure tones are introduced into the ear and the listener is asked to report the presence or absence of one or the other of the tones. These experiments demonstrate that the ear is not a perfect analyzer, for some tones obscure the perception of others. This interference is called *auditory masking.*

Auditory masking is usually defined as the shift of the threshold of audibility of the masked sound due to the presence of the masking sound. Following this definition, the measurement of auditory masking is a straightforward experimental procedure. First the just audible sound pressure is determined in the quiet. Then the interfering sound is introduced, and the listener's threshold is again determined. The difference, in decibels, between the quiet and the masked thresholds is the measure of the amount of masking produced by that particular type and intensity of interference for that particular masked sound. The notion can also be applied to the complex sounds of speech—the introduction of an interfering sound makes it necessary to raise the intensity of the speech for it to be understood.

Knowledge of the ear's susceptibility to masking is obviously a matter of considerable practical value. Much of our present knowledge has grown out of the job of developing the telephone, although research on communication problems in the Second World War supplemented the earlier investigations. In the course of this research many different masking sounds have been studied to determine the interference they can produce with the perception of many different masked sounds. The general principles involved can be demonstrated, however, by the masking effects of tonal and noisy sounds.

Masking Tones by Tones. The masking of tones by tones (monaural) is illustrated in Fig. 17 (Wegel and Lane, 1924). In the graph on the left there are four threshold curves. The lowest is the threshold measured in the quiet and is the same as the curve in Fig. 16. The next curve is the threshold as measured in the presence of a tone of 800 cps that is 20 db above the quiet threshold at 800 cps. In the presence of this faint masking tone there is a small increase in the threshold of audibility for other tones in the neighborhood of 800 cps. The masking effects do not extend far above or below the masking tone. The dip in the masked threshold indicates the region in which the masked and masking tones produced beats. The third curve from the bottom

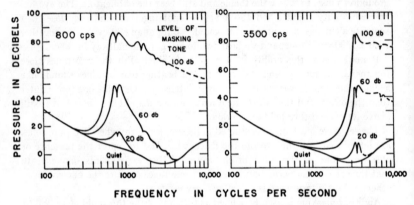

FIG. 17. Masking by pure tones. The change in the threshold of detectability produced by tones of 800 and 3500 cps. The parameter is the level of the masking tone in decibels above its own quiet threshold. (*After Wegel and Lane*, 1924.)

shows the threshold of audibility when the 800-cycle masking tone is increased to 60 db above threshold and the masking effects are more widely distributed. The top curve represents the threshold when the intensity is raised to 100 db. The graph on the right shows results obtained in an identical set of measures with the single difference that the masking tone was 3500 rather than 800 cps.

These thresholds show that the principal effects of a masking tone are produced in the range *above* the frequency of the masking tone. The shift in the threshold for lower tones is relatively slight. This one-way spread of masking means that tones of low frequency can mask out a larger part of the audible area than can tones of high frequency. The greater the loss in area, the less area there is left for communicative purposes. We predict, therefore, that low-frequency sounds will disrupt auditory communication more readily than will high-frequency sounds.

Masking Tones by Noise. Now we turn to the masking of tones by noise. There are an infinite variety of noises to study, but the noise of most general interest is *random noise*. Random noise is a hishing sound compounded of all frequencies of vibration in equal amounts. Because all frequencies are present, it is analogous to certain kinds of white light and so it is often called *white noise.* It sounds like /ꟗꟗꟗꟗꟗ/. Most experiments have not used noises that have extremely high or extremely low frequency components. Generally we work with a *band of noise* that extends from 100 up to about 10,000 cps. This covers all the component frequencies in speech and is adequate for our purposes. The fact that all the components are present in equal amount makes this a very convenient noise to work with. This means, for example, that half the power in the total sound is in the components below 5000 cps and half in the components above 5000 cps. The spectrum of such a noise is simply a horizontal line up to 10,000 cps.

The results obtained when such a noise of uniform spectrum is used to mask pure tones are shown in Fig. 18 (Hawkins and Stevens, 1950). When the over-all level of the noise is 0 db, we cannot hear it and so we turn it up to 10 db. At this level the noise is first detected, but the thresholds for the pure tones are not shifted. Turn the noise up to 30 db, and at this level some masking is produced. The tones in the region of 2000 cps, where the ear is most sensitive, are masked a few decibels, but the other tones are unaffected. By the time the noise is up to 60 db all the tones between 100 and 10,000 cps are masked in varying amount, and the general shape of the threshold curve is much more uniform for all frequencies. If we continue to increase the noise, the shape of the threshold curve remains uniform. For every 10 db increase in the noise we must increase the tone 10 db in order to make it audible. The effect of increasing the masking noise is to decrease the area available for communicative signals.

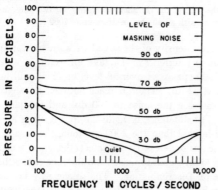

FIG. 18. Thresholds for pure tones when masked by white noise of uniform spectrum. Level of the masking noise is the parameter. (*After Hawkins and Stevens*, 1950.)

In Fig. 18 are shown the quiet and the masked thresholds. The difference between the masked thresholds and the quiet threshold is, as we have said, the measure of masking. Suppose we plot the masking for tones of 200 and 1000 cps as a function of the intensity of the noise. This will give us the sort of plot shown in Fig. 19, which, if we had more different tones plotted, would be essentially equivalent to Fig. 18. These two graphs contain similar information, but they are drawn with different coordinates.

For both masked tones in Fig. 19 the masking, once it is well under way, goes up the same number of decibels that the noise intensity goes up. If we put in 5 db more noise, we require 5 db more tone in order to hear it. This fact is often expressed by saying that the *signal-to-noise ratio* at threshold is constant for high noise levels. The signal-to-noise ratio is the difference in

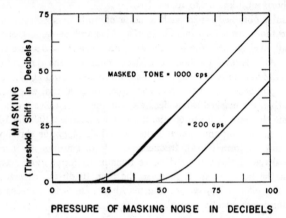

FIG. 19. Showing the shift of the threshold of hearing for two pure tones. The masking sound was a white noise with a uniform spectrum up to 7000 cps.

decibels between the intensity of the sound we want to hear and the intensity of the sound that is interfering. To take an example, a noise of uniform spectrum up to 7000 cps at an over-all level of 75 db will just mask a pure tone of 2000 cps at 52 db. The difference between the signal and the noise is 23 db. Now increase the noise to 100 db, and the just detectable tone must be 77 db. The difference is again 23 db. As long as the noise is less than 23 db more intense than the 2000-cps tone, the tone is audible. Thus the signal-to-noise ratio necessary to detect this tone remains constant at −23 db. At any lower signal-to-noise ratio the tone cannot be heard.

Effect of Noise on Discrimination. The reason why tones and noises produce masking can be phrased in the following way: Irrelevant noise from the world about us reduces the sharpness of our discrimination. Suppose the message spectrum contains energy at 1000 cps and that in order to know exactly which symbol it is we must discriminate rather accurately the magnitude of this 1000-cycle component. Now if a noise is present, it will also have energy in the range of frequencies around 1000 cps. Since the noise is random, we shall not know whether the noise energy is added to the signal (in phase) or whether the noise and the signal energy are canceling each other (out of phase). Therefore the noise adds a fuzziness to the amplitude of the 1000-cycle component in the signal. We are not able to tell precisely what the amplitude is, but only that it falls within a certain range.

If the noise is very faint and the signal is very strong, the fuzziness is negligible. Of course, if the noise is so faint that it makes the signal uncertain over a range smaller than the just noticeable difference, then the noise will have no effect at all. But as the intensity of the noise increases, the range of uncertainty grows larger and larger, until finally all information is washed away in the blur of randomness.

The number of discriminable amplitudes varies according to the amount of noise that is present. If there is much noise, a large change in the intensity of the signal is necessary before we can recognize the change as a symbolic rather than a chance occurrence. To take an example, suppose the maximum signal energy is 100 units of energy and the noise has 2 units of energy. The signal-to-noise ratio in decibels is then the logarithm of the ratio, or $10 \log_{10} {}^{100}\!/_{2}$, or 17 db. The maximum signal is 17 db more intense than the noise. Now ask how many different amplitudes of the signal can be distinguished. If the signal amplitude is 50 units, the listener may receive any value between $50 + 2$ and $50 - 2$ units. It will require a change of at least 2 units before he can be fairly sure the signal is different. The total range of energies he can receive extends from zero to $S + N = 102$ units. The size of a distinguishable change is N units. The total number of distinguishable steps is, therefore, $(S + N)/N$, or ${}^{102}\!/_{2}$, or 51.

Now notice what happens if the noise increases to 10 energy units while the maximum signal level remains the same. The new signal-to-noise ratio will be $10 \log {}^{100}\!/_{10}$, or 10 db. The signal energy can now be determined with an accuracy of only ± 10 units. The number of distinguishable steps is $(S + N)/N$, or $(100 + 10)/10$, or 11. By decreasing the signal-to-noise ratio we decrease the number of distinguishable steps and the number of alternatives that can be used for symbolic purposes.

As the noise increases, the listener's capacity to distinguish differences decreases, and so his ability to receive information also decreases. Thus the signal-to-noise ratio expressed in decibels is a very important concept in understanding communication.

If a language uses a great many different acoustic symbols, the listener needs to make very sharp distinctions in the intensities of the components in the various symbols. Such a language might work perfectly well in the quiet, but in a noisy situation these distinctions would become blurred and useless. Since noise is a regular hazard for our vocal acts, we must design our acoustic symbols to be noise-resistant, to be so different that noise will not confuse them. But if all the symbols must be very different, then there cannot be very many of them.

The occurrence of noise in our workaday world limits the number of speech sounds our language can conveniently employ. Our solution has been to use fewer different speech sounds and to rely more heavily upon the sequences in which these sounds are arranged.

Methods for the Study of Speech Perception

The discussion of hearing has, up to this point, been concerned with man's ability to hear pure tones in the quiet and in noise. Since complex sounds like speech can always be analyzed into pure-tone components, this discussion casts considerable light on the speech problem. Before proceeding to the perception of speech, however, the development must be interrupted at this point to say something about the methods used to study perception in general and speech perception in particular.

In principle, a perceptual experiment is quite simple. A subject is trained to respond in certain ways to certain patterns of stimulation. The physical dimensions of the stimulation are then varied. The question we ask is, Under what variations in the stimulation does the response remain invariant?

Suppose we want to know the threshold of hearing in some given organism. We first train this organism to lift a limb, press a key, wave a flag, or otherwise signal when a tone is on. We then vary the frequency and the amplitude of the tone systematically until the organism's response changes—fails to appear. The limits of the range over which the response occurs are the thresholds of hearing.

A more complicated perceptual experiment might ask what aspects of a melodic pattern of tones an organism discriminates. We could train the organism to make response *a* to pattern *A* and response *b* to pattern *B*. If the several aspects of the melodic patterns are varied systematically, some of the altered patterns may evoke response *a*, others *b*, and still others may evoke no response consistently. By determining what aspects of the stimulation can be changed without changing the organism's response, it is possible to discover those aspects which are crucial and those aspects which are irrelevant in the discrimination that the organism made between *A* and *B*.

The design of all perceptual experiments is similar; a discriminative response is established, the characteristics of the discriminated stimuli are varied, and the point at which stimulus variation begins to produce variation in the response is noted. How a discriminative response is established in any given organism is a problem that must be deferred to a later chapter.

The Articulation Test. It is not a difficult jump from perceiving melodic patterns to perceiving speech. We train the organism to make one response to the sound of the words 'Sit up' and another response to the sound of 'Lie down.' Then we vary the sounds—change their intensity, the fundamental pitch of the voice, the spectrum, the wave form, the duration, etc.—and see what the limits of the variation are. Such an experiment could be conducted with a dog, but if we want to expand the range of stimulus words, we must have the more intelligent human animal to make the discriminations. Fortunately, human listeners come to the experiment with a large vocabulary of discriminative responses that they can' make upon hearing certain acoustic stimuli. We do not need to train them so long as we confine ourselves to those acoustic patterns called words which have already been learned. We modify the stimuli, mix them with other sounds, or distort them in various ways. How much modification is possible before the stimuli fail to elicit the same responses that are elicited by the unmodified stimuli?

The experimental approach to the perception of speech is quite similar to the approach to other perceptual problems. The principal difference is that the discriminative responses have been learned in advance, and we can begin the experiment with a minimum amount of preliminary training. It is possible, however, to use nonsensical combinations of the speech sounds to avoid word combinations. In this case some preliminary training is necessary, for the listeners must learn to distinguish the speech sounds and to respond with the appropriate phonemic symbols. There are several types of nonsense syllables: Phonemes combined according to the rules of the language; phonemes combined in ways that violate the rules; and combinations of phones that do not occur in the language. In what follows we shall use the term to mean combinations of familiar phonemes that follow the rules of the language spoken by the listeners.

The experimental procedure, once the appropriate responses have been learned, is as follows: First the test material must be prepared. This may consist of nonsense syllables (syllables that are not words), monosyllabic or polysyllabic words, discrete sentences containing a given number of key words, or continuous discourse. A talker then reads these materials aloud. The speech sounds may go directly to the listener, or we may intercept them and pass them on to the listener after we have had a chance to modify them. To intercept them we put the talker and the listener in different rooms (or use a phonograph record of the talker's voice) and pick up the sound waves with a microphone which transforms the acoustic waves into electrical waves. The electrical waves then go through gadgets that may modify the wave form, or the spectrum, or the amplitude, etc. Then these modified electrical waves are turned back into acoustical waves by a loudspeaker or a set of earphones, and the sounds are introduced to the listener's ears.

The listener's job is to respond by writing the words or phonemic symbols that correspond to the sounds he hears. His responses are then scored, usually in terms of the number of responses that correspond to the items pronounced by the talker. The scoring may include the tabulation of responses that do not correspond to the words pronounced, since the analysis of errors gives us some notion of how the modified sounds are perceived. For some purposes, errors are as significant as correct responses.

This procedure is called an *articulation test* (Egan, 1948). This somewhat unfortunate name was adopted by engineers at the Bell Telephone Laboratories who first used such experimental methods on a large scale. Their interest was a practical one; they wanted to know whether or not their telephone installations were adequate. They thought of the earphone as speaking—articulating—to the listener. The tests were run to see whether or not the telephone's articulation was adequate for conversational purposes. These engineers were testing their equipment, whereas the psychologist's interest is not in the equipment but in the listeners themselves. With this different emphasis it might be better to call them speech-discrimination tests or speech-perception tests.

Intelligibility as a Function of Intensity. An obvious aspect of speech that we can vary is its intensity. Over a wide range of intensities listeners respond quite uniformly by writing down the words pronounced by the talker. At very low intensities, however, some of the speech sounds become inaudible,

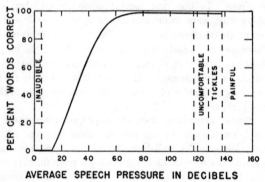

FIG. 20. The curve relates the per cent of monosyllabic words that can be recorded correctly to the intensity of the speech at the listener's ear. (*Data from Kryter*, 1946, *and Silverman*, 1947.)

and some of the words are missed. When the intensity of the speech is about 5 db above 0.0002 dyne/cm² , the presence of speech can just be detected but none of the words can be discriminated. At the high intensities the limiting factor is the listener's comfort. An intensity of 138 or 140 db is described as painful, and most listeners refuse to continue the experiment at higher intensities.

Figure 20 shows the relation between per-cent-words-correct and the intensity of the speech. The test words were English monosyllables. Over a range of almost 100 db, changes in intensity do not change a listener's ability to respond correctly. Over this range, therefore, intensity is not a crucial determinant of intelligibility.

The intensity values plotted along the bottom of Fig. 20 represent the intensity of the speech at the listener's ear, averaged over a large number of words. Any particular word may fall above or below this average because the speech sounds that make up the words have characteristically different intensities. The vowels should, since they have more power than the consonants, be correctly discriminated at intensities where the consonants are too weak to be heard.

If nonsensical syllables are used as test material and the listeners respond with phonemic symbols, we can determine the per cent of the times each speech sound is correctly perceived. The results of such tests are shown for several phonemes in Fig. 21 (Fletcher, 1929, 273–276). You will notice that,

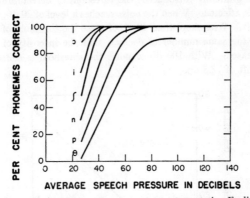

FIG. 21. The per cent of correct responses to some representative English phonemes is plotted against the average intensity for speech. These data were obtained from tests with nonsense syllables. (*Selected from Fletcher, 1929.*)

at an average speech intensity of 25 db, vowels are quite distinguishable but consonants are not. From the loudest vowel to the weakest consonant is a range of about 30 or 40 db.

The weakness of the consonant sounds is unfortunate. The consonants are more critical for the correct interpretation of speech. Comparison of the sentences '-a- -oe- -i- -ay?' and 'Wh-t d-s th-s s-?' shows that consonants minus vowels are more intelligible. In ancient Hebrew, in fact, no vowels were written—only consonants.

Some words are intrinsically more audible than others. 'Show' has far more power than 'theme,' for example. To make articulation tests representative of normal speech, therefore, we must be careful that all the sounds are represented about as often as they would normally occur in conversation. (The relative frequencies of occurrence of the different sounds is discussed in Chap. 4.) When the test material reflects correctly these relative frequencies, it is *phonetically balanced*, and we have some confidence in generalizing from phonetically balanced word lists to more practical situations.

The Masking of Speech

To apply the notion of masking to the perception of speech, we first determine the threshold of audibility for speech in the quiet. This value is about 5 db. Then the interfering sound is introduced, and the listener's threshold is again determined. With any appreciable intensity of noise the level of the speech must be increased to above 5 db to be audible. The difference, in decibels, between the quiet and the masked thresholds is taken as the measure of the amount of masking of speech produced by that type and intensity of noise.

As noise is gradually introduced, the threshold of detectability for speech is at first little affected. When the noise reaches a level of 20 db, the threshold begins to shift. With more than 40 db of noise the threshold of detectability increases by the same number of decibels that the intensity of the masking noise is increased. With 100 db of noise the threshold is shifted from 5 to 77.5 db, a shift of 72.5 db.

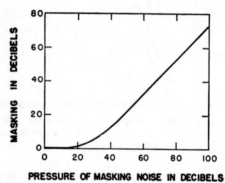

Fig. 22. The shift in the threshold of detectability for speech is plotted as a function of the intensity of white masking noise. (*After Hawkins and Stevens*, 1950.)

Notice that the curve in Fig. 22, which shows the masking of speech by a random noise of uniform spectrum up to 10,000 cps, is very similar to the curves in Fig. 19 for pure tones. As for tones, the signal-to-noise ratio necessary for the detection of speech is constant at high noise levels, and with this noise the speech is detectable so long as it is not more than 17 db less intense than the noise. Because of the general similarity between the masking curves for pure tones and for speech, it is possible to compute the masking of speech by any given noise if we know how this noise masks pure tones. This procedure is discussed in a later section.

The masking of speech depends upon three characteristics of the masking sound, (1) its intensity relative to the intensity of the speech, (2) its acoustic spectrum, and (3) its temporal continuity.

We have discussed the role of intensity for one type of interference, and its role with other types is similar; the more intense the masking sound, the greater the masking. About the spectrum of the interfering sound we can say that low-frequency noises cause more trouble than high-frequency noises but that the maximum masking is produced when the noise has a spectrum very similar to the spectrum of speech itself (Fig. 14). Interruptions in the continuity of the masking sound invariably lower its masking effectiveness.

Although we need not examine in detail all the varieties of masking sound that have been studied, at least one of them deserves special comment. Perhaps the most persistent noise we have to compete with is the sound of another person's voice. In considering other voices as sounds masking the desired voice, two things are obviously crucial. How many other voices is the speaker struggling against? And what are the other people saying? Articulation tests conducted under these conditions show that it is relatively easy for a listener to distinguish between two voices, but as the number of rival voices is increased, the desired speech is lost in the general jabber, even though the over-all intensity of the masking speech is held the same. Although the long-interval spectrum of a single voice is nearly optimal for masking, the spectrum at any moment does not include all of the necessary frequencies. The variations in the level of a single voice are great, and there are relatively long intervals during which no masking sound is present. With several voices a continuous masking signal is produced, and the babble of four or more voices going on at once will drown out the fifth voice about as effectively as any kind of noise we could find (Miller, 1947*a*).

The content of the masking speech—what the voices talk about—is a more difficult factor to evaluate. Masking voices speaking a foreign language have been used, but the masking was neither greater nor less than was obtained with an English babble. Laughter and improbable vocal effects also fail to change the results so long as the spectrum and the over-all intensity of the masking signals are the same. When the subjects are in a standard laboratory situation with a fairly objective attitude toward the test they are taking, the particular content of the masking speech does not influence significantly the amount of masking produced.

CHANGES IN THE SPEECH SPECTRUM

Over a very wide range of intensities a listener's ability to discriminate speech sounds is uniformly good. The presence of noise decreases the range of intensities available for communication, but noise does not distort speech or make it unintelligible if only the speech is loud enough. The speech spectrum should prove to be a more critical variable. The spectra of speech sounds are one of the principal aspects that serve to distinguish one sound from another. It may prove surprising, therefore, to learn how much the spectrum can be changed without destroying intelligibility.

To modify the spectrum of speech by known amounts and in known ways, we convert the acoustic waves into electrical waves, pass the electrical waves through an electrical filter that responds to certain frequencies but not others, then reconvert these filtered waves into acoustic waves for the listener to hear. We shall consider three types of frequency-selective devices: (1) filters that pass high frequencies more efficiently than low, (2) filters that pass low frequencies more efficiently than high, and (3) filters that pass intermediate frequencies more efficiently than high and low frequencies. We shall refer to these as *high-pass*, *low-pass*, and *band-pass filters*, respectively.

Consider the high-pass filter. As we raise the cutoff point below which no frequencies are passed, the per cent of the responses that are correct decreases. If we pass only those speech components above 6000 cps, for example, no words are correctly discriminated. With the low-pass filter we reduce the articulation score as we lower the cutoff point above which no frequencies are passed. When only the components below 200 cps are present, speech is an unintelligible, rumbling noise.

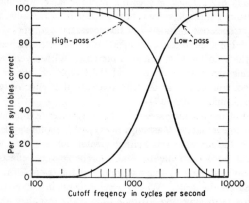

FIG. 23. Functions relating nonsense-syllable articulation scores to the cutoff frequency of high-pass and low-pass filters. For example, with a 1000-cps high-pass filter 90 per cent are correctly heard; with a 1000-cps low-pass filter only 27 per cent are correct. (*After French and Steinberg*, 1947.)

The exact number of words correctly reported will depend upon the intensity of the speech, whether men or women talkers are used, the experience of the test crew, the type of speech material, etc. The experiment has been carried out, however, with both men and women talkers speaking nonsense syllables to highly trained listeners. The speech intensity was maintained well above threshold. Under these conditions the results shown in Fig. 23 were obtained (French and Steinberg, 1947). In this figure the cutoff frequency of the filter is plotted along the abscissa, and the average articulation score is plotted along the ordinate. Looking at the curve for the low-pass filter, for example, we should read from the graph that when only the frequencies below 3000 cps were passed, 88 per cent of the syllables were correctly recorded by the listeners. This dropped to 27 per cent when only the frequencies below 1000 cps were passed.

The two curves cross at 1900 cps. If we pass all the frequencies *above* 1900 cps, listeners get 67 per cent of the nonsense syllables correct, or if we pass all the frequencies *below* 1900 cps, they get 67 per cent correct. The mid-value of 1900 cps is obtained when the results for men and women talkers are averaged together. With men alone, the center frequency is about 1660 cps.

Now it is a fact that under conditions where two-thirds of the nonsense syllables are heard correctly, connected discourse or ordinary conversation is perfectly intelligible. So we come to an interesting situation. We can communicate perfectly well with only the frequencies above 1900 cps present in our voices. But there is nothing peculiar about the frequencies above 1900 cps, because if we throw all these away and use only the frequencies below 1900 cps, we get along equally well. In other words, there is no particular portion of the speech spectrum that is crucial to discrimination.

The band-pass system is somewhat more difficult to discuss because here we have two cutoff frequencies instead of one. The simplest way to discuss it is to take the case where the center of the pass band is 1500 cps and the two cutoff points are varied symmetrically above and below this center. A band of frequencies 400 cps wide (1300 to 1700 cps) gives, if the speech is well above the threshold of hearing, an articulation score of about 10 per cent for nonsense syllables. A band 1000 cps wide will give about 45 per cent correct responses. A band 3000 cps wide will give about 85 per cent (Egan and Wiener, 1946).

It is clear that speech can limp along even when the most amazing changes are made in its spectrum. It does not sound natural, but it is intelligible.

ESTIMATION OF ARTICULATION SCORES

Almost any communication system that transmits the human voice introduces distortions into the spectrum. Not all frequencies are reproduced at their original intensities. It would be handy, therefore, to have some kind of theory that could predict how much interference any given kind of distortion would cause. We can get along without the theory, of course. We can conduct articulation tests with every communication system in order to see whether or not it is satisfactory. But this procedure is tedious and expensive. It would be far easier to measure the amount of distortion introduced and then simply to calculate the effect it has on intelligibility. Such a scheme for calculating articulation scores has been devised. The basic ideas of the theory are outlined in this section.

Division of the Spectrum into Equivalent Bands. The effects of frequency-selective systems upon the intelligibility of speech can be formulated in the following manner (Collard, 1930; French and Steinberg, 1947): Suppose that we have 10 band-pass filters, and the upper cutoff frequency of the first coincides with the lower cutoff frequency of the second, etc., so that with these 10 contiguous pass bands we cover the entire range of speech frequencies. Further suppose that we can vary at will the cutoff frequencies that separate adjacent bands.

Now we take each band separately and conduct articulation tests using only the speech components that lie in the range of frequencies passed by that band. At first we shall obtain higher scores with one band of frequencies than with another. So we readjust the cutoff frequencies, narrowing the bands that scored highest and widening the bands that scored lowest. By successive adjustments we can eventually establish a set of contiguous bands that all give the same articulation score.

Exactly what the score will be depends upon the nature of our tests, but suppose it turns out to be 20 per cent. The filter that passes the lowest band of frequencies permits 20 per cent correct responses, the filter that passes the highest band of frequencies permits 20 per cent correct responses, and each one of the 8 bands in between enables the listener to hear 20 per cent of the test items correctly. We have then determined experimentally the cutoff frequencies that divide the speech spectrum into 10 contiguous bands that *all contribute equally to the intelligibility of speech.*

The rest of the argument is simple. If we add all the bands together and pass all the frequencies, we get the highest articulation score—about 98 per cent. Let this maximum score equal 10 on a new scale that we shall call, arbitrarily, X. X is not the articulation score. $X = 10$ when all frequencies are passed. Each of the bands contributes equally to this value of X, and since there are 10 bands, each must contribute one-tenth of 10, or 1. If we put 2 bands together, $X = 2$, we may get an articulation score of 35 per cent. Combine any 3 bands, $X = 3$, and we get a score of, say, 50 per cent. By combining various numbers of the bands and conducting articulation tests we can go on to establish equations relating 4, 5, 6, 7, 8, and 9 bands to an articulation score. The relation between X and the articulation score would look something like Fig. 24. Within broad limits the contribution to X by any one band is independent of the contributions from the other bands.

We are now ready to tackle a practical problem. An engineer asks, "The communication system I propose to use will pass only the frequencies from a to b. Will speech be intelligible over this system?" To answer his question we get out tables and charts of the experimental results. One table shows the frequencies that divide speech into ten equivalent bands. A chart, similar to Fig. 24, shows the relation between the number of bands and the articulation score. In the table it says that between the frequencies a and b there are just

3.6 of our bands. Then we look up $X = 3.6$ in the chart and find that this corresponds to an articulation score of 60 per cent for the type of speech material we have used.

The engineer must say whether 60 per cent is adequate. Suppose it is not and that he asks, "How much will I have to broaden the system in order to raise the score to 95 per cent?" In the chart it says that 95 per cent requires at least 8.4 of the equivalent bands, and from the table again we see that this corresponds to a certain frequency range. In this way we find in a few minutes the answer to a problem that might have taken weeks to settle by means of articulation tests. The practical advantages of our experiments are obvious.

The scheme is, therefore, to divide the speech spectrum into a number of bands that provide equal degrees of intelligibility. Once this is done it is assumed that these bands can be added together and that the score obtained with one set of pass bands will be the same as the score obtained with another

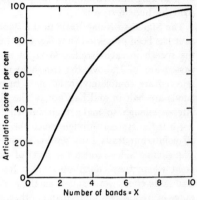

FIG. 24. Chart illustrating the kind of relation obtained between the articulation score and the number of equivalent bands passed by the communication system.

set of pass bands, so long as both sets contain the same total number of bands. The combination of the lowest and the highest bands, for example, should give the same articulation score as the combination of the two middle bands. To a close approximation this assumption is justified, and the bands do seem to add up. If $X = 5$, the articulation score will be approximately the same no matter which five bands are selected.

With this representation of the problem it is obvious that no single range of frequencies is indispensable for the discrimination of speech. The experiment has not been done exactly as described in the preceding paragraphs. The reasoning has been applied in a slightly different experimental form. The frequency of 1900 cps divides the speech spectrum into two bands that contribute equally to intelligibility. When we divide further to obtain 10 bands, we find that 5 of these bands lie in the range from 200 to 1900 cps and that the other 5 lie in the range from 1900 to 7000 cps. For this particular series of experiments, when $X = 5$ the articulation score (nonsense syllables) is 67 per cent. If the divisions are carried out, we find that the first band extends from 200 to 500 cps, the second from 500 to 800, then 800 to 1130, 1130 to 1500, 1500 to 1900 cps. The 5 bands above 1900 cps are divided at 2350, 2900, 3700, 4900, and 7000 cps. These 11 frequencies divide the spectrum into 10 bands that contribute equally to the factor X.

These frequencies, selected because they divide the speech spectrum into bands of equal importance for intelligibility, also divide the audible range into segments that contain approximately the same number of distinguishable tones. Where discrimination is most acute, there is (1) the greatest capacity for handling information and (2) the greatest contribution to the articulation score for human speech.

The Signal-to-Noise Ratio in the Bands. There is a snag in the argument as it has been presented thus far, and this snag has to do with the intensity of the speech in each band. So far it has been assumed that the frequencies passed are well above the threshold of audibility and that the frequencies rejected are completely inaudible. In most practical situations some of the bands are half in and half out of the picture; they may be present but not intense enough to make their full contribution to intelligibility. This can result if the system through which the speech passes does not have sharp cutoff points but trails away gradually on either side of the resonant frequency. The sloping sides reduce the level of the speech at some frequencies to the point where they contribute only a fraction of what they could contribute. The same effect can result from the presence of noise. Noise may affect one range of frequencies more than another, so that one band makes only a partial contribution while another contributes maximally. Before the computational system is suitable for most purposes, we must devise a *weighting factor* so that some bands can make a fractional portion of their maximum possible contribution to intelligibility.

The procedure for determining what fraction of its maximum each band contributes requires that we know the threshold of hearing in that band. Or if a masking sound is present, we must know the masked threshold of hearing in the band. It turns out that the speech energy in each one of the 10 bands must be higher than the threshold of hearing for a pure tone at the center of the band before the speech energy in that band can make any contribution to intelligibility. We disregard all the other speech components and measure only those within a given band. If the result of this measurement gives us a value below the threshold of hearing in that band—either the quiet or masked threshold—the band is no help to communication. If the result is more than 30 db above the threshold, the band makes its maximum contribution. As a general approximation, values between 0 and 30 db make a proportionate contribution; that is to say, if the speech in the band is 15 db above the threshold in the band, it contributes half its maximum, or if it is 6 db above, it contributes a fifth, and so forth.

To summarize: The factors of frequency selectivity, speech intensity, and masking can be combined into a single description by (1) dividing the speech spectrum into 10 frequency bands that contribute equally to intelligibility,

(2) weighting the contribution of each band according to how far the speech intensity in that band exceeds the threshold of hearing in the band, and (3) converting the total contribution of all 10 bands into an articulation score.

The reasoning behind this procedure is that the discriminative clues provided by one band of frequency components are independent of the discriminative clues provided by components outside the band. The listener responds most accurately when all the discriminative clues from all the bands are present, and as the number of discriminative clues is reduced, his accuracy is reduced. He will be right a small percentage of the time even when the discriminative clues are filtered or masked to a bare minimum. No particular frequency range is of indispensable importance, and the listener can use the clues he gets from one range of frequencies about as well as those he gets from another range.

An alternative way of expressing this notion is to say that undistorted speech contains many more discriminative clues than are actually necessary. By lavishing distinguishable differences all along the frequency scale we effectively take out insurance against distortion and masking. Many of the characteristic features may be distorted beyond recognition, but if we send enough different clues, some of them will probably get through. This is the secret of the resilience of the spoken word—it contains far more information than the listener actually needs. As a result the listener's response is invariant over a wide range of distortions, and not until nearly all of the clues are eliminated does the listener falter.

It is fortunate that speech intelligibility does resist the erosion of frequency selectivity, for our normal environment plays havoc with the speech spectrum. The world is full of objects, and the objects all cast shadows. Sound travels around corners, of course, but not all sound waves travel around corners equally well. Low frequencies get around far better than high frequencies. Consequently, the acoustic shadow of an object contains the low-frequency components of the sound while the high-frequency components are considerably attenuated. The speech spectrum behind a talker's head, for example, contains much less high-frequency energy than the spectrum in front of his head If speech were highly dependent upon faithful transmission of the spectra of the different speech sounds, it would necessarily reduce to a line-of-sight method of communication and many of the great advantages of vocal signaling would disappear.

Intelligibility and Information. It is instructive to compare this formulation of the articulation-test scores with the formulation given in Chap. 2 for the amount of information in a sound wave. There we found that

$$\text{Amount of information} = 2TW \log \frac{S+N}{N},$$

where $\log (S + N)/N$ can be taken as the signal-to-noise ratio in decibels, W is the width of the frequency band, and T is the duration of the message.

To calculate an articulation score also we need to know the signal-to-noise ratio in decibels and the width of the band of frequencies. The band-width factor X is multiplied by a weighting factor proportional to the signal-to-noise ratio. The duration does not enter the formula because we assume that all the test items last equally long. The similarity of the two formulations shows that the articulation score is a function of the amount of information the listener receives, when information is defined as in Chap. 2. However, the articulation score cannot be taken as a direct measure of the amount of information in the speech wave.

OTHER TYPES OF DISTORTION

Interruptions. A further illustration of the extravagant provision of discriminative clues in our vocal communication is the effect of *interruptions* of speech upon intelligibility. Suppose the talker is turned off completely for a certain per cent of the time. Under some conditions he can be understood satisfactorily even when his voice is turned off more than half the time. The number of discriminative clues provided during the short interval the speech is on is adequate for conversational purposes.

In one experiment the listener was prevented from hearing the first fractional portion of the nonsense syllable spoken by the talker (Steinberg, 1936, 931–932). A voice relay was used that did not complete the communication circuit to the listener until some fixed interval after the talker's voice had begun. The listener would then hear the nonsense syllable /fas/, for example, with a very short section missing at the beginning of the /f/. The average duration of the initial consonants was normally about 0.16 sec. When the first 0.08 sec of this consonant was lopped off, the listeners still got the sound right about half as often as they did when none of the consonant was missing. With the first 0.12 sec gone the listeners were right about 25 per cent of the time. If meaningful words were used in complete sentences, the whole consonant might be eliminated without disturbing the listener's response. Even in the absence of these contextual clues the listeners were able to discriminate individual consonants half the time when half the consonant was present.

Another type of experiment interrupts the circuit repeatedly at regular intervals but does not attempt to cut out any specific part of the words. Consider the case first where the speech is on as long as it is off—that is to say, the speech is turned on 50 per cent of the time. If the interruption is made at very slow rates—on for half an hour, then off for half an hour—the listener gets half as many words right as he would without interruptions, because only half as many words are presented to him. If the rate of interruption is speeded up, however, until the speech is turned on and off 10 times every second, then all the words are again intelligible. Interruption rates of 10 or more per second, where the speech is on 50 per cent of the time, do not lower materially the listener's ability to discriminate monosyllabic words (Miller and Licklider, 1950). Qualitatively, the interrupted speech seems hoarse or husky, as if the talker had some disorder of phonation. Nonetheless, the speech is surprisingly intelligible. The ear is very facile in patching together interrupted fragments of speech and in reconstructing the whole message from only half the original wave form.

We can hold the rate of interruption constant at, say, 10 interruptions per second and vary the portion of the total time the speech is on. It is not until 90 per cent of the speech wave is blanked out that none of the words can be discriminated. With only 25 per cent of the speech wave present it is possible to discriminate about 65 per cent of the monosyllabic words.

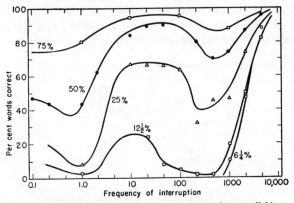

FIG. 25. Effect of interruptions of speech upon intelligibility of monosyllabic words. The articulation score is plotted as a function of the number of interruptions per second, with the per cent of the time the speech was on as the parameter. (*From Miller and Licklider,* 1950.)

The effects of interruption upon the intelligibility of monosyllabic English words are summarized in Fig. 25, where the per cent of the words heard correctly is plotted as a function of the number of interruptions per second. When the speech is on 75 per cent of the time and off 25 per cent, the frequency of interruption does not have any great effect; intelligibility is not greatly impaired. When the speech is on only one-eighth of the time, however, intelligibility is poor until the frequency of interruption reaches several thousand per second.

Time Delay. Another method of butchering the wave form of speech is to use different *time delays* for the different component frequencies. If we separate the speech spectrum into two parts, high frequencies in one and low frequencies in the other, we can delay one part by a small fraction of a second before we put the two halves back together again. This slight delay does not change the spectrum. But the low and high components now add together to give an entirely diffcrent wave shape. In experiments of this sort it has been found that a delay in half the spectrum of as much as 0.1 sec did not affect materially the intelligibility of speech (Steinberg, 1930).

Amplitude Selectivity. Even more radical alterations of the wave form can be produced by *amplitude selectivity*. It is possible with electronic circuits to devise a gadget that passes only certain portions of the wave, where the portion passed depends upon its amplitude. If, for example, the peaks of the speech wave vary from +10 to −10, we can select only that part of the wave between +5 and −5, while the peaks that extend beyond this range are thrown away. Or we can throw the center of the wave away and pass only the peaks.

Figure 26 illustrates these two types of amplitude selectivity. The usual wave form at the top is clipped electronically along the dotted line. If the center of the wave is passed and the peaks discarded, the wave is *peak-clipped*. If the peaks are passed and the center discarded, it is *center-clipped*.

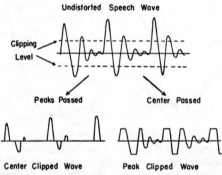

FIG. 26.   Two types of distortion of the wave form produced by amplitude-selective systems.

These two types of amplitude selectivity have quite different effects upon the listener's ability to respond. If we clip out the center of the wave, we do not need to go very far before everything is completely garbled. The peaks alone sound like static bursts. But if we clip off the peaks and pass the center, nothing happens to intelligibility. We can, in fact, strip the peaks down to practically nothing and use what is left to turn a switch on and off. This produces a square wave that crosses the time axis wherever the original speech wave crossed but that is otherwise unrelated to the speech wave. And, surprisingly, conversation can proceed under such distortion with little or no difficulty (Licklider, 1946).

Why does center clipping ruin intelligibility while peak clipping leaves it relatively unaffected? In the first place, vowels are much more intense than consonants. When we peak-clip, we affect the vowels but leave the consonants alone. When we center-clip, we cut out the consonants and leave the peaks of the vowels sticking up. Since the consonants are much more important for discrimination of speech, the center clipping, which throws the consonants away, quickly ruins our discriminative clues. With peak clipping the consonants actually become as strong as the vowel sounds, and a limited amount of peak clipping makes the speech sound crisp and clearly pronounced. In the second place, peak clipping does not change the spectrum as much as does center clipping. When the center is eliminated, the spectrogram we obtain from visible speech equipment is completely altered. But if the peaks are eliminated, the spectrogram is changed only in detail (Licklider, Bindra, and Pollack, 1948).

The fact that intelligibility is relatively impervious to peak clipping is convenient for the communication engineer. Speech comes in an unhandy sort of shape with peaks sticking out all over it. If he can shear these unhandy peaks away and get all parts to the same amplitude, he can put speech into a package that passes through his equipment more easily. For the psychologist, however, these studies imply that the shape of the wave does not uniquely determine the listener's response to speech.

The effect of peak clipping is greatly to simplify the speech wave. Extreme peak clipping, which produces a rectangular wave form, achieves the maximum simplification of the amplitude dimension of the wave. The wave form is reduced to one or the other of two alternative amplitudes. No further simplification of the amplitude dimension can be achieved. If the speech wave is to be further simplified, therefore, it is necessary to operate on the time dimension.

The peak-clipped wave crosses the time axis whenever the unclipped wave crossed. If we want to simplify it, we can force the wave to cross the time axis only at predetermined instants. At each such instant it either does switch, or it does not switch. For example, the output wave can switch at the end of an interval if, during the interval, the peak-clipped input wave has switched one or more times. If the instants at which we permit the wave to switch are very close together, none of the crossings in the original wave are lost. As the time between switching instants is increased, however, more and more of the crossings of the input wave will be deleted from the output wave. The question is, How far can we go in eliminating the crossings?

The experimental evidence indicates that if the switching instants are 0.0002 sec apart, it is possible to understand half of the monosyllabic English words uttered by the talker (Licklider, 1950). In other words, intelligible speech can be produced with a simple two-pole switch that can open and close 5000 times per second or more.

Frequency Changes. Still another kind of distortion is produced by *varying the fundamental frequency* of the talker's voice. From the lowest male basso to the highest female soprano is quite a range—from about 80 to 1000 cps—

and yet the intelligibility of their speech is unquestionable. The fundamental frequency of the voice is not critical for communication.

The relative unimportance of the fundamental frequency can be shown by varying the speed of rotation of a phonographic recording. This procedure is equivalent to *multiplying* all the component frequencies of the speech by a common factor. If the rotation is slowed down to half the normal speed, all the frequency components are multiplied by 0.5. The results of articulation tests conducted with this type of distortion show that an average person can interpret short sentences correctly over 90 per cent of the time even when the component frequencies of the speech are multiplied by a factor as low as 0.6 or as high as 1.8. With more elaborate equipment it is possible to *add* a constant number of cycles per second to all the component frequencies. Under these conditions a listener can respond correctly to short sentences over 90 per cent of the time even when the frequencies are shifted downward 250 cps or upward 400 cps (Fletcher, 1929). Thus we see that the listener's ability to discriminate words is relatively unaffected by large changes in the fundamental frequency of the talker's voice.

Speed of Talking. Variations in the speed of rotation of a phonographic recording vary the rate of talking in addition to changing all the component frequencies. How much effect does *speed of talking* have when the frequencies are not shifted? H. Goldstein (1940) reports a study in which paragraphs from reading-comprehension tests were read aloud at several speeds: 100, 137, 174, 248, 285, and 322 words per minute. The listeners were tested for their ability to understand the materials. Listening-comprehension scores remained remarkably high for the lower speeds and did not fall to zero even at the very rapid rate of 322 words per minute. Apparently, under otherwise optimal conditions, we could double our normal rates of talking without becoming unintelligible.

We have proceeded down the list of variables we can change in the study of speech perception, and none of them, taken alone, seems to be crucially important. Over very wide ranges of variation the intensity, the presence of noise, the shape of the spectrum, the shape of the wave, the pitch of the voice do not affect the listener's ability to discriminate words and to respond correctly on articulation tests. Consideration of the way speech can be mutilated and still survive as a means of communication increases considerably one's respect for the resilience and dependability of vocal signaling systems. We can throw away completely large portions of the speech without altering the listener's ability to interpret the speech correctly. The excessive number of discriminable aspects of the speech sounds makes the analysis of speech perception a difficult problem, but the practical usefulness of this multiplicity of discriminative clues is obvious.

In Chap. 2 we estimated that the amount of information in an acoustic wave is proportional to (1) the duration of the message, (2) the width of the band of frequencies, and (3) the signal-to-noise ratio in decibels. The results of the articulation tests confirm our belief that these are the three critical variables involved in the perception of speech, but the articulation score is not directly equivalent to the amount of information. Since we do not use all the potentially available alternatives, it is possible to lose some information in the noise and distortion and still get articulation scores near 100 per cent. It is not until the amount of information in the speech is dramatically mutilated that all of the discriminative clues are lost and the articulation score drops to zero.

THE TEST MATERIALS

At several places in the preceding pages it has been necessary to qualify a general statement by the phrase 'depending upon the specific nature of the test material.' An articulation score may be as low as 5 per cent or as high as 95 per cent under identical acoustic conditions. The difference lies in the test materials.

Figure 27 illustrates how important the test materials can be. These data were all obtained with the same test crew and the same communication equipment, but with three different kinds of test materials (Miller, Heise, and Lichten, 1951). In one case the test words were the digits from 0 to 9, in another case sentences were read and scored for the major words, and in the third case nonsense syllables were used and recorded in

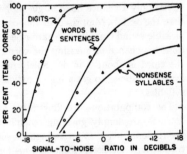

FIG. 27. Articulation scores obtained for different types of test materials. The same communication equipment and test crew were used for all three functions. (*From Miller, Heise, and Lichten,* 1951.)

phonemic notation. In order to get 50 per cent of the items correct, the nonsense syllables had to be 17 db more intense than the digits.

These large and consistent differences pose a problem. In Chap. 2 a formula is developed to express the amount of information carried by a sound wave. This formula says that the amount of information depends upon the length of the message, on the band width of the transmission system, and upon the signal-to-noise ratio in decibels. It does not say anything about the kind of verbal materials used to test the system. In these tests the duration of all the words was about the same, the band width of the communication system was from 200 to 3000 cps for all the tests, and the signal-to-noise ratios were those shown in Fig. 27. At any given signal-to-noise ratio, therefore, a constant amount of information reached the listener. When this amount of information was coded in nonsense syllables, however, the articulation score was far lower than when the same amount of information was coded in digits. Why does the articulation score vary even though the amount of information remains constant?

The principal factor at work is the restriction of the number of possible speech sounds a listener can insert to replace the inaudible portion of the utterance. A little calculation makes the point clear. Suppose we work with 25 consonants and 20 vowels and diphthongs as the building blocks from which our test material is constructed. If we build up only consonant-vowel-consonant (CVC) syllables, we can get $25 \times 20 \times 25 = 12,500$ different syllables. As a rough estimate only about 2000 of these will be found in a good English dictionary and can be called words. When the listener knows the test material is comprised of nonsense syllables of the CVC type, there is practically no anticipatory clue available to tell him what the third member is if he hears only the other two. If he misses the final consonant, for example, he has only 1 chance in 25 of guessing what it was. But if the listener knows that the test is comprised of monosyllabic words, about 85 per cent of the possible sound combinations are ruled out automatically. Under these conditions his chance of guessing the correct sound when he hears two and misses the third is about 1 in 4. Solely on the basis of probability, therefore, we expect a listener to get a higher articulation score for words than for nonsense syllables.

The computations are illustrative and should not be taken to imply that listeners are simply guessing machines. A multiplicity of factors influences the response made to an ambiguous sound. We do not know from this illustration how the listener changes his tendencies to respond in accordance with the nature of the material he expects. The expectation, or *set*, may be established by the experimenter's instructions, or it may come from the listener's previous experience in the situation. But in either case the listener who is set to discriminate among a small number of possibilities does better than the listener set to discriminate among a large number. It is for this reason that the Armed Forces standardize a small vocabulary and insist upon stereotyped procedures for all military communications.

Size of the Test Vocabulary. In order to estimate the importance of the size of the test vocabulary, articulation tests were run with test vocabularies of 2, 4, 8, 16, 32, 256, or an unspecified number of monosyllabic words (Miller, Heise, and Lichten, 1951). When the restricted vocabularies were used, the listeners knew exactly what alternatives to expect. They were required merely to decide which of the possibilities had really occurred. The results are shown in Fig. 28. As the size of the test vocabulary increases, it is necessary to increase the intensity of the speech relative to the noise in order to maintain a given level of accuracy.

These differences in perceptual accuracy cannot be explained in terms of the stimuli used. The sound patterns falling on the listener's ears were in all cases quite comparable. The difference lies, not in what words *were* spoken, but in what words *might have been spoken*. That is to say, the accurate perception of a spoken word depends not only upon the acoustic characteristics of the word as a stimulus but upon the frame of expectations in which that word occurs.

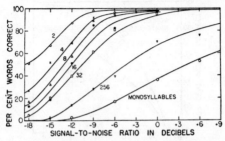

FIG. 28. Articulation scores are plotted as a function of the speech-to-noise ratio for test vocabularies containing different numbers of alternative English monosyllables. The function at the bottom was obtained with a vocabulary of approximately 1000 monosyllables. (*From Miller, Heise, and Lichten*, 1951.)

These considerations make it possible to say why the articulation score may vary even though the amount of information remains constant. When the test item is one out of a small number of possible items, it requires less information to perceive it correctly than when it is one out of a large number of possible items. If the sound wave carries one unit of encoded information, this unit may be sufficient for the accurate perception of one out of a small number of alternatives but insufficient for the accurate selection of one out of a large number of alternatives. Thus the logarithm of the number of items in the test vocabulary is a measure of the amount of information that the listener must receive in order to respond correctly.

Effects of Context. When larger units—phrases or sentences—are used, the listener is set to supply certain blanks in certain ways according to the words preceding and following the blanks. Here again an extravagant supply of discriminative clues is provided for the recipient. Whole words can often be replaced correctly when they are missing from a sentence. In connected discourse we are bound by syntactic rules. Verbs, adjectives, nouns, etc., appear in certain standard patterns in English. If enough of the discourse is perceived to reveal the basic pattern of the sentence, the range of possible words that can be substituted into the pattern is greatly decreased. Thus the probability of a correct guess is increased. For example, in the sentence 'He threw the . . . out the window,' we can immediately reject all parts of speech except nouns. Then we can reject all the nouns that are associated with unthrowable objects. Then we can give preference to certain things that people are known to throw—balls, rocks, bombs, etc. So we get down to a rather small number of possibilities. If we get the slightest clue from the acoustic pattern, we can choose one of these few alternatives. If it turns out that he threw some improbable object like a cow or a smile, we shall be wrong. But the odds are in our favor.

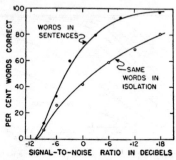

FIG. 29.   The effect of the sentence context upon the articulation scores for words. (*From Miller, Heise, and Lichten,* 1951.)

Figure 29 illustrates the value of the sentence as context for the correct perception of words. When the key words in the sentences are taken out of context and rearranged in a random order, these same words become much harder to hear.

Because the elimination of unlikely possibilities occurs so quickly and so automatically, it is difficult to imagine how the process takes place. The nature of the situation somehow influences what a listener expects, and from this relatively narrow range of expected events he chooses the one that seems to him most probable. Since connected discourse limits considerably the range of possible substitutions the listener can make, it yields test scores far higher than do nonsense syllables. We do not abandon a behavioral description when we talk about a listener's expectations; the word indicates merely that the likelihood of certain responses by the listener is very low and the likelihood of others is quite high. Exactly what goes on when the listener is set and how this set can be altered so readily are basic, unanswered questions in the psychology of perception.

In one experiment listeners were asked to repeat words and sentences in which certain consonants had been omitted by the speaker (Bagley, 1900). When isolated words were presented, the missing consonant was more often supplied correctly at the end of a monosyllable (13 per cent correct) than at the beginning (3.5 per cent). When the same mutilated monosyllables appeared in a sentence, however, the intended consonant was correctly supplied about three-fourths of the time. A somewhat vaguer set than the sentence could be supplied by giving the listener two words often associated with the mutilated word just before the test word was presented. The listener might hear 'water, hydrogen, ele–ents.' With the set so supplied he was much more likely to respond with 'elements' than he was when no set was provided.

When we are listening to a familiar language, therefore, it is possible for us to supply missing sounds and words and to respond adequately on the basis of extremely reduced clues. With an unfamiliar language—foreign or highly technical—the opposite may be true. If a listener is completely unprepared for the sequence of speech sounds that he hears, his ability to mimic the sounds is greatly reduced.

Perceiving speech is not a passive, automatic procedure. The perceiver contributes a selective function by responding to some aspects of the total situation and not to others. He responds to the stimuli according to some organization that he imposes upon them. And he supplements the inconsistent or absent stimulation in a manner that is consistent with his needs and his past experience.

DISCUSSION QUESTIONS

1. Does the reliance upon patterns (relative rather than absolute values of components of the stimulus) for vocal communication have any analogy in visual perception?

2. Would you expect to find the phenomenon of masking in visual perception? What is visual contrast?

3. Is the human voice properly engineered? Does it provide information in the ranges where the human ear is best equipped to handle information?

4. What effects would a deafness for high tones have on a person's ability to receive vocal symbols?

5. To what extent is the mistaken perception of speech responsible for changes in pronunciation during the history of our language?

6. To what extent can we evaluate a talker's personality merely from the sound of his voice? How are we able to make such judgments?

7. How would you go about selecting a vocabulary of highly audible words for communication in the presence of intense noise?

SELECTED REFERENCES

BORING, E. G., H. S. LANGFELD, and H. P. WELD. *Foundations of Psychology*. New York: Wiley, 1948. Chapter 14 provides an introduction to the psychology of hearing and supplements the more limited discussion given here.

FLETCHER, HARVEY. *Speech and Hearing*. New York: Van Nostrand, 1929. The last five chapters summarize the early studies on the perception of speech.

LICKLIDER, J. C. R., and G. A. MILLER. The perception of speech. In S. S. Stevens (Ed.), *Handbook of Experimental Psychology*. New York: Wiley, 1951. A brief summary of the experimental studies of speech perception.

STEVENS, S. S., and H. DAVIS. *Hearing, Its Psychology and Physiology*. New York: Wiley, 1938. An advanced but readable survey of auditory theory and research.

Chapter 4

THE STATISTICAL APPROACH

> Of all the acts of human behavior the stream of speech alone seems to constitute a continuum which with the minimum of distortion can be isolated from the total background of behavior and at the same time be labelled and studied statistically with a high degree of accuracy.
>
> —G. K. ZIPF

The work of the statistician has been likened to that of the map maker who presents a traveler with a sketch of the important highways, the locations of towns, and the major geographical features. The interesting details and beautiful scenery are deliberately omitted. Towns are dots and rivers are lines, and all features of human interest which constitute the traveler's real goals are missing. But just as the map is an aid to reaching these goals, so the statistical facts of a science provide an orientation for the workers in the science. The statistician gives averages, trends, variabilities, correlations, and the particular details are lost in the abstract summary. When we turn to statistical methods, therefore, we do so to gain a general orientation, and not to explain a particular event.

The statistical approach is most helpful when we have large masses of data to analyze. For example, it is impossible to remember the income of every individual in the United States. This great mass of figures is replaced by a few statistics that can be remembered and that are sufficient for most purposes. It is not surprising, therefore, to find that statistical methods are valuable in the study of verbal behavior. The quantity of verbiage spoken daily by the average citizen is so great that detailed analysis of his every utterance is almost unthinkable. Nothing less powerful than the simplifying abstractions of statistics can deal with the data.

What do people say? Even after we specify which people and under what conditions, the question is a hard one. It is not that we cannot record what they say, or that we cannot understand what they say, but that they say so much. Statistical simplification is imperative. We might make up a list that contained all the sentences we heard from the particular people under the given circumstances and check the appropriate sentence each time it occurred. If we did this for long, we should discover that some sentences occur relatively often, while others are rare, and some combinations of words do not occur at all. People do not often say, 'The green kangaroo writes textbooks of biochemistry,' and it is a safe gamble that this sentence would not occur in the list at all. What a man says is constrained in many ways: by the audience, by the grammar of his language, by his own needs and experience. Before we begin to consider some of the particular restraints imposed upon what people say, however, we need a general statistical orientation to tell us what kinds of utterances are important to consider.

One kind of constraint on the talker is the structure of the language he speaks. The successive words in an English sentence are not unrelated. Once a speaker has begun, 'She looked around the . . . ,' he is not free to open the dictionary at random to select the next word. The next word is determined, at least in part, by the context of the words around it. It is this notion of context, of interdependencies among successive items in a message, that we must examine. Obviously we cannot study every verbal context that could conceivably occur. What we can do is draw a statistical map of our communicative behavior and ask why we permit ourselves so little freedom in the choice of what we say.

A DEFINITION OF VERBAL CONTEXT

When psychologists refer to context, they usually mean the totality of conditions that affect an individual at a given time. In the study of learning, for example, it has been found that learned material is recalled more readily if the learner is trying to recall it in the same situation in which he learned it. Then we speak of contextual aids to memory.

By *verbal context*, however, we mean something more specific than the totality of conditions affecting the individual. Spoken language proceeds sound by sound, word by word, sentence by sentence. Whatever unit of language we choose, from the sine waves of Fourier analysis to the chapters of a book, the unit takes on different significance in different constellations. The verbal context of any particular verbal unit is made up of the communicative acts that surround it.

What a man says cannot be predicted entirely from the verbal context. A talker must have an audience to support his behavior, and his knowledge of that audience governs his choice of verbal units. His needs may lead him to choose certain verbal units to request or demand cooperation. His choice of verbal units is correlated with his perceptions, for he may comment upon the unusual or echo the words of another person. The talker's entire history contributes to the stock pile of verbal units he knows and the way he uses them. When we talk of verbal context we ignore, for the time, these important influences. The question under consideration is the extent to which any particular verbal unit is determined by the other verbal units that surround it. Speaking and writing are open to all the influences that affect all types of behavior, and a discussion of the complete context of a communicative act must include the talker's needs, perceptions, audience, and cultural background.   These factors are taken for granted in the present chapter.

The Units of Analysis.   The problem of verbal context implies the problem of *verbal units*, the elements that are arranged to provide the context.   Taken uncritically, behavior flows along more or less continuously.   To analyze the flow requires the definition of units of behavior.   These units are usually defined rather arbitrarily to suit the convenience of the particular analysis.   Sometimes the units are sharply restricted, detailed, specific, and *molecular*.   Sometimes they are general, goal-directed, *molar* units.   This is not a sharp distinction between molecular and molar units of behavioral analysis.   All that is usually meant by it is that one behavioral unit is more or less molecular than some other.   Compared with an analysis into word units, for example, physiological phonetics offers a relatively molecular approach to communicative behavior.   In the molar study of verbal behavior the physiological substratum is taken for granted; the emphasis is given to ordering the relations among larger units—sounds, words, sentences, complete conversations, or the like.   For a molar study it is sufficient to know the talker said such and such.   We do not need to specify that the abdominal walls braced at time t_1 followed by contraction of the internal intercostals at time t_2, etc.

There are many possible units—muscle contractions, sine waves, phonemes, morphemes, syllables, words, phrases, clauses, sentences, paragraphs, letters of the alphabet, parts of speech, or any one of several psychogrammatical categorizations.   The particular unit we choose depends on the purposes of the study.   If, for example, we want to study how children learn to spell, we use the letters of the alphabet as the units for the analysis.   If we try to determine how the phrasing of a question influences the results of a poll of public opinion, the phrase or sentence is the useful unit.   At one time we look at the talker as a generator of sound waves, and at another time he seems a fountain of prepositional phrases.   The choice depends upon the interest.   The only real restriction is that we must be able to recognize the unit whenever it occurs.

The most significant units into which the flow of English speech is commonly divided are phonemes, words, and sentences.   The rules defining the phonemes of any particular language are discussed in Chap. 2.   Can we find similar criteria for the definition of a word or a sentence?

The grammar of any language has two main parts: (1) *morphology* deals with the structure of words, and (2) *syntax* deals with the combinations of words in phrases and sentences.   To define what a word is in any given language is to describe the morphology of that language.   To define what a sentence is describes the syntax.

As we examine the recorded utterances of any language, we find that similar units occur again and again in similar situations.   On the basis of this recurrence the utterances can be analyzed into parts of various length.   Any part that can be spoken alone in normal speech is a *free form*.   A part that never appears alone in normal speech is a *bound form*. A free form that cannot be divided into smaller free forms is called a *minimum free form*, or a *simple word*. This definition is not completely satisfactory, however. In most languages some words can be analyzed into smaller parts. A word that is built up of a minimum free form plus a bound form is called a *complex word*. A word that is built up wholly of smaller words is called a *compound word*. In what follows we include minimum free forms, complex words, and compound words together when we refer to words in general. These rules for recognizing words are important when the language exists only in its spoken form. In order to develop a written version of the language, we use these rules for deciding what the words are. Most languages, however, have already taken the step from spoken to written form. When this step has already been taken, the rule for recognizing words is much simpler. We simply examine the written language; any sequence of symbols set off by a blank space at both ends is a word.

The analysis of the recorded utterances into sentences makes use of the pattern of intonation of the spoken language. Or if the written language exists, we look for the punctuation marks. The most common syntactic form in English is the *actor-action construction*. The first position in the sentence is given to the name of the actor; the second position is given to what the actor does. The two constituents are sometimes called the subject and the predicate. The majority of English sentences are modifications or elaborations of the basic actor-action construction.

Once the units of analysis are defined, the procedure is to count the number of times each unit occurs. Each particular occurrence of a speech unit is called a *token*, and all similar tokens classed together as one group are said to constitute a *type*. In the sentence 'There is no fool like an old fool' there are two word tokens that belong to the same type, so the sentence contains eight word tokens and seven word types. The number of word tokens is determined by the length of the passage counted. The number of word types is the number of different words that occur in that passage. When the number of occurrences of each word type has been determined, it is usually expressed as a percentage. In a passage of 1000 word tokens, for example, we might find 100 occurrences of the word type 'the.' In this case 'the' comprises 10 per cent of the total passage. Such a percentage value is referred to as the *relative frequency* of occurrence of the particular word type.

Patterns of the Verbal Units. In order to show how knowledge of the relative frequencies of occurrence of various verbal units contributes to the study of verbal context, we adopt a useful device from C. E. Shannon (1948).

Suppose that we hire a man who has no knowledge of the English language to write essays for us in English. We provide him with a complete list of all the English words and lock him up with the instruction that he must produce a passage *n* words long that is as much like English as he can make it. In his ignorance his best procedure is to draw words at random from the dictionary.

Since each word occurs once on the list, this procedure uses each word with the same relative frequency as every other word and the sequences are quite random. Such a sequence, based upon no knowledge of the statistical or grammatical structure of English, is called a *zero-order approximation* to English. It might read something like this: 'combat callous irritability migrates depraved temporal prolix alas pillory nautical,' etc.

To improve this performance we give the man statistical information about the relative frequencies of communicative units. Suppose we provide him with a list that tells how often each word is likely to occur in English. With this knowledge he is able to make a considerable improvement in the quality of his work. His procedure is still to draw words at random, but now he can assign reasonable likelihoods to the various words. He makes it much more probable to draw 'the' than to draw 'calisthenics,' for example. He writes each word on a slip of paper, puts all the slips into a huge urn, scrambles them, and draws. There are many more slips that have the word 'the' written on them than there are slips with 'calisthenics' written on them. In this way the relative frequencies are made to be the same as the relative frequencies in ordinary English. The result is a closer approximation to English, a *first-order approximation:* 'day to is for they have proposed I the it materials of are its go studies the our of the following not over situation if the greater,' etc.

The first-order approximation is still poor English, and so we must provide more statistical information. We give the man a tabulation of the relative frequencies of all *pairs* of English words. With the half-million words in the Oxford English Dictionary (more if different forms of the same word are considered) it would be possible to construct $500,000^2$ pairs. The size of this statistical job is so great that it has never been undertaken. But imagine that we have the list and give it to our employee. He continues to draw at random from the pairs of words as follows: Suppose the first pair of words he draws is 'goes down.' Next he draws one from all the pairs of words that begin with 'down.' 'Down here' turns up, and now the message reads 'goes down here.' Then he draws one from all the pairs that have 'here' as the first word and gets 'here is.' In this manner he proceeds to write his composition. This *second-order approximation* might turn out to be 'goes down here is not large feet are the happy days and so what is dead weight that many were constructed the channel was,' etc.

To obtain a *third-order approximation*, he must have a tabulation of the relative frequencies in English for sequences of three words. He might start with 'she was bent,' then draw from the triplets that start with 'was bent' and so obtain 'was bent and,' then draw from the triplets that start with 'bent and,' etc. A fourth-order approximation requires a knowledge of the relative frequencies of sequences of four words, and in general the *n*th-order approximation is based upon the relative frequencies of sequences of *n* words.

Higher order approximations to English do not qualify as great literature, but they come close to something that somebody might say, given the proper situation and motivation. A fourth-order approximation might run 'we are going to see him is not correct to chuckle loudly and depart for home,' etc., which can be punctuated to give two or three plausible sentences. A tenth-order approximation is still better, although the topic under discussion seems to change in odd ways.

Since tabulations of sequences of words do not exist, we require some practical way to construct these higher order approximations. There is a convenient procedure that yields satisfactory results. Several people cooperate to construct the sequence one word at a time. We ask each person to add one word to what the others have written. For a fifth-order approximation, for example, a subject sees four words and is asked to use them in a sentence. We take whatever word he uses after these four and add it to the sequence. Then the next person is given only the last four words and asked to compose a sentence, etc.

So far we have considered only words as the units of analysis. The choice of word units is not crucial. Other verbal units can be used equally well. For example, we might select the 26 letters of the alphabet, plus the space between words, as the units. With letter units a zero-order approximation to English is constructed by drawing letters at random from the alphabet. To construct a first-order approximation, we should draw letters according to their relative frequencies of occurrence in ordinary text. Thus the letters 'e,' 't,' 'o,' 'i,' 'a,' and 'n' would appear quite frequently, whereas 'z,' 'j,' 'q,' 'k,' and 'x' would be relatively rare. For a second-order approximation we should draw each letter according to its likelihood of following the one preceding letter. If the preceding letter was 't,' the most likely letter to follow is 'h.' For a third-order approximation we should draw each letter in the context of the two preceding letters. A fourth-order approximation would reflect the context of the three preceding letters, etc. Some samples of letter sequences constructed at different orders of approximation to English are the following:

Zero-order: xfoml rxklrjffjuj zlpwcfwkcyj ffjeyvkcqsgxydahnbix
First-order: tocro hli rgwr nmielwis eu ll nbnesebya tht eei ts
Second-order: on ei antsoutinys are t incore st be s deamy thall
Third-order: in no ist lat why cratict froure birs grocid ponde nome of
                demonstures of the reptagin is

This last is almost worthy of Lewis Carroll's jabberwocky.

These examples of statistical amphigory clarify the statistical notion of context. When separate units are selected in a contextual vacuum (zero- or first-order approximation), it is impossible to produce anything that looks like the language we daily use. As the amount of context that determines each unit is increased, however, the resulting sequences of words take on a more familiar aspect.

In order to control the extent of the verbal context and to evaluate quantitatively its influence, statistical information is needed about the relative frequencies of occurrence of the verbal units. We turn now to a brief review of some of the major statistical tabulations.

RELATIVE FREQUENCIES OF VERBAL ELEMENTS

Relative Frequencies of Phonemes. We have seen that approximately 40 phonemes are necessary for the transcription of English. Of these 40, nine make up more than half of our vocal behavior, and the most frequently used sound occurs more than 100 times as often as the least used sound. The relative frequencies observed by G. Dewey (1923) for standard English prose are given in Table 4. Very similar results were obtained by Voelker (1935; *vide infra*, Tables 11 and 12, Chap. 7). Attempts have been made to explain these differences in terms of the *articulatory complexity* of the sounds. For example, it can be argued that the production of a voiced consonant is more complex than the production of a voiceless consonant. If this is true, voiceless sounds should occur more frequently than voiced sounds. Zipf (1935) presents data drawn from 12 different languages showing that the voiceless plosives /p/, /t/, and /k/ occur more frequently than the voiced plosives /b/, /d/, /g/, respectively. A similar comparison of voiced and voiceless fricatives, however, gives more ambiguous results.

TABLE 4. RELATIVE FREQUENCY OF OCCURRENCE OF ENGLISH PHONEMES

(G. Dewey, 1923, p. 125)

Vowels and diphthongs				*Consonants*			
ɪ	8.53%	aɪ	1.59%	n	7.24%	p	2.04%
ə	4.63	oʊ	1.30	t	7.13	f	1.84
æ	3.95	ɔ	1.26	r	6.88	h	1.81
ɛ	3.44	ʊ	0.69	s	4.55	b	1.81
ɒ	2.81	aʊ	0.59	d	4.31	ŋ	0.96
ʌ	2.33	ɑ	0.49	l	3.74	ʃ	0.82
i	2.12	o	0.33	ð	3.43	g	0.74
e, eɪ	1.84	ju	0.31	z	2.97	j	0.60
u	1.60	ɔɪ	0.09	m	2.78	tʃ	0.52
				k	2.71	dʒ	0.44
				v	2.28	θ	0.37
				w	2.08	ʒ	0.05
Total — 38%				Total — 62%			

A significant thing to note in Table 4 is that the seven alveolar consonants, produced with the tip of the tongue near the gum ridge, are listed among the eight most frequent consonant sounds. These alveolar consonants comprise more than half the consonant tokens that we produce. It is characteristic of all these hard-working English consonants that they are produced with a slight flick of the tip of the tongue while the other articulators remain relatively fixed.

The preference for consonants all formed in a similar position is convenient for the listener as well as for the talker. Analysis of the confusions occurring in articulation tests conducted in the quiet with nonsense syllables shows that consonants are confused principally with other consonants produced in the same manner. Few confusions occur among consonants produced in a different manner in the same articulatory position. The voiceless plosives (same manner, different positions) are often confused with one another; the alveolars (different manner, same position) are seldom confused with one another. Since we tend to use principally the alveolar position, it follows that the manner of articulation must differ and that the listener seldom confuses these frequently used sounds. The preference for alveolar consonants derives from the fact that for English talkers they are both simple to produce and easy to hear.

What makes an articulation easy or difficult is a debatable matter. It is desirable to have some other measure of articulatory difficulty in addition to frequency of use. One possibility is to determine the relative number of errors that deaf children make in learning to produce different sounds (Hudgins and Numbers, 1942). The more errors they make, the harder the sound is to produce. A comparison of this sort has been made, and it is found that deaf children tend to have the most difficulty producing the sounds that normal adults use least. Although it is not a crucial test, this evidence supports Zipf's hypothesis in a general way. In spite of this evidence, however, we must reject Zipf's argument, for many languages are known to contradict it flatly, no matter what definition of articulatory difficulty is used.

A complicating factor in the analysis of consonants is the distinction between initial and final consonants. We use a wider variety of consonants at the beginning than at the end of our words. Only five different sounds make up more than 50 per cent of the final consonants, while eight are needed to comprise 50 per cent of our initial consonants. Also there is a division of labor among these sounds. Some, /w/, /j/, /h/, /b/, /g/, /f/, /p/, /ð/, /θ/, are used principally at the beginning, others, /ŋ/, /z/, /v/, /r/, principally at the end of words. The division is not perfect because some consonants, /t/, /n/, /l/, /m/, /d/, /k/, are handy on either end of a word, and some, /ʃ/, /ʒ/, /tʃ/, /dʒ/, are seldom used in either position. These characteristic differences provide discriminative clues that facilitate the perception of faint or distorted speech. They help us to determine, for example, why listeners are more successful in guessing final consonants than they are in guessing initial consonants (Bagley, 1900).

It can be shown that the most frequently used sounds are not those which babies babble earliest or most often (Irwin, 1947a, b, 1948; cf. Chap. 7). During the first two months of a baby's life the consonants it produces (other than crying) are principally glottal, /h/ and /ʔ/, with a few velar /k/ and /g/ thrown in. As the baby matures, the frequency of consonants formed farther forward in the mouth increases, until in adult speech the bilabial, labiodental, dental, and alveolar consonants predominate. The course of development of the consonants is, therefore, from the back of the mouth to the middle and front of the mouth.

As a child matures, the number of different sounds he produces also increases. At two months 87 per cent of an infant's consonants are either /h/ or /ʔ/. At the end of the first year the two most frequent consonants, /h/ and /d/, make up only 52 per cent of the child's consonants, and by 2.5 years the two favorites, /d/ and /t/, total only 26 per cent. The adult, who favors /n/ and /t/, uses these two sounds for 23 per cent of his consonantal behavior. It is interesting to note that the early appearance of /d/ makes it likely that a child will say /dɑdɑ/ before he says /mɑmɑ/—a fact that often puzzles devoted mothers.

Relative Frequencies of Syllables. *Syllable* counts show that we have a preference for certain syllables as well as for certain sounds (G. Dewey, 1923). The 12 most frequently used syllables—/ðə/, /ʌv/, /ɪn/, /ænd/, /ɪ/, /ə/, /tu/, /ɪŋ/, /ɚ/, /rɪ/, /ɪt/, /ðæt/—make up more than a quarter of our verbal behavior. Half of our speech uses only 70 different syllables, but 1370 syllable types are required before 93.4 per cent of English syllable tokens are included. The syllable /ðə/ alone makes up about 7 per cent of the syllables we utter and so must turn up on the average once in every 14 successive syllables. When this is compared with any one of the many syllables that turn up only once in several thousand successive syllables, it is quite clear that a certain few combinations of speech sounds tend to be repeated quite often.

Not all syllables are similarly constructed. One study, based upon the telephone speech of businessmen, showed that consonant-vowel-consonant (CVC) syllables comprised 33.5 per cent of all the syllable tokens spoken. CV syllables made up 21.8 per cent, VC 20.3 per cent, V 9.7 per cent, CVCC 7.8 per cent, VCC and CCVC each 2.8 per cent, CCV 0.8 per cent, and the complicated CCVCC syllables made up only 0.5 per cent (French, Carter, and Koenig, 1930). In all languages there is a tendency for vowels and consonants to alternate.

Relative Frequencies of Words. The favorite victim of the counting technique is the *word*. As early as A.D. 900 the Talmudists were counting the words and ideas in the Torah in order to find out how many times each word appeared and how frequently each word appeared in an unusual way. The modern respect for words as the obvious elements of language was certainly not shared by the ancients who first tried to represent speech sounds by a code of written symbols. Greek and Roman writing did not consistently separate words, and it was not until about the tenth century that the printer's pride in the legibility of his work led him to dignify word units by leaving space between them.

It is customary to distinguish between *words* and *lexical units*. A lexical unit is a single entry in the dictionary under which are grouped several related words. 'Give,' 'gave,' and 'given' are three different words, but a single lexical unit. Only the form 'give' is listed in the dictionary. Word counts are preferable to lexical counts. The lexical tabulation can be derived from the word frequencies, but the word frequencies cannot be deduced from the lexical frequencies.

In the Oxford English Dictionary there are nearly half a million lexical units. With no interruptions it would take about three solid days of filibustering to pronounce so many words. If the supply of different words were the only controlling factor, we could carry on our daily quota of verbalizations for weeks before we had to use the same word a second time. The statistical fact is, however, that we manage to get along for only 10 or 15 words, on the average, before we repeat ourselves. In writing, our favorite word is 'the.' On the telephone our favorite word is 'I.' The 50 most commonly used word types make up about 60 per cent of the word tokens we say and 45 per cent of those we write. Similar data for other languages show that the repetitious use of a few words is not peculiar to English.

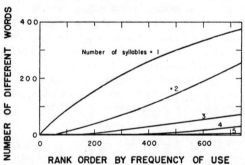

FIG. 30. The most frequent words are monosyllables. There are few words with three or more syllables among the 800 words used most frequently in telephone conversations. (*After French, Carter, and Koenig*, 1930.)

The majority of the commonly used words are monosyllables (Zipf, 1935). For example, when the words used in telephone conversations are listed in order according to frequency of occurrence, the first 30 are monosyllables. One might expect that a language like German, famous for its polysyllabic vocabulary, would be an exception, but the Kaeding count (Kaeding, 1897–1898) of nearly 11 million running words of written German shows that 50 per cent of these words are monosyllables and that words of four or more syllables form only 8.4 per cent. Many other languages give similar results. When a long word comes to be used very frequently in English, we tend to abbreviate it. 'Movie,' 'talkie,' 'gas,' 'auto,' 'hypo' are examples of abbreviation by truncation. Abbreviation also occurs by substituting shorter words for the longer ones. Abbreviatory substitutions may be either temporary, as in the case of pronouns, or permanent, as in the case of slang.

In Fig. 30 the number of monosyllables, of dissyllables, of trisyllables, etc., among the 800 most frequent words in telephone conversations are plotted against the rank order of the words from 1 (most frequent) to 800. The 200 most frequent words are nearly all monosyllables. Trisyllables are relatively rare on this list of overworked words. The efficiency of making the popular words short and the rare words long is obvious.

Frequency Distribution for English Words. The extensive use of some words and the neglect of others can be shown graphically by plotting the frequency of occurrence, f, against either (1) the number, n, of words that occur f times or (2) the rank order, r, of the words with respect to frequency of use.

The first of these two alternatives is usually called a *frequency distribution*. To take a concrete example, one student of newspaper writing counted 44,000 word tokens representing 6000 different word types (Eldridge, 1911). In this sample 2976 words were found to occur only once, and so this point would be located on a graph at 2976 on the abscissa (number of words occurring f times) and at 1 on the ordinate (frequency of occurrence, f). There are 1079 words that occurred twice, and so this point is located at 1079 on the abscissa and 2 on the ordinate. And so on for the 516 words that occurred three times, the 294 words that occurred four times, etc. The final point would represent the one word that occurred 4290 times. If we let the frequency of occurrence of any word type be represented by the symbol f and the number of words that occurred f times by the symbol n, then it is approximately true that the product of n and f^2 is a constant (Zipf, 1935):

$$nf^2 = K.$$

For the 2976 words that occurred once $(2976)(1^2) = 2976.$
For the 1079 words that occurred twice $(1079)(2^2) = 4316.$
For the 516 words that occurred three times $(516)(3^2) = 4644.$
For the 294 words that occurred four times $(294)(4^2) = 4704.$
For the 212 words that occurred five times $(212)(5^2) = 5300.$
For the 151 words that occurred six times $(151)(6^2) = 5436.$
For the 105 words that occurred seven times $(105)(7^2) = 5145.$
For the 84 words that occurred eight times $(84)(8^2) = 5376.$
For the 86 words that occurred nine times $(86)(9^2) = 6966.$
For the 45 words that occurred ten times $(45)(10^2) = 4500.$
For the 16 words that occurred twenty times $(16)(20^2) = 6400.$
For the 4 words that occurred thirty times $(4)(30^2) = 3600.$

And so on through the list until at the end we come to the one word that occurred 4290 times, and so its product is $(1)(4290^2) = 18,404,100.$

The product is approximately constant for the least frequent 5500 of the

6000 different words. But when we get to the last few words, which are used over and over, our rule breaks down completely and the product is far out of line. Even if we reduce the size of the exponent from 2 to about 1.5, say, we still are not able to describe all the frequencies of occurrence exactly. This equation has been debated by the verbal statisticians. It is so nearly correct that we hesitate to discard it, and yet it is so far wrong in a few instances that it cannot be considered the final formulation. Yule (1944) has reported some progress toward a more complicated, but probably more satisfactory, mathematical description.

Standard Curve for English Words. A second method of presenting these data is to plot the frequency of occurrence, f, of each word type against its rank when the words are ordered from the most frequent to the least frequent. In this same count of newspaper English the most frequent word occurred 4290 times, so it would be plotted at rank 1 on the abscissa and at frequency 4290 on the ordinate. The second most frequently used word occurred 2122 times and so would be plotted at rank 2 on the abscissa and at 2122 on the ordinate. And so on until we have constructed a plot of the sort shown in Fig. 31. You will notice that Fig. 31 is drawn with logarithmic coordinates; otherwise the points would be very difficult to read. This kind of representation is called by Zipf the *standard curve* of English words.

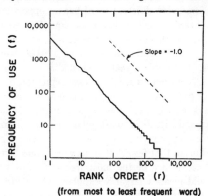

FIG. 31. The standard curve of English words. The frequency of occurrence of different words in American newspapers is plotted against the rank of the words when ordered with respect to frequency of occurrence. (*After Zipf*, 1935.)

The equation that has been used to represent the standard curve of Fig. 31 is

$$fr = C,$$

where f is still the frequency of occurrence of each word type, r is the rank of the word type when all the types are ordered with respect to frequency of occurrence, and C is a constant (Condon, 1928). We can test this equation in the same way we tested the preceding one: The first word occurred 4290 times, and so the product is $(4290)(1) = 4290$. The second word occurred 2122 times, so the product is $(2122)(2) = 4244$. The third word occurred 1375 times, so the product is $(1375)(3) = 4125$. And so on through the list. This time the formula seems to work a little better, but appearances must be deceiving because this is really the same formula we had before. The equation for the standard curve of English words is merely the integral of the equation for the frequency distribution.

A criticism of these equations is that they do not seem to apply well to all sizes of samples (Carroll, 1938). The formula predicts fractional words, of course, and so we must count a very large number of words before all the words have a chance to appear at least once. But if we count too many words, we exhaust the total vocabulary and even the rarest words begin to reappear several times. In either case, whether the number of words counted is too small or too large, the equation will not describe correctly the occurrence of the infrequent words. If we count a small sample, we find too many words occur only once, but for a very large sample too few words occur only once. There is an optimum size of the sample for which the equation gives the most accurate predictions. This optimum depends upon the number of different words in the sample. The larger the number of word types, the larger the sample must be before every different word has an opportunity to appear at least once. It has been calculated that these equations would give the best description of the frequencies of occurrence of different words in newspaper articles if the count were continued to about 120,000 words. With only 44,000 word tokens, the sample is really too small.

Whether or not this is the best mathematical representation, Fig. 31 makes it clear that certain patterns of speech sounds tend to recur with great persistence, while others must be neglected for long periods of time. One of the best ways to understand Fig. 31 is to ask yourself how our language would be different if the curve dropped with a steeper slope or with a gentler slope. A steeper slope would mean that fewer different words were being used and that the probability of occurrence of the most frequent word would be greater. A gentler slope would mean a larger vocabulary and a lower probability of occurrence of the most frequent word. If all possible sequences of speech sounds occurred equally often, the function would be a horizontal line.

Although it is obvious that certain words occur very frequently, we do not have any way of predicting how often any particular word will occur. The personal pronoun 'I,' for example, makes up 8.4 per cent of the speech of schizophrenics (H. Fairbanks, 1944), 5.0 per cent of our telephone conversations, 3.1 per cent of the speech of college freshmen explaining proverbs (H. Fairbanks, 1944), 1.2 per cent of written English, and 0 per cent in certain technical publications. The multiple factors influencing the probability of any individual word remain to be explored.

Effects of Context on the Standard Curve. Tabulations of verbal units longer than a word do not exist, because the variety of combinations of two or more words is so large that the project quickly gets out of hand. It is possible, however, to tabulate all the *pairs of words* beginning with a given word. Figures 32*A* and 32*B* show the results of such tabulations for 775 words following 'of' and 2000 words following 'the' in the writing in the *New York Times*. The dashed line indicates the slope predicted by Zipf's equation, $fr = C$. When the words are selected in this way, their relative frequencies do not distribute themselves according to this law. After 'of' the most frequent word is 'the,' which occurs almost ten times as often as any other word in that position.

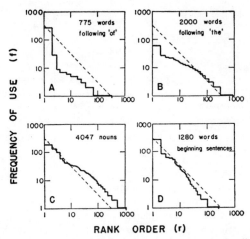

FIG. 32. The standard curves for selected words. *A* gives the curve for all words following the word 'of.' *B* gives the curve for all words following the word 'the.' *C* gives the curve for nouns (*after Yule*, 1944). *D* gives the curves for words standing at the beginning of sentences.

After 'the,' however, almost anything can happen, and there is a long list of nouns and adjectives that are about equally unlikely. Thus the standard curve of words following 'of' has a steep slope, while the standard curve of words following 'the' has a gradual slope. At the beginning of a sentence, however, we are relatively free of the contextual effects of surrounding words, and, as Fig. 32*D* shows, the standard curve for words appearing at the beginning of a sentence agrees more closely with Zipf's equation.

Figure 31 shows the likelihood that a certain word will occur *on the average*. It does not take into account the likelihood of the word's occurring in a specific context. Only tabulations of sequences of words or of sentences can reveal the finer structure of the statistical map of verbal behavior, and the magnitude of this task is a formidable obstacle.

Relative Frequencies of Parts of Speech. In Table 5 the words occurring in telephone conversations are classified according to *parts of speech* (French, Carter, and Koenig, 1930). The five minor parts of speech given in the last four lines of the table make up only 5 per cent of the different words and yet comprise 57 per cent of the word tokens we utter. Similar results have been obtained for schizophrenics and for college freshmen (H. Fairbanks, 1944).

TABLE 5. OCCURRENCE OF PARTS OF SPEECH IN TELEPHONE CONVERSATION

(French, Carter, and Koenig, 1930)

Parts of speech	Number of words		Type-token ratio
	Tokens	Types	
Nouns.	11,660	1029	0.086
Adjectives and adverbs.	9,880	634	0.064
Verbs.	12,550	456	0.036
Auxiliary verbs.	9,450	37	0.0039
Prepositions and conjunctions.	12,400	36	0.0029
Pronouns.	17,900	45	0.0025
Articles.	5,550	3	0.00054
Totals.	79,390	2240	0.028

The articles, prepositions, conjunctions, pronouns, and auxiliary verbs determine the general form of our statements, while the nouns, adjectives, adverbs, and verbs contribute the content. The different forms repeat themselves more often than do the different contents, and so the minor parts of speech compose the major part of our utterances. Language is based on a framework of a relatively small number of different words, arranged in many patterns, which supports the more variegated words that convey most of the information.

Differences in grammatical functions do not completely explain the data, however. Within any one part of speech, some members of the class are used much more than others. Nouns like 'thing,' 'man,' 'time,' 'day' receive far more than their fair share of attention. The social pressure for a common vocabulary and the convenience of monosyllabic words tend to restrict the variety of our responses, whereas the attempt to differentiate between similar statements expands the vocabulary and leads to the occasional use of polysyllabic words.

In Fig. 32C the standard curve for nouns is plotted in such a way that it can be compared with Zipf's general equation for all the parts of speech taken together. This count was made by Yule (1944) for Part I of Bunyan's *Pilgrim's Progress*. The curve is flatter than the equation predicts. When the little connective words that we use so often are taken out of the tabulation, we find a more equitable distribution of use. But even when we compare the relative frequencies of words that play the same grammatical role, it is apparent that some are used far more often than others.

It is a bit surprising to find that one's own verbal behavior follows such statistical rules with considerable orderliness. We select our words and arrange them to communicate with others with no consideration for relative frequencies of occurrence. Still, on the average, this apparently willful and conscious behavior of choosing words follows statistical rules with great regularity. Like the man who suddenly discovered he had been writing prose all his life, most of us find it rather wonderful that we can behave so lawfully with no trouble at all.

Content Analysis

What do people say? This question, which introduced the discussion of verbal statistics, can now be answered in part. People say some sounds, syllables, or words more often than others; the statistical outlines of their preferences are traced in the preceding pages. Unfortunately, the tabulation of all the sounds and sequences of sounds that are uttered runs into difficulties as the speech units grow longer because the sheer variety of possible sequences increases so rapidly. Just as we reach the point where we are ready to tabulate meaningful blocks of words, we find that the task has grown to unmanageable proportions. We know what words people say most often, but we do not have statistics to show how these words are fitted together.

In order to handle larger blocks of verbal materials in a statistical way, it seems necessary to reduce the variety of alternatives that must be tabulated. This can be accomplished by putting a wide variety of different word patterns into a single category. Then the relative frequency of occurrence of items in these categories can be found. For example, we can classify sentences as declarative, interrogative, imperative, or exclamatory and then count the number of each type that occurs in a particular kind of writing. Such a grammatical classification is not of particular psychological interest, however. We want classifications according to the ideas discussed, for then we can tabulate how often each idea appears. Unfortunately, however, nobody has proposed a general definition of the word 'idea' and nobody has developed an exhaustive classification of all the ideas that can occur.

No classification of the content of verbal behavior is scientifically acceptable unless its categories are derived on the basis of explicitly formulated rules. Any classification requires the considered judgment of a reader to decide which category includes any particular word pattern. If his judgments are to be at all consistent and repeatable by others, then the reader must make his rules of judgment explicit. When such rules are plainly stated and the frequency of occurrence of word patterns in each category of a classificatory scheme is counted, the result is called a *content analysis*. We have previously discussed the measurement of the *amount* of information; in this section we turn our attention to the techniques for discovering the *content* of the information.

Communication content is so varied, and our interest in analyzing it may spring from so many different sources, that no one system of categories can be devised to describe it. For a particular kind of material and with a specific aim in view, a classificatory scheme can be devised to do the job. But if new materials or new interests develop, a different system of categories is required. Flexibility of the classification is unavoidable if we are not willing to make an exhaustive study of all the possible patterns of words. Since the complete tabulation is too large a task, we ignore many of the distinctions and lump different word patterns together in a single category in order to reduce the number of categories that must be listed. The distinctions that we ignore in one study, however, may become the distinctions of principal interest for the next. As attention is shifted from one aspect to another, the classificatory abstractions must change.

The way categories grow out of the questions asked can be demonstrated with a simple example. The example is taken from an analysis of the treatment given different ethnic groups in popular magazine fiction (Berelson and Salter, 1946). The study began with a general question, How do popular magazines describe the different ethnic groups in fiction? The question defines the material to be analyzed and the general interest in it.

The next step is to formulate specific hypotheses to be tested with the material. A sample hypothesis is the following: The great majority of the major characters in magazine fiction are from the majority group in the culture; these characters are approved and treated sympathetically; the minorities are more likely to be represented by minor characters who do not behave according to the approved standards of the culture. The problem is to test this hypothesis. Ordinarily there is a list of 10 or 20 such hypotheses. They are specific propositions that we hope to support or refute.

Next, the categories necessary for testing the hypothesis are listed. The example yields three categories: (1) the ethnic group of the character, majority or minority group; (2) the role in the story, major or minor; (3) the degree of approval, sympathetic or unsympathetic. Now specific indicators for each category are selected. The criteria that place a fictional character in one or the other of these categories are stated. To decide his ethnic group, we draw up a list: explicit mention, surname, appearance, membership in voluntary organizations, etc. To decide his role in the story, we can take some measure of the amount of space devoted to him or the number of sentences involving him in any explicit way. A list of words or phrases indicating social approval or disapproval can be compiled.

In this way a general problem is transformed into specific questions; the questions suggest categories to be studied; the categories are defined by suitable indicators. The frequency of occurrence of indicators in each of the categories is counted, and the results provide a test of the hypotheses. Obviously, a different interest or hypothesis would lead to a different scheme of classification.

Content analysis is a technique of investigation. The present discussion of content analysis is consequently limited to illustrative examples. Current interest in the method derives from a growing concern with propaganda and public opinion and the emergence of radio as a mass medium for communication. Content analysis illuminates the cultural or personal conditions under which the material was produced, reveals stylistic features, exposes propaganda techniques, helps to trace the development of interests, describes trends in communication content, etc.

Here is an example. There was a general decline between 1900 and 1930 in the status of religion in the United States. This decline can be traced in a quantitative way by counting the number of approving or favorable references to organized religion that appeared in general magazines during this period. In 1905, 78 per cent of the references were favorable. In 1920, 53 per cent of the references were favorable. By 1930, only 33 per cent of the references were favorable. In the more intellectual magazines during the same period the corresponding percentages are 57, 27, and 18 (Hart, 1933). By such analyses of content it is possible to survey the changing attitudes and interests of the times and to reveal the cultural patterns as they are reflected in the popular publications.

In the words of one proponent of content analysis (Lazarsfeld, 1948):

> Our economic statistics are today quite well advanced. We know how much pig iron is produced every month and how much meat is exported every year. But we still have very little bookkeeping in cultural matters. The content of mass media of communication is an important and readily available source of social data, and it will not be surprising if its analysis becomes a regular part of our statistical services in the not-too-distant future.

Of more direct psychological interest are studies that reveal consistencies in the verbal productions of one individual. For example, a study of the letters of a domineering mother adopted the techniques of content analysis to check the results of a more intuitive interpretation (A. L. Baldwin, 1942). It is assumed (1) that the frequency of a certain class of items in the letters is a measure of its importance and (2) that if two kinds of items occur near to one another quite often, these items are related for the person. The study distinguished 15 different topics of discussion, and every comment related (in the opinion of the judge) to any one of these topics was singled out and classified. In addition, each of the topical categories was further subdivided into attitudinal categories according to whether the writer considered the topic to be favorable, unfavorable, neutral, dependent, independent, honest, dishonest, etc. If the frequency of occurrence of certain kinds of items was very low, they were dropped on the assumption that they were unimportant. The frequently occurring items were examined to see which ones were consistently referred to in the same paragraph. This examination revealed, for example, that unfavorable remarks about her son were coupled with unfavorable comments about women too often to attribute their contiguity to chance.

Since the case material that psychologists and psychiatrists must evaluate often comes to them in the form of autobiographies, diaries, or other personal documents, content analysis of these materials may prove to be of considerable value. The techniques can be further adapted to objectify the interpretation of the psychoanalytic interview. Lasswell (1938) suggests a scheme of classification for such interview materials that does not need to be redesigned for every different interview. In outline, the scheme is: The statement to be classified says that the (talker-listener-another) holds a (favorable-unfavorable) attitude toward the (talker-listener-another). Thus the statement 'He said you were nice' is classified, 'Another person holds a favorable attitude toward the listener' or, more briefly, 'pro-listener by another.' Although the proposal includes refinements, it is basically the statistical tabulation of the occurrence of proper nouns and pronouns together with complimentary and derogatory adjectives and adverbs. The usefulness of such a tabulation remains to be tested.

These examples show that, although a complete tabulation of all possible sequences of words is seldom feasible, a tabulation of certain kinds of words and their occurrences together may suffice to answer specific questions. The scheme of classification must be carefully considered, however, and is most important to the success of the analysis. The general principles dictating the proper kind of scheme for any job have yet to be derived. It is still a debatable point whether we can eventually evolve a general set of psychological categories for verbal materials comparable with, say, the grammarian's classification of the parts of speech.

DISCUSSION QUESTIONS

1. To what extent has the tendency to use lingua-alveolar consonants been responsible for changes in pronunciation during the history of our language?

2. If you were trying to transcribe an unfamiliar language in phonetic notation, would you break it up into word units? What criteria would you use to decide what were words?

3. Try to write a long passage that uses each word just as often as every other word.

4. Can you think of an English word spelled with a 'q' that is not followed by a 'u'? How much information is conveyed by the 'u' in this position?

Selected References

Fries, C. C., and A. A. Traver. *English Word Lists*. Washington, D.C.: American Council on Education, 1940. Reviews the available word counts and evaluates them as teaching aids.

Thorndike, E. L., and I. Lorge. *The Teacher's Word Book of 30,000 Words*. New York: Bureau of Publications, Teacher's College, Columbia University, 1944. This book presents the results of several extensive counts of the frequency of occurrence of English words.

Zipf, G. K. *The Psycho-Biology of Language*. Boston: Houghton, 1935. The results of statistical analysis are applied to problems in linguistics.

———. *Human Behavior and the Principle of Least Effort*. Cambridge, Mass.: Addison-Wesley, 1949. Zipf's contributions to the statistical study of language are summarized, and the general principles derived are applied to a wide range of problems.

Chapter 5

RULES FOR USING SYMBOLS

Our problem may be stated as follows:—

Given some statement in a language of which we know the grammar and the syntax, but not the vocabulary, what are the possible meanings of such a statement, and what are the meanings of the unknown words that would make it true?

The reason that this question is important is that it represents, much more nearly than might be supposed, the state of our knowledge of nature.

—BERTRAND RUSSELL

In order to understand a language, we must know its grammar as well as its vocabulary. It often happens in English that a string of words can make a sentence that is true when the words are in one order but false in another order. A simple example is 'Brutus killed Caesar.' The same words in the opposite order, 'Caesar killed Brutus,' say something quite different. A reader who knows all about killing and knows who Brutus and Caesar were still does not know the meaning of 'Brutus killed Caesar.' In order to know who did the killing and who got killed, he must know something about the order of words in English. He must know the rules of the language.

The rules that govern the use of symbols in a language have important effects upon the statistical properties of the language. In order to understand these effects, we must first extend our ideas about the amount of information. So far we have talked about the amount of information as the logarithm of the number of alternative symbols, and we have made the implicit assumption that all the alternatives were equally likely to occur. Chapter 4 shows quite clearly that the alternative symbols of English are certainly not all equally likely. When we extend our definition of the amount of information to fit these new facts, we discover that English uses far more symbols per message than would be necessary if all symbols could be used equally often. This fact leads us to say that English is highly redundant. The amount of redundancy in any language depends upon the rules for using its symbols. Some rules increase redundancy, some rules decrease it. The notion of redundancy and the ways it is kept under control by the rules of the language are the subject of the present chapter.

INFORMATION, NOISE, REDUNDANCY

Information is something we need when we face a choice. What specific information we need depends upon the situation, but whatever its source or content, the amount of information required depends upon the complexity of the choice to be made. If we face a wide range of equally likely alternatives, if anything can happen, we need more information than if we face a simple choice between two alternatives, either this or that.

The Mathematical Expression for Amount of Information. In Chaps. 2 and 3 the definition of the amount of information was introduced and developed for the acoustic information encoded in a sound wave. Now the same definition can be used again, but instead of the sine waves that Fourier analysis uses for its building blocks, the concern is with the range of alternatives provided by more molar verbal units. If phonemes, for instance, are selected as the units for the analysis, we can ask how many phonemes there are, how they are arranged in patterns, and how many alternative patterns there are. In this way we can arrive at an estimate of the amount of information that can be encoded in such a system of phonemes.

The amount of information, therefore, is proportional to the logarithm of the number of alternatives in the set from which any particular message is drawn, *where the alternatives are all equally likely and independent.*

By 'equally likely' we mean that every symbol appears as often as every other symbol if we count the number over a long period of time. And by 'independent' we mean that the occurrence of one symbol does not alter the probabilities of occurrence for the next symbol.

Consider a language of equally likely symbols in which successive symbols are chosen independently. Suppose the language has a different symbols— different letters, sounds, words, or the like—and that the occurrence of a particular one of these a alternatives in no way influences the probabilities for the next symbol. For this language the probability $p(x)$ of occurrence of any particular symbol x at any position in a sequence of symbols is always $1/a$. If there are 100 different symbols, then each symbol has one chance in 100 of occurring in any context. The fact that a particular symbol may just have occurred does not give it any more or less of a chance to be the next symbol in the sequence. It also follows that all *sequences* are independent and equally likely, and the chance of getting any particular sequence of n symbols in a row is $(1/a)^n$.

A meaningful message could be composed in this language of independent and equally likely symbols by the simple procedure of putting all the symbols into a hat and drawing (and replacing) them at random. It is obvious that this peculiar language has little resemblance to the language we speak, for if we hire a man to produce English essays in this manner, his results are gibberish. This strange language has no contextual determination, no preferred symbols or preferred sequences of symbols. The only thing that recommends this language to us is that it is a simple matter to determine the amount of information per symbol the language can encode.

By definition, the amount of information in a language of independent and equally likely symbols is given by the logarithm of the number of alternatives:

$$\text{Amount of information} = I = k \log a^n = -nk \log p(x).$$

In this expression I is the quantity of information; k is a constant of proportionality that determines the size of the unit of measurement; a is the number of different verbal units; n is the length of the sequence; $p(x)$ is the probability of occurrence of symbol x and is equal to $1/a$.

This equation is simple for the unusual language we have imagined, but difficult to apply to languages that are actually spoken. In the first place, not all symbols are used equally often. Some are much more probable than others. And, second, some sequences of symbols are much preferred to other sequences, and so it is impossible to say that successive symbols are independent.

We know how to specify the amount of information in a language of equally likely and independent symbols. We want to know how to specify the amount of information in a language with unequal and dependent probabilities of occurrence of its symbols. Can we transform a language with unequal and dependent probabilities into an equivalent language with equal and independent probabilities? The answer is yes. We can transform a choice among unequally probable alternatives into an equally uncertain choice among a smaller number of equally probable alternatives. In the language of equally probable symbols we take the logarithm of the probability of occurrence of a symbol; with unequal probabilities we take the *average value* of all the logarithms of the probabilities of the different symbols. When the likelihood of occurrence of different symbols is different, it is still possible to say, 'If this language of unequally probable symbols is translated into a language that carries the same amount of information but uses all symbols equally often, the average amount of information is such and such.'

The Definition of Redundancy. By favoring some sequences of verbal units more than others, we effectively reduce the amount of information that is encoded per unit. Take a simple example. Suppose the various possible messages in a language consist of sequences of three digits: '1–9–3' or '8–7–0,' etc. So long as each digit in the message is unrelated to the other two, we can send any one of 10^3, or 1000, different messages. If the symbols are not independent, however, but if some fixed relation exists among them, the number of alternatives is reduced. If the sum of the digits is always 16, or if the third digit is always 9 minus the second digit, etc., our freedom of choice is restricted and the message cannot convey as much information.

The results of some actual calculations can illustrate this argument. The study of the relative frequency of English speech sounds distinguished 41 phonemes. If these phonemes could be spoken equally often and in any order at all, they could convey log 41 units of information per phoneme. However, some of the phonemes are more frequently produced than others. When the average value of the logarithms of their probabilities is calculated, the result is only log 28 units of information per phoneme. In other words, we could convey just as much information per sound with a language that has only 28 sounds but uses them all equally often as we can with our present language of 41 sounds that are not used equally often.

The calculations can be repeated for sequences of two or more phonemes. Since our preferences for certain sequences of sounds are even more striking than our preferences for individual sounds, the amount of information per phoneme is further reduced when we consider sequences. As the statistical analysis is extended to longer and longer sequences of symbols, the effect of the increasing context is to restrict our freedom of choice more and more; the reduction in the amount of information per symbol becomes more and more apparent.

If the successive units in a message are related, if the probability of a unit depends upon the units that precede it, these relations reduce the amount of information that a single unit can carry. When any restricting relations of this sort exist, it means that the same amount of information could be coded more rapidly in a language that had the same number of independent alternatives. In a sense, therefore, contextual dependencies mean that the message source is repeating itself. More symbols are being used to encode the message than are theoretically necessary. We express this fact by saying that most languages are *redundant*. The major generalization to be drawn from the statistical studies in Chap. 4 is the high redundancy they reveal.

Redundancy has its advantages, and a large degree of interdependence among the successive units of a language means that parts of the message can be lost or distorted without causing a disruption of communication. Any missing portions can be supplied by the receiver on the basis of the surrounding portions, on the basis of contextual clues. Although a redundant language is necessarily more verbose than a language of independent units, it is more dependable under adverse circumstances. And since our nervous systems seem to absorb new information slowly, if at all, we suffer little inconvenience in going slower while we gain considerably in reliability.

So long as a language contains fewer symbols than there are things to be symbolized, the symbols must be arranged in patterns. Thus every symbol occurs in a context of other symbols, and its symbolic role changes as the context changes. When not all the possible patterns are used by the language, we know there must be contextual restraints operating to make the language redundant. If, for example, we are able to replace a missing or distorted portion of a message, we can do so only because we know that some sequences are probable and others are improbable.

Reduction of Errors through Redundancy. The usefulness of redundancy becomes apparent when we consider the matter of mistakes. Mistakes in communication can arise from a variety of sources. It is convenient to call anything that produces a random, unpredictable alteration in a message *noise*. We do not need, for the present purpose, to distinguish the different kinds of noise. All we want to say is that we put a certain sequence of symbols into the communication channel and some of them are different when they come out. Unpredictable differences are mistakes, and whatever causes them is noise.

All channels of communication are noisy, all channels are subject to mistakes. There seems to be no way of avoiding this situation. It is necessary, therefore, to design our languages in such a way that the inevitable mistakes can be discovered. Errors can be corrected, of course, if their position is known. But one of the characteristics of noise is its unpredictability. We have no way of deciding which items in the sequence have gone wrong.

When a message passes through a noisy channel, therefore, we suspect that errors are introduced, but we do not know where the errors are. How is it possible to discover the mistakes and eliminate them? The secretary who said, 'I've added this column of figures six times and here are the six answers,' had the right idea, although her noise level was too high for success. What we must do when we suspect an error is to repeat the process. Repetition is the only way we have to catch a mistake.

The problem of errors is especially important in a nonredundant language. If the language uses symbols independently and equally often, any sequence of received symbols is a possible message in the language. Any sequence at all makes sense. The only way we can be sure that every symbol is received correctly is to ask the source to repeat the message several times. Then by a statistical study of the several received versions the probability of an error can be made very small.

Note that a nonredundant language may not save time even though every symbol seems to carry the maximal amount of information. If there is any chance of error, the communication must be repeated and the various received versions compared. And there is always a chance of error, even in the most elegant communication machinery.

Repetition catches mistakes, and repetition is redundancy. By sufficient repetition the probability of an error can be made as small as we please, and even a little repetition is a help. A language must contain a certain amount of redundancy if it is to be a reliable means of communication.

Examples of Rules Introducing Redundancy. Messages can be repeated in many ways. We may use several channels simultaneously and compare the several received messages. Multiple channels save time if they are available. More often it is necessary to use a single channel several times in a row. Thus the entire message may be given and then repeated, or one section of the message may be repeated before proceeding to the next section. It is usually desirable to introduce the repetitions as soon as possible, for two reasons. In the first place, if we wait too long to give the repeated message, the listener will have forgotten the first one that he is supposed to compare with it. And second, it is usually desirable to catch the mistakes as we go in case the communication is unexpectedly interrupted. We might, therefore, repeat each individual symbol several times in a row. The sequence of numbers '1–0–3' would then be sent as '1–1–1–1–1–0–0–0–0–0–3–3–3–3–3,' where every symbol is given five times running.

See what the repetition has done to the probabilities of the sequences of symbols in the message. The successive numbers may have been independent in the original message, but they are certainly not independent in the repeated message. In the example, the most probable symbol to follow '1' is another '1.' Consequently, we can no longer claim that successive symbols are independent. The chances are 4 to 1 that any symbol will be the same as the symbol that preceded it. If a sequence like '1–2–3' is received, we know immediately that there has been an error, for this sequence violates the rules of this repeating language.

A subtler kind of redundancy can be illustrated as follows: Suppose we are encoding information in a binary language, *i.e.*, a language with only two symbols. Let the two symbols be '1' and '0,' and suppose that there are four different messages we want to send. In a nonredundant language the four messages could be encoded as '0–0,' '0–1,' '1–0,' and '1–1.' Any mistake, however, transforms one message into another and gives the recipient no chance to detect the occurrence of an error.

To introduce redundancy, we must allow for repetition; we must consider longer sequences. There are eight possible sequences of three symbols: '0–0–0,' '0–0–1,' '0–1–0,' '0–1–1,' '1–0–0,' '1–0–1,' '1–1–0,' and '1–1–1.' We want to select four of these eight in order to encode the four messages. Which four shall we take? We should select them in such a way as to make the four alternatives as different as possible. Then when an error occurs, it will not be so likely to turn one message into another. The situation is illustrated in Fig. 33, where each of the three successive symbols is indicated as '0' or '1' along a different coordinate in three-dimensional space. The eight corners of the cube formed in this way indicate the eight alternative sequences of three symbols. We want to take four of these points that are as far from one another as possible in this space. If we select the four points indicated by the large symbols ('0–0–0,' '1–1–0,' '1–0–1,' and '0–1–1'), we have an optimal solution. For this set of messages, a single error in any one of the three places turns the message into an impossible form; two errors must occur before one of these four is converted into another. The entire message is carried by the first two symbols, or by the second two symbols, or by the first and last symbols. This is an ideal kind of repetition of the information.

A poor solution is to choose four numbers on a single face of the cube, *e.g.*, '0–0–0,' '1–0–0,' '0–1–0,' and '1–1–0.' In this set of messages the third symbol is always '0,' and so it carries no information. This is a way of introducing redundancy without gaining any advantage against error; the first two symbols are doing all the work.

Repetition reduces errors by making some sequences of symbols more likely than others. We may try to devise a more efficient language by reducing redundancy, but as soon as we try to use this new language in a noisy situation,

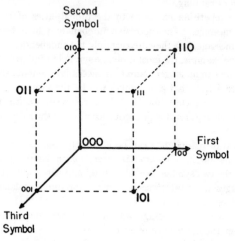

FIG. 33. Graphical representation of the eight messages that can be formed with two symbols used in sequences of three at a time. The problem is to select four of these eight in such a way as to make the occurrence of errors most easily detectable.

the redundancy has to be put back in. In one form or another every language, if it is to be reliable, must be redundant. There is no other way to catch mistakes. Thus the time spent redundantly is not wasted, for it serves to make the language a dependable channel for communication.

A SAMPLE LANGUAGE

The ways redundancy is introduced into English are much more complicated than a simple rule to repeat everything five times, but the effect is similar. Just how redundancy should be introduced into a language depends upon what kinds of mistakes are likely to occur. The alteration of a message by the noise should turn the message into some unlikely sequence of symbols. An error should not change the message into another likely sequence.

There are three kinds of rules that are usually distinguished by students of language, and as we shall see, all three can lead to redundancy. There are, first, the *semantic* rules that relate the symbols to the things symbolized and that state when one symbol can be replaced by another. The *syntactic* rules govern the relations among symbols. And the *pragmatic* rules govern the relations between the symbols and the user of the symbols (Morris, 1938). Since verbal symbols do not exist without organisms to generate and perceive the symbols, the pragmatic rules of language are, in a sense, fundamental to the semantic and syntactic rules. The psychologist's principal interest is in the pragmatic dimension of language, but he cannot afford to ignore the semantic and syntactic dimensions.

In order to illustrate the operation of linguistic rules, we shall invent a language to talk about. It is convenient in these matters to have two languages, one to talk *in* and the other to talk *about*. Both in logic and in psychology it is important to distinguish what is said from what is said about what is said.

The language we use to talk about a language is usually called the *metalanguage*. The language that is talked about is called the *object language*. We use the metalanguage to avoid confusion in discussing the object language. It is possible to construct a metalanguage to talk about English. We might use French or German for this purpose, but then the audience would be limited to bilingual readers. The procedure that we shall follow here is to keep the familiar English language as the metalanguage and use it to discuss some simple, well-defined object language.

The sample language is the language chess players use to record the course of play of the game of chess. We have, therefore, the English metalanguage to talk about the chess language that talks about the moves of the pieces on the chessboard. The chess language is simple and can be learned quickly by those who know nothing of the game of chess. There are, in fact, two chess languages, the English and the German. The German is simpler, and so we adopt it with several modifications.

Now the problem can be stated directly. We want to examine the semantic, syntactic, and pragmatic rules of the language of chess, with English as the metalanguage. From this discussion we can discover sources of redundancy in the chess language. By analogy it will become clear how redundancy is introduced into other languages. Then, having shown how redundancy is introduced, we can proceed to show how further rules are invented to reduce redundancy.

A chessboard is divided into 64 squares, 8 to a side. The chess language must have some way of designating each one of these squares. A semantic rule is needed to establish a fixed relation between certain symbols and certain squares. This is done in the following way: Starting from the lower left square in front of the player who has the white pieces, (1) the columns are designated from left to right by the letters 'a,' 'b,' 'c,' 'd,' 'e,' 'f,' 'g,' and 'h,' and (2) the rows from the bottom to the top are designated as '1,' '2,' '3,' '4,' '5,' '6,' '7,' and '8.' With these semantic rules it is possible to indicate any one of the 64 squares. The square e3 is in column e and row 3, and it cannot be confused with any other square because only the one square is in both e and 3.

See what the semantic rules have done by way of limiting sequential possibilities. We cannot write 'eg' in this language because 'eg' does not designate anything, just as 'blau' does not designate anything in English. The alternatives that can follow a letter are limited to the set of eight numerals. With a different semantic rule these 16 different symbols could be arranged in any one of 256 pairs that might designate 256 different things. The language does not use all the possibilities available. Therefore, redundancy has been introduced.

Furthermore, a syntactic rule has been introduced. Should the square that is common to column e and row 3 be designated by 'e3' or '3e'? Or should both be allowed as synonyms? The syntactic rule states that the column letter must be written in front of the row numeral. Thus 'e3' is admitted to the language, while '3e' is excluded. A comparable situation in English is the syntactic rule that adjectives must precede the nouns they modify, and so 'early bird' is admitted while 'bird early' is relatively rare. The rule for English is not, of course, unbreakable.

Each player in the game of chess has 16 pieces, or men, that he moves about the board. The semantic rules for designating these men are: (1) the king is symbolized by 'K,' (2) the queen by 'Q,' (3) the two bishops by 'B,' (4) the two knights by 'N,' (5) the two rooks by 'R,' and (6) the eight pawns by 'P.' These six rules are not sufficient, however, because it is necessary to designate which piece of a certain kind is meant. It is not enough to write 'P,' for this might symbolize any of the eight pawns. The distinction is made by indicating the square the particular man is sitting on. A rule of the game is that only one man can be on any square at any particular time, and so there is no chance for confusion here. Thus 'Pf2' designates the pawn that is on square f2. Here a further syntactic rule is added that the symbol designating the man must be written in front of the symbols designating the square that the man is sitting on.

These rules seem reasonable and, at first glance, necessary in order to keep track of the various men. But note the redundancy. It is not necessary to have symbols for the pieces at all. Only one man can sit on a square at a time. This man can be unambiguously indicated by naming the square. Nevertheless we introduce the additional symbols.

Two kinds of moves can be distinguished in chess. (For simplicity we can ignore the special cases that arise when castling or when a pawn is exchanged for a queen.) One kind occurs when a man moves to an unoccupied square. This kind of move is designated by '-.' 'Pd2-d4' says that the pawn on square d2 moves to the unoccupied square d4. The second kind of move occurs when a piece is captured. In this move the capturing piece moves onto the square previously occupied by the opposing piece, and the captured piece is removed from the board. The capturing move is designated by 'x.' 'Pd4xBc5' says that the pawn on square d4 moves onto and captures the bishop on square c5. These symbols for the moves are the verbs of the chess language.

This chess language has 24 different symbols: eight lower-case letters for columns, eight numerals for rows, six upper-case letters for pieces, and two symbols for moves. Used equally often and independently, one of these symbols could designate any one of 24 alternatives. With the semantic and syntactic rules of this language, however, the number of alternatives is reduced to only 6 or 8 per symbol.

As yet practically nothing has been said of the rules of the game. These introduce further redundancy. The rules say, for example, where all the pieces must be situated when the game begins and how the various men can move. The bishop's rule is that he can move only on diagonals, but he can travel as far as the diagonal is unobstructed. The pawns can only move forward, never backward, but they can capture pieces only on the diagonals. These rules of the game can also be considered as linguistic rules that exclude a great many sequences of symbols from the chess language. 'Pe2xBe3' cannot occur in the chess language because it is against the rules of the game for pawns to capture in this manner. We shall not even try to estimate how much redundancy such rules introduce.

As soon as a player becomes familiar with some of the fundamentals of chess, he sees that some moves are good and some are bad. If he persists in moving his king to the center of the board where it is exposed to attack, he does not win many games. Eventually he either gives up the game or begins to select moves that offer him a better chance of winning. Exactly what moves he thinks will achieve this end depend upon his skill and experience, and no formal statement can be made about them. But it is clear that the player's desire to win will lead him to select certain moves and to reject others, thus limiting still further the range of symbol sequences that are likely to occur in the chess language. From the point of view of the chess language, therefore, these selections act like pragmatic rules and add further redundancy. Other pragmatic illustrations are the use of an exclamation mark to indicate a strong move and a question mark to indicate a poor move. Our selection of letters for the pieces is also influenced by our knowledge of their English names.

At almost every step in drawing up this object language the rules have introduced more symbols than necessary. Symbolic freedom is limited by rules relating symbols to things, by rules relating symbols to symbols, and by rules relating symbolizers to symbols. The constraints of context are the result of these rules. Unequal and dependent probabilities are just what we must expect from the kinds of rules we impose.

DEFINITIONS AND ABBREVIATIONS

How can redundancy be weeded out of a language? As rules pile up, they usually manage to constrain more and more our freedom in using the language. Unless we can somehow cut through these rules, the redundancy may grow out of all proportion to the likelihood of an error. The weapon against too much redundancy is *abbreviation* (Zipf, 1949).

In the chess language we might want to write 'Pe4xPf5.' An examination of the board reveals that there are no other pawns located so that one can take the other. No ambiguity will result if we simply write 'PxP.' The abbreviated sentence could not, in the context of this game, refer to the wrong pawns.

Abbreviations can be used whenever the information is carried by the context and there is little chance of a mistake. When 'television picture' becomes very frequent, we abbreviate it to 'telepic.' More common abbreviations are the pronouns. A man's name is mentioned and quickly changes to 'he,' 'him,' or 'his.' Pronouns, especially 'they,' are sometimes used because the full information cannot be supplied. More often it is laziness or impatience that leads to pronominal substitution.

Definitions. A large group of abbreviations are called *definitions*. Take the chess language again. With competent players the sequence of moves at the beginning of the game is relatively stereotyped. There are perhaps 100 different sequences that are likely to occur in the first 10 moves of the game. We could take advantage of this fact to give each of these opening sequences a number from 0 to 99. If two players followed one of these sequences for the first 10 moves, we could indicate the fact by writing its number and beginning the detailed record with the eleventh move. Of course, it is not certain that only these 100 possibilities will occur. A game may follow one of them for 5 moves and then depart into an improbable sequence. Consequently a final digit is needed to tell us how far the particular opening was followed. Thus 337 says that the game followed opening 33 through 7 moves and that the detailed record begins with the eighth move. In this way a sequence of three digits could often replace a sequence of 80 letters. This is definitional abbreviation.

In the chess language this form of abbreviation reduces redundancy. The frequently used sequences are replaced by new terms; the definitions of the new, shorter terms are given by the longer sequences they replace. In these situations the definition is a rule for avoiding the use of a symbol. The definition gives an equivalent means of symbolizing the information.

There are two kinds of definitions. In the chess language we use both kinds. The semantic rules that related numbers and letters to rows and columns are definitions of one kind, and the abbreviatory use of numbers to replace other symbols at the beginning of the game illustrate definitions of a second kind. The first is sometimes called an *extensional* or *ostensive* or *pointing definition*. The second is called an *intensional* or *dictionary definition*. More precisely, an extensional definition lists or points to every object the symbol designates; an intensional definition is another alternative set of symbols for the same things signified by the symbol being defined.

Intensional definitions serve to reduce redundancy, but they may lead to confusion if they are misused. Abstract nouns cause much trouble because we learn to use them without learning the full sequence of symbols they are intended to replace. Then we begin to disagree with others on how to replace them and perhaps decide eventually that no acceptable definition exists. In order to avoid such confusion, it is sometimes argued that every intensional definition should be reducible to an extensional definition. Then all abstract words could be traced to the particular objects or events from which the abstraction was formed, and thus our language would be much better anchored in reality (Korzybski, 1933). A little reflection shows, however, that this procedure cannot work. In practice we often know a great deal about a class of objects without being able to give an extensional enumeration of the members of the class. We can give an intensional definition of 'men' as 'the class of featherless bipeds,' but no one would undertake to enumerate all men. It is not necessary to have an extensional definition in order to use a word unambiguously. And when we consider classes with an infinite number of members, extensional definitions are out of the question. It is impossible to define the word 'integer' by listing all of them (B. Russell, 1919).

Definitions are often dismissed as merely verbal arguments. Definitions are not trivia; wars have been fought over the proper definitions of 'salvation' and 'freedom' and the like. Abbreviation is convenient to keep redundancy under control, but when the definition of the abbreviation is unknown, the resulting nonsense and misunderstanding may lead to all kinds of trouble.

Dictionaries. It is widely recognized and usually forgotten that modern dictionaries of English are based on usage rather than fiat. The lexicographer collects many sentences by writers of literary or historic importance who have used a certain word. He then proceeds to classify these sentences into groups that seem to use the word similarly. For each group he writes a short phrase that can be substituted into the sentences in place of the word itself. A dictionary definition is, therefore, an alternative verbalization derived from the contexts in which the word has been used previously. A given word may have a variety of definitions inferred from the variety of contexts in which it appears.

Consider the verb 'take.' In the Oxford English Dictionary there are 317 definitions of this word, 317 verbal alternatives that can be substituted for it. This is a confusing state of affairs. To find an analogy, suppose that 'da-di-dit' in the International Morse Code usually represented 'D' but under certain conditions might represent almost any other letter in the alphabet. How could one tell which letter was intended? A set of rules saying that 'da-di-dit' is 'D' unless used before one thing or after another, etc., would be required. The decoding would get much more complicated.

Why do people tolerate such ambiguity? The answer is that they don't. There is nothing ambiguous about 'take' as it is used in everyday speech. The ambiguity appears only when we, quite arbitrarily, call isolated words the units of meaning. It is possible to draw up a dictionary using some other verbal unit—the syllable, say, instead of the word. Sentences that include a certain syllable can be collected and classified into groups that use the syllable similarly. Phrases to be substituted for the syllables can be composed. One entry would be the syllable 'sent,' for example. This would have in its list of verbal equivalents certain ones that apply when the syllable stands alone, others to be used when the syllable is preceded by 're' or 'dis,' still others to be used when the syllable is followed by 'ence' or 'inel,' etc.

Most people object to such a syllable dictionary. It is useless, they feel, because syllables standing alone have no meaning. Or if they do have meanings, the meanings are so many and so ambiguous that it is impossible to know what any syllable means unless you know what other syllables precede it and follow it. The answer to this objection is that it applies also to word dictionaries. Words standing alone have no meaning either or, more precisely, have no single meaning. The dictionary definitions are derived from the contexts in which the word occurs.

There are no meanings in the dictionary. There are only equivalent verbalizations, other ways for saying almost the same thing. There is a common belief that to define a word is to give its meaning. It is healthier to say that by defining the word we substitute one verbal pattern for another.

Of the several definitions listed for each word, some are used more often than others. The relative frequencies of occurrence of the different definitions have been studied by Lorge (1937) and Thorndike and Lorge (1944). After counting through a sample of several million words these workers were able to compile lists showing the frequency of occurrence of the definitions given in the Oxford English Dictionary. For example, of the 317 definitions given for the word 'take,' Lorge and Thorndike found 171 represented in a sample 3504 'take's.' Seventeen of these definitions were found more than 20 times in 1000 uses of the word, and the most frequently used definition occurred on the average 85 times per 1000 'take's.' When the definitions are ranked in order by frequency of occurrence and the frequency is plotted against the rank, definitions are found to follow the same sort of law that governs the frequency of occurrence of words (Zipf, 1945). It is also possible to show that the most frequently used nouns and verbs and adjectives tend, on the average, to have the greatest number of definitions.

These statistics, which are usually referred to as a *semantic count*, provide a basis for producing a more functional dictionary. In some of the more recent dictionaries, for example, only the most frequent words are given, and for each of these only the most frequent definitions are listed. This manner of selection would seem to rid the dictionary of esoteric, obsolescent, archaic, and provincial words and definitions. On the other hand, these are just the words we often have to look up in a dictionary.

Agreement in the Use of Symbols. There have been various attempts to determine uniformity in the use of words and to express the degree of uniformity in a quantitative way. The maximum possible number of agreements can be calculated, and the ratio of the number of agreements actually obtained to this maximum number can be taken as an *extensional agreement index* (W. Johnson, 1944). This index shows how well people agree in enumerating a certain thing as a member of the class of things symbolized by the word. More specifically, suppose we ask 100 people whether Herbert Hoover is a member of the class of liberals. If 50 say 'yes' and 50 say 'no,' we have the smallest possible number of agreements. If 100 say 'yes' or if 100 say 'no,' we have the largest possible number of agreements. When this was tried, 95 out of 100 people refused to call Hoover a liberal, which shows rather good agreement in the use of this term as applied to this man. When Thomas E. Dewey was considered, however, 47 answered 'yes' and 53 answered 'no.' Here is considerable disagreement. If we got so much disagreement over the objects designated by words like 'chair' or 'lamp,' we should probably have to abandon the whole language as a bad job.

A somewhat similar index can be used to quantify the degree of agreement in defining a word—the *intensional agreement index*. This index shows how well two or more intensional definitions agree. In one study, psychology texts were searched until six definitions of each of four terms ('learning,' 'perception,' 'emotion,' 'personality') were found. A similar search of texts in biochemistry produced definitions of five biochemical terms. All words were eliminated from the definitions except nouns, verbs, adjectives, and adverbs. Then an agreement index was computed for each term according to the number of words common to the six definitions. For the psychological terms the indices averaged 0.012. For the biochemical terms the average was 0.092. Thus it is possible to show a measurable difference between the two fields in the degree of terminological uniformity that has been achieved to date.

It is fairly clear, both from the many definitions per word in the dictionary and from the low agreement indices, that there is little uniformity in our use of individual words. The information we convey is coded into a pattern of words. The relations among the components of the pattern must be known before the individual components can be decoded.

LANGUAGE ENGINEERING

Probably we shall never be able to cure everyday speech of vagueness and misunderstanding. The usual solution is to invent a new language whenever a situation calls for greater precision than ordinary speech can achieve.

Scientists, for example, develop their own notation and draw heavily upon the mathematical and logical languages when they want to say something accurately. Some scholars have tried to imagine what a perfect language would be like. These attempts to meddle with and modify existing languages for special purposes are examples of language engineering (Miller, 1950).

For more than a thousand years educated Europeans were tied together by their common knowledge of Latin. After the Reformation the use of Latin began to decline. A substitute was needed for international communication. Volapük, Esperanto, Ido, Esperantido, Interlingua, Novial, and other artificial languages had adherents, but none seemed to catch on. A fairly recent and apparently very successful contender is Basic English. Many of the proposed international languages are based to a high degree on Latin. English may have an advantage over Latin because it seems to be freer of redundancy. Complex and redundant rules for inflections are largely nonexistent in modern English.

Some linguists believe that languages evolve from long, elaborate phonetic patterns with little communication content toward short units combined according to rules to convey much more content per element (Jesperson, 1922). In statistical terms, the evolution of language shows a progressive decline in redundancy. This speculation can be examined in several ways. For example, redundancy is reduced by abbreviation. Abbreviation produces shorter words. If linguistic evolution is toward less redundancy, a trend toward shorter words should be evident. Table 6 gives some relevant figures. The approximate numbers of syllables needed for the Gospel of St. Matthew in 10 different languages are listed (Baker, 1950). French, which is derived from Latin, uses fewer syllables than Latin to say the same thing. Similarly, modern English uses fewer syllables than Anglo-Saxon. Linguistic evolution does seem to decrease redundancy.

TABLE 6. NUMBER OF SYLLABLES IN GOSPEL OF ST. MATTHEW IN 10 LANGUAGES
(Baker, 1950)

Greek	39,000	French	33,000
Latin	37,000	Danish	32,500
Swedish	35,000	Gothic	31,100
German	34,000	English	29,000
Anglo-Saxon	34,000	Chinese	17,000

To illustrate the decay of English prefixes and suffixes, it is sufficient to compare the proportion of monosyllables in English with the proportions in other languages. A word count of some verses from the Bible shows 90 per cent monosyllables in the English version, 75 per cent monosyllables in German, 65 per cent in French, and 30 per cent in Latin. With the decay of the linguistic rules governing affixes has come a greater freedom in the use of words. Thus words like 'promise' or 'hope' serve as nouns or verbs, and only their position in a pattern of words indicates which function they serve. In most languages this information is given by affixes as well as by context. Similarly, English nouns often function as adjectives. The freedom from rigid, unbreakable rules makes it relatively easy to manipulate the statistical structure of the English language.

Basic English. Basic English is an interesting attempt to take advantage of the statistical aspects of language. The proponents of Basic English point out that there are approximately 1500 languages at present spoken by approximately 2300 million people. The lack of a common coding procedure is a barrier to international communication and understanding. To provide an international language Ogden (1934) has proposed an adaptation of English that is adequate for communication and that can be learned easily and quickly. The adaptation consists in limiting the language to 600 nouns, 150 adjectives, and 100 additional words (verbs, prepositions, conjunctions, pronouns, articles) that put these nouns and adjectives together so the whole system can work as normal English. These 850 lexical units were carefully chosen so that by combinations they could be made the equivalent of a much larger vocabulary. For technical writing, however, an additional handful are permitted. To quote Ogden:

> We are so accustomed to multiplicity of terms in certain fields that we are apt to regard their absence as a sign of weakness. Often, however, the elimination of all but one has been the outcome of a long process of linguistic development. . . . Various kinds of animals and humans which for the highly civilized Frenchman might merely *crient*,* are found to call, shout, yell, shriek, bawl, mew, scream, screech, croak, roar, bellow, low, etc., as soon as they cross the Channel. In Basic they are content to *make sounds* and *noises* in various ways—which is, in fact, all that they do in real life. . . . The real statistical task of linguistics is not so much the determination of the number of words actually used by any particular person or class of persons as the study of how a reduction may be effected in the number of words that need to be used; *i.e.*, how a given field of reference may be covered with the greatest economy. . . . What is really required is, in fact, a scientifically selected vocabulary minimum; and it is this selection that Basic claims to provide.

Of the many proposals for language reform, Basic English has attracted the widest attention and support. By reducing the number of word types to 850 lexical units the potential size of the audience is greatly increased. This

---

* Ogden exaggerates the simple uniformity of French expressions. It is true that the French word '*crier*' has a wider use than any English parallel, but the highly civilized Frenchman would probably use commonly the words '*hurler*,' '*vociférer*,' '*mugir*,' '*rugir*,' '*aboyer*,' '*miauler*,' '*croasser*,' '*coasser*,' '*hennir*,' '*brailler*,' '*beugler*,' and '*meugler*.' To illustrate how fine the distinctions are, '*meugler*' is used for the sound of a cow and '*beugler*' for the sound of a bull.

substantial gain exacts a certain toll, however, for we cannot throw away 95 per cent of our vocabulary without losing something. The loss appears in the form of idiomatic constructions and clauses that lengthen sentences and often make them seem out of focus to the reader accustomed to old-fashioned Complex English. 'A delicious aroma' might become 'a very good smell,' or 'blood, sweat, and tears' might become 'blood, body water, and eye water.'

An interesting but debatable economy in Basic English is the treatment of verbs. In Basic the equivalent of a verb is a general *operator* combined with a qualifying word or expression. For example, movements through space can all be indicated by the operator 'go' with qualifications to describe how the movement was accomplished. Thus the word 'walk' becomes unnecessary because we can say 'go on foot.' 'Wander' also disappears to be replaced by 'go from place to place without aim.' The Basic equivalents get a little long-winded, but communication is certainly possible. Some critics feel that Basic's 18 operators are too economical and that a few more verbs might be added to avoid unfortunate idiomatic constructions. For example, Basic English does not use the verb 'try.' For the various uses of this word Basic would substitute 'make an attempt at' or 'put to the test' or 'be the judge of.' A foreigner may be puzzled that he cannot 'put an attempt' or 'make to the test.' For English-speaking people, Basic is a handy auxiliary language that lacks the richness of Complex English. For the businessman dealing in foreign markets, for the diplomat arguing via translators, for the aviator landing at a foreign airport, etc., richness can be sacrificed for direct communication.

Whereas the emphasis in Basic English has been placed on reducing the size of the vocabulary, there has been an artistic and scientific swing in the opposite direction. The desire for verbal diversification in literature is typified by James Joyce. One word may be the logical equivalent of another word, but not, it is argued, the psychological equivalent. Paralleling the neologisms of the artist is the continued growth of the scientific vocabulary. The scientist often resorts to long and unusual words in order to express himself with greater precision. The price of verbal diversification, however, is a reduced audience.

There seems to be a kind of linguistic equilibrium. An increase in the size of the vocabulary is balanced by a decrease in the size of the audience. A decrease in vocabulary is balanced by an increased audience. There seems to be no simple way to have a large vocabulary and a large audience at the same time.

It is a feature of Basic English that it takes advantage of the relatively low redundancy of normal English. The principal difficulties with normal English are the tremendous size of its hybrid vocabulary and the irregularities of English spelling. These difficulties lose their significance in Basic. As an auxiliary international language and as an introduction to English for foreigners, Basic English can be a useful contribution. And the American or Englishman who studies Basic carefully will be rewarded by a clearer understanding of the way his own language works.

Enthusiasts sometimes claim that Basic should replace, rather than merely supplement, the many languages of the world. This is a dangerous idea. The Indo-European languages, with their actor-action structure and their Aristotelian logic, give a rigid scaffolding for our thought. Before we put all our eggs in this one linguistic basket, we must know the basket is sound and sturdy. We must be sure that other structures and other logics are dispensable (Whorf, 1941). The language engineers are not yet wise enough to settle this question.

Phonemes Available for an International Language. One of the worst barriers facing the designers of auxiliary international languages is the difference in phonemic habits among the potential customers. The Chinese who tries to learn Basic English does not find that its reduced vocabulary helps him to pronounce English words more accurately. What is the common core of speech sounds that all peoples could be expected to produce and distinguish? Trubetzkoy (1939) suggests that the designers of international languages should limit themselves to the following 14 phonemes: the 5 vowels /u/, /o/, /ɑ/, /e/, and /i/; the 9 consonants, /p/, /t/, /k/, /m/, /n/, /j/, /w/, /s/, and /l/. These sounds, or recognizable approximations to them, can be found in all languages of major importance. However, not all combinations can be admitted. Only two diphthongs, /ɑi/ and /ɑu/, are common enough to be acceptable. Of the 45 possible consonant-vowel combinations, all but 5, /wu/, /ji/, /tu/, /ti/, and /ki/, are acceptable and would not often be confused. All vowel-consonant combinations except /ij/ and /uw/ can be included. Only 7 of the consonant-consonant combinations are admissible: /mp/, /nt/, /nk/, /ns/, /mw/, /nj/, and /nl/. Vowel-vowel combinations connecting adjacent syllables should include only /oɑ/, /oe/, /ɑo/, /ɑe/, /eo/, and /eɑ/. No word should start with a double consonant. Every word should end with a vowel or with a vowel followed by /n/. Within the limits of these rules, designed to select only features common to all the world's languages, Trubetzkoy calculated that over 10,000 one- and two-syllable words can be constructed.

A language built to be pronounceable by all the peoples of the world would have to be completely artificial. No existing language satisfies all the requirements listed above. At the present time it seems unlikely that any completely artificial language can gain sufficient support to be adopted.

DISCUSSION QUESTIONS

1. What is the difference between redundant and irrelevant information?
2. Musical notation is a language for writing about music. Distinguish some pragmatic, semantic, and syntactic rules that constrain the possible sequences of symbols in this language.

3. Is it necessary to be more redundant in spoken than in written language?

4. List the contextual influences, other than the verbal context, that go to determine verbal behavior.

5. Could a group of listeners make a higher articulation score, as a group, if they were allowed to compare their answers? In what sense would this procedure introduce redundancy?

Selected References

BODMER, F. *The Loom of Language.* New York: Norton, 1944. A popularized introduction to the languages of the world. Chapters X–XII are particularly relevant to the present discussion.

JESPERSEN, O. *Language: Its Nature, Development, and Origin.* New York: Macmillan, 1922. An introduction to linguistics for students who wish to pursue this topic further.

MILLER, G. A. Speech and language. In S. S. Stevens (Ed.), *Handbook of Experimental Psychology.* New York: Wiley, 1951. Applies information theory to estimate the redundancy of connected discourse.

OGDEN, C. K. *The System of Basic English.* New York: Harcourt, Brace, 1934. A connected and relatively complete account of the system of Basic English for English-speaking readers.

———— and I. A. RICHARDS. *The Meaning of Meaning* (Rev. Ed.). New York: Harcourt, Brace, 1947. A pioneering work in the analysis of language, and a statement of the philosophy behind Basic English.

Chapter 6

INDIVIDUAL DIFFERENCES

Language most showeth a man; speak that I may see thee.

—BEN JONSON

According to the Book of Judges (xii: 4–6) Jephthah managed to separate his Gileadites from the Ephraimites by taking advantage of differences in verbal behavior. The Gileadites took the passages of Jordan before the Ephraimites. When an Ephraimite said, 'Let me go over,' the men of Gilead asked, 'Art thou an Ephraimite?' If he said, 'Nay,' they persisted, 'Say now Shibboleth,' and he said 'Sibboleth,' for he could not pronounce it. Then they took him, and slew him at the passages of Jordan: and there fell at that time of the Ephraimites forty and two thousand.

Individual differences in verbal behavior seldom have such drastic consequences, but they go far to put us in our social niche. In addition to the information we intend to convey, our speech inadvertently helps the listener guess our nationality, sex, age, region of the country, social background, and education. Whether we like it or not, our listeners type us—stereotype us —according to the impression they gain from our verbal habits (Pear, 1931). Every word we speak is a shibboleth.

Thus far our concern has been with language in general. The particular talker has been ignored in favor of an imagined average talker. Often, however, we are interested in a particular individual's verbal behavior—is he above or below the average in some respect, and how does this relate to other facts known about him?

The fact that different peoples talk different languages is perhaps the most glaring source of individual differences. The language we speak is a part of our social inheritance and is not particularly diagnostic of what is called our personality. Jespersen (1923) has suggested that one cannot expect much vigor or energy in the people who speak the musical, vowel-dominated languages of Spain, Italy, or Hawaii, but such suggestions do not seem to lead anywhere. In this chapter we are more concerned with the differences that exist among people who have been exposed to nearly the same cultural background. These can be referred to as differences in verbal *style*.

It is apparent that people differ in their verbal styles and that these differences are fairly consistent. Suppose, for example, that we conduct the following experiment: A group of subjects writes short essays or themes that we collect. Some time later we repeat this procedure. Now take the two sets of themes, and carefully remove all marks of the authors' identities. Will trained psychologists be able to match the first theme any given individual wrote with the second? If so, we have demonstrated a recognizable consistency in the verbal behavior of the essayists. The experiment has been conducted with nine themes collected from each of 70 college students over a period of 8 months (Allport, Walker, and Lathers, 1934; Vernon, 1936). The investigators attempted to group together all the themes written by each college student. While their groupings were by no means perfect, they did succeed far better than would be expected on the basis of chance. The immediate question to ask is, How did the investigators do it? What clues did they find in one theme that made them say it was written by the same person who had written another theme? Unfortunately they themselves were unable to answer this question. Like artists, they succeeded intuitively, which means simply that they were unable to formulate in words all the factors that influenced their decisions.

There is a problem here. Can verbal style be studied profitably by quantitative procedures, or must it be approached through intuition and inference? If mechanical carriers of style can be used in an objective way, the intuitive judgment may become more retraceable and more communicable.

STATISTICAL INDICATORS OF STYLE

What statistical aspects of language are most diagnostic of individual differences in verbal style? There is a wide range and variety of statistical indices available. Some of these statistics have been explored more thoroughly than others (Sanford, 1942a). One that has received considerable attention is the *size of the vocabulary*.

Vocabulary Size. Most of us are sensitive about the number of words we recognize and use. We are entreated to take steps toward a more powerful vocabulary, told to use the dictionary more often, quizzed by feature writers in magazines, and generally made to feel inferior if we fumble an unusual word. This lexicographic propaganda is based on some very reasonable considerations. In the discussion of the amount of information, a fundamental notion was that we must enumerate the set of possible alternatives, and the amount of information we can convey per word is thus related to the size of our vocabulary. The analysis proposed by Zipf also places the size of the vocabulary in an important theoretical position. Ogden and Richards are much interested in the matter, and the reduction of the vocabulary is one of the most important features of Basic English. The psychologists who measure intelligence find that estimates of vocabulary size are among the most dependable indicators they possess. Both theoretical and practical considerations urge the study of vocabulary size.

In view of its importance it is unfortunate that it is so difficult to obtain a reliable estimate of the number of words a person knows. One difficulty arises because we have several vocabularies, one for talking, one for writing, one for reading, etc. In the count of 80,000 words of telephone conversation, for example, there were only 2240 different lexical units, or about 5000 different words. If this is an estimate of the size of the speaking vocabulary, it is necessary to conclude that there are many words we know but never speak. A reasonable extrapolation based upon small samples can be made from the type-token ratio, and this would indicate a writing vocabulary of about 10,000 words in good fiction. James Joyce's 29,899 different words in *Ulysses* is unusually high (Hanley, 1937). If we ask about the size of the recognition vocabulary, however, the estimate may soar as high as 200,000 words.

One of the better vocabulary tests for older children and adults was devised by Seashore and Eckerson (1940). These investigators began with the Funk and Wagnalls unabridged dictionary. They divided the words in this dictionary into (1) *basic*, or *root*, words (lexical units) and (2) *derivative* words (compound and complex words) formed by a slight variation of the basic words. The test was made up of both types of words. For the basic words, college students checked one of four possible alternatives (the scores were corrected to take account of guessing). For the derivative words, the students were asked to check those words which they recognized and could use in a sentence. Of the 166,000 basic words in the Funk and Wagnalls dictionary, the test included 330, or $\frac{1}{505}$ of the total. In order to estimate the number of basic words, therefore, the score on the test is multiplied by 505. Derivative words were tested similarly. The test sampled $\frac{1}{4550}$ of all the derivative words in the dictionary, and so the number of such words recognized was multiplied by 4550.

According to this test the average college student can recognize 35 per cent of the basic words and 47 per cent of the derivative words. Thus his vocabulary is estimated at nearly 60,000 different lexical units, or a total of 156,000 words. The lowest 10 per cent recognized 112,000 words, the highest 193,000. These figures may seem too high. Certainly the vocabulary *used* by these same students over some given period of time would be much smaller.

The differences in the size of the several vocabularies of a single person are larger than the differences in the size of the same vocabulary for different people. It is a general rule of verbal learning that recognition is easier than recall—a word is recognized even though we could not have used it ourselves. A large recognition vocabulary along with relatively small talking and writing (recall) vocabularies is insurance that we shall understand a wide range of talkers even though we should not have used their words.

Intelligence, age, and education are the principal factors correlated with differences in the size of vocabulary. Since age is such an important variable, we shall postpone further consideration of the matter to Chap. 7.

Verbal Diversification and the Type-Token Ratio. The writer or speaker who uses a large vocabulary has a more diversified style than the man who restricts himself to a small vocabulary. Various methods of determining indices of *verbal diversification* are available. One method is to determine the standard curve for a particular writer (cf. Chap. 4). For newspaper writing it was found that the slope of the curve relating frequency of use to rank order (Fig. 31) was approximately −1 on logarithmic coordinates. Changes in this slope are associated with changes in verbal diversification.

In order to indicate that the slope of the function in Fig. 31 might change, the equation for the standard curve of English words must be rewritten $fr^x = C$, where the new term, x, is related to the slope. In Chap. 4 we assumed implicitly that $x = 1$. This assumption is approximately true for most of the samples that have been counted. If a person uses a wide range of different words and does not tend to repeat certain words very often, the value for x for that person falls between 0 and 1. If a talker has a limited vocabulary and so must repeat the few words he knows over and over, the value of x falls between 1 and 2. In short, the more diverse vocabulary produces a gentler slope for the function. Thus the slope constant can be used as an index of diversification.

An alternative way to estimate the degree of verbal diversification has been proposed by Carroll (1938). If a person has a limited vocabulary, he will, in the course of a long message, re-use a word sooner on the average than will the person who has a large vocabulary. If we choose the most frequent word in the message and count the number of words that separate successive occurrences of this word, we find that, on the average, there are more words intervening between successive occurrences if the talker has a diverse vocabulary. The advantage of this index of verbal diversification is that we do not need to make a complete tabulation of all the words in the sample. Since the average value does not change systematically with the length of the sample, it is possible to estimate the diversification from a short passage and to compare the result directly with the results obtained with longer passages under other conditions.

Since 'the' is usually the most frequent word in written material, we might arbitrarily choose it as the word to look for in all cases. Then we determine the average number of word tokens intervening between successive occurrences of 'the.' The result, which is usually somewhere in the neighborhood of 10 to 15, is the index of diversification.

A closely related index, called the *type-token ratio* (TTR), provides a more direct measure of diversification (W. Johnson, 1941). The TTR is the ratio of the number of different words (types) to the total number of words (tokens) in the passage. In the count of newspaper English, for example, there were 44,000 tokens and 6000 types, and so the TTR is $6/44$ or 0.136.

One difficulty with the type-token ratio is that it gets smaller as the size of the sample gets bigger (Estoup, 1917). If the passage contains only one word, this one word is one type and one token and so the TTR must equal 1.00. If the passage consists of two word tokens, these two tokens will probably be different types. We must take a passage of about 10 tokens before one type occurs more than once. As the length of the passage is increased it becomes more likely that words will be repeated and less likely that new, unused words will occur.

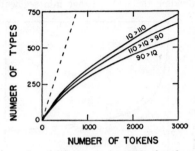

FIG. 34. The average number of different word types is plotted against the total number of word tokens for bright, average, and dull school children. (*After Chotlos,* 1944.)

The fact that the number of tokens increases more rapidly than the number of types is shown graphically in Fig. 34. These data were obtained for the writing of grade-school children between the ages of eight and twelve (Chotlos, 1944). The purpose was to discover whether or not children with a high intelligence quotient (IQ) show the greatest verbal diversification, the highest type-token ratios. The three functions in Fig. 34 show the results for superior, average, and inferior groups of children. On the average the written material of the more intelligent children contained a larger proportion of different words than did the written material of the children with low IQ's. There were, however, considerable differences among individuals.

If the middle curve from Fig. 34 is plotted as a ratio, it becomes clear that the type-token ratio changes continually as the length of the passage is increased. The ratio has been plotted in Fig. 35. Since the TTR decreases in this manner, TTR's for different people can be compared only if the number of words counted for both is the same. This comparison for different lengths would be possible if we knew how to translate a ratio for one length to what it would have been if a different length passage had been used. The translation could be accomplished if we could give an accurate equation for the curves of Figs. 34 and 35. Several attempts have been made to find a satisfactory equation (Carroll, 1938; Chotlos, 1944).

The type-token index of verbal variability can be used in several ways, and W. Johnson (1946, 500–502) has defined four such ratios that need to be distinguished. (1) The *over-all TTR* is determined for an entire language sample

—a novel, essay, sonnet, or whatever is of interest. The over-all TTR is of little value unless the length of the sample is also given. (2) The *mean segmental TTR's* are determined by dividing the total passage into segments of equal length, then determining the TTR for each segment and averaging these several values together. (3) The *cumulative TTR* curve is determined by computing successive TTR's as the passage grows longer and longer. The curve in Fig. 35 represents such a cumulative TTR. (4) The *decremental TTR* curve is determined by dividing the total passage into segments of equal length,

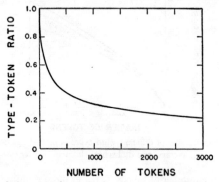

FIG. 35. The cumulative type-token ratio plotted as a function of the length of the passage. Drawn from the middle function of Fig. 34. (*After Chotlos*, 1944.)

counting the new words in each that have not appeared before in any preceding segment, and plotting the ratio of the number of new types per segment to the length of a segment (not to the total length of the passage up to that point). The decremental curve shows directly the rate at which new words are introduced into the passage.

The cumulative and decremental curves can be compared in an imaginary example. Suppose a particular writer uses 60 different word types in his first 100 word tokens and 40 more new words in his second 100 words. The cumulative TTR at the end of 100 words is 60/100, or 0.6, and at 200 is 100/200, or 0.5. The decremental TTR, for segments of 100 words, is 60/100 for the first 100 words and is 40/100, or 0.4, for the second 100 words. In more technical terms, the decremental curve is the absolute value of the first derivative of the cumulative curve.

There is, of course, no need to limit the type-token ratio to word units. The ratio can be used just as well with other verbal units. Chen and Irwin (1946), for example, have used such ratios among phoneme tokens and types to study the increase in the variety of speech sounds produced by infants as they learn to talk.

Sentence Length. Another widely used statistic is *sentence length*. Very consistent individual differences have been reported for this measure. Writers and talkers vary widely in their willingness to use short sentences. In one count of popular magazines (Gray and Leary, 1935) the median number of syllables per sentence ranged from 13 for *All-Story* magazine to 33.5 for *Review of Reviews*. The *Saturday Evening Post* was near the middle of the range with 21 syllables per sentence. Similar large differences are found in the writing of different authors. Sir William Petty used about 60 words per sentence, while Macaulay scraped by on 22. Comic strips use about 8 words between periods.

An interesting use of the statistics of sentence length occurs in cases of disputed authorship. One statistician (Yule, 1938) was able to show that the disputed *De imitatione Christi* was written with sentences whose lengths were approximately the same as those in the writings of à Kempis and were shorter than those used by Gerson. Assuming a certain consistency in the styles of these two authors, it is more likely that à Kempis wrote the *Imitatio* than that Gerson did.

A stylistic device used by some authors is to vary the lengths of their sentences. A long sentence may be followed by a short, abrupt statement that emphasizes some point or creates some definite effect. This sort of variation is reflected quantitatively in the amount of dispersion around the average (C. B. Williams, 1940). G. K. Chesterton and G. B. Shaw, for example, use about the same number of words per sentence, but Chesterton places his periods with considerable regularity, while Shaw varies widely from sentence to sentence. If we draw up a frequency distribution of sentence lengths, plotting the number of one-word sentences at one, the number of two-word sentences at two, the number of three-word sentences at three, etc., Chesterton's plot will be very tall and thin, while Shaw's plot will be short and broad. If we redraw this same plot using the logarithm of the number of words per sentence, the plot becomes very nearly what statisticians call a *normal probability distribution*. For curves with this general shape statisticians know many tricks, and it has been proposed that the root-mean-square deviation from the logarithmic average (the standard deviation) should be used as a convenient measure of the verbal change of pace.

It is worth while to try to catalogue some of the factors that tend to lengthen sentences. The principal reasons would seem to be abbreviation and qualification. Abbreviation may seem a paradoxical reason for long sentences, but it happens this way. We have several things to say about Joe. We could say 'Joe lives in Boston. Joe writes books. Joe has a hat. Joe's hat is brown.' But this seems choppy, and we seem to be using the word 'Joe' more than necessary. We can mention Joe only once, thus abbreviating, if we say 'Joe, who lives in Boston and writes books, has a brown hat.' The four original sentences had a total of 15 words, while the single longer sentence gets by with 12. So abbreviation—the reduction of redundancy—can produce long sentences. Not all long sentences result from an attempt to abbreviate. Often we find long sentences that can be chopped into shorter ones with an actual saving in the total number of words.

Words must be spoken one at a time, and this is often a considerable inconvenience. In thinking we may succeed in solving a problem because we were lucky enough to consider several things all at the same time. The structure of the solution is clear, but it must be translated into a succession of logical steps before we can communicate it to anyone else. This translation is not always easy. One statement must qualify another in such and such a way, and the implication of something else must be remembered throughout, etc. If the translation is not fully achieved, the result may be a single sentence that tries to say everything at once. Then actors and actions are torn apart, intermingled, and patched together with empty phrases like 'in accordance with the fact that it seems to be the case that,' etc. The desire to qualify one sentence with another need not force the writer to make one sentence out of two, but it usually has that effect.

Mimicry can also produce long sentences. The man who writes for a scientific journal will read the journal and probably adopt its style. Vanity may lead a writer to impress his reader with intricate prose. Or the writer may feel that the reader will escape if a period offers him the chance. And, presumably, some people write long sentences because they *like* long sentences.

Styles in Punctuation. One way of looking at the average sentence length is that it measures the writer's willingness to use periods. It is possible to explore other *punctuation marks* in a similar fashion (Summey, 1949, especially the Appendix, pp. 157–163). Do different authors punctuate differently?

Fashions in punctuation have changed considerably in the course of a few centuries. For example, more than 10 per cent of the punctuation marks in the first folio of Shakespeare (1623) and the first printing of the King James Bible (1611) were colons. Today the colon makes up about 1 per cent of all the punctuation marks in books, magazines and newspapers. The use of a string of dots, '. . . ,' shows the opposite trend. First used to signify the omission of letters in a word, or words in a sentence, then used occasionally in the nineteenth century to indicate an incomplete thought, '. . .' has in the twentieth century become quite fashionable. For some writers it supplants more conventional dashes, exclamation points, 'etc.,' phrases, or nothing at all. An example of devotion to '. . .' is found in *Superman*, a picture-story magazine that charms childish minds, young and old. A count of punctuation marks in this writing showed 9 per cent of them were '. . . .' This refutes the conviction of many perplexed readers that '. . .' represents a meditative pause by someone, the character, the author, or the reader, for Superman seldom pauses for meditation.

Punctuation profiles for 14 authors are given in Table 7 (Thorndike, 1948). Clear stylistic differences are apparent. Some of these differences depend upon what sort of persons and events the author writes about and what sort

TABLE 7. RELATIVE FREQUENCIES PER 1000 PUNCTUATION MARKS

(Thorndike, 1948)

	,	.	;	:	—	( )	. . .	?	!
18th century:									
Daniel Defoe	718	134	121	10	4	3	0	8	2
Samuel Richardson	534	161	85	37	65	34	0	33	51
Henry Fielding	584	198	119	14	22	19	0	28	13
Jane Austen	522	270	92	6	31	4	0	2	4
19th century:									
Walter Scott	687	177	58	1	48	1	0	12	12
W. M. Thackeray	569	213	64	22	44	20	0	30	3
Charles Dickens	583	233	57	12	35	20	0	25	34
George Meredith	466	336	58	25	29	4	6	32	44
Thomas Hardy	510	323	55	9	41	6	3	31	20
20th century:									
Edith Wharton	433	302	65	31	70	7	15	50	27
H. G. Wells	441	337	30	3	53	1	32	30	31
Arnold Bennett	440	368	31	20	19	8	7	37	69
John Galsworthy	447	292	61	28	58	5	1	38	70
Angela Thirkell	586	368	4	5	3	2	0	28	9

of readers he writes for. Some differences are merely the operation of fashions in punctuation. But even when allowances are made for these factors, large stylistic differences remain. In artistic writing, punctuation does more than guide the reader's pauses and aid his recognition of grammatical structure; punctuation influences emphasis, movement, style.

Verb-Adjective Ratio. Some verbal statistics are designed to reveal individual differences in the frequency of use of different parts of speech. Busemann (1925, 1926; Stern and Busemann, 1925) has suggested that the occurrence of verbs and adjectives in a person's speech is somehow related to his emotional stability. He counted the number of qualitative and active constructions in stories told by children. The qualitative category included adjectives and also all the participles and nouns used as adjectives. The active category included all verbs except the auxiliaries. The *verb-adjective ratio* is the quotient obtained when the number of active constructions in the story is divided by the number of qualitative constructions.

Busemann also had teachers rate the children for emotional stability. Comparison of the verb-adjective ratio with these ratings indicated that the children who showed a change toward greater emotional instability showed a corresponding change toward more active constructions. Children whose emotional stability increased showed fewer active constructions. Presumably the active style correlated with mobility, emotion, lower objectivity, less concreteness, and less intellectuality.

The verb-adjective ratio is usually higher for spoken than for written language. The more time we have to produce the symbols, the more qualifications we put on them.

In an analysis of a wide range of American writing Boder (1940) compared the ratios (1) for one person at different times, (2) for different people, and (3) for different types of writing. For a comparison of one person with himself Boder used Emerson's *Journals*, which begin in 1820 and continue until Emerson's death in 1876. The results give a rather irregular curve that seems to increase with age. When he was sixteen, Emerson used about 2 verbs for every adjective, but as a sexagenarian he used almost 3 verbs per adjective.

Large differences can be found for different authors, even when they are writing a similar kind of material. For example, Mencken's articles in the *American Mercury* ran about 1.4 verbs per adjective, whereas Brisbane's column had about 2.2 verbs per adjective.

The comparison of different kinds of writing showed the largest variations. For example, the dialogue in plays increases their ratio to 9 verbs per adjective, while scientific writings showed only 1.3. Legal statutes, which deal with the acts of human beings, have 5 verbs per adjective. Fiction has about 3 verbs per adjective. It is interesting to note that theses written for the master's degree have 1.5 verbs for every adjective, but by the time the candidate reaches his Ph.D. thesis he manages to reduce the ratio to 1.1. In one Ph.D. thesis a cautious writer used two qualifications for every active construction, a verb-adjective ratio of 0.5.

The most important factor that influences the verb-adjective quotient is the type of writing. One person generates different ratios depending upon the task he faces. The ratio cannot be used to indicate reliably changes in emotional stability or the like unless the verbal tasks are carefully equated.

A Comparative Case Study

Although there have been numerous studies that treated a single statistic of verbal behavior, there have been relatively few studies that use a wide variety of statistical indices on the same people. The aspects of language that can be classified and tabulated easily are not particularly sensitive, and it would be amazing if any single index could give all the information we need. As an illustration of a more comprehensive attack upon individual differences in verbalization we shall consider in some detail a study reported by Sanford (1942b). Through an intensive study of the speech of two subjects, dubbed Chatwell and Merritt because those are not their names, Sanford develops a method to deal with linguistic style and attempts to paint an objective picture of the linguistic traits characterizing these two individuals. He writes,

The style that survives statistical analysis seems less rich and less complete than the style we intuitively perceive in talking with these men. The calculating machine misses a great deal that would register on the human brain, and the delicate texture of style appears to be easily injured by our crude analytical devices. But an analytical and quantitative picture of the individual's manner of speaking, though it may lack the subtler shades of the original, will have a certain utility. It will enable us to apply the language of science to the phenomena of style.

Chatwell and Merritt were both college sophomores, both twenty years of age, both had approximately the same grades for their college work, both chatted freely, and neither showed an awe of the psychologist and his lair. Both subjects commented on paintings, described familiar scenes, elaborated narratives from text islands of 3 words and 10 words, reconstructed a semi-narrative piece of writing they had read at the experimenter's request. These samples of their conversational speech were recorded phonographically. In addition, samples of their written language were obtained. There were, in all, 11 samples of speech or writing from each subject.

The dissection of style was based for the most part on conventional grammatical and lexical devices. Added to these basic categories were a number of mechanical variables relating to the speed, quantity, etc.; a group of psycho-grammatical variables, created by fusing grammatical with psychological concepts; and a number of composite categories set up by combining certain of the grammatical and lexical categories in ways that seemed to be reasonable. The grammatical categories were used because they were available, but Sanford found them clumsy tools.

The first step in the analysis was to score both men for each of more than 200 variables on each of the 11 samples of speech. In treating the number of cognitive verbs, for example, there were 11 counts of Chatwell's cognitive verbs, and similarly there were 11 counts of Merritt's. In other words, there were 11 comparisons to be made between the two talkers. In 8 of the samples Merritt had more cognitive verbs. In 2 of the samples Chatwell had more. And in 1 sample both scored the same. We can indicate this difference by writing (8-2). Similar comparisons were made for all the variables studied.

Once the speech is thoroughly dissected and reduced to a set of numbers, how do we put it back together again to resynthesize the talkers' distinctive styles? The first step was the compilation of two lists, one containing all the linguistic constructions that Chatwell used more frequently than Merritt, the other containing the usages occurring more frequently in the speech of Merritt. Upon inspection the items in each of the lists lent themselves to classification under several general headings. By selecting variables that seemed to cohere meaningfully, the experimenter emerged with a group of linguistic traits for Chatwell and another group for Merritt.

Consider Merritt's style. His verbal responses are highly complex; he has many subordinate clauses (10-0), many complex (8-3) and compound-complex (9-2) sentences; the sentences are long (9-1) with many more statements of relation than of description (8-2); and he uses many parenthetical clauses

(8–2). Speaking, for Merritt, is a highly involved affair, and the task of getting from one end of a sentence to the other requires many detours into subordination, many interpolations. The intricacy of responses is probably his outstanding linguistic characteristic.

Merritt perseverates. He repeats frequently (7–0) and continually returns to examine a previous response and to rephrase it (6–3). He tends to use the same word frequently and so has a low type-token ratio (2–8). He repeats content (8–2), has many phrases referring to what he has just said (6–0), and makes liberal use of the word 'very' (8–0). Merritt is thorough; he uses few implicit constructions (2–9), many transitive verbs (8–1), and all his productions are lengthy. He seems, on the statistical evidence, to lack coordination. He hesitates (7–2), repeats (7–0), rephrases (6–3), is grammatically awkward (8–1), and starts talking quickly with little planning (7–2). There is little overt action represented in Merritt's speech. His characters rarely act without first thinking it over. He uses few action verbs (3–7), many infinitives (8–1) and psychological verbs (9–2). And when his characters do act, the action is given future, perfect, or pluperfect reference (6–2). Merritt is, however, very clear and precise. He uses many restrictive adjectives (7–2), many pointing words (7–4), and many concrete nouns (8–2). He is cautious and qualifies his statements by 'It seems . . .' (9–1).

In summarizing Merritt's style of speech, the statistical evidence says that it is complex, perseverative, thorough, awkward, cautious, static, and highly definitive. He is cautious and indirect, but once he makes a judgment he explains it and presents all aspects of it, leaving little for the imagination and little to be questioned.

What about Chatwell, the second subject? We could continue through the statistical picture of Chatwell's speech, presenting evidence that it is colorful, emphatic, direct, active, progressive, coordinated, and confident. Chatwell uses speech not so much to describe the external world and its relations as to express his own individuality and to impress the auditor. But by now you see how a clear picture of a talker can emerge from the pages of facts and figures.

The synthesis of the statistical data suffers, of course, from the fact that each subject was compared only with the other. It would be desirable to have such a painstaking analysis of a larger group, with an eye toward setting up averages representing the college population. Also, the comparisons and groupings are somewhat arbitrary. But these difficulties can be ironed out in further research. The important thing is the success of the statistical method in revealing individual differences and giving pictures of style which have a decided ring of validity. By a multiplicity of statistical devices Sanford was able to give a more complete and rounded picture of the person's speech than could be obtained from any single index. The description of the speech at many points reads like a description of the person.

A similar sort of analysis has been made of the speech of neurotics (Balken and Masserman, 1940). Fifteen neurotic patients, classified as cases of conversion hysteria, anxiety state, and obsessive-compulsive neurosis, made up stories about pictures. The stories were then analyzed according to 85 different statistical variables. Of these 85, 10 gave objective and significant differences among the various neuroses. The obsessive-compulsive, for example, gave the longest phantasies, which supports the observation that such a neurotic feels it is necessary to rationalize and elaborate in detail. That he is inclined to feel uncertain is revealed by his lavish use of qualifications and of words indicating improbability. The cases representing conversion hysteria used many adjectives and few verbs, used few words indicating uncertainty, seldom spoke in the first person, and generally manifested the reduced anxiety that accompanies the conversion of repressed needs into organic dysfunctions. The stories in an anxiety state were brief, the verb-adjective ratio was high, and special expressions connoting vagueness, hesitation, and fear were freely used.

Such observations confirm the notion that personality is reflected in the manner of speaking as well as in the content of the speech. Whether like Merritt we are cautious and long-winded or like Chatwell we are emphatic and direct, our verbalizations reveal consistent and repeating patterns from day to day. By going further afield we could find even more dramatic illustrations of the reflection in the speech of the speaker's personality. Schizophrenics, for example, withdraw into a world of their own, regard their conversational partner with contempt, and often speak an incomprehensible language of their own invention, filled with neologisms and discordant relations.

READABILITY

An important dimension of language along which people differ is the difficulty of their verbal patterns for a reader or listener. Anyone who has struggled with government forms, insurance policies, legal contracts, scientific papers, or philosophic arguments knows that English words can be combined in sequences that would baffle the wisdom of Solomon. What makes some English difficult, and what can be done to make it simpler and easier?

The Teacher's Word Book. There are two ways to attack the problem of readability. One way is to educate the reader, the other is to simplify the material. The principal proponent of the first method is E. L. Thorndike, a psychologist whose influence on modern educational theory and method has been profound. Thorndike sees the problem through the eyes of the teacher in the elementary grades. What should children be taught in order to prepare them to communicate with others? Thorndike's answer is simple and straightforward. A child should learn those words which he will encounter most frequently. The child's education should progress from the common to the uncommon words.   He should not be asked to learn words like 'psychophysiology' before he learns words like 'table.'

To implement this approach, Thorndike and Lorge have counted millions of words to find the 30,000 most common word types.   The results are contained in their *Teacher's Word Book of 30,000 Words*, which tells anyone who wishes to know about a word how common that word is in standard English reading matter.   According to the authors,

> A teacher should decide, concerning many words which occur in books or articles to be read by the class, whether to have the class learn the word well enough so that the ability to know the sound and the important meaning or meanings of the word when they see it will be a permanent part of their stock of word knowledge, or merely inform them of its meaning temporarily so that they can understand and enjoy the reading matter in which it occurs.   This book will answer the question wisely for most words for most classes.

In grades 1 and 2 the word should be taught permanently if it is one that the book says occurs more than 100 times in every million words.   By grade 3 the words that occur 50 times per million should be taught permanently, and by grade 11 the child should have worked down to all the words that occur 3 or more times per million.   The authors suggest that "graduation from senior high school may be made conditional upon knowledge of at least 15,000 words."

Communication depends upon a common core of signals that all the communicators can encode and decode in the same way.   It is essential that children be taught this common core, and we can be thankful that Thorndike and Lorge have provided the necessary information.   But the problem does not end here.   The words are used in combinations, and a high-school graduate who has memorized permanently his 15,000 words may be completely stumped when he runs into a sentence like 'Unless you don't approve of saying no, you won't refuse.'   There is nothing uncommon here in the way of words, but it is an uncommonly difficult sentence to translate.

Tests of Reading Comprehension.   A writer must cooperate if he expects to be read.   Not only must he stick to fairly common words, but he must put these words together in standard ways.   Most of us think of grammar as providing these standard ways; sentences have a subject and a predicate, adjectives stand in some definite relation to the things they modify, etc.   But grammar does not ensure readability.   As an example we might mention the writing of Henry James, who, for artistic reasons, spins out grammatical sentences that sometimes take the average reader minutes to decipher.   What we want to know are the psychological rules for readability, not the grammatical rules for correctness.

One approach to the problem is to take various samples of written English, have people read them, then ask simple questions about what was read (Vogel and Washburne, 1928; Dale and Tyler, 1934; Gray and Leary, 1935; Lorge, 1939, 1944). If the readers answer the questions quickly and correctly, it is considered an easy passage. If the readers make mistakes in answering the questions, the passage is considered difficult. In this way a scale of readability is constructed; the various samples are arranged in order from the most difficult (greatest number of errors) to the most readable (fewest errors). Defined by such a procedure, readability means the accuracy with which readers can answer questions, not the artistic merit of the passage. We are concerned here with the effectiveness of the communication process qua communication, and not with the writer's ability to create a mood, stir the emotions, or inflame the imagination. An easy passage may be pretty dull stuff, but this does not worry us for the present.

The development of a test of reading ability is in itself a difficult undertaking. What questions should we ask about the passage? The sort of questions we ask determines whether we test a reader's ability to repeat, parrotlike, the literal words of the passage or his ability to reorganize the general content into different words and equivalent expressions. The philosophy governing the construction of reading tests has been that both (1) the ability to get the sense of what is read and (2) the ability to recall specific elements are of major importance. It is generally assumed that comprehending fiction is not a fundamentally different process from comprehending nonfiction. The reading test is constructed experimentally. Passages and questions are tried and the reliable, discriminating ones are retained, while the unreliable ones are dropped. By this trial-and-error procedure the experimenter evolves a dependable test containing items that range from very easy, remembered correctly by everyone, to very difficult, remembered correctly by no one.

Statistical Indices of Readability. The next step, once the passages are ranked for difficulty, is to analyze the passages statistically. Can we derive a simple statistical index closely correlated with difficulty? If we discover that hard passages always score low on some particular index, we have a way of predicting the readability of the passage and of estimating how many people can read it and respond appropriately to it. If this index is then placed in the hands of the aspiring writer, he can evaluate for himself the difficulty of his writing and the size of the audience to whom he can appeal. Used properly, such an index can be a valuable aid to the efficiency of our verbal communications.

What measurable aspects of written language might be related to readability? There are a great many aspects we could measure; percentage of frequently used words, number of different hard words, number of words not known to sixth-grade children, number of different words, number of monosyllables or polysyllables, number of first-, second-, or third-person pronouns, number of complex sentences, number of figures of speech, etc. Once a list of statistical indices is compiled and the scores on the various passages are known for each index, the scores are correlated with the scores on readability. If a coefficient of correlation is near $+1$ or -1, the statistical index is measuring something related to readability. If the correlation is near zero, the statistical index is unrelated to readability. By analyzing the correlations obtained it is possible to select four or five indices that seem most important. In considering the results of these studies we shall confine our attention to those indices which have paid off.

All the studies seem to agree that *short, familiar words* make a passage easy, while long, unfamiliar words make it difficult. The major disagreement has been which measure of familiarity should be adopted. In some cases lists of easy words have been compiled, where 'easy' is defined in terms of frequency of use and familiarity to grade school children. The necessity for such a list cuts down the convenience of the index.

An alternative is to count the number of different words, or to determine the type-token ratio for samples of a given length. Vogel and Washburne (1928), in their pioneer study of readability, found that a type-token ratio was their best indicator. If a writer has a large number of different words, a large type-token ratio, he is probably using unfamiliar words to increase his verbal diversification. The number of difficult words and the size of the type-token ratio should be closely correlated. Although the type-token index does not require the verbal statistician to have a special check list of words available, it is still a tedious procedure to keep track of each word. One suggestion is to count the number of affixes (prefixes and suffixes) per 100 words. Since many rare polysyllabic words are built up from a common root word by adding 'un-' or 're-' or 'a-' in front of the root and '-ism' or '-ology' or '-ence' at the end of it, counting affixes is another way of estimating the proportion of hard words. Still another alternative is to count the total number of syllables per 100 words. Rare words are usually polysyllabic.

The basic facts are that the frequent words are the familiar words, and the frequent-familiar words are short words, and the frequent-familiar-short words have few affixes, and the writer who uses frequent-familiar-short-affixless words has a low type-token ratio. A statistical measure of any one of these attributes of words is closely related to statistical measures of the other attributes. Consequently, if one of these measures is correlated with readability, all of them are probably correlated with readability.

A second factor that turns up consistently is *sentence length*. Here again there are various possible measures. Is it better to count the number of words or the number of syllables in the sentence? It can be shown that passages with a large number of prepositional phrases are more difficult than passages with few prepositional phrases. Is this because prepositional phrases are hard to read, or because they make the sentence longer? The two measures seem to be related, although it is possible to write short sentences with prepositional phrases or long ones without them.

A third factor that turns out to be related to readability is the number of personal pronouns or *personal references*. People are better at reading about other people than about anything else. This device is commonly used to make dull topics more interesting and to hold the reader's attention. Newspapers use eyewitness reports or interviews, news magazines emphasize personal anecdotes, and everyone knows about human-interest stories.

The Estimation of Readability. At least half a dozen formulas are available to the interested writer who wants to apply the scientific yardstick to his work. All of them rely upon one or more of these three aspects: word complexity, length of sentences, human interest. Probably the best publicized formula is that of Rudolph Flesch, who took his own research seriously enough to write a highly readable little book called *The Art of Plain Talk* (1946).

The particular readability index discussed below is selected because it is convenient to use and probably about as accurate as the more complicated formulas (Flesch, 1948). It is based upon the reading-comprehension scores of children in grade school (McCall and Crabbs, 1926). The index comes in two parts. The first, called *reading ease*, is a score that varies from about 0 to 100. A high score is supposed to indicate easy reading. The prediction of reading ease takes account of word length and sentence length. The second part of the index uses a scale from 0 to 100 to estimate the degree of *human interest* in the material. The human-interest score depends upon the relative frequencies of personal words and personal sentences. The scoring rules are given in the following eight paragraphs:

1. Unless the entire piece of writing is to be tested, the first step is to select samples at random. For instance, take every third paragraph or every tenth page. It is important to go by some numerical rule and not to try to select typical passages. For an article at least 5 samples should be selected, and at least 30 are needed to test an entire book. Every sample should start with the beginning of a paragraph.

2. For each sample, count off the first 100 words. Contractions and hyphenated words are counted as one word. Numbers or letters separated by a space also count as one word.

3. The next step is to compute the *average number of syllables per* 100 *words* (W). Count the number of syllables in a number according to the way the number is pronounced. Thus '1918' is scored as four syllables.

4. Find the sentence in each sample that ends nearest to the 100-word mark. Count the number of sentences up to that point, and divide the number of words in those sentences by the number of sentences. Usually sentences are marked off by periods, but sometimes they are divided by colons or semicolons. If two sentences are joined by a conjunction, however, they count as one sentence. This gives the *average sentence length* (S).

5. Figure the *average number of personal words per* 100 *words* (w). Personal words are all nouns with natural gender, all pronouns except neuter pronouns

(unless they refer to people rather than things), and the words 'people' (used with a plural verb) and 'folks.'

6. Figure the *average number of personal sentences per* 100 *sentences* (*s*). Personal sentences are spoken sentences marked by quotation marks or otherwise; questions, commands, requests, and other sentences addressed directly to the reader; exclamations; and grammatically incomplete sentences whose meaning must be inferred from the context. If a sentence fits two or more of these criteria, count it only once.

7. Figure the reading ease by inserting the average number of syllables per 100 words (W) and the average sentence length (S) in the following formula:

$$\text{Reading ease} = 206.84 - 0.85W - 1.02S.$$

A score of 0 is practically unreadable. A score of 100 is easy for any literate person.

8. Find the human-interest score by inserting the percentage of personal words (w) and the percentage of personal sentences (s) in the following formula:

$$\text{Human interest} = 3.64w + 0.31s.$$

A human-interest score of 0 indicates no personal references, while a score of 100 indicates that the passage is full of human interest.

In order to illustrate the use of the scale, it is applied to the following two passages. The first is from *The Education of T. C. Mits* by H. and L. Lieber, a delightful little book on mathematics for the celebrated man in the street.

They are the theoretical men—they ask the most 'useless' questions. For instance: "What happens when you mix sugar and water and lemon?" They call it 'Sugar Hydrolysis' instead of 'Lemonade.' They study it in different solutions, carefully varying the relative amounts of the substances involved, and examine them with a polariscope for days and days, years and years, keeping careful records and publishing the results in scientific journals. Will these investigations make them rich? Or fat? Or benefit them in any 'practical' way? Not at all. Then why do they do it? The answer is that they are just driven by curiosity.

This passage of 104 words is made up of 11 sentences, which gives an average sentence length of 9.5 words. The first 100 words contain 158 syllables. Substituting these values into the formula for reading ease,

$$\text{Reading ease} = 206.84 - 0.85(158) - 1.02(9.5) = 63.$$

A score of 63 indicates standard difficulty; the passage could be read by about 75 per cent of American adults.

There are 10 personal words in the first 100 words, and 6 of the 11 sentences (55 per cent) fall under the definition of personal sentences. Substituting these values into the formula for human interest,

$$\text{Human interest} = 3.64(10) + 0.31(55) = 53.$$

A score of 53 can be called highly interesting and compares with the style of the *New Yorker* magazine.

Now contrast this sprightly passage with one from the *Federal Register*.

The maximum price for a primary fish shipper sale of fresh fish or sea-food (except shrimp, salmon or halibut) to a retailer or purveyor of meals where the sale is negotiated or made at a branch warehouse as herein defined and where the fish or seafood is sold and delivered from the stock of a primary fish shipper wholesalers branch warehouse which is remote from his main place of doing business, and at which warehouse the primary fish shipper employs two or more full-time employees who are stationed at and engaged in making sales and performing services solely for the primary fish shipper from such warehouse, is the price listed in Table D in 22 plus the allowance provided in 6 for a service and delivery sale where such sale is made, plus the transportation allowance in 9 plus the appropriate container allowance in 21.

This one sentence has 145 words. There are 159 syllables in the first 100 words. By the formula,

$$\text{Reading ease} = 206.84 - 0.85(159) - 1.02(145) = -76.$$

The sample is so ridiculously difficult that nobody could answer a question about it correctly after a single reading. When scores go below zero, it is convenient to assume the readability score is zero. Such negative scores are unusual, and a fair selection of samples would probably show that even the *Federal Register* does not maintain this pace indefinitely.

There is one personal reference, and the one sentence does not qualify as a personal one. The formula for human interest thus gives

$$\text{Human interest} = 3.64(1) + 0.31(0) = 4.$$

Thus the passage is neither readable nor interesting.

The scores for reading ease and human interest can be referred to Tables 8 and 9. These tables give Flesch's interpretations of the scores. If a rough estimate is sufficient, it is often satisfactory to count only the sentence length and to check this figure against the third column of Table 8. Sentences that run longer than about 30 words usually must be shortened before an average reader can make much sense of them.

The writer who limits all his sentences to five words in length finds he has relatively few different sentences at his command. The writer who uses fifty words in every sentence has a tremendous range of different patterns available. Long sentences often arrange words in patterns that are strange to the reader's verbal habits, whereas short sentences cannot. In a long sentence the qualifications can split apart words that function together. The reader's memory span is limited, and he is apt to forget the noun before he discovers a verb that goes with it. Long sentences that result from an attempt to abbreviate may be difficult because they give too much information per word. If every word in the sentence is packed with significance, you can bet that the average reader misses most of what is said.

TABLE 8. INTERPRETATION OF READING-EASE SCORES

(Flesch, 1948)

Score	Description of style	Average sentence length in words	Syllables per 100 words	Typical magazine	Potential audience (typical audience one step above) School grade completed	Typical magazine	Per cent of United States adults
0 to 30	Very difficult	29 or more	192 or more	Scientific	College	Scientific	4.5
30 to 50	Difficult	25	167	Academic	High school or some college	Trade	24
50 to 60	Fairly difficult	21	155	Quality	Some high school	Digests	40
60 to 70	Standard	17	147	Digests	7th or 8th grade	New Yorker	75
70 to 80	Fairly easy	14	139	Slick-fiction	6th grade	Fiction	80
80 to 90	Easy	11	131	Pulp-fiction	5th grade		86
90 to 100	Very easy	8 or less	123 or less	Comics	4th grade		90

TABLE 9. INTERPRETATION OF HUMAN-INTEREST SCORES

(Flesch, 1948)

Score	Description of style	Percentage of personal words	Percentage of personal sentences	Typical magazine
0 to 10	Dull	2 or less	0	Scientific
10 to 20	Mildly interesting	4	5	Trade
20 to 40	Interesting	7	15	Digests
40 to 60	Highly interesting	11	32	New Yorker
60 to 100	Dramatic	17 or more	58 or more	Fiction

It should be emphasized that the use of short sentences, simple words, and personal references does not automatically make the writing good. It merely avoids one common way in which writing is bad. The highest score is not always the best writing. A score of 100 would probably insult the readers of scientific journals. A high score does not ensure that readers will enjoy what you write or that you will enjoy writing it. But it goes a long way toward ensuring that people can, if they must, answer questions about it.

In summary, then, we can say that written communication can be made more reliable (1) by educating the reader and (2) by simplifying the writing. The two approaches together have much to contribute to the practical and persistent problem of letting the people know.

Discussion Questions

1. A man's speech is affected by the structure of the language he speaks, by the situation in which he is placed, and by personal reactions that depend upon his own particular past. Can any one of these aspects be studied without considering the others?

2. How would you devise a test to measure how effectively a person uses words in combinations? Would this test show a high correlation with an intelligence test that estimates the size of the person's vocabulary?

3. Could you devise scales to measure aspects of language other than difficulty? What aspects do you suggest? How would you proceed?

4. What statistical indices would you use to make a quantitative comparison of the verbal habits of psychotics and of the average person?

5. Are grammatical categories the best possible ones for the psychological analysis of language? Can they be used in modified forms, or would you attempt to create entirely new categories?

Selected References

FLESCH, R. *The Art of Plain Talk*. New York: Harper, 1946. A readable book that tells you how to write readable English.

GRAY, W. S., and B. E. LEARY. *What Makes a Book Readable*. Chicago: University of Chicago Press, 1935. This exploratory work provides a gold mine of information on verbal statistics and readability.

SANFORD, F. H. Speech and personality. *Psychol. Bull.*, 1942, *39*, 811–845. A thorough review of research on individual differences in verbal expression.

Chapter 7

THE VERBAL BEHAVIOR OF CHILDREN

> He that attentively considers the state of a child at his first coming into the world, will have little reason to think him stored with plenty of ideas.
>
> —JOHN LOCKE

The world's 1500 languages give noisy testimony to the fact that speech is learned, not instinctive. Nevertheless, the successive stages in the development of verbal behavior are much the same in all children, regardless of their parents' language. The agreement between German, French, and American studies indicates that the development of speech depends upon the prior development of the child's anatomical and neuromuscular systems. In the early stages of development there is relatively random vocalization. Control of these vocalizations awaits the slow process of physical growth.

The old argument about the relative importance of heredity and environment is still unsettled, but now the debaters know that the process of development is too complex and baffling to yield its secrets either to a list of hereditary instincts or to a list of conditioned reflexes. Growth and learning complement one another in normal development. Growth is not limited to certain activities nor to certain times of life. The most we can say is that there seem to be critical periods in the growth of an organism when it is most susceptible to certain kinds of stimulation from the environment. The critical period for one activity may occur at an entirely different time from the critical period for another activity.

The role of maturation in the development of speech can be seen in many ways. For example, the area in the brain that controls speech (Broca's area) develops later than the other motor centers (de Crinis, 1932). Not until 17 months after birth does it reach that degree of anatomical differentiation that can be observed in the other motor centers by the eleventh month. Changes in the structure of the speech apparatus also play a role; the resonating cavities change in size and shape. Everyone is familiar with the embarrassing change in the pitch of the male voice that accompanies a sudden lengthening of the vocal folds at adolescence.

If identical twins are given different opportunities to learn to speak, the differences that result must be due to the effects of these environmental influences. One study used twins just on the threshold of speaking at the age of eighty-four weeks of age (Strayer, 1930). Beginning with the eighty-fourth week, one of the twins was given elaborate training. Objects were presented and named, the child was encouraged to imitate, simple commands were learned, pictures were identified. At the end of 5 weeks the child's total vocabulary had grown from 1 to 35 words. The second twin was kept in reserve during these 5 weeks. This child heard no speech at any time but lived in a wordless world from his eighty-fourth to his eighty-ninth week. Then, when the first child had completed 5 weeks of training, the second began. The second twin learned faster than the first. At the end of the fourth week the second twin knew 30 words. The experiment was discontinued at this point. Several months later the differences between the two children had disappeared.

Experiments of this sort suggest that the more mature child profits more from training than the less mature child. With special attention an immature child can be pushed ahead of his normal development, but even a hard push by a conscientious teacher has little permanent value. When the child is ready to talk he begins to talk, provided a normal verbal environment is at hand. Training is necessary, of course, but intensive training at an early age is less rewarding than the same training given when the child has reached a more advanced stage of physical and neural development.

A child cannot learn verbal responses until he is old enough and mature enough to learn them. Maturation sets the pace. With a normal environment the child's speech awaits a step-by-step unfolding of the growth process. Consequently we find a succession of developmental stages that are quite similar in all children. By manipulating the language environment of the child we can modify or delay the development, but we shall never teach a baby to utter prepositional phrases before he begins to babble. The successive stages of language development are similar in all normal children, and it is to these developmental stages that we turn first.

PRELINGUISTIC STAGES

Successive stages in the development of speech are indicated in Table 10. This table has been compiled from eight major studies of child development (McCarthy, 1946). The length of the bars represents the approximate range of times reported by the various studies for the onset of the different stages. The agreement among the studies is rather good, but it would be misleading to indicate the onset in a more definite manner.

In the words of one reviewer (E. Dewey, 1935, 251):

The literature is in general agreement that the first sounds of the newborn infant are the overt elements from which speech develops, that vocalizations are used as means of communication before words proper are used; that comprehension appears before the use of words; that the normal child has a repertoire of a very few words by one year of age, that development is slow in the first months of the second year, but that toward the end of that year a great increase in the speed of progress appears;

TABLE 10. COMPOSITE TABLE SHOWING AGE IN MONTHS AT WHICH SELECTED ITEMS ARE REPORTED IN EIGHT MAJOR STUDIES OF INFANT DEVELOPMENT

(McCarthy, 1946)

Age in months

Behavior	0	6	12	18	24	30
First noted vocalizations	xxxxxxxxxx					
First responds to human voice	xxxxx					
First cooing	xxxxx					
Vocalizes pleasure	xxxxxxxx					
Vocal play	xxxx					
Vocalizes eagerness and displeasure		xxx				
Imitates sounds		xxxxxxxxx				
Vocalizes recognition		xx				
Listens to familiar words		xxxx				
First word		xxxxxxxxxx				
Expressive sounds and conversational jargon			xxxxxxxxxxxxxxxxxxxx			
Follows simple commands			xxxxxxxx			
Imitates syllables and words			xxxxxxxx			
Second word			xxxxx			
Responds to "no" and "don't"			xxxxxxxxxxxxx			
First says more than 2 words				xxxxx		
Names object or picture				xxxxxxxxxxxx xx		
Comprehends simple questions				xx		
Combines words in speech					xxxxxxx	
First uses pronouns					xxxxx	
First phrases and sentences					xxx	
Understands prepositions					xxx	

that words are first used in a generalized sense, and that their use for specific meanings is a developmental process; that name words appear first, verbs and adjectives later, relational words still later, and pronouns are just beginning to be used by the most advanced children by the end of the second year; that the first words have the force of a phrase or sentence, and combinations of words do not begin for some time.

Motor Development. The birth cry is the first vocalization. Although crying has received considerable attention from physicians and parents, it probably has little significance for the development of speech. Crying has been observed in premature babies and persists long after language habits are established. The birth cry is evidence that the baby enters the world with the rudimentary respiratory and laryngeal equipment he will need later for speaking, and it is produced as well by a child without a cerebrum as by a child with one.

For the first 9 months after birth the infant grunts, coos, gurgles, babbles, hiccoughs, snorts, and, of course, cries. The earliest sounds are principally reflexive. They are associated with breathing, swallowing, hiccoughing, etc., and no specific sounds are associated with specific situations. The parent who claims to be able to tell from the baby's cry whether it is hungry, stuck by a pin, or in need of a change is probably judging on the basis of his knowledge of the situation rather than the sound of the crying. Parents and trained nurses fail to differentiate these cries in laboratory tests (Sherman, 1927).

During this prelinguistic period there are consistent changes in the sounds that the infant produces. The very young baby utters far more vowels than consonants. The first vowels are those which adults form in the front of the

mouth, and the back vowels become more frequent as the child develops. Consonants, on the other hand, first appear as glottal and velar sounds formed in the back of the mouth. The order of development of the consonants progresses from the back to the front of the mouth (Irwin, 1947).

The vowel-to-consonant ratio has been proposed as a developmental index during the period of prelinguistic vocalization (Irwin and Chen, 1946). Infants a month old have a ratio of almost 5 vowels to 1 consonant. Adults (in their telephone conversations) have a ratio of 1 vowel to 1.4 consonants. Feeble-minded children four years of

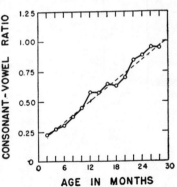

FIG. 36. The increase in the consonant-vowel ratio during the first 2.5 years of life. (*After Irwin and Chen,* 1946.)

age, but under 50 IQ, had a ratio of 2 to 1 (Irwin, 1942). In Fig. 36 the consonant-vowel ratio is plotted as a function of age in normal children.

Tables 11 and 12 present the results of a careful study of the frequency of

TABLE 11. CONSONANT PHONEME PERCENTAGES

(Irwin, 1947)

	Age, months															Adult
	2	4	6	8	10	12	14	16	18	20	22	24	26	28	30	
p	0.10	0.20	0.30	1.13	0.67	1.63	1.07	2.10	1.27	2.73	4.17	4.32	3.57	3.63	4.47	2.41
b	0.19	1.54	2.50	4.47	7.97	9.79	9.48	11.95	14.95	13.38	13.52	8.97	8.81	7.34	7.64	3.18
m	0.21	0.66	3.07	5.21	7.53	6.69	9.23	5.74	5.43	7.38	8.45	8.41	7.14	7.29	7.99	4.47
w	0.07	1.10	1.49	0.96	2.64	3.31	4.36	4.55	7.02	4.61	5.19	6.42	5.77	3.83	3.31	2.99
hw	....	....	....	....	0.02	0.08	0.34	0.05	0.04	0.15	0.20	0.03	0.21	0.11	0.20	0.60
f	....	....	0.27	0.56	0.73	0.37	0.45	0.47	0.63	0.81	1.37	1.18	2.19	1.73	1.79	3.48
v	....	0.16	0.16	0.90	1.22	1.03	0.44	0.42	0.29	0.49	0.29	0.52	0.68	0.57	0.63	2.52
θ	....	0.40	0.39	0.49	1.49	0.85	0.67	0.38	0.29	0.36	0.11	0.36	....	0.06	0.14	1.06
ð	....	0.37	0.34	0.30	0.17	0.34	0.43	0.30	0.36	0.56	0.61	0.61	0.68	0.62	1.70	5.13
t	0.17	0.39	0.22	1.05	1.68	4.34	3.96	4.14	4.61	5.57	7.43	8.31	10.12	11.17	11.68	11.66
d	....	2.64	2.06	6.46	15.73	20.58	19.42	20.04	20.56	18.45	15.07	15.31	14.25	16.20	13.98	8.28
n	0.14	0.35	0.52	1.68	1.03	2.65	2.07	3.11	5.38	7.89	8.85	9.74	9.31	10.07	9.49	11.85
s	....	0.05	0.20	0.17	1.65	3.45	2.81	3.08	3.59	3.51	6.06	7.42	7.98	8.11	6.87	7.54
z	....	0.07	....	0.12	5.21	0.56	0.69	1.23	1.00	1.14	0.65	0.51	0.58	0.23	0.41	3.48
ʃ	0.17	0.09	0.02	....	0.33	0.37	0.25	0.29	0.41	0.50	1.08	0.84	1.40	0.93	0.82	1.64
ʒ	....	....	....	0.12	....	0.10	....	0.02	0.11	0.04	0.07	0.09	0.07	....	....	0.67
l	0.21	0.99	0.23	0.51	1.37	0.96	0.57	1.57	1.04	1.47	1.93	2.08	2.51	3.06	3.37	6.32
r	....	....	0.15	....	....	0.10	0.18	0.53	1.09	0.99	1.54	2.67	3.96	4.12	4.64	10.51
j	....	0.72	1.12	1.14	2.15	1.77	3.78	2.29	1.95	2.80	1.64	1.73	1.69	2.04	1.50	1.89
ç	....	0.09	....	0.06	0.16	0.06	0.11	0.29	....	0.02	....	....	0.06	0.09	0.10	....
ŋ	....	0.26	0.17	0.80	0.03	0.33	0.31	0.03	0.14	0.42	0.31	0.62	0.84	0.99	0.48	1.68
k	8.80	2.78	4.90	2.05	1.82	2.12	2.36	2.76	2.73	4.04	6.04	4.36	6.74	6.16	6.98	4.15
g	2.79	11.73	7.46	5.43	4.12	4.15	4.91	5.55	5.17	4.46	4.47	2.67	3.33	3.18	4.05	1.75
x	....	0.04	0.10	0.01	0.14	0.08	0.05	....	0.02	0.09	0.04	....	0.07	0.03	0.03	....
h	44.22	59.88	61.93	57.87	41.29	31.77	29.75	26.69	20.75	16.29	9.84	10.93	7.53	8.14	7.65	2.66
ʔ	42.91	15.48	12.41	8.51	5.84	2.52	2.31	2.19	1.12	1.85	1.07	1.90	0.44	0.22	0.07	....

TABLE 12. VOWEL PHONEME PERCENTAGES

(Irwin, 1948)

	Age, months															Adult
	2	4	6	8	10	12	14	16	18	20	22	24	26	28	30	
	Number of infants															
	62	80	75	64	62	62	57	55	50	41	37	31	32	24	19	
i	0.14	1.10	1.77	1.80	2.09	4.15	4.32	6.62	7.05	7.63	9.71	11.42	11.63	12.16	13.44	7.40
ɪ	27.39	21.89	24.82	24.96	22.22	23.02	23.13	24.96	22.46	20.61	17.27	19.22	18.42	21.07	18.38	20.56
e	0.16	1.08	1.58	2.04	2.85	3.25	3.25	3.24	3.07	3.01	2.64	3.11	4.20	2.54	2.70	5.21
ε	42.98	33.91	31.27	31.40	32.35	27.56	27.03	22.00	18.17	14.34	12.51	12.19	8.72	8.94	7.48	7.98
æ	1.82	2.65	2.62	3.13	2.72	4.13	2.25	2.97	3.22	3.83	3.85	4.38	4.30	4.89	4.63	8.06
ʌ	25.18	25.56	23.44	19.65	16.80	16.17	16.58	15.13	15.73	16.16	14.65	13.15	13.58	12.63	13.43	1.12
ə	.....	0.23	0.25	0.15	0.18	0.20	0.40	0.80	0.77	1.03	1.55	1.02	1.04	1.95	3.24	17.76
a	0.21	2.18	1.52	2.17	5.34	6.48	6.64	6.58	8.37	10.98	11.73	13.09	13.43	14.95	13.67	10.85
ɔ	.....	0.10	0.20	0.22	0.47	0.64	0.80	0.67	1.61	1.63	2.30	3.08	2.27	1.52	2.54	5.58
o	.....	0.18	0.17	0.30	0.68	1.33	1.17	2.25	3.76	3.08	5.29	4.54	6.58	5.27	6.74	5.54
ʊ	1.75	7.70	8.20	10.12	10.24	7.71	8.79	8.88	10.44	11.57	10.97	10.27	10.59	9.42	9.51	4.60
u	0.31	3.41	4.17	3.88	4.06	5.36	5.69	5.92	5.32	6.10	7.49	4.50	5.24	4.58	4.19	5.21

occurrence of English vowels and consonants in the first years of life (Irwin, 1947*a*, *b*, 1948). There is a rapid increase in the variety of sounds, and by the end of the tenth month all of the different sounds have appeared. Phonetic transcription of the infant's babbling is a difficult task, for he has no special preference for English speech sounds. Children who are hearing only English often make German umlaut sounds, French guttural /r/, and a wide variety of sounds that they are not able to produce as deliberate phonemes. It is improbable that a child babbles such phones by imitation; they seem to occur spontaneously in the course of his experimentation with his developing vocal equipment. The child's early babbling is so complex that only a linguist with a well-trained ear can make the distinctions necessary for a narrow phonetic transcription. Although there has been some interest by linguists in this developmental process (*e.g.*, Jakobson, 1941; Leopold, 1937–1949), the relatively broad transcription by the psychologist Irwin and his colleagues, for American children, is at present the only large-scale statistical study, and it does not try to distinguish accidental phones from intentional phonemes.

Perceptual Development. While the motor side of the child's verbal behavior is developing and expanding through vocal play and random experimentation with sounds, the perceptual side is also making progress. Two months after birth the baby attends to—stops or changes activity, or turns toward—the sound of the human voice. By the sixth month the baby seems to distinguish a friendly tone of voice from a scolding tone. When he is about nine months old, he begins to pay attention to a few familiar words and seems to have more interest in some words than in others. By this age he usually responds to 'bye-bye' and he begins to react appropriately to gestures. In the tenth month he can make different adjustments to certain words. Before his first birthday he can stop when told 'no' and can follow some very simple commands. By fifteen to seventeen months he understands 'Give me that' when it is accompanied by a gesture, and at eighteen months he can point to his nose, eyes, or hair on command. It is generally agreed that a child understands the language of others considerably earlier than he is able to use the same words himself.

It is not clear just how important the early babbling is for the development of words, nor just how the vocal play changes into the verbal habits of a particular language. It is not uncommon to find that a child has produced /l/ and /r/ during its infantile babbling, but that later, at the age of two or three years, he is unable to produce these sounds correctly in English words. It would seem reasonable to expect the child to select the phonemes he needs out of his large repertoire of babbled phones, but this does not seem to be the case. The child must tediously relearn these sounds as parts of the connected stream of speech in his native tongue (Jakobson, 1941). He is not able spontaneously to use the phonetic elements of his babbling as the phonemes of his language.

Learning phonemes as parts of words represents a convergence of the babbling development with perceptive development. The evidence for this convergence is the appearance of *imitation*. By twelve months of age the child repeats a pattern produced by an adult. At two years the child repeats words over and over. There is a clear tendency for children to make *echoic responses* to their own voices or the voices of others. That is to say, the child repeats, like an echo, the sound that he hears.

The Circular Reaction. In order to account for the echoic responses of children many psychologists have assumed that some kind of *circular reaction* is set up (J. M. Baldwin, 1895). This circular reaction provides the first real guidance of the motor development by the perceptive development. F. H. Allport (1924, 181–189) gives a detailed account of how a circular reaction might be established and how it could account for vocal imitation. When the baby utters a syllable, he stimulates himself kinesthetically and acoustically. This returning stimulation tends to produce another response, and since the particular syllable just spoken is in a state of readiness, it occurs again. Again there is returning stimulation that discharges through the same behavior. The cycle continues and the baby is trapped by his own voice until the cycle is broken by some distraction. The repetitive babbling produced by the circular response provides practice and fixes the association between vocal responses and acoustic results.

Once the ear-to-voice link is well established for a variety of sounds, it is no longer necessary for the child himself to speak the stimulating sound. If the sound is spoken by another and it starts the child's circular reaction, the effect is as if the child imitated the sound it heard. The child does not imitate exactly the sound he hears; he replies with the nearest similar ear-to-voice link that he has been able to fixate. The sounds of 'doll' would probably evoke [dɑ].

As soon as the parent can touch off circularly established ear-voice reflexes, the process of teaching names of objects can begin. Now the doll itself is held up for inspection while the child repeats the word pronounced by the adult. Eventually the object alone becomes a sufficient stimulus to set off the appropriate response.

The circular reaction to the sound of his own voice does not stop when the child begins to learn words. Echoic responses comprise a statistically significant portion of a child's utterances up to about thirty months of age. Zipf (1949) analyzed some of Fisher's (1934) data to see whether or not the equation $fr = C$ applies to young children as well as to adults (cf. Chap. 4). Zipf quotes the following passage recorded for a child twenty-two months old:

Grandma. Grandma. Buggy. Baby. Baby crying. Baby crying. Baby crying. Grandma. Grandma here. My ball. Baby girl. Munner. All through. Yes. Grandma. Grandma. Grandma. Grandma. Grandma. Grandma. Grandma. Grandma. Stand up. Stand up. Grandma. Grandma. Grandma. Grandma. Grandma. Grandma. Grandma. Grandma. Grandma.

Bill's hat. Coat. Coat. Put my sweater on. Put my sweater on. Grandma sit down. Grandma sit down. Grandma [14 times]. I got blocks. I got blocks. Hat. My ball. Look. Look. Look. Ball. Ball. Mary. Ball. Ball. Ball. Ball.

And so on. When all the words in such a passage are counted, the result agrees rather well with Zipf's equation. If the echoic responses are deleted, the distribution of word frequencies does not satisfy the equation. Zipf concludes that the echoic responses are an integral part of the stream of speech and important for the proper equilibrium in the child's behavior. The direct repetitions of the young child give way slowly to the more intricate redundancies of adult speech.

THE GROWTH OF VOCABULARY

The time of occurrence of the first word is not easy to recognize and specify. It is tempting to see significance in the early babblings that happen to coincide with certain events. If, for example, the father walks into the room with a bottle of water for the baby, he is very likely to catch baby saying [dæ], or [bɑ], or [wɑ], any of which can be taken to represent the baby's approximation of 'daddy,' 'bottle,' or 'water.' The father, who has been anticipating conversation with his son and heir, jumps to the conclusion that the baby has begun to talk. We must take a dim view of the parents' reports and rely more upon the judgments of trained psychologists. These observers place the first word at about twelve months of age for the average child and as early as the ninth month for exceptional children.

The first word is almost always a reduplicated monosyllable: 'bye-bye,' 'mama,' 'dada,' 'bebe,' 'tick-tick,' etc. It is used as a sentence is used, and by supplementing the word with gestures and different intonations it can serve in a variety of situations. 'Baba' may be the equivalent of 'Where is the ball?' or 'There is the ball,' or 'I want the ball,' depending upon the inflection and accompanying behavior. Possibly these early words are used to designate objects only secondarily, and their principal function is to express the emotional state of the child.

Although individual differences are large, in the average child the vocabulary appears to increase rather slowly at first, then rapidly between the ages of two and eight years, and then more slowly until maturity. Exactly how we should measure this growth is a controversial problem. The observer must decide whether or not the child is using each word appropriately. Some criterion must be set: is a word part of the child's vocabulary if he responds correctly when he hears it, or should we wait until the child uses the word in his own spontaneous vocalizations? It is necessary to distinguish between spoken, written, reading, and listening vocabularies. It is necessary to distinguish between root and derivative words, between different uses of the same word, and between generally used words and words used by the child only with its parents. Since the observer's time with each child is limited, he may not hear all the words that the child can use. Because of these many difficulties the various estimates of the size of vocabulary differ widely among themselves. The answer we get depends upon the way we measure, and it is useless to quote any given number of words without stating how this number was obtained.

One of the first extensive studies of the growth of vocabulary was conducted by M. E. Smith in 1926. A sample of 203 words was selected from Thorndike's (1921) list of 10,000 most frequent words. Pictures were then obtained which would lead the child to use the selected words. For about half the words, if the child did not use the word when he was asked simple questions about the pictures, the examiner then used the word in a question. The child was said to know the word if he used it or if he answered correctly questions about the word.

The scores obtained from Smith's test are relative scores and do not tell us the size of the average child's vocabulary. However, Smith argues that total vocabulary can be estimated with this test; when the total score on the test was multiplied by an appropriate multiplier, the results agreed fairly well with actually known total vocabularies. By such approximations the test scores were interpreted to mean that the average child knows 3 words on his first birthday, 272 on his second, 1540 on his fourth, and 2562 on his sixth. Somewhat higher figures have been reported by Grigsby (1932), who used a revised and standardized version of the test (Williams and McFarland, 1937). The figures are not easy to interpret; probably we should regard them merely as indicators of the relative rates of verbal development at different ages.

The vocabulary does not stop growing at the age of six years, but the agreement among the vocabulary estimators is, if anything, worse for older children and adults than it is for preschool children. As a general rule, the estimated size of the vocabulary is proportional to the size of the dictionary used to supply the test words; the estimates range all the way from 5000 to over 200,000 words. The Seashore-Eckerson test has been adapted for use in the lower school grades, and the results obtained with a large sample of children are shown in Fig. 37 (M. K. Smith, 1941). The lower curve represents the average number of root words, and the upper curve represents the average size of the total vocabulary (basic plus derivative words). The average child in the first grade recognizes almost 24,000 basic and derivative words. This figure is a little startling if we recall that the early estimates of the adult vocabulary used to be well below 24,000!

A persistent headache and source of error in studies of the verbal behavior of children is the incomprehensibility of much juvenile speech. One study (Betts, 1934) compared five methods of recording the utterances of children in the fourth through the sixth grades. Phonographic recordings provided the standard by which the accuracy of the other four methods could be estimated. Court reporters made the most complete records, but even so they missed 20 per cent of the material. Shorthand writers scored next, getting 53 per cent. Longhand writing caught only 32 per cent. Phoneticians had the most incomplete records, for they noted only 15 per cent of the material. The accuracy of transcription was about the same (85 per cent) for all four methods. In order to make any precise and reliable statements about what a child has said, phonographic recording techniques are indispensable.

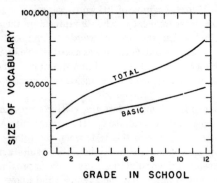

Fig. 37. The basic and total (basic plus derivative) recognition vocabularies, plotted as a function of school grade for the average child. Seashore-Eckerson test. (*After M. K. Smith,* 1941.)

The most serious problem is provided by the speech of children less than 2 years old. One observer (McCarthy, 1930) reported that only 26 per cent of the verbal responses of 18-month-old children were comprehensible. This figure rises to 67 per cent at 2 years, 89 per cent at 2.5 years, 93 per cent at 3 years, 99 per cent at 3.5 years. These percentages agree fairly well with the estimates of other observers. At most age levels the speech of boys was less well understood than that of girls.

The estimation of the intelligibility of children's speech and the establishment of norms for average children is a practical problem. Such information makes it possible to detect slow development and defects of speech and hearing at an early age (Wellman, Case, Mengert, and Bradbury, 1931; E. A. Davis, 1937).

INCREASING COMPLEXITY

The increase in the quantity of a child's speech is one of the most obvious indications of his verbal development. The average two-year-old speaks about 80 words in the course of an hour of free play (M. E. Smith, 1926). At four years he speaks 400 words under the same play conditions. Children vary widely on both sides of these averages, however, and a measure of the sheer quantity of talking is not a reliable index of the child's verbal development. A loquacious child will talk many times as much as a taciturn child.

A more dependable index is the length of the individual response. The earliest sentences are *holophrases*—one-word sentences. By the fifth year the spoken sentence has lengthened to about 5 words for the average child or to about 10 words for the superior child.

Sentence Structure. Not only do the number and length of the child's verbal responses increase; they become increasingly complex. The early holophrases are largely replaced with simple sentences during the second and third years. From the age of four on, the relative frequency of simple sentences declines as more complicated constructions come to be used. Figure 38 shows this development in the form of curves compiled from the results of two different studies (McCarthy, 1930; Davis, 1937).

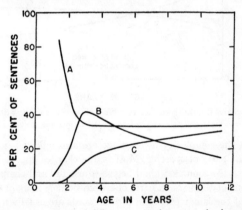

Fig. 38. The relative frequencies of different types of sentences in the speech of children under twelve years. Curve *A* represents sentences that are functionally complete but grammatically incomplete. Curve *B* represents simple sentences. Curve *C* represents all sentences more elaborate in structure, *i.e.*, containing prepositional phrases, complex or compound sentences. Between 10 and 20 per cent of all sentences were functionally incomplete, and so the three curves do not add to 100 per cent. (*After data from McCarthy*, 1930; *Davis*, 1937.)

Simple sentences without prepositional phrases are the first patterns to be learned. Variations on this basic theme do not begin to appear until the child is about 2 years old. According to the norms for intelligence tests, the child's *memory span* for digits increases from 2 to 6 between the ages of 2.5 and 10 years. This increase in the ability to repeat immediately a sequence of sounds spoken by the experimenter is accompanied by an increased ability to turn out long patterns of words. Here again linguistic development seems to depend upon maturation.

The increasing complexity of verbal behavior in older children is shown by the studies of their written compositions. Figure 39 shows the relative frequency of simple, compound, and complex and compound-complex sentences in compositions written by children between the ages of eight and fourteen years (Heider and Heider, 1940). The proportion of simple sentences continues to decline; more intricate patterns of words make up about three-fourths of the sentences of fourteen-year-old writers.

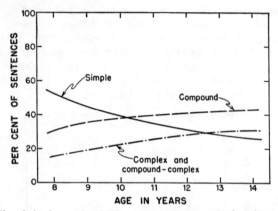

FIG. 39.   The relative frequencies of different types of sentences in the written compositions of children between eight and fourteen years. (*After Heider and Heider*, 1940.)

Changes in the complexity of language are also reflected in the incidence of the different parts of speech. Most of the changes appear before the age of three years. As soon as a child begins to use full and complete sentences, the proportions of the various parts of speech become more or less set by the conventions of the language. The earliest words are usually nouns, although the child uses them as complete sentences. Verbs, adjectives, and other parts of speech do not appear in their proper role until the child is about three years old.

Identification of Words from Context.   Once a child has acquired the grammatical habits of the language, it is possible for him to learn new words by their appearance in the familiar patterns. The ability to define an unfamiliar word on the basis of its contextual associations has been studied in children from eight to thirteen years of age (Werner and Kaplan, 1950). The child's task was to define an artificial word that appeared in six different contexts. For example, 'corplum' appeared in the first set of six sentences; the contexts were:

1. 'A corplum may be used for support.'
2. 'Corplums may be used to close off an open space.'
3. 'A corplum may be long or short, thick or thin, strong or weak.'

4. 'A wet corplum does not burn.'
5. 'You can make a corplum smooth with sandpaper.'
6. 'The painter used a corplum to mix his paints.'

The experimenter's translation of 'corplum' is not important; the interesting point is how the child's synonym for corplum evolved, not whether it eventually became 'stick.'

After the task was explained, the child was given a card on which the first sentence was printed. He responded and was asked how and why his definition fitted into the sentence. Then the second sentence was given while the first remained in view. After the child responded to the second sentence he was again asked how and why it fitted and also whether it could be applied to the preceding sentence. This procedure was continued until all six contexts had been presented.

Many of the responses from the younger children showed that they did not differentiate clearly between a word and the context in which the word occurred. For instance, one sentence was 'People talk about the bordicks of others and don't like to talk about their own.' One child responded, 'Well, bordick means people talk about others and don't talk about themselves; that's what bordick means.' That this child seriously thought that 'bordick' meant the whole sentence became clear when he tried to fit this response into the context, 'People with bordicks are often unhappy.' To this context he responded, 'People talk about others and don't talk about themselves; they are often unhappy.' To the question 'How does this fit?' he answered, 'Say this lady hears that another lady is talking about her, so she'll get mad at her and that lady will be very unhappy.'

Another kind of response was to give a general phrase rather than a specific synonym. To the sentence, 'The way is clear if there are no ashders,' one child responded, 'The way is clear if there are no parts of a radio that don't fit in right together.' This definition of 'ashder' was broad and fluid; it could change in range from sentence to sentence.

Both of these kinds of responses decreased in frequency as the children became older. The confusion of the word and its context disappeared around the ten- to eleven-year level; the use of broad, modifiable phrases decreased more slowly. These results indicate that there is a growing comprehension of the sentence as a stable, grammatical pattern. Younger children manipulated the sentence as a fluid medium; they frequently altered the grammatical structure of the test sentence in order to give their response. The older children had a more adult respect for the context given.

The Duration of the Developmental Process. Prolonged training is necessary before a child masters his mother tongue. Increases in skill are evident over a period of at least 15 years. The continued growth of verbal skills is shown by the growth of vocabulary (Fig. 37) and by the increasing complexity of sentence structure (Figs. 38 and 39); neither of these achievements is finished before high school. A similar statement can be made about reading skill. The prolonged growth of reading ability has been demonstrated by studies of eye movements during reading. In Fig. 40 there are shown three measures of eye movements during reading by children from the first grade through college (Buswell, 1922). The average number of fixations per line of type (the number of points along the line where the eyes paused to focus) decreases

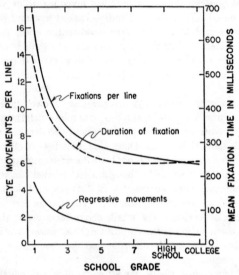

Fig. 40. Increase in reading skill as a function of school grade. Number of fixations and regressive movements decrease, and fixation times become shorter. (*After Buswell*, 1922.)

from 15 or 20 in the first grade to about 6 in college. The average duration of a fixation (the length of the pause while the eyes are focused on a particular point) decreases from 500 milliseconds to about 250. The average number of regressive movements per line (movements to reexamine words or phrases previously fixated) decreased from 5 to less than 1.

When we talk about the development of language, we are apt to think of a process that, like learning to walk, is over and done by the time a youngster is five years old. All the evidence is against this attitude. Learning our language takes 15 or 20 years of full-time study and never really ceases.

EGOCENTRIC VS. SOCIALIZED SPEECH

Many psychologists have puzzled over the role of language in the child's life. Why does he bother to talk? What good does it do him? Does he learn to talk so he can order his parents about? Is he trying to express a rich inner world of experience? Or does he want to give and receive information?

The early investigators classified responses as declarative, exclamatory, interrogative, or imperative. These classes are difficult to apply to the utterances of children. The one-year-old says 'mama,' and the observer must decide from his knowledge of the child and the situation whether this utterance is a declarative sentence ('There is Mother'), an interrogative sentence ('Is that Mother?'), an exclamatory sentence ('Imagine seeing Mother!'), or an imperative sentence ('Mother, come here'), or not a sentence at all. Children at all ages are supposed to make far more declarative sentences than any other kind; this conclusion gives little insight into the function of language in the child's life.

A new approach to the problem was provided in 1924 by Piaget. Piaget distinguishes two functions of language, the social and the egocentric. *Egocentric*, or self-centered, speech shows no concern for the audience—"the child does not bother to know to whom he is speaking nor whether he is being listened to. He talks either for himself or for the pleasure of associating anyone who happens to be there with the activity of the moment." *Socialized* speech shows a consideration of the audience—"the child addresses his hearer, considers his point of view, tries to influence him or actually exchange ideas with him."

Piaget distinguishes various subclasses of response. Socialized responses can take the form of informational statements, criticism, commands, questions, and answers. Egocentric speech is manifested in echolalia, monologues, and collective monologues. According to his records of the verbal behavior of two six-year-old children at La Maison des Petites, 38 per cent of their remarks were egocentric, 45 per cent were spontaneous socialized remarks, and 17 per cent were answers to questions. Almost half of the spontaneous utterances of these two children were egocentric. From the ages of three to five years the egocentric function was more important than the social function. According to Piaget, a definite socialization of the child's speech does not occur until the age of seven or eight. He implies that adult speech is highly socialized. Thus egocentric speech is a symptom of psychological immaturity.

Piaget's work was hardly published and read before American psychologists repeated it in bigger and better ways. One study used 140 children, several judges, and Piaget's exact definitions of his categories, in an attempt to establish reliable norms for average children (McCarthy, 1930). This work did not confirm the high percentage of egocentric speech. The discrepancy aroused considerable interest and discussion, and the experiment has been repeated in America, Japan, and Germany, but seldom with Piaget's results. Seldom do more than 10 per cent of the responses fall under Piaget's definition of egocentricity. It has been suggested that the children Piaget studied were somewhat unusual, for the institution in which they lived was reputed to encourage individuality and independence and to discourage social intercourse.

According to the later studies, almost two-thirds of the normal child's speech is concerned with the exchange of information: naming, comments on the immediate situation, comments on things associated with the situation, and general information statements not related to the situation. Naming is very prominent in the speech of young children, but by the age of five years naming is relatively infrequent. The older child recalls information, uses it in the present situation, and looks ahead to future events.

The frequency of emotionally toned speech—commands, threats, complaints, whining—also declines with age. Questions seem to increase until the age of five and then become less frequent. The young child may often ask a question to which he knows the answer. He does this to gain attention and to confirm the adequacy of his verbalization. Tentative statements, made in the interrogatory form, invite rejection or corroboration by others. Most of the child's questions relate to human actions or plans. It is not until the seventh or eighth year that the child begins to expect a cause-and-effect explanation in answer to 'why.'

These forms of socialized speech comprise most of the child's remarks, and there is little evidence to support the idea that the normal child talks *to* himself as much as he talks to others. The normal child talks *about* himself at great length, and if we change the definition of egocentric to include all statements referring to himself, we find between 30 and 40 per cent of the child's remarks in this category. This new definition of egocentricity is not a sign of immaturity, however, for adults show very nearly the same percentage of references to themselves as do children (Henle and Hubbell, 1938).

We can conclude, therefore, that speech in the child serves primarily a social role. Perhaps even the monologues that Piaget called egocentric are in reality the expression of a desire to feel closer to others.

INDIVIDUAL DIFFERENCES

There are many possible measures and indices of a child's verbal development: size of vocabulary, length of sentence, consonant-to-vowel ratio, intelligibility of speech, complexity of sentences, egocentricity, etc. If the various indices are closely related, it should be possible to estimate the degree of development and to express this in terms of a single coefficient.

Take the *intelligence quotient* (IQ) as a model. A series of tests are developed, and the average ages at which children are able to succeed on the tests are determined. From these averages the mental age of a particular child can be determined. The IQ is simply this mental age divided by his chronological age, and the result multiplied by 100. If we could devise a similar series of speech tests and determine the average ages at which these tests are passed, we could establish a similar speech quotient: speech age divided by chronological age, and the result multiplied by 100.

The available evidence indicates that some such scheme is feasible. One study (H. M. Williams, 1937) found that accuracy of articulation, correct usage of words, length of sentences, completeness of sentences, and complexity of sentences all correlate with one another. A child who scores high on one of these measures tends to score high on all of them. However, there is little relation between these speech measures and the size of the child's vocabulary. The size of the vocabulary correlates closely with the child's mental age and so is an excellent test of intelligence. But size of vocabulary does not seem to be related to other measures of speech development.

What factors in a child's background and environment are associated with the rapid development of speech? Girls have a slight advantage over boys in their speed of development in nearly all the aspects of language that have been studied. Deaf children are greatly handicapped, but the blind may develop more rapidly because of the special care given them and their verbal dependence upon others. Children in families with low incomes tend to be neglected, and their linguistic retardation is the most noticeable aspect of their generally retarded development. Children in more favored homes develop speech much faster. Children who are associated primarily with adults develop rapidly, and thus single children outstrip children with many brothers and sisters. Children from multiple births and children from polylingual homes are often retarded.

If we tried to picture the most precocious child orator, we should think of a blind girl, the only daughter of wealthy parents. The child with the greatest handicap would be a hard-of-hearing boy, one of a pair of twins, born into a large family with poor parents who speak two or three languages.

DISCUSSION QUESTIONS

1. Do children learn words first and then learn the rules for combining them? Or do they learn to speak sentences, and only later learn to analyze these sentences into the component words? What kinds of observations might settle this question?

2. What kinds of speech defects can be detected very early? What factors delay the recognition of the other difficulties?

3. Do you think the course of development of language in the child recapitulates the development of language in the race?

4. What is the difficulty score, as estimated by Flesch's scale, for the passage on page 147 quoted from a 22-month-old child?

5. What is the advantage of using identical twins to study the development of language?

6. Are gestures important in the development of the child's ability to communicate?

SELECTED REFERENCES

DEWEY, E. *Behavior Development in Infants.* New York: Columbia University Press, 1935. A valuable compendium of research on behavior development from fetal life to the end of the second year.

LEOPOLD, W. F. *Speech Development of a Bilingual Child,* Vols. I–IV. Evanston, Ill.: Northwestern University Press, 1937–1949. A linguist's record of the development of his child's speech. A model for the careful study of a single case.

LEWIS, M. M. *Infant Speech.* London: Kegan Paul, Trench, Trubner & Co., 1936. In spite of its self-contradictory title, this book gives a careful description of the early stages of linguistic development.

MCCARTHY, D. Language development in children. In L. Carmichael (Ed.), *Manual of Child Psychology.* New York: Wiley, 1946. Pp. 476–581. This manual is the basic English reference for child psychology. McCarthy gives a thorough review of studies of language development.

PIAGET, J. *The Language and Thought of the Child* (translated by M. Warden). New York: Harcourt Brace, 1926. This work provided an important stimulus to experimentation, but more careful experiments did not support his broad generalizations.

Chapter 8

THE ROLE OF LEARNING

"Looky here, Jim; ain't it natural and right for a cat and a cow to talk different from us?"

"Why, mos' sholy it is."

"Well, then, why ain't it natural and right for a Frenchman to talk different from us? You answer me that."

"Is a cat a man, Huck?"

"No."

"Well, den, dey ain't no sense in a cat talkin' like a man. Is a cow a man?—er is a cow a cat?"

"No, she ain't either of them."

"Well, den she ain't got no business to talk like either one er the yuther of 'em. Is a Frenchman a man?"

"Yes."

"Well, den! Dad blame it, why doan' he talk like a man? You answer me dat!"

—MARK TWAIN

The process by which the sounds of a language come to acquire meaning is called learning. Any scientific theory of language and meaning must have something to say about the learning process. It is the purpose of this chapter to trace some of the implications of modern learning theory for the psychology of communication.

MEANING AND REFERENCE

When a child learns a language, what is it that he has learned? The easy answer is that he has learned the *meanings* of the words and sentences of the language. If this answer is to be useful, we must decide what a meaning is and how we know when a person has learned one.

It is convenient to distinguish different attitudes toward meaning: the *magical*, the *subjective*, the *logical*, the *behavioral*. The magical attitude is a belief in some intrinsic connection between the symbol and the thing symbolized, a connection independent of the people who use the symbol. The magical attitude is common among primitive peoples. It is seen most clearly in the common belief that operations upon the name of a thing can somehow affect the thing named.

The subjective attitude toward meaning is a belief that meanings are personal experiences. This attitude, which to most people is obviously correct

159

and a matter of simple common sense, is inadequate for any scientific analysis. Personal experiences are private and cannot enter the public domain of science. The pursuit of these personal, subjective meanings leads immediately to such unanswerable (therefore useless) questions as 'How do we know that your meaning is the same as my meaning?' or 'Can the true meaning be translated from one language to another?'

Since common sense often leads to fruitless controversy and unanswerable questions, logicians have searched for a more profitable approach. A logician might want to split the problem of meaning into two parts. The first part deals with the problems of *reference;* what does a name name? For example, it is a useful question to ask under what conditions we are willing to call a sentence 'true.' A sentence is true if it satisfies certain criteria of reference. Some logicians contend that a proposition is meaningful only if it is verifiable as true or false. Other logicians reply that verification is just as hard to define as meaning, and so little progress is made in this way. The second half of the logician's question concerns *synonymy:* when do two statements mean the same thing? For example, a logician would say that these two sentences are synonymous: 'Either the girl is not singing or Bill is deaf,' and 'If the girl is singing, then Bill is deaf.' A logician might define what he considered a meaningful sentence by simply listing all of them. Sometimes he is able to devise rules for generating meaningful statements, so that any statement that breaks the rules is meaningless. Such lists or rules usually produce a static, logical language quite different from the ever-changing, often illogical language we ordinarily use.

The behavioral attitude toward meaning leads the psychologist to try to stick close to what he calls observable facts. Logic is more an analysis of the way things should be than of the way they are. Logic helps us to avoid mistakes, but the psychologist is as much interested in mistaken behavior as in correct behavior. A person's behavior toward an object changes with prolonged acquaintance. He builds up certain set ways of responding to such familiar kinds of stimulation. In this attitude we argue that the meaning of anything to a person is the total history of his interaction with that thing. The meaning of a man's speech is given by the totality of conditions that lead him to speak.

The remainder of this chapter is devoted to an elaboration of the behavioral attitude toward meaning. The discussion follows lines developed by B. F. Skinner (1947). The central question is 'How can we specify all the conditions leading to the commission of a verbal act?' Since the theory of learning plays a central role in this discussion, we begin with a distinction between two kinds of learning theories.

TWO KINDS OF THEORIES

It is as difficult for psychologists to agree about learning as it is for a group of theologians to agree on a definition of sin. It is possible to distinguish at least 10 theories of major importance (Hilgard, 1948), and each of these 10 undergoes modifications in the hands of its different proponents. To simplify the situation, we shove all the various theories into one or the other of two categories. From each category we then synthesize a theory that the different theorists endorse in spirit if not in detail.

The first type of theory has behind it two centuries of philosophical and psychological speculation. It analyzes behavior into elements, studies the elements independently, and discovers laws governing the combinations of elements. Originally the component elements were ideas and images, but the modern proponents of *association theory* prefer to speak of more tangible stimuli and responses. It is typical for association theorists to emphasize the importance of learning as an explanation of behavior, and to talk of the stimulus-response connections that a person acquires during the course of his life.

The alternative view, *field theory*, is a protest against association theory. Field theorists do not build the action pattern out of its component parts. The parts, they feel, have significance only in terms of the total configuration of the parts, and a change in any part of the whole may affect all the parts. They feel no compulsion to use only behavioral evidence, and some of their best examples derive from an introspective account of personal experiences. They tend to emphasize the structure or configuration of the organism at the time an act is performed; the history of the organism is not the most fruitful way to describe its present state. Since the organismic configuration is principally inherited and subject to only minor variations in different environments, they tend to emphasize the importance of hereditary factors as an explanation of behavior.

Association Theory. An experiment that association theorists like to conduct runs as follows: (1) an animal is deprived of food, water, or sex, or made generally uncomfortable by electric shock, (2) a bar or lever is provided which the animal can push, and (3) pushing the bar provides a partial or temporary alleviation of the animal's needs. The variables to be studied in this simple situation include the nature and amount of the deprivation or shock, the force required to move the bar, the spatial arrangement of the bar and the reward, the temporal delay in reward, the nature and amount of reward provided, etc.

To make the example specific, suppose the animal is a hungry rat and that each time the rat depresses the bar a pellet of food drops into a tray. The first step is to teach the rat to eat from the tray, and in a very short time the association between the stimulus object of the tray and the response of approach is established. At this stage we might write

tray (stimulus) associated with *approach* (response)
leads automatically to
food (stimulus) associated with *seizing* (response)

The next step is to supply food by operating the magazine. This device will usually work with a clicking sound, and the rat comes to respond to the tray only when the sound is produced.   The final step is to present the lever for the rat to push.   If the lever is presented near the food tray, the rat will explore it, eventually press it.   Pressing leads to food, and the response is quickly established.   At this point we write

> *lever* (visual stimulus) associated with *raising up* (response)
> leads automatically to
> *lever* (tactual stimulus) associated with *pressing* (response)
> leads automatically to
> *tray* and *sound* (stimuli) associated with *approach* (response)
> leads automatically to
> *food* (stimulus) associated with *seizing* (response)

In commenting upon this analysis Skinner (1938) writes, "What we have is a chain of reflexes, not a 'chained reflex.'   The connections between parts are purely mechanical and may be broken at will.   Any section of a chain may be elicited in isolation with the same properties that characterize it as part of the total chain.   There is no reason to appeal to any unique properties of the whole sample as an 'act.'"

The rat must be hungry or the correlations indicated by this analysis will not appear.   This fact leads to the concept of *reinforcement*.   Whenever a series of stimulus-response units leads to reward, the association between the stimuli and their responses is strengthened.   The probability is increased that on subsequent occasions the same stimuli will evoke the same responses.

A closely related process is *secondary reinforcement;* when a stimulus is strongly associated with a response that leads to reward, the stimulus itself takes on the character of a reward and can be used to strengthen other stimulus-response units.

When no reinforcement is given for a response, this response becomes less and less frequent; this process is called *extinction*.

Suppose that pressing the bar leads automatically to food only when it is dark.   When a bright light is on, pressing the bar has no effect.   Under these conditions a rat learns to press the bar in the dark and has little interest in the bar when it is light.   In a very dim light the rat responds more often than he does in the bright light but less than he does in the dark.   The brighter the light gets, the less he responds; the darker it gets, the more he responds.   Such data are taken as an indication of *generalization;* if a response is associated with one stimulus, it will also be associated with all similar stimuli, and the greater the similarity, the stronger the association.

Field Theory.   What do field theorists say about this?   They say the lever-pressing example is a poor experiment.   The relation between pressing a bar and being fed is senseless.   It depends upon the operation of a complex device that a rat cannot possibly comprehend (Adams, 1929).   The field theorist objects to analyzing the lever-pressing response into a chain of discrete reflex units. The adjustments of the animal to the situation must be considered as a whole. That any portion of the chain can be studied in isolation is a claim he thoroughly disbelieves. He is also dubious of reinforcement; the mechanical stamping in of associations seems a dangerous oversimplification. He prefers to think that perceptual configurations leave a trace in the brain and that some need like hunger or thirst serves either to provide the opportunity to use the information or to cause the organism to pay attention to the relevant aspects of the situation.

Field theorists favor a different kind of experiment. For example, a hungry animal is placed inside a three-sided pen. Through one side it can see food. In order to reach the food, it must turn and go in the opposite direction. The animal must restructure the situation, reorganize it with respect to the barrier. Different animals behave differently in this detour situation. A chicken may get excited, dash back and forth along the barrier, crane its neck through the wires. The chicken would starve to death in sight of food if its excited activity did not land it, apparently by accident, outside the barrier. Dogs or chimpanzees grasp the spatial relations, turn about quickly and go around the obstacle. A very young child may behave like the chicken, but a normal five-year-old will have no difficulty.

This experiment is characteristic of field theory in several respects. Comparison of different animals reflects a concern with hereditary factors. There is little necessity to talk about learning; the solution is attained by sudden insight and is remembered and recognized in similar situations in the future. Here is no patching together of chains of reflexes. If the motivation is strong, the animal's solution is usually delayed. Instead of speeding the learning process and stamping in the associations, the animal's needs can sometimes interfere with learning.

Association theorists see no need to abandon their chains of reflexes and the strengthening effects of reward in order to account for the results of this experiment. They assume that the subject has had considerable experience in moving toward goal objects before he comes to the experimental situation. Experience has taught that the larger the angle at the beginning of the path, the longer the path to the goal. In general, movements straight at a goal have been rewarded more quickly than movements along any other path. The subject comes equipped with a strong tendency to go straight to the goal and a much weaker tendency to approach the goal indirectly. The experimenter then proceeds to extinguish the chain of stimulus-response units that leads directly to the goal. When the direct-approach responses are weakened to the point that they are no more probable than the indirect responses, the detour can be made (Hull, 1938). This is merely a special case of *discrimination learning*, *i.e.*, learning to associate different responses with different stimuli.

We shall have little to say about field theories and much to say about association theories. As a matter of fact, we shall ignore field theories until

Chap. 11.   Chapter 11 is concerned with thinking, and on that topic no existing psychological notions are completely satisfactory.   Thinking, particularly
productive or creative thinking, is one of the most challenging puzzles of psychology; we shall need any ideas, field or association, that we can get.   But
until we reach that topic, association theory provides a better orientation
toward the known facts of verbal learning.

ASSOCIATION THEORY AND VERBAL BEHAVIOR

Field theorists, because of their dislike for analysis into smaller elements or
response units, have not attempted to account for the specific and detailed
development of verbal responses.   They argue that the total configuration
can be preserved while the specific parts change.   It is not the particular words
we utter but the concepts that these words symbolize that are of interest.   The
words or sentences can change while the functional signification is retained.
Consequently, the field theorist has studied thinking, insight, conceptual
behavior, and the like, without worrying about the language by which thoughts,
insights, and concepts must be expressed.   They assume what we have called
the subjective attitude toward meaning.

For a detailed account of the particular forms of verbal behavior we must
turn to association theory.

The association theorist approaches the problems of language as he approached the lever-pressing rat.   His variables are of three kinds: stimulus
variables, response variables, and reinforcement variables.   His question is,
'How can we control the occurrence of any given verbal response by manipulating the stimulus and reinforcement variables?'   His observations are expressed, 'When the stimuli *ABCD* are present, they tend to be associated with
the responses *MNOP* if they lead to reinforcements *WXYZ*.'

Verbal behavior is a form of social behavior.   Social behavior necessarily
develops out of stimulus-response associations that *depend upon another
organism for their reinforcement*.   In the response chain discussed above the
successive stimulus-response units were connected by the statement 'leads
automatically to . . . .'   Pressing the lever led automatically to reinforcement as the pellet of food was produced by the machine.   Many of the things
human beings learn depend on just such automatic reinforcement.   But if a
child says [mɪ] and no adult pays attention to it, the response is not reinforced.
If the adult provides milk and praise to reinforce the response, it tends to
occur again whenever the child wants milk and the adult is present.   The
choice of the response [mɪ] is made by the adult and is purely arbitrary; any
other response would serve as well.   The important thing is that such responses
have no reward associated with them unless another person cooperates.

By stipulating the conditions for reinforcement the association theorist
defines a special field of verbal behavior.   Instead of a chain of stimulus-

response associations that involve a single organism, there is a chain that crisscrosses back and forth between two people.

Individual A	*Individual B*
Individual B and *book* (visual stimuli) associated with *saying*, '*Hand me that book*' (verbal response)	

leads automatically to

sound of words and *sight of book* (stimuli) associated with *approach to book* (response)

leads automatically to

book (tactual stimulus) associated with *grasping* and *turning* (responses)

leads automatically to

sight of individual A (stimulus) associated with *approach and saying*, '*Here it is*' (responses)

leads automatically to

sound of words (auditory stimulus) and *book* (tactual stimulus and secondary reinforcement) associated with *grasping* and *saying*, '*Thank you*' (responses)

leads automatically to

words (auditory stimulus and generalized reinforcement)

The reinforcement of A's verbal behavior depends upon B's responses, and the reinforcement of B's behavior depends upon the rather peculiar satisfaction he gets from A's gratitude and 'Thank you.' If the necessary stimulus-response associations are not established in both participants, the chain is broken. If, for instance, individual C is a Frenchman and does not associate the stimulus word 'book' with the response of approaching the book, individual A's verbal behavior is not reinforced. A's verbal behavior is strongly influenced by his audience, for some utterance that B might reinforce could not be used successfully in the presence of C.

A listener, in so far as he only listens, does not exhibit verbal behavior. This analysis leads us to put the greatest emphasis upon the role of the talker, the producer of verbal responses. The listener has the important but often non-verbal job of reinforcing the talker's behavior.

A talker is capable of millions of responses, if we include all the different sentences he might say. These responses have different likelihoods of occurrence. The job for the association theorist is to describe all the factors that make one response more probable than another.

CLASSIFICATION OF VERBAL RESPONSES

What variables control the likelihood of a verbal response? The simplest instance is the response that has its origin in the needs of the talker. 'Give me an apple' is controlled by the state of hunger and by the presence of an audience to reinforce the response. All such requests, demands, commands —Skinner has called them *mands*—vary in likelihood according to variations in the needs of the speaker. Mands are comments about the needs of the speaker. If they are reinforced, they tend to recur.

Not all verbal behavior has this command character. Many of our statements are of the form 'This is an apple' or 'This apple is red.' These are comments about the world. In Skinner's terminology, comments about the world are called *tacts*. Whereas the mand is a response to a need, the tact is a response to a stimulus. Since a tact does not lead to the gratification of needs, it is reasonable to ask what reinforces the tact response.

In order to understand the motivation underlying tacts we must develop the notion of *generalized* reinforcement. When some stimulus is associated with a reinforcement, this stimulus tends to become reinforcing when presented alone. This is referred to by association theorists as secondary reinforcement. Now suppose that the stimulus is associated over and over again with the satisfaction of a wide variety of different needs; the secondary reinforcement is greatly strengthened and is generalized to almost any state of need. For human beings, generalized reinforcement is provided by money, by 'thank you,' by smiles of approval, etc., which have in the past been associated with a variety of reinforcements.

A mand benefits the speaker; a tact benefits the listener. The problem is to explain why a speaker bothers to emit tacts. Imagine a mother who is very anxious to see the postman but needs to work in the kitchen. She stations her child by the window and tells him to let her know when the postman comes. The child is then rewarded for the response 'The postman is here.' The reward may be a smile or a piece of candy. There is no particular need involved, and the child's response depends upon a complex stimulus situation. His response is not directly rewarded but is strengthened by the secondary, generalized reinforcement of approval.

After long training in making informational statements and receiving approval the tendency to comment becomes quite strong. If you want a person to utter the word 'chair,' one of the best ways is to let him see an unusual chair. This stimulus will evoke a tact, because he knows that in the past comments about unusual things have usually led to approval and generalized reinforcement.

Mands and tacts are responses to essentially nonverbal conditions, to the needs of the person or the state of the world about him. Other responses are elicited by the verbal situation itself. *Echoic responses* are the simplest examples. Apparently the repetition of a pattern of sounds carries a certain satisfaction in and of itself, whether the stimulus sounds are originated by another talker or by the imitator. Children exhibit marked tendencies to repeat sounds and words. Adults often repeat a difficult question, authors and poets may repeat for artistic effects, an unusual word may be repeated many times once it pops into a conversation. The tendency to repeat is not so obvious in adults as in children because it is deliberately discouraged, regarded as unproductive, and dismissed as childish. Nevertheless the echoic response plays an important role in the development of verbal habits.

Closely related to echoic responses are the verbal responses to written language. These can be called *textual responses*. Most people have a demonstrable tendency to read, often out loud, any words they see. This tendency helps to support advertising agencies and keeps our highways cluttered with billboards.

A large class of responses are called *intraverbal*. An example is provided by the study of history. No modern historian can make verbal responses to George Washington. The best he can do is to make verbal responses to the records of other verbal responses to Washington. A dictionary or a thesaurus is a systematic collection of intraverbal connections. All of us are stuffed with memorized connections between words—poetry, aphorisms, mathematical tables, grammar, and the like. Once a memorized pattern of words begins, it will run off according to form. If I say 'red, white, and . . . ,' you will probably say 'blue.' To say anything else seems strange, perhaps humorous. Much wit consists in upsetting established intraverbal connections.

We often underestimate the degree to which verbal behavior is elicited by prior verbal behavior and we often confuse statements about words for statements about things and events. The modern man cannot verify all the verbal behavior he perceives, and so he comes to accept words with an alarming credulity. For instance, most of us accept the verbal pattern 'The world is round' and think the ancients naïve for saying, 'The world is flat, with edges.' Yet who is the more credulous? The ancient can defend his statement by saying, 'Look at it.' How would we defend ours? For most of us, 'The world is round' is a purely verbal proposition, supported by enough intraverbal connections with Newton and Columbus to satisfy our demands for consistency.

GENERALIZATION AND ABSTRACTION

Generalization is the rule rather than the exception. When an organism learns to make a particular response in the presence of a particular stimulus, this learning generalizes to a wide range of other stimuli. A child who learns to say 'kitty' for one four-legged furry animal generalizes this response to mice, rats, dogs, etc. Special training is required to make the child *discriminate* more accurately; reinforcement of the response to a narrow range of stimuli is accompanied by extinction of the response to stimuli outside that range.

Nothing in the world is reacted to as special or different from anything else until reinforcement depends on its differentiation.

An *abstraction* is a response to a property isolated from its context; 'red' is a response to redness wherever it occurs. Before an abstraction can occur, however, the response to the property must be consistently reinforced in a variety of contexts. This differential reinforcement is more readily supplied by another organism than by the automatic reinforcements provided by inanimate nature.

Most of our abstractions are social products. A man who lived his entire life alone would not react differently to different colors; nothing in his contact with the automatic reinforcements of the physical world would reward him for abstracting the concept of color. (Curiously enough, a solitary man would have no vocabulary about himself, for the concept of self is a social phenomenon.) Some native tribes are known to have no names for part of the visible spectrum, yet they are able to see these colors. Their culture does not reinforce them differentially for making the distinction. On the other hand, things intimately related to the daily work and acquisition of food are meticulously discriminated because such abstractions are reinforced. When husbandry and hunting were more important to the average man, English distinguished among 'herd,' 'flock,' 'bevy,' 'school,' 'brood,' 'drove,' 'covey,' 'swarm,' and 'pack.' Today these distinctions are relics and could all be replaced by 'group.' Modern English, however, is careful to distinguish among terms closely related to modern life; for example, the distinctions among 'car,' 'coupé,' 'sedan,' 'taxi,' 'bus,' 'roadster,' 'convertible,' 'automobile,' 'truck,' 'racer,' and 'station wagon' are perfectly clear.

Formation of Abstractions by Animals. Abstractions are built up by repeated reinforcements of discrimination. A response to a given property is reinforced in a variety of contexts until the subject discriminates that property from all other irrelevant contextual details. The way such training can operate is demonstrated by experiments with monkeys (Harlow, 1949). A monkey was shown two objects and allowed to select one of them. If the monkey moved the correct object, he discovered food underneath it. He was then given a second trial with the same pair of objects. The position of the correct object was shifted randomly from left to right on successive trials.

Each discrimination problem was repeated for several trials, and then a new problem with two new objects was begun. In one experiment 344 different discrimination problems were learned, one after another. With repeated training the animals learned to learn; on the first 8 problems the monkeys improved from 50 per cent (chance success) on the first trial with a new problem to 53 per cent correct choices on the second trial. On these first problems the learning was slow, and the monkeys seemed quite stupid. On the last 56 problems, however, the monkeys improved from 50 per cent correct on the first trial with a new problem to 97 per cent correct choices on the second trial. At this point the monkeys learned each new problem in one trial, and their behavior seemed intelligent and insightful. Similar data were obtained for children whose ages were between two and five years.

In this series of problems the monkey evolved a concept we can call 'similarity of objects.' He learned to respond to the same object that had been reinforced on the previous trial regardless of what the object was. He learned to respond to similarity in a variety of contexts (*i.e.*, regardless of the particular objects), and this is the behavioral definition of an abstraction.

Once this first abstraction was learned some of the monkeys were taught a new abstraction, 'similarity of position.' A run of problems required these monkeys to pick objects in the same position on every trial. Then a third series of problems again required the monkeys to pick the same object. After several alternations between these two kinds of problems the monkeys learned to switch quickly from one abstraction to the other.

These experiments show that monkeys can develop abstractions and behave in apparently insightful ways. This abstract, insightful kind of response does not appear, however, unless some human being makes reinforcement depend upon discrimination and recognition. Presumably this kind of training goes on continually in a child's development. Each contact the child has with an object represents a single specific learning trial. Each object represents a separate problem. Learning to react verbally to one object is followed by learning verbal reactions more rapidly to the next object encountered. Eventually the child's verbal responses to new things are acquired so rapidly as to appear almost instantaneous.

Limits on the Accuracy of Reinforcement. A parent, by the use of generalized reinforcement, trains a child to make distinctions and to form abstractions that automatic reinforcement could not support. However, there are limits to the kinds of abstractions a parent can reinforce. One major limitation depends on the parent's ability to perceive the same stimuli that the child perceives. Suppose a child looks at a chair and says, 'That is a chair.' The parent can respond to this tact immediately with reinforcement by saying, 'Yes, that's right, that is a chair.' The child turns and looks out the window and says 'That is Mr. Smith.' Now the parent is at a disadvantage for he cannot see out the window. He can go over and look, thus exposing himself to the same stimuli that the child sees. Or he can fall back upon what he knows of the situation, Mr. Smith's habits, and the child's acquaintance with Mr. Smith, in order to estimate the chance that Mr. Smith is outside the window. The second alternative is less reliable, but in many instances it is the only alternative available. When the child says, 'I am thirsty,' it is impossible for the parent to expose himself to the same stimuli that are controlling the child's behavior; he cannot look through the child's window. He must estimate the likelihood that the child is thirsty, the likelihood that the child really wants attention, balance the two, and reward according to his best estimate.

The accuracy with which a parental audience can infer the stimulus conditions associated with a given verbal response by their child varies considerably for different situations. Their reinforcements must be differential and consistent, or the response is not associated with the proper aspects of the situation. Teaching a child to say 'dog' is relatively straightforward. But how does the child learn when to say 'truth,' 'beauty,' 'love,' 'justice'? The situations in which these words are used are so complex that we seldom manage to attain agreement. Confusion and uncertainty can result when we try to train a child to use certain responses in association with certain states inside himself. The word 'happy' provides an example. To teach the child to use this word, we could decide what situations reduce a need and then always use the word in these situations. The child's facial expression—a part of his gesture language —may provide additional clues, but in general the parent must give or withhold reinforcement for 'happy' according to the situation rather than according to the child's private reaction.

Because of this limitation the language of emotions and desires is vague and unreliable. In order to talk about a complicated feeling, we usually resort to a description of situations that would produce similar feelings. We may say metaphorically, 'I felt like I was trying to repair a watch with gloves on.' We probably could not agree on the name, but the feeling is vaguely familiar. Thus we talk about feelings in terms of situations and activities, for these are the stimulus conditions that can be used by the audience as a guide for the differential reinforcement of our verbal behavior. The metaphor depends upon generalization and extension of the discriminative stimuli associated with the response.

THE ORGANIZATION OF VERBAL BEHAVIOR

So far the theoretical account of verbal behavior has avoided the problem of verbal organization. Any language has two basic components, its vocabulary and its grammar. We have considered in detail how the vocabulary might be acquired but have said little about how to learn the rules for combining words. How are words arranged into phrases and phrases into sentences? Is association theory adequate to explain the organization of verbal behavior?

One conceivable explanation is that we learn every possible English sentence individually and so learn to associate a particular sentence with every situation. This explanation can be rejected immediately; there are too many sentences to learn, and we coin new ones constantly. An alternative explanation is that we learn rules for forming sentences. If by rules we mean explicitly verbalized formulas, this explanation can be rejected too. Everyone learns to speak long before he goes to school and reads the explicit rules in a grammar book. The only reasonable explanation is that we learn the rules implicitly; how this could occur is the process we must explain.

Logical Words. Logical terms serve to state relations among other words or groups of words. The organization of verbal behavior is intimately connected with the use of logical terms. A partial list of logical terms is as follows: 'is,' 'all,' 'any,' 'some,' 'not,' 'or,' 'and,' 'if,' 'the,' 'true,' 'false,' and punctuation marks.

Logicians illustrate the importance of these little words in the following way: Suppose we learn on good authority that all mantelops are lespeads and that all lespeads hile. We can conclude immediately that all mantelops hile and that any grimpet that does not hile certainly is not a mantelop. There may, of course, be lespeads that aren't mantelops, so hiling is not a sure sign of mantelopicity. The fact that we have no idea what we are talking about does not stop us from talking. We simply operate on names and properties according to the rules governing the use of logical terms. A logician has been defined as a man who never knows what he is talking about.

Once we have learned the patterns of a language, we can deduce a great deal about a new word or phrase by the way it turns up in familiar patterns. Perhaps the word 'polity' is unfamiliar, but after we have seen it in 'The national polity of the United States is Republican,' and 'The two churches agree in polity though they differ in faith,' and in a few other contexts, we learn to use the word in the correct places; this is indirect or implicit learning from the intraverbal context. In this way it is easy to acquire general impressions about words before we are able to use the words correctly. Often these impressions are hopelessly wrong.

Logical terms are verbal responses; they must be responses *to* something. Clearly they are not responses to the talker's needs, or to any objects in his environment, or to any other person's verbal behavior. One can conclude that *logical terms are responses to other words* that the talker himself is saying. For example, what does 'is' refer to? 'Is' refers to the words that accompany it and serves to notify the listener that these accompanying words form an assertion. 'Is' is the speaker's assurance to his hearer that the statement can be trusted. 'Not' serves the opposite function; it is a negation that refers to the words associated with it. It is usually learned first in the familiar parental mand 'Don't!' which has the effect of inhibiting any concomitant activities.

In the sentence 'There is not a book on the table,' what stimulus conditions elicit the response? It is not the absence of the book that determines the response, or otherwise we should respond continually to all the things that are absent at the time. Before we say, 'There is not any book on the table,' other variables must strengthen the assertion 'There is a book on the table.' Some one has said so, or we need one there, or we remember putting one there, etc. The response is, therefore, a response to the other aspects of the situation that would lead us to say, 'There is a book on the table,' plus a qualifying comment, 'not,' which is added to the statement. 'Not' thus plays the role of a response to the other verbal behavior that accompanies it. We can achieve exactly the same result by saying, 'It would be false to say that there is a book on the table.' In this case it is clear that 'It would be false to say that . . .' is a comment about the verbal behavior that is to follow.

We can analyze the word 'all' in the same way. Clearly the stimuli for saying, 'All dogs have four legs' do not include all dogs. The 'all' is a comment about the statement 'dogs have four legs.' An equivalent expression is 'It is always safe to say that dogs have four legs.'

To recapitulate, we began by asking how we learn to follow the grammar of our native language. This question turns into a question about the use of logical terms. Logical terms are responses to the words they accompany. Now if we can understand how people come to make responses to their own responses, we shall have the key to the problem of verbal organization.

The Talker as His Own Audience. Speech has the interesting characteristic that it affects the talker acoustically in much the same way it affects the listener. Since every talker is his own listener, it is as natural for a person to respond to himself as to respond to others. Indeed, a kind of circular reflex to respond to sound with sound is one of the simplest explanations of the echoic behavior of babies. Young children can be observed to talk to themselves about what they are doing—to respond verbally to their own responses. As the child matures, these private conversations do not appear overtly; crowded schoolrooms require quiet children. Society forces this speech to become subvocal; we suppose that it must continue even though we cannot observe it.

Some of our responses to our own behavior get out where the listener can hear them. Phrases like 'It seems to me that . . .' or 'It is interesting to note that . . .' or 'In conclusion let me say that . . .' are obviously comments about, or responses to, the verbal behavior that is to follow. 'I believe that . . .' warns the listener that other people may not agree with what is coming. Other examples of talking about our talking are less obvious. The words 'like' or 'as though' or 'sort of' warn the listener that the verbal behavior that follows is not to be taken literally but that a metaphorical generalization is intended. Thus 'like' is a comment about the words to follow, not a comment about the nonverbal world.

We have a large number of verbal responses that we use to push other responses around, and these pushing, manipulative responses are used to control and order the flow of responses to needs, things, events, etc. Thus the talker does not resemble a boiling kettle of responses that pop out automatically and unedited. The adult responds to what he is saying, sometimes before he says it, sometimes as he is saying it. His own response to what he is saying may be to suppress it, to amplify it, or to qualify it—to push or pull it around to where the listener will reinforce it.

In summary, the association theorist seems to have reasonable answers for most of the questions we can ask about meaning. The answers can be elaborated in greater detail; in broad outline, they are as follows: A special area of behavior is marked off because it depends entirely on the intervention of another person for its reinforcement. Stimulus-response associations formed in this way vary in strength (likelihood of occurrence) from moment to moment. The variables that control the responses and determine their strength are the talker's needs, the stimuli affecting the talker, the opportunity to echo or read, the interconnections of one verbal response with other verbal responses, the presence of an audience to provide reinforcement. The organization of these response tendencies into acceptable linguistic patterns is accomplished by a self-editing process; the talker reacts to and comments on the responses that are currently strongest.

DISCUSSION QUESTIONS

1. Why are puns funny?

2. Can you suggest a definition for verbal context in terms of intraverbal responses?

3. How is it possible for human beings to span a long period of time between the occurrence of a stimulus and their response to the stimulus? Under what conditions could animals successfully span such a gap in time?

4. Was Aristotle as intelligent as Einstein? If so, why could not Aristotle solve the problems that Einstein solved? How does a system of symbols increase the range of learning and problem solving?

5. Could you develop the ideas presented in this chapter without appealing to the concept of reinforcement? What assumptions would you use in place of reinforcement?

6. How do people come to make deliberately false statements? What is the referent for a false statement?

7. Consider the definition: A word is a logical term if and only if it is a response to a relation. Can you find any exceptions to this definition? How does it differ from the suggestion made in this chapter?

SELECTED REFERENCES

BLOOMFIELD, L. *Language.* New York: Holt, 1933. A classic text in linguistics which favors the behavioristic description of verbal behavior.

HILGARD, E. R. *Theories of Learning.* New York: Appleton-Century-Crofts, 1948. Reviews the several attempts to provide a theoretical interpretation of the facts of learning.

MORRIS, C. W. *Signs, Language and Behavior.* New York: Prentice-Hall, 1946. Chapters I, II, and the Appendix provide an example of the use of association theories in the discussion of verbal behavior.

Chapter 9

VERBAL HABITS

> I vainly strove to recall the name of the master who made the imposing frescoes of the "Last Judgment" in the dome of Orvieto. Instead of the lost name—Signorelli—two other names of artists—Botticelli and Boltraffio—obtruded themselves. The forgetting of the name could not be explained until after I had recalled the theme discussed immediately before this conversation. In these sentences we can find the words and names: Bosnia, Herzegovina and Herr, which may be inserted in an association series between Signorelli, Botticelli and Boltraffio. The name Signorelli was thus divided into two parts. One pair of syllables (elli) returned unchanged in one of the substitutions, while the other had gained, through translation of signor (Herr), many and diverse relations.
>
> —Sigmund Freud

Verbal behavior is an adaptation to the social environment. Because reinforcement is given or withheld by parents, teachers, and friends, a child is able to draw distinctions and to develop concepts that would never be differentially reinforced by the inanimate environment. Reciprocal reinforcement in a social situation supports the evolution of complex communicative behavior. Some of the consequences of this social adaptation are worked out in the preceding chapter. We turn our attention now to the experimental study of the literate adult, the socialized product of years of reciprocal reinforcements. The verbal habits he has acquired from his social environment can be explored in a variety of ways, and they can be shown to be related to the way other psychological functions are performed. The question we shall raise in this chapter is: What verbal habits does the literate adult possess and how can we measure them? In Chap. 10 we ask: How are these established habits related to his perceptions, his ability to learn, and his memory? The discussion of the effects of verbal habits on thinking and problem solving are deferred to Chap. 11.

Associative Strength

We have seen that a reasonable account of communicative behavior can be built from a consideration of the associations between stimuli and responses. Some of these associations are reinforced until they become quite *strong;* other associations are seldom or never reinforced and so remain quite *weak.* When the same stimuli present themselves again, the stronger associations dominate and occur first. If they are not successful, they are not reinforced; if they are not reinforced, they are extinguished; as they are extinguished, the weaker responses begin to dominate. The strong associations occur most frequently, but some relatively weak associations occasionally appear. This is exactly the picture we discovered by statistical analysis; some patterns of symbols occur much more frequently and so are much stronger than other patterns of symbols.

In order to examine this matter of relative strengths in more detail we must ask how the strength of a verbal response is influenced by the other verbal responses that accompany it. For example, the word 'I' might have a relative frequency as high as 0.1 (every tenth word) in conversation or letter writing but drop as low as 0 in dignified, impersonal scientific writing. How, then, do we specify the strength of this response? On a more molecular level, 'I' seems to vary widely in strength from instant to instant. It is a very improbable response to 'Who was the first king of England?' and a very probable response to 'Who wants a million dollars?' Statistical summaries of the sort discussed in Chap. 4 describe verbal strengths in a general way. To be more specific we must study the bonds between words.

The simplest assumption we can make about the bonds between words is that groups of associated words increase or decrease together in their probability of occurrence. When a particular symbol becomes highly probable, there is a set of associated symbols that also becomes more probable. Skinner (1936) has expressed the notion as follows:

. . . when a member of a group [of related responses] is elicited, all members of the group are temporarily strengthened relative to their normal latent strengths. Thus, if I say *hire*, all my responses which resemble that response are temporarily strengthened—particularly the response *hire* itself, which is likely to be elicited again sooner than its resting strength would dictate, and *higher*, which leads me to pun. Also strengthened are all words beginning with *h* (hence alliteration) and all ending in *ire* (hence rhyme) . . . . My response *hire* strengthens all responses associated with its referent, and I am likely to 'go on' to speak of labor, wages, and so on.

The Word-association Test. Experimental attempts have been made to explore these groups of related responses. Probably the simplest and most straightforward is the *word-association test*. Sir Francis Galton (1879; cf. Woodworth, 1938, Chap. 15), English scientist and cousin of Charles Darwin, was the first to try the word-association experiment. He wrote each of 75 different words on a separate card and filed the cards away for several days. Then he looked at the cards one at a time. He timed himself with a stopwatch, starting it the moment the word caught his eye and stopping it as soon as the word had suggested two different ideas. He recorded these ideas as he went through the list but refused to print them. "They lay bare," he commented, "the foundations of a man's thoughts with a curious distinctness, and exhibit his mental anatomy with more vividness and truth than he would probably care to publish to the world."

Psychologists quickly adopted Galton's experiment, extended it, and modified it. It was used by C. G. Jung (1918) to explore the emotional responses of his patients. Delayed or unusual responses indicate that the stimulus word is associated with some emotional complex or guilty knowledge. (This interpretation is not accepted by all psychologists; cf. Lorge and Thorndike, 1941.) In order to know what responses are unusual, however, it is necessary to know what the popular responses are. This means that the test must be given to large groups of people and their accumulated responses used as the basis for discovering individual peculiarities. These data have been collected, and our present interest is in the relative frequencies of occurrence of the various responses to the same stimulus word.

In one experiment (Kent and Rosanoff, 1910) the subject was seated with his back toward the experimenter and was instructed to give "the first word that occurs to you other than the stimulus word." The list of 100 stimulus words, nouns and adjectives, was then read aloud, and the subject's response to each word was noted. This procedure was repeated with 1000 men and women of different occupation and education. The results are assembled in tables that give all the different responses to each word along with the number of people who gave each response. The results for 2 of the 100 stimulus words are shown in Table 13.

Certain associations are quite common. For 'lamp' 650 subjects out of 1000 replied 'light.' (Note also the effects of technology on word association — 'oil,' 'chimney,' and 'wick' are not so frequent today as in 1910.) For 'chair' the response was 'table' for 191 subjects. The distribution of frequencies is very similar to the distribution obtained for words in connected discourse (Skinner, 1937; cf. Chap. 4). The results are evidence for the uniformity of our verbal habits. Not only do we use certain words over and over, but the same word associations are given time after time by different subjects.

Word-association data have been obtained for other large groups of subjects (Woodrow and Lowell, 1916; O'Connor, 1928). It is interesting, for example, to compare the responses of children with the responses of adults. This comparison is made for a few words in Table 14. The children tend to give a word that completes or enlarges upon the stimulus word. The adults jump to a related but parallel word. Apparently there are systematic changes in word associations as a function of age.

The more homogeneous the subjects' backgrounds, the more similar their verbal associations. For example, the responses of professional groups have been compared (Foley and Macmillan, 1943). Lawyers respond more like other lawyers than they do like doctors. When the responses of members of the same family are examined, the correspondences are even more striking. Some examples are given in Table 15. The best and most uniform agreement

TABLE 13. FREQUENCY OF WORD ASSOCIATIONS IN 1000 MEN AND WOMEN
(Kent and Rosanoff, 1910)

Stimulus—lamp

650	light
49	oil
37	chimney, shade
23	wick
20	burn
13	candle
12	bright
10	burning
8	glass, table
7	globe, kerosene
6	articles
5	black, electric, fire, post
4	gas, lighted, night, smoke
3	brightness, burner, dark, high
2	chandelier, darkness, furniture, illumination, large, lights, lit, reading, room, see, stand, useful, vessel
1	Aladdin, arc, blaze, brass, burns, cheer, convenience, crockery, dangers, daylight, distance, dull, evening, flame, full, glaring, home, hot, house, lantern, library, lighten, match, nickel, ornament, petroleum, pretty, red, Rochester, shadow, small, smokes, smoking, smoky, stove, student, tall, warmth, wisdom

Stimulus—chair

191	table
127	seat
107	sit
83	furniture
56	sitting
49	wood
45	rest
38	stool
21	comfort
17	rocker
15	rocking
13	bench
12	cushion
11	legs
10	floor
9	desk, room
8	comfortable
7	ease, leg
6	easy, sofa, wooden
5	couch, hard, Morris, seated, soft
4	arm, article, brown, high
3	cane, convenience, house, large, lounge, low, mahogany, person, resting, rung, settee, useful
2	broken, hickory, home, necessity, oak, rounds, seating, use
1	back, beauty, bed, book, boy, bureau, caning, careful, carpet, cart, color, crooked, cushions, feet, foot, footstool, form, Governor Winthrop, hair, idleness, implement, joiner, lunch, massive, mission, myself, object, occupy, office, people, place, placed, plant, platform, pleasant, pleasure, posture, reading, rubber, size, spooning, stand, stoop, study, support, tables, talk, teacher, timber, tool, upholstered, upholstery, white

is found among parents and their children of the same sex. The children differ more from the father than from the mother; the daughters' approximate more to the mothers' responses than to the fathers'. The more the subjects' past experiences with language overlap, the greater the similarity of their word associations.

The responses are quite similar even if objects or pictures are used instead of words (Karwoski, Gramlich, and Arnott, 1944). The reaction time is

TABLE 14. WORD ASSOCIATIONS FROM DIFFERENT GROUPS OF PEOPLE

(Woodworth, 1938)

Stimulus	Response	1000 children	1000 men and women	1000 men in industry
Table............	Eat	358	63	40
	Chair	24	274	333
Dark.............	Night	421	221	162
	Light	38	427	626
Man.............	Work	168	17	8
	Woman	8	394	561
Deep...........	Hole	257	32	20
	Shallow	6	180	296
Soft............	Pillow	138	53	42
	Hard	27	365	548
Mountain........	High	390	246	171
	Hill	91	184	364

TABLE 15. SIMILARITY IN RESPONSES OF MOTHER AND DAUGHTER

(Jung, 1918)

Stimulus word	Mother	Daughter
Angel....................	Innocent	Innocent
Haughty....................	Bad boy	Bad boy
Stalk....................	Leek's stalk	Stalks for soup
Dance....................	Couple	Man and lady
Lake....................	Much water	Great
Threaten....................	Father	Father
Lamp....................	Burns bright	Gives light
Rich....................	King	King
New....................	Dress	Dress
Tooth....................	Biting	Pains
Take care....................	Industrious pupil	Pupil
Pencil....................	Long	Black
Law....................	God's command	Moses
Love....................	Child	Father and mother

shortest when the stimulus is a word, longest when the stimulus is a picture. Presumably some extra symbolic process intervenes to mediate the verbal association to objects and pictures.

The general result of word-association tests is that the stimulus words elicit a rather small sample of response words. This supports the notion of relatively stable connections among words. If the response words of any given subject or group of subjects seemed chosen at random from the pages of a dictionary, we should have to abandon the notion of associative bonds between words.

What happens when the subjects are told to respond with completely *un*associated words? Even with these instructions it is possible to trace the associations that guide the replies (Atherton and Washburn, 1912). The subjects' responses are made by phonetic associations, by perseveration from recent experiences or from words that occurred earlier in the experiment, or by obvious associations that they somehow overlooked. Some subjects rely on *mediated associations*—for example, if the stimulus word is 'sheep,' they repress the associated response 'wool' but use it as another stimulus word to suggest 'cotton.'

Classification of Word Associations. The question naturally arises as to whether we can classify different kinds of associations. The responses are so various that no single classification has gained universal favor, but it is worth while to examine some of the types of associations that occur. Some responses are related to the stimulus words by *contrast* ('wet-dry,' 'black-white,' 'man-woman'). Others are *similar* ('blossom-flower,' 'pain-hurt,' 'swift-fast'). Some are *subordinate* to the stimulus words ('animal-dog,' 'man-father'), while others are *coordinate* ('apple-peach,' 'dog-cat,' 'man-boy'), and still others are *superordinate* ('spinach-vegetable,' 'man-male'). There are also examples of *assonance* ('pack-tack,' 'bread-red'), of *part-whole* ('petal-flower,' 'day-week'), of *completion* ('forward-march,' 'black-board'), of *egocentrism* ('success-I must,' 'lonesome-never'), of *word derivatives* ('run-running,' 'deep-depth'), of *predication* ('dog-bark,' 'room-dark'). Apparently words are related to one another in an amazing number of ways (cf. Karwoski and Berthold, 1945; Karwoski and Schachter, 1948).

Woodrow and Lowell (1916) classified responses for their own data on 1000 children and for Kent and Rosanoff's data on 1000 adults. They classified every response that was given by 10 or more of the 1000 subjects. These popular responses made up about 80 per cent of the total number of responses. The 21 categories they used are given, along with examples, in Table 16. The examples are drawn from the published classification. The categories are listed in order in Table 16 according to their relative frequencies of occurrence among adults. The relative frequencies of each type of response are listed for both adults and children. The task of sorting all the various response words into 21 types of response forces the judge to make many arbitrary decisions. The selections of stimulus words and of subjects also have marked effects on the results. The percentages reported in Table 16, therefore, must be regarded as approximations, not precise measures, of the strengths of the several types of association.

TABLE 16. RELATIVE FREQUENCIES OF WORD ASSOCIATIONS OF DIFFERENT TYPES FOR ADULTS AND CHILDREN

(Woodrow and Lowell, 1916)

Class	Examples	Relative frequency	
		Adults	Children
Coordinate	Table-chair; deep-low; house-barn	10.9	6.0
Contrast	Dark-light; sickness-health; deep-shallow	10.6	1.3
Similarity	Dark-black; sickness-illness; mountain-hill	8.9	8.6
Superordinate	Table-furniture; music-sound; house-building	7.6	3.7
Adjective-noun	Deep-hole; soft-bed; black-dress	6.9	11.2
Verbs	Table-eat; dark-see; music-play	6.4	10.2
Contiguity	Table-dish; dark-night; sickness-doctor	6.0	15.3
Noun-adjective	Music-sweet; mountain-high; house-big	4.3	7.8
Cause-effect	Sickness-death; lamp-light; bath-clean	2.5	1.9
Whole-part	Table-leg; music-notes; mountain-rocks	2.1	3.6
Participles	Music-singing; eating-drinking; chair-sitting	1.9	0.9
Subordinate	Music-song; sickness-fever; fruit-apple	1.6	2.1
Part-whole	Fruit-tree; foot-limb; soldier-army	1.1	0.4
Material	Table-wood; needle-steel; lamp-glass	1.0	0.9
Verb-object	Eating-bread; wish-fairy; hammer-nails	0.9	1.7
Completion	Table-cloth; wish-bone; spider-web	0.77	1.04
Effect-cause	Sleep-tired; hungry-appetite; afraid-burglar	0.4	0.5
Noun-abstract attribute	Mountain-height; butterfly-beauty; eagle-flight	0.25	0.05
Assonance	Table-able; dark-mark; short-port	0.07	0.43
Pronouns	Woman-she; stomach-mine; thirsty-me	0.05	0.22
Miscellaneous		4.7	5.5
Sum	....	78.94	83.34

Response Latency. The relative frequency of a response is only one of several indices of associative strength. Another kind of measure that is often used is *latency* (or *reaction time*). The latency of a stimulus-response association is the time that elapses from the onset of the stimulus to the onset of the response. If an association is relatively strong, the response occurs quickly. If several responses are weakly associated with the stimulus at about the same strength, the response occurs with a longer latency.

If frequency of occurrence and latency are both measures of the strength of an association, they should be closely correlated. Thumb and Marbe (Woodworth, 1938) seem to have been the first to investigate the relation between the time it takes a subject to respond and the number of other people who give the same response. Marbe's law says that the more frequent responses are quicker. Schlosberg and Heineman (1950) measured association time and communality of response for 204 subjects and 25 monosyllabic stimulus words. They found a coefficient of correlation of -0.80 between the two measures.

Verbal Generalization. Still another method of probing for the associations among words is to take advantage of generalization. In Chap. 8 we noted that a response associated with one stimulus is also associated with all similar stimuli, and the greater the similarity, the stronger the association. This phenomenon is referred to as generalization. As the similarity decreases, generalization decreases. This relation is usually called a *gradient* of generalization. Some association theorists speak of a *semantic gradient* of generalization that operates in verbal behavior. A response established to the name of an object generalizes to the object itself, and vice versa (Cofer and Foley, 1942), thus illustrating semantic generalization. *Phonetic generalization*— as in alliteration, rhyming, and punning—can also be distinguished (Skinner, 1937, 1941).

If the generalization depends upon previous learning by the subject, it is usually referred to as *mediated generalization*. Intraverbal associations provide the best example of the operation of mediated generalization. If the word 'vain' occurs and its occurrence somehow makes the word 'conceited' more likely to occur, generalization from one to the other has been mediated by previous learning. The sounds of the two words are not similar; their similarity must be learned. Clearly the generalization can extend through several steps, from 'vain' to 'conceited' to 'pompous' to 'pampas' to 'steppes' to 'steps' to 'stairs' to 'stares' to 'looks,' or can go off in some quite different gradient, from 'vain' to 'fruitless' to 'sterile' to 'barren' to 'baron' to 'nobleman' to 'lord,' etc. Actually to trace out all the various gradients, even for a few steps, is an extensive undertaking.

If one views the bonds between words as paths along which generalization can occur, then the methods developed for simpler cases of generalization can be applied to the verbal case. The *conditioning experiment* has been used in this way with human subjects to explore the web of intraverbal bonds along which generalization can occur. In one study, for example, the subject was conditioned to give a *galvanic skin reflex** (GSR) when certain printed words were presented (Riess, 1940). This was accomplished by showing the words at the same time a loud buzzer startled the subject. After several repetitions the GSR, which appeared originally in response to the buzzer, began to appear in response to the word alone. Once the GSR was conditioned to these words, the next step was to test for generalization to associated words. If the stimulus was 'urn,' would the word 'earn' also elicit a GSR? The answer is that it did. There was also a response to the synonym 'vase.' A response conditioned to 'urn' generalizes to words associated with it. Adults usually show greater generalization for synonyms than for words that sound alike (Razran, 1939; Riess, 1940), but children tend to generalize more readily to words that sound alike. This tendency disappears at about eleven years of age (Riess, 1946).

The conditioning technique has also been used to illustrate the notion of *unconsciousness* (Diven, 1937). The GSR was recorded as the experimenter called out a series of words: 'one, two, three, five, nine, four, buildings, red, *barn*, east, subway, hay, pavement, red, *barn*, easy, cloth, horse, city, plow, red, *barn*, book, tin, cow, streetcar, pasture, stores, advertisement, red, *barn*, number, wagon, red, *barn*, soft, office, sheep, red, *barn*.' The list is built around the word 'barn,' which is always preceded by the word 'red.' The subject was asked to respond, as in the word-association test, with any words that occurred to him and to continue until the experimenter told him to stop. The conditioning was produced by giving the subject an electric shock after he had made several verbal responses. Every time 'barn' occurred in the list, the subject began responding with associated words, then received a shock.

The subjects quickly began to give a GSR whenever 'barn' occurred. This was true of all subjects, even though about half of them were unable to report at the end of the experiment that 'barn' was always the critical word. These subjects responded to 'barn' with a GSR, but could not respond to 'barn' with the verbal response, 'Barn is always followed by shock.' This is an interesting case; they obviously *knew* what led to shock because they responded to it with a change in skin resistance. At the same time they obviously *did not know* what led to shock because they were not able to report it at the end of the experiment. Here is an example of unconscious behavior; the subjects were unable to respond verbally to their own responses.

The strengths of the associations among the words in the list were shown by the generalization of the GSR to other rural words. The responses to 'horse,' 'plow,' 'cow,' 'pasture,' and 'sheep' were not as great as to 'barn' but were larger than the responses to other words in the list. The rural words

---

* The galvanic skin reflex (GSR) is a change in the electrical resistance of the skin. Changes in resistance follow the physiological activity of the autonomic nervous system, and thus the GSR is often considered to be an indicator of emotional responses by the subject.

had not been associated with shock; they were associated with the word that had been associated with shock. The response also generalized to the word 'red' that always preceded 'barn' in the list.

Razran (1949) used *salivary conditioning* to map out the verbal generalization to a variety of words related in different ways to the conditioned word. First, subjects were conditioned to salivate when certain words were presented; this was accomplished by showing the words while the subject ate. (The subjects were misinformed about the purpose of the experiment.) After the salivary response was established, other words were presented and the amount of salivation was measured. The salivation was greatest in response to the conditioned words; the amount of generalized salivation is expressed as a percentage of the amount of conditioned salivation. Thus '50 per cent generalization' means that the magnitude of the response to the associated word was half the magnitude of the response to the conditioned word. For example, one of the conditioned words was 'dog.' The generalization words and the relative magnitudes of the responses they evoked were 'animal' 22.2 per cent, 'cat' 38.1 per cent, 'terrier' 50.3 per cent, and 'bark' 56.8 per cent. The strength of the association between 'dog' and 'bark' is greater than between 'dog' and 'animal.'

TABLE 17. PER CENT GENERALIZATION OF SALIVARY CONDITIONING
FOR DIFFERENT KINDS OF ASSOCIATIONS

(Razran, 1949)

Word derivative	64.5
Subordinate	42.5
Antonym	40.5
Part-whole and whole-part	39.1
Coordinate	38.2
Predication	35.0
Assonance	26.1
Superordinate	22.9
Completion	12.6

In all, 12 different words were conditioned, and 32 associated words were tested. The different kinds of associations were classified, and the average amount of generalization for each class of associations was computed; these are summarized in Table 17. It is instructive to compare these results with results given in Table 16 for the word-association test. (1) The greatest generalization was obtained to derivative words ('take-took'), although such responses are not common in word-association tests. Apparently a subject who is told to give the first word he thinks of that is different from the stimulus word does not consider derivatives to be different words. (2) There is nearly equal conditioned generalization for contrasts and coordinates. This finding shows a correspondence, since the frequencies of these categories in word-association tests are nearly equal.

The most unexpected results of the conditioning experiment were (3) generalization to superordinates was only half as large as to subordinates and (4) there was hardly any generalization from the first to the second word in the completion of a compound of two words ('Yankee-doodle,' 'mineral-water'). The small generalization to superordinates seems to contradict the results of association studies. The absence of generalization from the first to the second word of a phrase violates our notions of the ongoing habits of normal speech. Both discrepancies make sense, however, when we realize that the generalization experiment works in the opposite direction from the word-association experiment.

For example, 'animal' is a common superordinate response to 'dog' in the word-association test. When 'animal' is the stimulus word, however, the subordinate response 'dog' is relatively rare. Thus we have, for the word-association test:

$$\text{'Animal'} \rightarrow \text{'dog' (weak association)}$$
$$\text{'Dog'} \rightarrow \text{'animal' (strong association)}$$

Now remember what happens in the generalization experiment. A response is conditioned to 'dog.' To test the generalization from 'dog' to 'animal,' the word 'animal' is presented. We find there is little generalization from 'dog' to 'animal'; as in the word-association test, when 'animal' is presented, the association to 'dog' is weak. In the word-association test, the *association* from 'dog' to 'animal' is tested by presenting the word 'dog.' In the generalization experiment, the *generalization* from 'dog' to 'animal' is tested by presenting the word 'animal.' When this notion of the direction of association is introduced, the two experiments no longer seem contradictory.

The same explanation, involving the direction of association, also accounts for (4). If 'doodle' is presented on a word-association test, subjects do not normally respond 'Yankee,' although the reverse association, 'Yankee-doodle,' is quite common. When the conditioning procedure is to condition a response to 'Yankee,' then test by presenting 'doodle,' the presentation of 'doodle' is not associated with 'Yankee' and so a small response is obtained. When the procedure is reversed—when 'doodle' and 'water' are conditioned, and 'Yankee' and 'mineral' are presented as the test words—the generalization jumps from 12.6 to 53 per cent.

The generalization experiment can be summarized in this way: (1) a response is conditioned to A; (2) B is presented; (3) B is associated with A; (4) a generalized response to B occurs at a magnitude determined by the strength of the association from B to A. The magnitude of the response to B is not determined by the strength of the association from A to B. The association, like a vector, has both magnitude and direction.

Three measures of associative strength—frequency, latency, and generalization—give related results. The experimental agreement lends assurance that verbal associations are stable patterns of response built up by reciprocal rein-forcement in much the same way for all speakers of one language. The fact that these associations have a directional aspect becomes especially significant when we begin to analyze the sequential habits that enable us to patch sounds and words together in connected discourse.

Studies of verbal generalization use a number of similar stimuli to evoke a single, conditioned response. The magnitude of this response to the various stimuli indicates degree of generalization, or associative strength. The word-association test, on the other hand, uses a single stimulus to evoke a number of similar responses. The frequencies and latencies of the various responses indicate associative strengths. Both methods reveal associative clusters—groups of words that are all strengthened when any member of the group is strengthened.

Analysis of Errors. Another way to probe these associative clusters is to analyze the errors that occur during learning and remembering. Underwood and Hughes (1950) had subjects study syllable-adjective pairs, such as '*xan*-musty,' '*ceg*-horrid,' etc. The list of pairs was presented once; then the non-sense syllables were presented alone, and the subjects were asked to write the adjectives. Then the list of pairs was presented again, and again the subjects were asked to write the adjectives, etc. Five presentations of the list of pairs were given. The errors were recorded during this original learning session and again during a memory test held 1 week later. If they could not remember, the subjects were told to guess. The question is, How similar are the wrong responses to the correct response?

The errors were rated by a group of 40 judges. Of the errors made during the original learning, 47 per cent were rated as homophones (words alike in sound, but different in meaning), 46 per cent as synonyms, and 6 per cent as antonyms. Of the errors made at recall 1 week later, 18 per cent were rated as homophones, 34 per cent as synonyms, and 4 per cent as antonyms. The errors at recall were less similar to the correct adjective than were the errors during learning. For both learning and recall, however, analysis of the errors showed that subjects often remember the associative cluster to which the correct response belongs although they are not able to recall the exact word. In other words, a subject may have considerable information about the correct response, for he can narrow the search down to a small number of alternatives; but he may not have sufficient information to narrow it down to the one word that is the correct response. This difficulty is often seen in a more acute form when brain damage produces a condition known as aphasia (Chap. 11).

GRAMMATICAL HABITS

By grammatical habits we mean the operation of contextual constraints upon the sequence of symbols. Referring to these habits as grammatical does not imply that some habits are good grammar and others bad. Matters of taste are not the issue.　The question is, What grammatical habits do we have, and how do we measure them?

Grammatical habits are made of the same stuff as associative connections. A word-association test shows relatively unstructured verbal habits.　Any word at all is acceptable as the subject's response.　Now we want to extend the analysis to more specific sequences of behavior.　The distinction is sometimes drawn by separating *free* from *controlled* association.　Free association is the kind discussed in the preceding section; the subject is free to give any response that occurs to him.　In controlled association his response is restricted not only by the stimulus word but also by specific instructions given by the experimenter.　Thus we might tell the subject to give only superordinate words, or only words beginning with /p/, etc.　Then the response is constrained by a more specific context.

Controlled associations are quite similar to the choice of successive words in speech.　As we talk, the specific words we use are not chosen before we begin. They occur as needed, usually without any reportable searching.　Established habits determine the choice of words as the response sequence moves from one set of verbal bonds to the next.　In controlled association it is as though the subject had spoken all but the last three words of 'A word that is superordinate to . . . is . . . .'　The occurrence of the reaction word is as natural and automatic as the occurrence of the word in a sentence.

The Influence of Context.　It can be shown that the verbal context influences the choice of the reaction word even when subjects are not explicitly told to choose their response from a limited set.　We can let the subjects hear a sequence of four words but instruct them to give their response only to the last word in the sequence (D. H. Howes and C. E. Osgood, unpublished data). They listen carefully to all four words but respond to only the fourth word. They write the first response to the fourth stimulus word that occurs to them. Howes and Osgood, in their version of this experiment, varied the degree of association among the first three words.　For example, 'devil—fearful— sinister—*dark*' has three context words that form an associated cluster.　In other cases the sequence might be 'devil—fearful—basic—*dark*' with two associated and one neutral word, or 'devil—eat—basic—*dark*' with only one associated word in the context, or '429—124—413—*dark*' with no associated word in the context.　The total cluster of response words associated with 'devil—fearful—sinister' were, according to the judgment of the experimenters, 'bad,' 'evil,' 'fear,' 'fright,' 'ghost,' 'gloomy,' 'hell,' 'mysterious,' 'scared,' 'scary,' and 'shadow.'　Ordinarily these words do not occur frequently in response to the word 'dark.'　The question is whether the associated context makes the words in this cluster appear more frequently than they would without the context.

When the context was neutral—nonsense syllables or numbers—only 5 per cent of the responses fell into the chosen clusters.　With one word from the cluster placed in the context, 10 per cent of the responses fell into this group. With two words from the cluster placed in the context, 22 per cent of the responses fell into the cluster, and with all three contextual words chosen from the cluster, 34 per cent of the response words were in this group. For example, if the word 'sleep' followed a context of 'eternal—deep—death,' the chance of getting 'Christ,' 'church,' 'crypt,' 'death,' 'depth,' 'God,' 'life,' 'mortal,' 'inescapable,' 'reincarnation,' 'profound,' 'universal,' or 'winter' as the response was increased about sevenfold.

By manipulating the context we manipulate the relative strengths of associative connections. This apparently goes on automatically and unconsciously to determine a subject's reaction to the stimulus word. It is not necessary to constrain the associations by explicit instruction; they can be modified implicitly by context. This is the way context operates in ordinary speech.

Sentence Completion. The effects of context in constraining association can also be explored with the *sentence-completion* test. First devised in 1897 by Ebbinghaus, the procedure was later adapted as a clinical test (Trabue, 1916; Kelley, 1917; Tendler, 1930; Symonds, 1947). The subject is given a suggestive start, like 'The fact that he failed . . . ,' and asked to go on.

In one form of the experiment a number of sentences are selected from contemporary writing or composed for the special purpose. All of the sentences use a certain word. This word is replaced in all the sentences by a blank or an unfamiliar group of letters. The subject is then asked to guess what word has been removed. He reads the first sentence and makes his response, then perhaps modifies this response when the second sentence is given, and so proceeds through the list until he decides upon a response that can always be substituted (cf. Werner and Kaplan, 1950). Commonly used words usually require only one or two sentences, but infrequently used words are more difficult and require many sentences before the correct intraverbal connections are formed (Miller, unpublished data). An analysis of the responses that precede the final decision of the subjects reveals words that have associative bonds with one another and with the missing word. For example, in a group of sentences where 'sorrow' had been removed, readers substituted for it 'anger,' 'hatred,' 'loneliness,' 'longing,' 'confusion,' 'destruction,' 'horror,' 'fear,' 'grief,' 'pain,' 'anxiety,' 'doom.' When the missing word was 'red,' presolution responses included 'pale,' 'bright,' 'hot,' 'large,' 'green,' 'brown,' etc. This procedure yields a group of related responses that are, to varying degrees, interchangeable in many contextual settings. The verbal context that makes one of the group probable also makes the others probable.

In one study (Selfridge, 1949) a group of 36 subjects was asked to guess at the successive words in a continuous passage. The subjects were told all the words in a story up to a certain point. At this point they were asked to guess what the next word would be. After each guess was made they were told the correct word and asked to guess the next. In this way the subjects proceeded word by word through a long passage. The material was simple prose, an account of the boyhood of Robert Schumann written for children. The distribution of responses is illustrated by the following excerpt:

Rows: he–13, then–5, there–5, when–4, the–3, surprise, it, Robert, in, seeing, (–).
of: of–32, his, upon, I, (–).
black: keys–12, white–6, strings–4, black–3, dusty–2, ivory–2, type, wires, little, gleaming, (–), (–).
and: and–21, keys–10, objects, hammers, book, hair, wires.
white: white–34, ivory, brown.
keys: keys–33, books, strips, squares.
stared: were–12, met–3, appeared–3, stared–3, greeted–2, confronted–2, invited, faced, which, placed, exhibited, lives, caught, lay, (–), (–), (–), (–).
back: at–20, up–9, him–3, back–2, forth, (–).
at: at–35, from–1.
him: him–36.

Notice the variation in the range of guesses. The word 'him' is determined by context for all 36 subjects and the author, while the context for 'stared' elicited 14 different alternatives and 4 'don't know's.' The word 'him' conveys little information, for all the readers know what is coming, but 'stared' was selected out of a wide range of possibilities and so carries considerable information.

Sentence-completion tests differ from the word-association tests because they supply more context and so limit further the range of possible responses. In both cases, however, the results show groups of words that function together, that lead to ready transitions, and that become likely or unlikely in similar contexts. And both tests show that these groupings, with minor individual variations, are common to all users of the language.

Analysis of Errors. *Mistakes* often provide an indication of associative connections. Among the first to become interested in linguistic lapses and to collect instances of them were Meringer and Mayer (1895). They classified the mistakes they found as inversions of word or sound order, anticipations of words to come later, substitutions of incorrect words or sounds, etc. Their evidence convinced them that the errors were always similar to the correct response; the associations between the two are usually strong.

This interpretation of mistakes did not seem complete to Freud (1914). Any word has multiple associations with other words. What selective factors determine that one confusion rather than another will occur? Freud looked for the factors in the motives of talkers. He was able to convince himself—and his account is generally accepted—that the form of linguistic lapses is not accidental, but highly diagnostic. As an example of the sort of mistakes Freud emphasized, consider the woman who said, 'Near the mountain loin,' when asked where her summer cottage was. The substitution of 'loin' for 'lane' is attributable, according to the Freudian interpretation, to the repression of memories of where the prying and lustful hand of another had touched her.

Analysis of mistakes illustrates the multiple determination of verbal behavior. The significance for clinical psychology is that mistakes often reveal desires or fears that are unacceptable to the talker, or the audience, or both. Their significance for the analysis of verbal habits is that even when an accident occurs, it is guided by established associations. Even when the talker's editing of his speech lets down, verbal habits can carry the utterance on to a grammatical conclusion.

Automatic Writing. The notion that the verbal machinery can run on by itself without any deliberate guidance by the person is more dramatically illustrated by *automatic writing.* An early study by L. M. Solomons and Gertrude Stein (1896; Skinner, 1934) serves to illustrate how automatic writing can be developed. Solomons and Stein were interested in the fact that people often go through a series of complex movements and are later unaware that they have done so. Often they stop in the middle of the activity and realize with some surprise what they were doing. These acts are performed without the accompaniment of the person's verbal responses to them. They usually occur when the person is deeply involved in some other problem; his subvocal responses are otherwise engaged. Solomons and Stein wondered if this automatism could be cultivated with practice. Would it be possible to go through a series of writing movements so automatically that there would be no awareness of them until the written words were later discovered? Such writing should give a look at the response tendencies in the writer before even the writer has had a chance to edit them.

The experiments began by exploring movements that occur without any reportable effort of will. The suspended arm gets uncomfortable after a while, and if it is given a slight movement, it tends to continue moving. The subject reports the rather distracting impression that his arm is moving by itself and that he has nothing to do with it. If he reads an interesting story, all this goes on unknown to him. The next step is to supply the subject with a pencil that he moves over a paper as though writing, although he is meanwhile engaged in reading a story. The writing movements quickly become automatic and do not prevent him from giving full attention to the story. Under these circumstances there is a decided tendency to write words read, especially simple words such as 'the,' 'in,' 'and.' The subject usually knew that he had written a word, but he could not report the fact that he was going to write a word.

The second step suggested the third. Since the reading was too rapid for the pencil to follow, the subject was instructed to write at dictation. His attention was occupied as fully as possible in reading. He kept the pencil going constantly, scribbling when no dictation was going on. The authors report that "these experiments were by far the most difficult we attempted, and required the most training." At first the subject is unable to continue reading and stops to write every word. But after a few hours' practice he becomes very adept at shifting attention back and forth from reading to writing every 15 or 20 sec. The feeling of effort disappears first, and then the whole process becomes automatic. The word is heard and the subject knows that he has written; that is all. Real automatism, where the subject has no recollection of the event, comes only at intervals and for short periods of time. After long practice these periods of complete automatism might extend for as many as five or six words. Under these conditions "the subject was absolutely unable to recall a single word written, but nevertheless felt quite certain that he had been writing."

The next experiment concerned automatic reading. The subject reads in a low voice something rather dull while the experimenter reads to him an interesting story. "If he does not go insane during the first few trials he will quickly learn to concentrate his attention fully on what is being read to him, yet go on reading just the same . . . . One remembers having read something at the beginning of the paragraph and suddenly finds himself at its end. All between is blank."

After this training the experimenters found that spontaneous automatic writing became quite easy after a little practice. Miss Stein often found it sufficient distraction to read what her arm wrote, but following three or four words behind her pencil. They noted a marked tendency for repetition, as if a verbal response that was strong enough to appear spontaneously would persist for some time before another response displaced it. And they also noted that memorized poems could be readily produced without any attention on their part. There were flashes of consciousness every six or seven words which, they felt, might have supplied a certain amount of continuity. Here are a few specimens of the stuff that came out:

Hence there is no possible way of avoiding what I have spoken of, and if this is not believed by the people of whom you have spoken, then it is not possible to prevent the people of whom you have spoken so glibly. . . .

When he could not be the longest and thus to be, and thus to be, the strongest.

This long time when he did this best time, and he could thus have been bound, and in this long time, when he could be this to first use of this long time . . . .

One feels a certain similarity between these samples and the vocal ramblings of a drunken actor. Except for the marked tendency toward perseveration, these have a structure similar to a third- or fourth-order approximation to English (cf. Chap. 4).

The clinical psychologist has shown more interest in automatic writing than his experimental colleague. A large literature, both clinical and spiritualistic, awaits the interested explorer (Mühl, 1930). Some people are particularly gifted and acquire the knack of writing automatically with little training. These people often believe quite sincerely that they have spiritualistic gifts and that the voices of the dead can make themselves heard through this avenue. The difficult clinical question of the so-called split personality that such productions often reveal is not well understood.

The value of automatic writing for the study of verbal behavior is that it demonstrates the operation of grammatical habits in the absence of the writer's reactions to his own behavior. The words run along in reasonable short sequences, but the total effect is usually confused or even unintelligible. The verbal connections seem to be operating almost at random. When a response reaches threshold and is written, it may recur several times in a boring fashion. The writer who is able to react to his own reactions censors and manipulates these rambling connections in order to elicit some more gratifying reward from his audience.

The Eye-Voice Span. A more experimental approach to the study of grammatical habits is provided by tests of reading ability. In reading aloud a person responds to visual stimuli with vocal responses. If the material is familiar, he is able to handle it in fairly large chunks; if it is unfamiliar, he may be forced to slow down and pronounce each syllable separately. With the familiar materials, grammatical habits lead him to expect certain sequences, and several syllables or several words can be taken at a glance. As he pronounces one word, his eyes move several words ahead to secure the stimuli for succeeding responses.

It is a simple matter to measure how far the eyes are ahead of the voice. This measure is called *eye-voice span*. While the subject is reading aloud, the light is suddenly extinguished; the reader continues to say the words as far as he had seen them. Educated adults reading familiar materials can continue for about five words on the average (Quantz, 1897). More elaborate measurements (G. Fairbanks, 1937) show that a good reader stays about 20 per cent of a line ahead of his voice, as compared with only 15 per cent for poor readers. The eye-voice span is quite elastic. On a difficult word it may shrink to zero; on simple materials it may expand to include a whole line.

Measurements of eye-voice span have been used to study reading ability, but they have not been sufficiently exploited in the study of sequential verbal habits. It would be interesting to know, for example, whether the length of the span is greatest for those sequences of words which can be most accurately anticipated in the sentence-completion experiment. The eye-voice span should be shortest where the information per symbol is greatest. If it existed, such a correlation would be valuable, for it would provide a simple and continuous estimate of the relative redundancy of different passages.

The input to the reader stays about five words, or 2 seconds, ahead of the output. Are these values comparable with the span by which thought normally outruns speech? If so, a fifth-order approximation to the statistical structure of English word sequences should read quite naturally. Consider the following fifth-order sample (Miller and Selfridge, 1950):

house to ask for is to earn our living by working towards a goal for his team in old New York was a wonderful place wasn't it even pleasant to talk about and laugh hard when he tells lies he should not tell me the reason why you are is evident.

Each word was chosen in the context of the preceding four by a different person. Since each person talked about something different, the subject seems to jump about in odd ways. This can be controlled by giving all the contributors the same general topic. When contributors were told to give words about baseball, the following fifth-order sample was produced:

the umpire quickly shouted that Durocher had made his men work to perfect their skill at fielding is very good when the team isn't in the lineup today is one of the greatest players stood amazed at the plate while the batter swung at the pitch.

When successive words are constrained by a general topic, as well as by the verbal context, a fifth-order approximation begins to sound almost reasonable. It takes only a little editing to get several plausible sentences out of the second sample. Thus it is not too difficult to imagine that the average talker needs to plan his sentences, on the average, only about five to ten words ahead of his voice. Such estimates are, of course, pure speculation and should not be taken too seriously. Their principal value is to demonstrate that sequential, grammatical habits can be discussed within the framework of an association theory of verbal behavior.

In Chap. 8 we saw that grammatical habits are intimately related to a small group of logical terms that we use with great frequency. These logical terms manipulate the other words and shove them into standard sentence forms. The variety of sentence forms that a talker uses is not great, and probably the lengths of the patterns that are fitted together into these forms seldom exceed 5 or 10 words. The process of forging sentences is not inexplicable, and a clear formulation of what we need to know should lead to better observations and, eventually, better explanations of our grammatical habits.

To summarize: The existence of grammatical habits imposes restrictions upon a talker's freedom in selecting successive symbols. He has learned a complex set of intraverbal associations. These associations have the effect that if one member of a group of symbols is strengthened, associated symbols in the group are also strengthened. The occurrence of a particular symbol or sequence of symbols limits the range of alternatives from which the talker can choose succeeding symbols because he must proceed in accordance with the verbal associations he has learned. The talker is not completely constrained by his intraverbal associations, for every word has numerous dimensions along which other words are associated with it. Which particular association occurs to a talker depends upon his needs and his audience. The personal factors guiding his choice are of interest to the clinical psychologist, and most of the methods for exploring intraverbal associations have found wide use in the clinics. Nevertheless, *the striking thing about these studies is not the individual differences that occur, but rather the great uniformity in the verbal habits of all normal members of the language community.*

ARTIFICIAL LANGUAGES

How can we trace the *development* of verbal associations in the course of learning a language? This can be done by a careful study of children or students of foreign languages, but here the situation is most complex. So many uncontrolled factors influence the learner, and the language has so many symbols that the relations among them quickly grow beyond our ability to tabulate them. A way out of this difficulty is to construct an *artificial language* that can be as simple as we like. Verbal associations can then be studied in a manageable situation. Unfortunately, relatively little has been done by psychologists with artificial languages. A beginning has been made, but only a beginning. The studies that do exist are directed toward understanding the changes that occur in the history of any language (Esper, 1925; Wolfle, 1932).

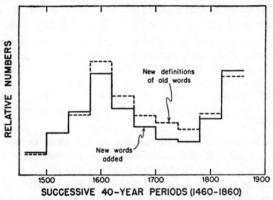

FIG. 41. Rate of permanent additions of new words to English over a period of 400 years. (*After Thorndike*, 1947.)

Kinds of Linguistic Change. All living languages are constantly changing. New words are added, old words are dropped, other words are generalized to new situations or are pronounced in new ways. For example, Fig. 41 graphs the rate of permanent additions of new words to English over a period of 400 years. The data were obtained from a random sample of the dated words in the Shorter Oxford English Dictionary (Thorndike, 1947). The Elizabethan peak at 1600 greatly enriched the language with personal words for acts, feelings, occupations, qualities, and with literary words. The more recent boom has come in the names of material objects.

Once a word has been accepted by a language community, there are three ways in which it may be modified. *Semantic changes* occur when the word is extended analogically as a response to a new situation. An example of this sort of change is 'persona-person-parson,' a change that can be seen at a glance in the following table (Ogden and Richards, 1947, 129):

1.	A		Mask
2.	$A + B$		Character indicated by a mask
3.	B		Character or role in a play
4.	$B + C$		One who represents a character
5.	C		Representative in general
6.		$C + D$	Representative of church in parish
7.		D	Parson

The successive changes seem to be molded by changes in the verbal connections of this word with other words. Figure 41 also shows the rate at which new definitions have been given to old words in English. Possibly the same factors that lead to the invention of new words also lead to the elaboration of old ones, for the two curves of Fig. 41 are quite similar.

Phonetic changes are more difficult to trace in the history of a language because writing usually lags far behind pronunciation. The sort of evidence we have for phonetic change is characterized by Bloomfield (1933, 346).

In our Old English records we find a word stan, 'stone,' which we interpret phonetically as [stɑn]; if we believe that the present-day English word stone [stoʊn] is the modern form, by unbroken tradition, of this Old English word, then we must suppose that Old English [ɑ] has here changed to modern [oʊ]. If we believe that the resemblances are due not to accident, but to the tradition of speech-habits, then we must infer that the differences between the resemblant forms are due to changes in these speech-habits.

The modern linguist has tried to evolve rules to classify phonetic changes. Thus unvoiced plosives in other Indo-European languages are usually paralleled in the Germanic languages by unvoiced fricatives, and so on.

The third type of change, also a change in the pronunciation of a word, is known as *analogic change* and is usually attributed to the interference of some associated word. For example, when such words as 'length,' 'breadth,' 'width,' and 'depth' make us pronounce 'height' as if it were 'heighth,' then 'height' has undergone analogic change. Similarly when, on the basis of such plurals as 'hands,' 'toes,' 'shoes' and 'toys,' the child says 'foots,' he is illustrating an analogic formation.

The Experimental Approach. A method for studying analogic change consists in teaching an artificial language to a group of subjects, then carefully studying the analogic tendencies that develop. It has been shown with artificial languages that the changes that occur frequently while the subject is first learning the language are the same changes that recur after the language is well learned. If this applies to English, it would mean that the child who, in first learning the words, frequently confuses 'uncle' and 'aunt' is the one who later will be most apt to show this confusion and interference by a mixture of the two.

In one experiment (Wolfle, 1932) a group of eight subjects was taught an artificial language that consisted of the nonsense names of nonsense figures. There were 16 figures consisting of four sizes of each of four shapes. A nonsense-syllable name was applied to each size and to each shape. The names of the individual figures consisted of the combination of the size name and the shape name. The size name was regularly pronounced first, as in ordinary English; one looks at a figure and says, 'a large square.' The names of the figures, however, were not all left in this systematic form. Six of them were altered somewhat. In 2 of the names a vowel was changed, in 2 a consonant was changed, and in 2 the syllable order was reversed. Thus there were 10 names that conformed perfectly to the regular pattern and 6 that were partially unsystematic, or did not conform to the pattern of the language as a whole. The names used are shown in Table 18.

TABLE 18. THE VOCABULARY OF AN ARTIFICIAL LANGUAGE—
PHONETIC SPELLING OF THE NAMES OF 16 FIGURES

(Wolfle, 1932)

Size name	Shape name			
	A. poʊf	*B*. sɛb	*C*. grtʃ	*D*. lʊd
1. vʊs	vʊskoʊf*	sɛbvʊs*	vʊsgrtʃ	vʊslʊd
2. nɑs	nɑspoʊf	sɛbnɑs*	nɑsgrtʃ	nɑɪslʊd*
3. zɪg	zɪŋpoʊf*	zɪgsɛb	zɪggrtʃ	zɪglɔd*
4. tɑv	tɑvpoʊf	tɑvsɛb	tɑvgrtʃ	tɑvlʊd

The names of the four shapes, [poʊf], [sɛb], [grtʃ], and [lʊd], are given horizontally at the top of Table 18. The names of the four sizes, [vʊs], [nɑs], [zɪg], and [tɑv], are given vertically at the left. The names of the individual figures are given in the body of the table. The six starred names are the ones altered from their systematic form. Thus the four sizes of the shape [poʊf], given in the second column under [poʊf], were [vʊskoʊf] where the systematic name would be [vʊspoʊf]; [nɑspoʊf]; [zɪŋpoʊf] where the systematic name would be [zɪgpoʊf]; and [tɑvpoʊf].

The procedure used to teach the figure-name relations was as follows: Two learning series, each consisting of all 16 figures, were shown to the subject while the names were pronounced by the experimenter. The subject repeated the name while still looking at the figure. This method provided a combination of visual, auditory, and kinesthetic (speech movements) stimulation. As the third series was shown, the subject was instructed to call off the names of the figures without prompting. Two more learning series were shown, then another recognition series, and so on, until the subject was able to name correctly all 16 figures in one recognition series.

The order of the figures in these series was determined by chance. The subjects never saw the same order twice. The learning was continued until the subject had given six consecutive errorless series on each of 3 successive days. The speed of the exposure apparatus was then increased and the same criterion of learning demanded. This done, learning was considered complete. Thereafter, the subject never heard the names of the figures given by anyone other than himself.

During the postlearning period the subjects were required to name all 16 figures six times each day. Regardless of how many errors were made, no learning series were ever introduced.

A comparison of the learning curves of the subjects used in this experiment with those of another group of subjects to which a different artificial language was taught is shown in Fig. 42. The language learned by the second group of

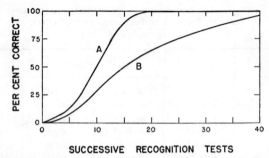

SUCCESSIVE RECOGNITION TESTS

FIG. 42. Average learning curves for systematic (*A*) and unsystematic (*B*) artificial languages. (*After Wolfle*, 1932.)

subjects was more systematic or homogeneous than that of the present experiment. While both languages were fundamentally of the same type, none of the words in the systematic language was altered from its regular form. The systematic language was essentially such a language as would result from making the six starred names in Table 18 conform perfectly to the pattern set by the size and shape names. The symmetrical curve, labeled *A*, is for the systematic language. The unsymmetrical curve, labeled *B*, is for the unsystematic language of the present experiment. Both languages are learned slowly at first, with increasing rapidity until the inflection point is reached, and then with decreasing rapidity until learning is complete.

During the course of learning the language, and after it is quite thoroughly learned, many errors are made in naming the figures. The errors are primarily of two kinds: (1) a subject might see one figure and give it the correct name of another, or (2) he might give one figure a mixture of the correct name and another name. Thus if the figure [nɑsgrtʃ] is shown to the subject, [nɑsgrtʃ] is the correct and most frequent response. But sometimes the name [naɪslʊd] is the response. This is an error of the first type. Sometimes the response is [naɪsgrtʃ]. This is a mixture of the two names, or an error of the second type.

Making either of these types of error indicates that for the subject [naɪslʊd] and [nɑsgrtʃ] are interfering with each other. This interference is the condition that may lead to analogic change. The first kind of error (giving some other name) indicates the possibility of analogic change, while the second kind of error (giving a mixture of the two names) is an actual case of analogic change.

Very few analogic changes are made in the names of those figures which are members of the size category [tɑv], and relatively few are made in the shape category [grtʃ]. From Table 18 it may be seen that the members of these categories are all left unaltered. The fact that few analogic changes are made in these systematic categories does not mean that few errors are made in naming them. Actually, nearly as many errors are made to these figures as to any others, but the errors consist of the proper names of other figures. The irregular forms lead to analogic errors.

Analogic changes are generally changes in the direction of greater regularity or systematization. Sometimes these changes bring one of the irregular names into conformity with the remainder of the system. Sometimes the changes bring the rest of the system into conformity with one of the irregular names. Either type of change, if allowed to become permanent, makes the language a simpler, more systematic one. Not only in this experiment, but in changes in living languages as well, one of the characteristics of analogic change is that it is generally a change from irregularity to regularity. Analogic change tends to systematize a language.

It is unfortunate to find that psychologists have done so little with artificial languages. Language engineers have demonstrated the enormous possibilities that exist and the practical consequences that such research can have. As international cooperation becomes more and more of a problem, the need for such information becomes increasingly clear. The reasons why so little has been done are probably the magnitude of the job and the fact that several disciplines must cooperate to carry it off successfully (Miller, 1950). If cooperative research continues to increase in popularity, perhaps the future will see an increased interest in the business of creating new languages for special purposes.

Discussion Questions

1. How would you classify the various dimensions along which words can be interconnected? Of what use is such a classification?

2. What factors, other than the purely verbal context, go to make up the total context in which a particular word can occur?

3. Would the cluster of associations to an English word be similar to the cluster of associations to a corresponding word in another language?

4. Did Gertrude Stein abandon her interest in automatic writing when she left college?

5. To what extent is it permissible to say that the cluster of associations to a particular word defines the meaning of the word?

Selected References

Jung, C. G. *Studies in Word-association* (translated by M. D. Elder). London: Heinemann, 1918. A basic reference on word associations, particularly their clinical applications.

Woodworth, R. S. *Experimental Psychology*. New York: Holt, 1938. Chapter 15 summarizes the psychological literature on word associations; Chap. 27, on reading.

Chapter 10

SOME EFFECTS OF VERBAL HABITS

> The old idea that words possess magical powers is false; but its falsity is the distortion of a very important truth. Words *do* have a magical effect—but not in the way that the magicians supposed, and not on the objects they were trying to influence. Words are magical in the way they affect the minds of those who use them.
>
> —ALDOUS HUXLEY

Why is sense easier to remember than nonsense? Such a simple question seems hardly worth the asking. It is like asking why apples fall downward out of trees or why day is different from night. That is just the way things are. But there is one very important thing about such simple questions: sometimes we can answer them. And after we have answered enough of these simple questions, we can usually go on and answer some that are not so simple.

Take the question seriously. The first point it raises is, What is the difference between sense and nonsense? Things are sensible if they are familiar, habitual. Things are senseless if they are strange, unpredictable. The difference between sense and nonsense boils down to a matter of habits. The habits we have formed determine for us what is sensible and what is senseless. When the strange, unpredictable, senseless event occurs, we cannot perceive it accurately, remember it accurately, or think accurately about it. Our habits make us see it as something else, distort our memory of it, and lead us to wrong conclusions about it.

All of our habits have the effect of making us more efficient in familiar situations but of betraying us when the unfamiliar occurs. In this chapter and the next we shall explore the ways in which certain particular habits, our verbal habits, influence what we see, what we learn, what we remember, and what we think.

EFFECTS OF VERBAL HABITS ON PERCEPTION

The intimate relation of verbal habits to the way we perceive the world about us is a familiar fact to psychologists. Many of the differences we perceive among things and events would not be noticed if society had not forced us to learn that they have different names. The process works both ways. (1) The perceptual objects we deal with daily come to possess a unity and continuity that demand they be named. We discriminate an object or a class of objects as distinctive, then learn the name. (2) Most people are less aware, however, that knowing the name makes the object easier to recognize. The earliest demonstration of this idea was given by Lehmann (1889), who found that if subjects were taught numbers for each of a set of nine shades of gray, they could identify these shades with considerable accuracy. If the subjects did not learn the numerical names, their success was little better than chance. The grays were not discriminated until a verbal response to them had been learned.

The most startling effects of verbal habits on perception occur in the perception of the sounds of speech and the marks of writing. Compare the American's perception of a Chinese newspaper with his perception of an American newspaper. The Chinese printing looks like blobs and scratches of ink scattered systematically over the page, but the American newspaper is organized in familiar, easily distinguished units. In our native language we know what to expect; in a foreign tongue anything can happen.

During the organism's long training with common stimulus objects his nervous system builds up patterns of activity that change in about the same way the stimulation changes. When the events in the world start a familiar sequence of stimuli $A, B, C, \ldots$, the events in the brain run through a similar series of states $a, b, c, \ldots$. The central activity in the nervous system supports the incoming sensory activity. This central support of a sensory process is *attention*. Some sensory processes go on without support from parallel processes in the nervous system; then we say that we are not paying attention to the sensory processes. When the sequence of states in the brain gets ahead of the sequence of stimulus events, we call it *expectation* (Hebb, 1949). When we read a familiar sequence of wiggles or hear a familiar sequence of sounds, the central activity of the brain can run slightly ahead of the stimulus sequence and so lead us to expect certain stimuli before they occur.

In Chap. 3 it is pointed out that the kind of verbal materials used in an articulation test is an important determinant of what the listener hears. If the test word is one out of a large number of alternatives, the subject's hearing must be quite acute. If the test word is one out of only a few alternatives, the word can be heard more easily. The difficulty of hearing the words correctly is directly related to the range of alternatives that the listener expects. These observations are relevant to the study of verbal habits because *in normal discourse the range of alternatives that the listener expects is determined by his established verbal habits*. The fact that it is easier to hear a word correctly in the context of a sentence than in isolation is a simple demonstration that verbal habits influence perception.

Tachistoscopic Experiments. The influences of verbal habits can be demonstrated just as convincingly for visual perception as for auditory perception. As early as 1885 James McKeen Cattell reported that speed of reading varies according to the familiarity of the language and that letters are easier to read when they form a word than when they stand in isolation. Cattell compared single letters with short words (1) by measuring the subject's reaction time and also (2) by determining the shortest exposure time that is necessary for correct recognition. At short exposure durations where only 4 or 5 random letters could be recognized it was possible to read as many as 3 short words that all together contained more than 4 or 5 letters. These results indicated that words are perceived as a whole and are as unitary in character as single letters. Somewhat later it was noted (Dodge and Erdmann, 1898) that a word can be read at a distance at which its individual letters are unrecognizable.

Short exposures have been widely used for the study of visual perception. The instrument used to obtain brief exposures of variable duration is called a *tachistoscope;* the method is referred to as *tachistoscopic presentation* of the visual stimulus. The experimental problem is to determine the shortest duration at which the items can be correctly identified. This minimal duration necessary for accurate perception is called the *duration threshold.* In many respects this experiment is the visual counterpart of the auditory articulation test. From the large literature of the tachistoscopic experiments we can review here only a few of the more recent studies that reveal most clearly the influence of verbal habits.

If words can be perceived under conditions where scrambled letters cannot, it is natural to ask just how scrambled the letters must be. Is there some peculiar property about words, or can the difference be obtained with letter sequences that preserve the statistical structure of English but do not happen to form words? This question was explored by constructing pseudo words at different degrees of approximation to English and presenting them tachistoscopically (Miller, Bruner, and Postman).

The pseudo words shown to the subjects each consisted of a sequence of 8 letters. These sequences were composed on the basis of zero-, first-, second-, and fourth-order approximations to the statistical structure of English. For the zero-order words, letters were selected at random from the alphabet. For the first-order words the letters were selected according to their relative frequency of occurrence in written English. For the second-order words the relative frequency of pairs of letters was observed, and for the fourth-order words the relative frequency of sequences of four letters was observed. The following samples illustrate the results of this procedure:

Zero-order	First-order	Second-order	Fourth-order
yrulpzoc	stanugop	wallyoff	ricaning
ozhgpmtj	vtyehulo	therares	vernalit
dlegqmnw	einoaase	chevadne	mossiant
gfujxzaq	iydewakn	nermblim	bittlers
wxpaujvb	rpitcqet	onesteva	oneticul

These pseudo words were presented in a random order. The subjects were instructed to fill in the eight blanks on the answer sheet with the letters they saw. They were further instructed to place each letter in its correct position. The exposure durations were 10, 20, 40, 100, 200, and 500 milliseconds (1 millisecond = 0.001 sec). Responses were counted as correct only if the letters were placed in the correct positions.

The results are shown graphically in Fig. 43. As the exposure duration is lengthened, the percentage of letters correctly placed increases for all four types of pseudo words. The fourth-order words are consistently easier to recognize than the nonsensical zero-order words, and the first- and second-order words fall in between. This result agrees with the findings of Cattell and others. More letters can be perceived if they form a familiar sequence.

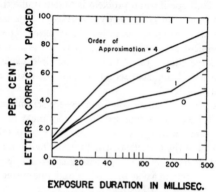

EXPOSURE DURATION IN MILLISEC.

Fig. 43. Tachistoscopic presentation of eight-letter pseudo words constructed at four orders of approximations to the statistical structure of English. At all durations of exposure more letters were correctly placed for the higher than for the lower orders of approximation. (*After Miller, Bruner, and Postman.*)

It should be noted that getting more *letters* does not necessarily imply getting more *information*. The information per letter is less for the higher order approximations. When the redundant effects of context are allowed for, it appears that about the same amount of information per exposure was perceived for all orders of approximation. Under given conditions of illumination, size of type, and flash duration, an observer is able to absorb a certain fixed amount of information. If the information is encoded in a familiar, redundant pattern, the observer will be able to write more letters correctly, but the extra letters do not represent more information to him.

Frequently used words are more readily perceived than infrequently used words (Howes and Solomon, 1951). The duration threshold is an approximately rectilinear, decreasing function of the logarithm of the relative frequency of occurrence in English writing. As the frequencies of use of the test words go up, the time needed to read a word goes down. Correlation coefficients on the order of -0.70 indicate that the frequency of use affects perceptual accuracy.

Such a close correlation is rather surprising when it is noted that the two measures, frequency and threshold, come from different sources. The relative frequency of occurrence in standard English writing of any particular test word is only a rough estimate of the relative frequency with which that word has been seen by a particular subject. The correlation between frequency and threshold might be even higher if we could take account of each observer's reading habits. Note, however, that we do not want to correlate the duration threshold with the frequency of use in the observer's own speech. The tachistoscopic task is a reading task. Thus the frequency with which the words are seen by the subjects in standard writing is a better correlate than the frequency with which the words are spoken by the subjects.

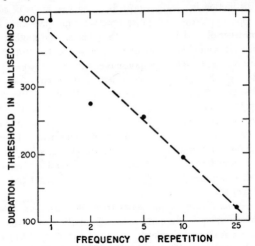

Fig. 44. Duration threshold as a function of the frequency of repetition of Turkish words. (*Previously unpublished data, courtesy of R. L. Solomon.*)

One way to obtain known frequencies is to give the subjects new words that they have never seen before and to control their familiarity by controlling the number of times they are read. This experiment was done with a set of 7-letter Turkish words (R. L. Solomon, unpublished data). A pack of cards with the Turkish words printed on them was given to each subject. Two of the Turkish words appeared 25 times in the pack, 2 appeared 10 times, 2 appeared 5 times, 2 appeared twice, and 2 appeared only once. Each subject was told that the experiment was a test of his ability to pronounce Turkish words. His task was to proceed through the deck one card at a time, spell each word aloud, then pronounce it, then go on to the next. After he had gone through the deck once, duration thresholds were measured for the 10 words. The results, averaged for five subjects, are shown in Fig. 44. Over the range of frequencies tested the relation is rectilinear; the coefficient of correlation is -0.96. The stronger the association between the visual stimulus and the vocal response, the shorter the exposure time needed for correct recognition.

Reaction Times. In addition to the tachistoscopic evidence, *reaction times* to words also show effects of verbal habits on perception. A distinction is usually drawn between *simple* and *complex* reaction times. The simple reaction uses a single stimulus and a single response. For example, a light flashes on, and the subject lifts his hand as soon as he sees the light. The latency between the onset of the light and the beginning of the hand withdrawal is the reaction time. Such simple reactions are usually accomplished within 0.1 to 0.2 sec.

A further distinction is usually drawn between two kinds of complex reaction times. One kind, the *associative* reaction time, has already been discussed as a measure of associative strength. The second kind is called a *disjunctive* reaction; it is an either-or affair. For example, the stimulus is either a white light or a red light, and the response is either with the right hand or with the left hand—right hand for white light, left hand for red. As a general rule, the more similar two alternatives are, the longer is the disjunctive reaction time. It takes longer to distinguish between two stimuli that are nearly identical than two that differ greatly (Lemmon, 1927). This relation is easy to demonstrate so long as there is a straightforward index of similarity. Many of the discriminations we are interested in, however, are among stimuli that differ in several respects and for which no simple index of similarity exists. In such a situation it is sometimes profitable to try to imagine what the answer might be like if it did exist.

Suppose the stimuli are simple geometrical designs that differ from one another in three respects. Suppose that each of the three attributes can be measured along a scale and that every stimulus can be said to have a certain amount of each attribute. We can then imagine that the three scales are laid off along the three coordinates of ordinary space. In this three-dimensional space defined by the three coordinates, each stimulus is represented by a point; the point is given by the three values that the stimulus has for each attribute. Then the distance between any two points can be used as a measure of the degree of similarity of the two geometrical designs. Such an arrangement is depicted for two stimuli in Fig. 45.

Now we ask a subject to discriminate between two stimuli that are represented by points in this space. If the two points are close together, the discrimination is difficult and the disjunctive reaction time is long. If the two points are far apart, the discrimination is easy and the reaction time is short. So long as we consider only two stimuli to be distinguished, the two can be made quite different. What happens, however, if we increase the number of alternative stimuli among which the subject must discriminate? As we put more and more points into the same space, it is obvious that the average distance between points must get smaller and smaller. In other words, as the number of alternative stimuli gets larger, the differences among the alternatives must get smaller. Smaller distances mean harder discriminations and longer reaction times. As the number of alternatives increases, disjunctive reaction time also increases. Although the spatial representation is harder to visualize, this general argument can be applied when the stimuli differ in more than three dimensions.

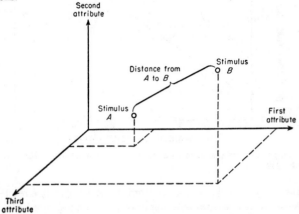

FIG. 45. Two stimuli which differ from one another in three respects are plotted as points in a three-dimensional space. Stimulus A is low on all three attributes, whereas stimulus B is high on all three. The distance between A and B indicates how easy it is to tell them apart. As more and more stimuli are put into the same space, the average distance between points will decrease, *i.e.*, discrimination will become more difficult. (Compare Fig. 33, p. 106.)

The relation between the number of alternatives and the disjunctive reaction time is one of the oldest established facts of experimental psychology (Merkel, 1885; Woodworth, 1938). In the original experimental demonstration 10 stimuli were used: Arabic numerals 1 through 5 and Roman numerals I through V. The 10 fingers were assigned to the 10 stimuli: those of the right hand, in order, to Arabic numerals, those of the left hand to Roman. The subject's response was to press a key with the appropriate finger as soon as a numeral was exposed for him to see. Different numbers of alternatives, from 1 through 10, were used in different experiments. The averaged results for nine subjects are shown in Fig. 46, where reaction time is plotted against a logarithmic scale of number of alternatives. Reaction times get longer as the alternatives become more numerous. These results are related to the linguistic problem because they show that the reaction time (up to 10 alternatives, at least) is a linear function of the amount of information. As the number of alternative stimuli increases, the amount of information carried by the occurrence of a particular stimulus increases.

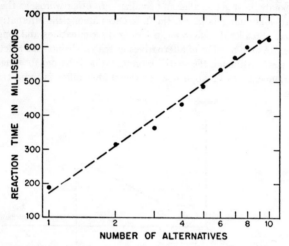

FIG. 46. Disjunctive reaction time as a function of the number of alternatives. (*After Woodworth*, 1938.)

The time it takes to read a printed word is also a disjunctive reaction time. The alternative stimuli are quite numerous; any English word is a possible stimulus. The alternative responses are equally numerous; the observer speaks one out of all the possible English words. If the test vocabulary is limited in advance to a single word, there is no need for discrimination among words and the observer can respond correctly as soon as he sees a flash. Under these conditions the experiment reduces to a measurement of a simple reaction time. If the test vocabulary includes two different words, the observer must discriminate between them. Under these conditions we measure a disjunctive reaction time, and the response is somewhat slower. If the test includes four different words, the discrimination must be more acute and the disjunctive reaction time becomes still longer. When the stimulus can be any one of several thousand words, we expect to find a very slow reaction indeed.

The fact of the matter is not quite so simple. Some words can be recognized much more quickly than others. The reaction time is not only a function of the number of alternatives; it is also a function of the likelihoods of the various alternatives. The familiar words which occur frequently in English writing can be read much more quickly than the rare words (Howes, 1950). The often-perceived words presumably have strong associations and so occur more quickly. These results for disjunctive reaction times to verbal stimuli bear out the tachistoscopic evidence that common words can be perceived at shorter exposure durations.

The Summation of Verbal Associations. Strong verbal associations—those which occur most frequently—lower perceptual thresholds and shorten the time needed for discrimination. One gets a picture of a large number of tendencies existing at different strengths. A strong association is easily elicited; a weak association appears only under special conditions. These tendencies to respond are in constant flux as the stimulus conditions and verbal context change. When the stimuli and the context are controlled in an experimental situation, it is possible to trace out some of the associative bonds and to estimate their relative strengths under the stated conditions. In the uncontrolled flow of normal discourse, however, these response tendencies vary according to the nature of the talker's needs, the kind of audience he has, the stimuli that he receives, the verbal connections he has formed. All these factors which influence the choice of a particular utterance can be thought of as summing together to give a total strength that lies above the *threshold* for a verbal response. So long as the response tendencies are so weak that no one exceeds this imagined threshold, no verbal responses occur. When all the factors add up, however, the strength of the response tendency rises above the threshold value and the person begins to talk.

Some verbal response tendencies never become strong enough to exceed the threshold. No matter how the situation, needs, and context change, there are some things that a person does not say. He may say them to himself, subvocally, but he does not say them aloud. We can imagine that in many situations the threshold for subvocal speech is somewhat lower than that for vocal speech. But there must be many possible utterances that never become strong enough even for subvocal speech. These constitute a reservoir of response tendencies of which the person is entirely unconscious. Some of these unconscious response tendencies may be associated with emotional experiences in the person's life. There may be an active process that weakens these associations and keeps them below the threshold. Psychoanalysis provides a situation in which these emotionally loaded associations can occur and can be explored by the patient.

The way in which a verbal association and a stimulus can combine to push a response over the threshold when neither is adequate alone is illustrated by the following experiment (Ohms, 1910): Pairs of nonsense words were studied and later tested by presenting one of the words and asking the subject to recall the other. When the subject failed to recall a word, it was spoken to him over a poor telephone. Ordinarily the subject could not understand the nonsense words over the telephone. But when the inadequate memory and the inadequate auditory stimulus came together, the subject was usually able to produce the correct response. The period of study increased the probability of a verbal association just enough to make the perceptual process possible.

The summation of the different factors affecting the strength of a verbal response has been used as the basis for a technique to explore latent response tendencies (Skinner, 1936). The technique is similar to an articulation test, but the discriminative clues are reduced to a bare minimum. The listener who tries to make sense out of a faint, mumbling voice supplies short statements of his own invention in the full conviction that these were spoken by the voice. When something is missing, the listener adds whatever seems probable to him. If the subject thinks the experimenter is interested in his ability to discriminate speech sounds, he may cooperate to give the experimenter a glimpse of latent response tendencies; he may reveal tendencies that are not normally strong enough to appear overtly in behavior.

The materials are phonographically recorded vowel sequences: [ə-o-ə-ɑ-ɑ], or [ə-ə-aɪ-i-ə], etc. The vowel sequences are reproduced at a very low intensity, and a given sequence is repeated over and over in a near monotone. The listeners are told that the experiment is to study the clarity of speech and that they are to listen until they get the phrase that is being repeated.

An average of 11 repetitions was needed before a response was given. There was little duplication by different listeners of responses to the same sounds. While the stimuli averaged 4.4 syllables in length, the average response was only 4 syllables. The relative frequency of occurrence of different words followed the same general rule that applies to normal samples of speech; some words are much more probable than others.

What the listeners reported could often be attributed to fortuitous external stimuli. For example, the sound of an automobile horn outside the building led to the response 'an automobile.' Loud talking in the hallway gave 'loudmouth.' The manner of presentation was responsible for 'Call them louder' or 'We ought to hear him.' The effect of the experiment upon the state of the listener lay behind some of the responses: 'We wanted to sleep,' or 'Time will soon pass.'

Here is a situation in which a man makes a statement about something in his environment, fully believing that he is repeating what is being said by a phonograph. He may immediately notice the connection and comment on the coincidence. It is traditionally assumed that we notice connections and then speak of them, but the reverse order—that we speak and then notice the connection—has much to recommend it.

Once a word or theme occurred in a listener's responses, it might persist for some time before it disappeared. The responses themselves set up a condition that affected subsequent responses. Perseveration appeared in grammatical structure, dialect, language, alliteration, rhyming. As an example of the way successive responses were occasionally chained together, one listener reported that the voice said 'My eye's on the rope,' then 'What did he do?' and finally 'He pulled the rope.'

If we single out a certain word in a subject's record, we find that it varies in strength over a long series of responses. The word may appear in five or six responses in a row and then disappear for an equal number before it turns up again. The perseveration of certain responses once they occur is very similar to the perseveration noted in automatic writing. The picture of the intraverbal connections that we get from this experiment is that stimulus-response associations exist, they are interconnected in very complicated patterns, and they vary in strength from moment to moment depending upon a wide range of conditions.

Attempts have been made to use the verbal summator as a technique in the psychological clinic (Trussell, 1939; Shakow and Rosenzweig, 1940; Grings, 1942). The general principle of the verbal summator—that weak, ambiguous stimuli can summate with latent response tendencies—is the basis for the many *projective tests* that have in various forms proved so useful for clinical diagnosis. The verdict seems to be, however, that this form is of limited value for diagnostic purposes.

EFFECTS OF VERBAL HABITS ON LEARNING

In order to pose the problems of the present section, it is convenient to begin with a distinction (somewhat arbitrary) between long-term learning and short-term learning. In the preceding pages we have discussed ways of measuring long-term verbal learning, learning that began in infancy and continues daily. By such learning we acquire reaction tendencies that guide every new task we tackle. Short-term learning, on the other hand, is a more temporary thing. We need a bit of information for a few seconds or a few days. Once the particular situation is past, the need for the information is gone and we are glad to forget.

Short-term learning undoubtedly leaves some long-term traces, and so no sharp distinction can be drawn. The dichotomy between long-term and short-term memory is most clear for a calculating machine. The permanent memory of the machine is determined by the way it is built. Its structure is relatively permanent and contributes to all the subsequent behavior of the machine. Its short-term memory holds an intermediate result until it is needed and then forgets it. At the end of a computation the machine's temporary memory can be cleared and a new problem begun. Unlike the machine, the human system is never completely cleared. It is as if the machine was started on new problems without first clearing out the instructions and results for preceding problems.

With this rather hazy distinction in mind we can phrase the present problem as the study of the effects of long-term verbal learning on short-term verbal learning.

Short-term learning is relatively easy to study. A subject is made to memorize verbal materials, usually nonsense syllables. We may ask him to learn to recite a list of nonsense syllables in their proper order, or to learn to give one nonsense syllable as the response whenever some other nonsense syllable is presented as the stimulus, etc. Nonsense syllables are supposed to minimize the effects of long-term verbal learning and to give different sets of materials of equal difficulty. When meaningful text is memorized, established verbal habits have their maximum effect. In order to see the effects of verbal habits on learning, therefore, we compare the results obtained for nonsense with the results obtained for meaningful materials. This comparison has been made for a variety of conditions, for different tasks and methods of learning.

Amount of Material. Consider first the *amount of material* to be learned. It does not take an elaborate experiment to convince us that long passages are harder to learn than short ones. The more we have to memorize, the harder we must work. The purpose of the experiments is to discover just how much harder the longer passages are. The general conclusion of these experiments is that two units are more than twice as hard to learn as one unit. As the amount of material to be learned is increased, the difficulty of learning it increases disproportionately.

What is the longest list that can be learned completely in a single presentation? This length is usually called the *span of immediate memory*. The answer to the question depends on the kinds of materials and the method of administration (Guilford and Dallenbach, 1925; Blankenship, 1938). If the span is defined as the number of digits that can be remembered correctly 50 per cent of the time, the average college student has a span of about eight digits. Other types of material generally give different estimates. Brener (1940) presents the comparison summarized in Table 19; his subjects were college students.

TABLE 19. AVERAGE MEMORY SPAN FOR DIFFERENT TYPES OF MATERIALS

(Brener, 1940)

Material	*Average span*
Simple sentences (whole)	1.75
Simple commands (correctly executed)	2.42
Nonsense syllables (whole CVC)	2.49
Paired associates (whole pairs)	2.50
Abstract words (visual)	5.24
Simple geometrical designs	5.31
Abstract words (oral)	5.58
Concrete words (visual)	5.76
Concrete words (oral)	5.86
Colors	7.06
Consonants (oral)	7.21
Consonants (visual)	7.30
Digits	7.98

The sentences contained 6 words and 8 syllables. Thus 1.75 sentences correspond to 10.5 words and to 14.0 syllables of connected prose. When the words are disconnected, only 5.6 words could be recalled.   Reed (1924) reports an even larger difference; his students had a memory span of 6.55 for disconnected words, but they recalled 25.36 words in ordinary sentences.   These differences suggest that the limiting factor may be the amount of information stored rather than the total number of items.   In general, if the items are selected from a wide range of alternatives, we cannot remember as many as we can if the items are selected from a limited range of alternatives.   And if the items occur in the familiar context of our language, we can remember more of them than if they are chosen freely and at random.   The amount of information per item is defined as the logarithm of the number of alternative items. Some rough-and-ready calculations of the number of alternatives in Brener's materials lead to the estimate that about $\log 10^{10}$ units of information can be stored after a single presentation.   In other words, the average subject remembers 1 out of about 10 billion alternative sequences of symbols that might have been presented.   Although this is necessarily a crude estimate of information storage, it gives some idea of the capacities of the human nervous system.

If the length of the message extends beyond the span of immediate recall, the material becomes progressively harder to remember.   The number of items that can be remembered after one presentation increases as the length of the message is increased, but the percentage of the total message decreases.

The time it takes to memorize the material to a criterion of errorless recall increases disproportionately as the passage is lengthened.   Thus the time per item also increases.   For nonsense materials the time per item increases approximately as the square root of the number of items in the passage (Thurstone, 1930).   The longer time per item is probably due to increasing interference between parts of the passage and to the wasted time spent repeating portions of the material that are already learned.

TABLE 20.   TIME TO LEARN VARYING AMOUNTS OF MATERIAL

(Lyon, 1914)

Number of nonsense syllables	Total time, min	Number of words of prose	Total time, min
8	0.13	50	2.25
12	1.50	100	9.00
16	3.67	200	24.00
24	5.00	600	84.00
32	6.00	1,000	165.00
48	14.00	3,000	780.00
72	25.00	5,000	1625.00
104	37.00	7,000	2065.00
200	93.00	10,000	4200.00
300	195.00	15,000	5475.00

In Table 20 the results for a single highly trained subject on nonsense syllables and prose are presented (Lyon, 1914). Examination of these data indicates that (1) the connected discourse is far easier to learn and (2) the time per item increases more rapidly with nonsense syllables than it does with prose as the amount of material is increased. Apparently the interference effects pile up more rapidly when we try to learn unfamiliar sequences of letters. Not all prose is equally easy, however. Reed (1924) found that his subjects could memorize an easy prose passage in 111 sec but a difficult prose passage of the same length took 261 sec. It would be interesting to compare such measures of learning time with the indices of readability discussed in Chap. 6.

Kind of Material. It is clear that a greater number of items can be learned in a fixed amount of time if the items fit into the established pattern of intraverbal connections. This very fact has proved to be a complicating factor in studies using nonsense syllables. Psychologists turned to such syllables in order to have a large quantity of relatively homogeneous items that were not influenced by previous learning. All subjects start in equal ignorance. A little experience with nonsense syllables, however, quickly establishes the fact that they are not all equally nonsensical. Some have very definite associations for the learner. Practically everyone reports that *bel, duc, gym, jan, vik,* or *wil* suggest words. In an effort to find even more unfamiliar materials, groups of three consonants have been used. Things like *qjf, zgj,* or *xfq* have few associative connections with words, but everyone recognizes *dnt, drk, swm,* or *whp* (Glaze, 1928).

Suppose we ask a subject to learn a list of 10 items. We make up several kinds of lists, (1) one of three-letter words, (2) one of nonsense syllables that have associative values for everyone, (3) one of nonsense syllables that have associative values for about half the people asked, and (4) a final list of nonsense syllables that have associative values for no one. We give the subject a list and let him study it for 2 minutes. Then we take it away and ask him immediately to recall as many of the items as he can. This experiment has been conducted with a large group of subjects (McGeoch, 1930). It was found that they recalled, on the average, 9.1 of the words, 7.4 of the 100-per-cent syllables, 6.4 of the 50-per-cent syllables, and 5.1 of the 0-per-cent syllables. In other words, the greater the associative value, the easier the learning.

This observation is common in learning experiments. Whenever intraverbal connections are available, it is as if some of the learning had already occurred before the experiment began. This previous learning is transferred to the new situation. One of the most useful tricks for learning material rapidly is to associate it with something you have already learned.

In Chap. 4 we saw that various approximations to English can be constructed by permitting contextual dependencies to work over longer and longer sequences of symbols. If we deal with word units, a zero-order approximation picks words at random from the dictionary. A first-order approximation reflects the relative frequencies of occurrence of the individual words. A second-order approximation reflects the relative frequencies of occurrence of pairs of words. And so we proceed to higher orders of approximation. As the amount of contextual determination is increased, the approximations to English change from sheer gibberish to something very like human writing. The constraints of context are gradually introduced, and the sequences become more familiar. Speaking loosely, we generate a continuum between sense and nonsense. The more the material respects established verbal connections, the more sensible it seems.

What happens when subjects try to learn materials constructed in this fashion? An exploratory experiment has been done with zero-, first-, second-, third-, fourth-, fifth-, and seventh-order approximations to English and with passages from connected text. Lists of 10, 20, 30, and 50 words were used

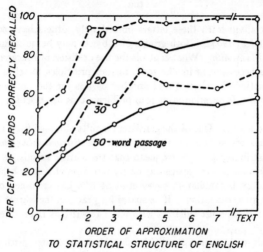

FIG. 47. Accuracy of recall is plotted as a function of the order of approximation to English sentence structure. For all lengths of passages from 10 to 50 words the recall was more accurate for high than for low orders of approximation. (*From Miller and Selfridge*, 1950.)

(Miller and Selfridge, 1950). Subjects heard the words read aloud once and attempted to recall them immediately afterward. The per cent of words correct (regardless of order) is shown in Fig. 47. The greater the contextual constraint, the easier it is to remember the material. By the time the fourth- or fifth-order approximation is reached, there is little further improvement. It is the short-term dependencies that are most important for recall. A fourth-order approximation is still nonsense, but it is rememberable nonsense. It is apparently not important that the sequence of words has a meaning. It is sufficient that it does not violate familiar intraverbal connections extending over sequences of only four or five words.

It must be added, of course, that the presence of intraverbal connections in the materials is of little value to the subject who does not suspect their presence. They do not operate automatically—they must be discovered. Suppose we ask subjects to memorize the following groups of letters:

> und
> era
> spr
> ead
> ing
> che
> stn
> utt
> ree
> the

Some subjects will learn these letters immediately; others have considerable difficulty (Snygg, 1935). Both groups of subjects may be quite familiar with *The Village Blacksmith*. What controls the use or disuse of *Blacksmith* associations? It is necessary to invoke some further principles to tell us when one set of associations is relevant and another useless for the problem at hand. The pursuit of this question leads into problems that are discussed more fully in Chap. 11.

Method of Study. One of the consistent results obtained from the memorization of nonsense syllables is the superiority of *distributed* over *massed practice*. By distributed practice we mean that the learner spends his study time in short intervals of work spaced apart by intervals of rest or other activity. Massed practice is familiar to every student who has crammed on the final night before an examination. If he spaces his practice, the learner can usually master a list of nonsense syllables with fewer repetitions than if he masses his practice.

This result with nonsense syllables is seldom duplicated with meaningful materials. Some experimenters have even found evidence that massed practice might be better than distributed practice for memorizing prose or poetry. The discrepancy between the relative efficiencies of these two study methods for nonsense and meaningful materials is illustrated nicely by an experiment of Tsao's (1948). Four lists of 11 nonsense syllables were used. The syllables were selected, on the basis of a previous study (Hull, 1933), in such a way as to give two lists of syllables with low associative values and two with high. The lists are given in Table 21. The syllables were exposed one at a time by a special exposure device. The exposure time for each syllable was two seconds with half-second intervals between successive syllables. The subjects were required to anticipate the occurrence of the next syllable, and a correct response consisted in speaking the next syllable before it actually appeared in the exposure window. Ten trials were given to each list. In distributed prac-

TABLE 21. LISTS OF NONSENSE SYLLABLES HAVING LOW AND HIGH ASSOCIATIVE VALUES

(Tsao, 1948)

Low		High	
jid	zik	dap	han
fap	fep	wim	yis
tev	koy	lub	jur
buw	mev	rej	vap
vip	pob	tus	reb
zoy	huj	hab	dut
pes	wib	kip	nev
wof	vak	baf	loy
yut	yuf	noy	tav
kef	bej	yas	fid
haj	tiv	vol	pum

tice a one-minute rest interval was interposed after every two successive trials. In massed practice the readings were continuous. Different subjects learned the lists in different orders, and every list was learned once by every subject.

The average number of correct anticipations on each trial is plotted in Fig. 48. As we would expect, the high-associative-value syllables (HAV) were

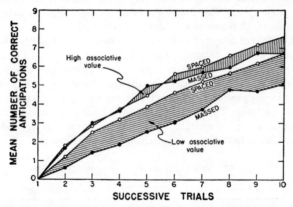

FIG. 48. Learning of a list of nonsense syllables is plotted as a function of successive presentation of the list. Spaced practice is advantageous for nonsense syllables with little associative value but makes little difference for nonsense syllables with high associative value. (*After Tsao*, 1948.)

learned more easily than the low-associative-value syllables (LAV). The curves also show that spaced practice gave higher scores than the massed, for both the HAV and LAV lists. The point is that the difference is large and important for the LAV lists, but small and insignificant for the HAV lists. Spacing the practice trials produced relatively more rapid learning of the LAV lists, but not of the HAV lists. The difference is easily seen by comparing the sizes of the shaded areas in Fig. 48. The associative value of the learning material is a major factor that determines the relative efficiency of spaced and massed practice.

What happened during the one-minute rest intervals between every two trials of the LAV lists? And why did it fail to occur with the HAV lists? One might think that this interval allows the subject to forget what he is doing and so might actually slow up his learning. As an answer we can postulate that a sort of confusion effect, an interference of response tendencies, occurs with the unfamiliar syllables and that this effect decreases during the rest interval. Perhaps learning involves the inhibition of responses as well as their elicitation, and the inhibition has time to dissipate during a rest interval. Presumably these competing or inhibitory tendencies are less important for familiar materials. One result of our long-term verbal habits seems to be the reduction of these interference effects when we have too much to learn too rapidly.

Still another place where long-term verbal habits manifest themselves is in their effects upon the value of recitation during learning. In a classic experiment on this question (Gates, 1917), school children were given 9 min to study, but this time was divided between reading and recitation (with prompting) in different proportions. The results obtained with eighth-grade children memorizing a list of 16 nonsense syllables and 170 words of prose are shown in Table 22. The advantage of recitation is greater for nonsense than for prose. The nonsense syllables demand considerable organization by the learner, and apparently recitation leads him to organize in a more active way than does quiet reading. The prose passages, on the other hand, are already organized in a familiar way; recitation does not help the learner to make the material over into a pattern. To the extent that the learner anticipates the words he reads there is a kind of recitation going on during the reading, and a more deliberate kind of recitation does not change the conditions radically.

TABLE 22.   THE VALUE OF RECITATION IN MEMORIZING

(Gates, 1917)

Method	Per cent learned	
	Nonsense syllables	Prose passages
No recitation..................	35	35
⅕ time reciting................	50	37
⅖ time reciting................	54	41
⅗ time reciting................	57	42
⅘ time reciting................	74	42

Individual differences in learning ability also reveal a contrast between nonsense and meaningful learning. Subjects who are able to learn nonsense materials most easily are not necessarily the same subjects who learn meaningful materials most easily (Welborn and English, 1937). When a group of subjects is given a variety of learning tests, scores on the different nonsense tests correlate rather closely and so do the scores on the meaningful tests. But scores on the two kinds of tests show only a small positive correlation with each other. It is as if two different abilities were involved; abilities that are only slightly related.

The effects of verbal habits on learning can be summarized as follows: First, materials that permit the operation of established verbal habits are far easier to learn than materials that violate these habits. With familiar materials much of the learning has already occurred before the experiment starts. The familiar materials convey less new information per symbol to the learner. It may prove true that when the materials are compared in terms of amount of new information, the difference will disappear; it will certainly decrease. At present, however, adequate data for the quantitative comparison of the storage facilities for information encoded in different ways are not available. Second, the interference effects among the parts of the learning task seem far less severe for familiar materials. These effects seem to accumulate less rapidly during the learning of long, meaningful passages and do not dissipate during the interposed rest periods. And, third, meaningful materials do not demand the kind of organizational learning that is necessary for nonsense. We might separate the learning of *content* from the learning of *pattern;* meaningful tasks require principally the former, nonsense tasks require both.

Obviously the story is not complete. We are not yet able to say what size packages of information fit best in the mnemonic warehouse. The outlook is hopeful, however, for the question is under continual experimental attack, and with better quantitative control of the familiarity of the materials we may soon be able to answer it definitively.

Effects of Verbal Habits on Memory

William James once pointed out that if we remembered everything, we should be as ill off as if we remembered nothing. It would take as long to recall a space of time as it took the original to elapse, and we should never get ahead with our thinking. Forgetting is, however, a mixed blessing. The real trick is to remember just those things we need to know at some later date and to forget the irrelevancies. In a limited way, this is exactly what we do. If a bit of knowledge is important, it tends to recur again and again so that it is always fresh and new; the irrelevant details do not recur and are forgotten.

Quantitative studies of forgetting show that it proceeds most rapidly immediately following learning. After the first few hours the rate of forgetting becomes slower, and the knowledge that survives this first rapid decrement is likely to stay with us for weeks or months to come. This general result is obtained for wide varieties of materials and methods of measurement. The loss is usually more gradual for familiar materials than for nonsense.

Why do we forget? The most natural answer is that if an associative bond is never used, it grows weaker and weaker until eventually it disappears through sheer disuse. On closer inspection, however, this notion that the passive passage of time can cause forgetting seems naïve. The real question is, What goes on during this time that causes forgetting? Time itself causes nothing; time merely permits other factors to operate.

Retroactive Inhibition. The search for an active agent behind passive forgetting has led to the notion that new learning unravels the old. If we could somehow stop the physiological processes temporarily so that no new learning occurred, we should expect to find the memories as fresh as ever when the processes were started up again. Sleep may provide such a temporary block. Forgetting during sleep seems to proceed more slowly than during the waking hours (Jenkins and Dallenbach, 1924). This difference is quite dependable when the lesson consists of nonsense syllables. Where meaningful stories are recalled, however, the details essential to the story are remembered as well after waking activity as after sleep; the irrelevant details are recalled better after sleeping than after waking (Newman, 1939).

The notion that forgetting is a function of the kinds of activity that intervene between learning and remembering is easily tested. Subjects learn a lesson, then occupy themselves in various ways until they are asked to recall or relearn the original task. The intervening activity may be light reading or new lessons. If the subjects are required to learn new things during the interval, they are usually less able to remember the original material than if they had spent the same time resting or reading jokes, light fiction, etc. The new learning interferes with the memory of the old learning. The process underlying this interference is usually called *retroactive inhibition*.

The amount of interference produced by the interpolated learning depends upon the relation between the old and the new lessons. Not all tasks produce interference. An obvious example of an interpolated task that *facilitates* is the original task itself. If the intervening period is spent in continued study, recall is improved. It is necessary, therefore, to know something about the *similarity* of the two tasks before we can predict whether forgetting will be speeded or retarded. But what about the two is similar? The original lesson presumably establishes certain stimulus-response associations; the interpolated lesson establishes further stimulus-response associations. The two may have identical stimuli but call for responses that are more or less similar. Or the responses may be identical and the stimuli varied. Or both stimuli and responses may vary in their degree of similarity. The various possibilities can be schematized as follows for different stimuli (S) and responses (R):

	Original lesson	Interpolated lesson	Retested on
(1)	$S_1 \rightarrow R_1$	$S_2 \rightarrow R_1$	$S_1 \rightarrow R_1$
(2)	$S_1 \rightarrow R_1$	$S_2 \rightarrow R_2$	$S_1 \rightarrow R_1$
(3)	$S_1 \rightarrow R_1$	$S_1 \rightarrow R_2$	$S_1 \rightarrow R_1$

The results with situation (1) usually show facilitation, the amount increasing with increasing similarity between S_1 and S_2. In situation (2) there is usually interference, the amount increasing as the similarity between S_1 and S_2 increases. In situation (3) there is usually facilitation if R_1 and R_2 are very similar, but interference if the responses differ appreciably (Osgood, 1949).

The relation of interference to similarity is not a simple one. Discussion of the relation usually gets difficult when we try to say precisely what we mean by similar learning materials. Two different definitions can give quantitative scales of the similarity of two lessons. One definition is for *formal similarity;* the two stimuli or two responses have certain elements in common. Thus in 'vop' and 'vup' two out of three elements are identical, whereas in 'vop' and 'zap' only one element is shared. 'Elegant' and 'elephant' are quite similar in this formal sense, and 'elegant' and 'stylish' are dissimilar. The second definition is for *functional similarity.* Two *stimuli* are functionally similar to the extent that (1) they tend to evoke the same responses or (2) the response to one of them serves as a stimulus to evoke the response usually made to the other. Two *responses* are functionally similar to the extent that they provide similar stimuli for other people. Functional similarity can be measured in terms of amount of generalization.

Functional similarity is the more general of the two definitions. To the extent that generalization occurs to stimuli or responses with identical elements, formal similarity is simply one dimension along which functional similarity can be measured. There does not seem to be any way, however, to reduce all the functional similarities to identical elements of stimuli or responses. So long as we deal only with unfamiliar nonsense syllables, the two definitions give nearly the same results; generalization from one nonsense syllable to another can be predicted fairly well in terms of the number of elements common to both syllables. But when words or connected materials are used, the learner's established verbal habits introduce generalizations that cannot be explained in terms of formal similarities.

We have already discovered the complexity of intraverbal bonds and have noted that when some stimulus increases the likelihood of a particular response it also increases the likelihood of associated responses. If we have learned to respond 'elated' whenever the stimulus 'green' occurs in the experimental situation, we have also strengthened the tendency to respond with all functionally similar words like 'happy,' 'joyous,' 'high,' 'dejected,' 'delighted,' 'eluded,' etc. (Underwood and Hughes, 1950). Now suppose that, following experiment (1) schematized above, 'green' is changed to 'red,' a similar stimulus word, but 'elated' is unchanged.   Practicing the association 'red-elated' does not interfere with our memory of 'green-elated.'   In fact, since 'red' and 'green' are functionally similar, the interpolated study may prove helpful.   If instead of 'red' some unassociated word like 'large' is substituted for 'green,' the new learning is simply unrelated and has no more effect on the 'green-elated' memory than an equal period of rest.   But now suppose the experiment follows plan (3).   Instead of 'elated' we are made to learn 'green-happy.' At the end of this second learning period we have two responses of nearly equal strength.   These responses compete; remembering 'green-elated' takes longer and is less certain than if we had spent the time resting.   The interference is even greater if some unassociated word like 'whole' is substituted for 'elated.'   Apparently in order to learn 'green-whole' it is necessary to weaken the prior 'green-elated' association more than is necessary in order to learn 'green-happy.'

In spite of its central importance for a theory of memory, retroactive inhibition is not yet well understood.   Even the simple relations indicated in the preceding paragraphs are not above dispute.   The interference of new learning with old memories depends upon a great number of variables: the method of measurement, the nature, amount, conditions, and completeness of the original learning, the nature, amount, conditions, and completeness of the interpolated learning, the time of introduction of the interpolated learning, the similarity of the materials, the personal characteristics of the learners, etc. To work out all the combinations of these variables is a job for the future. For the present it is very difficult to compare two different experiments unless they are carried out under almost identical conditions; since few such studies exist, our conclusions must be quite tentative.

Forgetting Meaningful Materials.   The evidence that similarity has something to do with the amount of interference with verbal memory is based largely on results obtained with nonsense syllables or isolated words learned serially or in pairs.   When the original learning is for connected prose or poetry, intervening study produces small amounts of retroactive inhibition and similarity may have little to do with it.   For example, in one study subjects learned poetry or prose.   The interpolated materials were of two kinds: another selection from the same work, or nonsense syllables.   Both kinds of interpolated materials produced the same amounts of interference (McGeoch and McKinney, 1934a, b).   The stimulus-response associations are not easily analyzed in such an experiment, and so precise predictions from the simpler experiments are not possible.   Even so, we might have expected that such large differences in similarity would have some effect.

Connected, meaningful passages are more resistant to interference effects, both during learning and during retention.   It is as if our verbal habits provide pigeonholes where information can be stored away in relative isolation.

Another source of knowledge about the effects of verbal habits on memory comes from the studies of *testimony*. Given sufficient time and incentive a person of average intelligence can store away large quantities of information. In many situations, however, the necessary repetitions are not possible. A very practical case is the matter of legal testimony. A man witnesses a wreck or a robbery. Later he is asked to testify in court about what he saw. How accurate is his eyewitness account likely to be?

The accuracy of testimony has been studied experimentally by psychologists (Stern, 1902), and their findings make one wonder how justice is ever done in a court of law. Both pictures and actual events have been used in these studies. Witnesses have been permitted to give their accounts immediately or after a period of time has elapsed. They have been permitted to recall freely without interference or they have been cross-examined. There is much that the witnesses do not witness at all, and as time elapses, the report becomes even more fragmentary and schematic. Inconsistent details are forgotten, or altered to fit the general theme of the account, or sharpened until they color unduly the entire testimony. Cross-examination can make a witness even more unreliable, for he is forced to make definite statements about facts he remembers only dimly. The same kind of omissions, inaccuracies, and distortions occur in remembering the plot of a story or play (Bartlett, 1932). Apparently the memory of an event is changed to what the rememberer considers a sensible interpretation.

A major source of distortion is the language used to describe the event. The particular phrase that the person chooses may be remembered after the event itself has become quite vague. If the word is poorly chosen or suggests additional features, recall is distorted by the operation of verbal associations. In one experiment (Carmichael, Hogan, and Walter, 1932) subjects were asked to remember several visually perceived forms. Each was drawn to suggest two different objects. One group of subjects saw the figures with one name attached; another group saw the same figures with different names. The subjects were then asked to draw as many of the figures as they could remember. The subjects' reproductions conformed to the name that the experimenter had suggested. Two circles joined by a line were drawn as eyeglasses by subjects who had seen that label, but as a dumbbell by subjects who had the different label. By influencing the verbal responses associated with the figures the experimenters were able to control the kinds of distortions that were introduced into the figures. In this way established verbal habits can modify the remembrance even of nonverbal materials.

Perceiving, learning, and remembering are all modified by the associative habits built up through communication. Under some circumstances these habits assist us toward an easier and more accurate use of the psychological functions. Under other conditions the same habits can interfere and distort. The facilitating or inhibiting effects of verbal habits seem even more striking when we consider that most obscure psychological function, thinking. This is the problem described in Chap. 11.

DISCUSSION QUESTIONS

1. Nietzsche wrote, "By the grammatical structure of a group of languages everything runs smoothly for one kind of philosophical system, whereas the way is barred for certain other possibilities." Are philosophers the only victims of established intraverbal habits?

2. Does the limit imposed by the span of immediate memory have any implications for the way words should be combined into sentences?

3. Why are nonsense syllables harder to memorize than an equal number of adjectives?

4. Is it possible for learned material to be retained even though the learner can no longer recall any of it? If he could relearn it more quickly, would this be evidence of retention?

5. What would happen to the duration threshold if emotionally loaded words were exposed? Would the threshold be longer, shorter, or about the same as for neutral words?

SELECTED REFERENCES

HOVLAND, C. I. Human learning and retention. In S. S. Stevens (Ed.), *Handbook of Experimental Psychology*. New York: Wiley, 1951. Includes a short review of human verbal learning, more recent and more readable than most.

McGEOCH, J. A. *The Psychology of Human Learning*. New York: Longmans, 1942. A thorough review of the experimental studies of human verbal learning.

THORNDIKE, E. L. *The Fundamentals of Learning*. New York: Bureau of Publications, Teachers College, Columbia University, 1932. A gold mine of experimental ideas and data on verbal learning. Experiments on "belonging" of associations are particularly pertinent.

Chapter 11

WORDS, SETS, AND THOUGHTS

> By relieving the brain of all unnecessary work, a good notation sets it free to concentrate on more advanced problems, and in effect increases the mental powers of the race . . . . It is a profoundly erroneous truism, repeated by all copy-books and by eminent people when they are making speeches, that we should cultivate the habit of thinking of what we are doing. The precise opposite is the case. Civilization advances by extending the number of important operations which we can perform without thinking about them. Operations of thought are like cavalry charges in a battle—they are strictly limited in number, they require fresh horses, and must only be made at decisive moments.
>
> —A. N. WHITEHEAD

Language develops in a social situation and functions to spread information through a group. It enables one person to take advantage of the experience of other persons, and it is our principal weapon for welding a group together for cooperative action. Social control is impossible without a signaling system; even the social insects have a kind of language. Although the social implications must be kept foremost in understanding language, the possession of language offers advantages to the individual other than those it offers to him as a member of a group. A child learns its language in a social situation and for social reasons, but once he has learned it, his whole personal orientation toward himself and his own problems is altered (cf. Mead, 1925).

One of the nonsocial consequences of language is the user's ability to talk to himself. This ability aids him to pose and to solve problems. By means of the language a problem can be described with a set of symbols. The symbols can be manipulated more easily and quickly than can the components of the original problem; many solutions can be tried symbolically before any action is taken. This is not to say that all thinking is verbal manipulation; but certainly the results of thinking are influenced by our symbolic acts.

Thinking is never more precise than the language it uses. Even if it is, the additional precision is lost as soon as we try to communicate the thought to someone else. The importance of a precise language is most clearly demonstrated by the value of mathematical language in science. It is only necessary to compare the Arabic with the Roman system of numbers in order to recognize the tremendous advantage a good notation has over a poor one.

Just how much emphasis to place on language in the study of thinking is still a debatable issue in psychology. Opinions range all the way from

J. B. Watson's (1924), who said thought *is* implicit movement of the speech musculature, to the modern field theorists, who write long treatises about thinking with scarcely a mention of verbal behavior (Wertheimer, 1945). No one denies, however, that many people converse with themselves. If they are interrupted, they will say they are thinking. These subvocal monologues do not comprise the entire area that we want to call thinking, but they merit our attention.

EARLY STUDIES OF THINKING

The Determining Tendency. Before the experimental evidence began to accumulate, it was assumed by psychologists that thought is the succession of ideas that pass through consciousness. This view is probably the popular one even today among people who have not tried to test it. It seems a simple matter to subject thinking to scientific scrutiny. People are given a task to think about and then asked to introspect—to describe what ideas passed through their conscious minds. The thinker's task must be simple so that he can remember everything that goes on, and it should permit a free flow of ideas and images. One experimenter (Marbe, 1901) asked his thinkers to make simple judgments: to compare weights, to sing the tone of a tuning fork, to add numbers, to answer simple questions. Then the subjects gave a full, introspective account of what had gone on. This seems simple enough, but the observers discovered, much to their own astonishment, that there are no psychological conditions of judgment, there is no psychological judgment process, there is nothing that in direct experience marks a judgment as judgment. All that the subjects could report were attitudes toward the judgment —doubt, uneasiness, difficulty, uncertainty, effort, etc., or their opposites— and memories of the instructions, the situation, or other attendant features of the experiment. But no judgments or thoughts.

In another study (Mayer and Orth, 1901) the word-association test was used, and the subjects gave introspective details of how they got the associated word with which they responded. Quite frequently the subjects found they had nothing to report. When they examined this blank interval, they reported that their experience consisted of certain conscious processes that defied description. Thus they came to speak of "the lay of consciousness" (*Bewusstseinslagen*).

Still other experimenters (Watt, 1905; May, 1917) used a variation of the word-association test in which the subjects are told to respond with a word that stands in a certain relation to the stimulus word. Sometimes they are asked for a superordinate response ('dog-animal'), sometimes for a subordinate response ('dog-collie'), sometimes for a coordinate ('dog-cat'), sometimes for a whole, a part, or another part of a common whole. Since his predecessors had discovered how difficult it is to find judgments and associations in consciousness, Watt asked the subjects to pay attention to and report in full on a small segment of the total process. The process was dissected into four parts, (1) the preparatory period, (2) the appearance of the stimulus word, (3) the search for the reaction word, and (4) the occurrence of the reaction word. Little conscious content was reported during the period of search, although adequate reports were obtained for the other periods. The word usually came without hesitation, and there was nothing in consciousness that reflected any searching.

Essentially similar conclusions must be drawn from the introspective accounts of the world's greatest creative thinkers. When they grow too old for more profitable work, mathematicians sometimes turn their attention to the stages involved in inventive thinking. These men have firsthand experience in finding new and important answers; who should know better than they the anatomy of thought? The peculiar fact is that they are as ignorant as any psychologist. Their accounts describe a long period of preparation, a frustrating inability to find the answer, a retreat from the problem, a more or less sudden insight, a final burst of work to verify and express the solution. But when they are asked to tell exactly what went on to produce the insight, they speak of unconscious work or the chance association of ideas or in some other phrase confess that the machinery is not accessible to introspective peeping (Hadamard, 1945).

These observations let loose a flood of controversy and printer's ink. The battle raged around two main issues: (1) Is it possible to think without having conscious images in the mind? (2) How is the process guided to a successful completion? The controversy over imageless thought seemed to get nowhere. Either there are large individual differences in the use of imagery, or else people describe their experiences in quite different ways. A certain practical impatience with this image quibbling probably contributed to the widespread popularity in America of a behavioristic psychology that rejected all mentalistic controversies as meaningless.

The positive contribution of the early thought experiments came via the concepts of task, set, and determining tendency. According to the usual formulation, the *task* gives the subject a particular *set*, and this set influences his associative sequence by means of unconscious *determining tendencies* that guide the process to its proper completion (Selz, 1922). These concepts bear a very close resemblance to what we have called, in preceding chapters, contextual constraints or associative connections. Determining tendencies must operate in the extemporaneous patching together of words in ordinary speech.

The determining tendency is, of course, a much broader concept than verbal context. The early thought experiments are but one source of evidence that a subject's predispositions affect his subsequent actions. Determining tendencies were first encountered in the laboratory in experiments on reaction time, but after 1910 they passed into the general armamentarium of psychology. The terms *Bewusstseinslage, Aufgabe, Einstellung, determinierende*

Tendenz, etc., have since been collected under the general heading of *attitudes*, and their influence is recognized in all areas of psychology (G. W. Allport, 1935). Verbal context is one illustration of the more general problem.

Syllogistic Reasoning. Since the simple word-association test does not produce thoughts that we can study, more complicated tasks may be needed. Störring (1908) met this need with the syllogism. He showed the subject the major and minor premises from which a conclusion was to be drawn. The subject read these carefully and gave an introspective account of how he reached the answer. For example, the subject would be shown:

All *i* belong to the class *o*. All *z* belong to the class *i*. Therefore . . .

The subject read these premises, then introspected, 'What are you doing with the second statement? You have to relate it to the first premise. How do you do that? Where was *i* mentioned in the first premise?' He then found the place where it said 'all *i*' and so went on to see that all *z* belong to *i*, and therefore *z* was to be put in place of all *i*. All this went on without any particular references to the class *o*.

Störring collected extensive protocols with these syllogistic problems. Sometimes the subject visualized the solution, sometimes the conclusion was reached by purely verbal means. Unfortunately, however, the results do not seem to lead to any generalizations about how people think or where successful hypotheses come from. They do show, however, that *the laws of logic are not the dynamic laws of thought*. Everyone obeys the law of gravitation, but we are all likely to disobey the laws of logic. The syllogism is a reconstruction of a devious psychological process.

Verbal habits have a marked effect on the syllogizing reasoner. Some conclusions are drawn because they sound all right in the light of established verbal connections. The logician's trick of removing words and substituting letters is the principal source of the layman's confusions. The logician gains generality by the substitution, while the layman loses contact with familiar phrases. The letters *i*, *o*, and *z* in the preceding syllogism do not have established intraverbal connections with the words. The subject who relies on these connections finds that almost any answer sounds all right, and so he goes astray.

In another form of the experiment a subject is shown a single premise and asked to continue (Wilkins, 1928; Eidens, 1929). For example, what can you say about *B* if you know that all *A* are *B?* Subjects tend to continue, "Then all *B* are *A*." The typical responses to four initial premises are as follows:

1. If all *A* are *B*, *then all B are A.*
2. If no *A* are *B*, *then no B are A.*
3. If some *A* are *B*, *then some B are A.*
4. If some *A* are not *B*, *then some B are not A.*

Only (2) and (3) are valid, but all four occur frequently in the responses of naïve subjects. The subjects tend to convert statements into like statements. For the letters A and B the conversions sound plausible enough. If words are substituted, however, the habitual verbal associations make the false conversions sound ludicrous. The person who accepts (1) would never accept 'If all flowers are plants, then all plants are flowers.' Nor would the person who accepted (4) find it natural to say, 'If some plants are not flowers, then some flowers are not plants.' The statements rephrased with words are not structurally different. The difference is that the subject recognizes the intraverbal connections and accepts the familiar statement regardless of the logical form. These intraverbal connections can betray the subject even when familiar words are used. For example, 'If some flowers are not plants, then some plants are not flowers' is not a valid statement for the logician but would be acceptable to many nonlogicians. Again, 'If some fish are airplanes, then some airplanes are fish' is logically impeccable, but most laymen find the conclusion absurd (it violates familiar intraverbal bonds) and reject the entire suggestion as obviously false.

The Atmosphere Effect. The experiments with syllogisms are full of demonstrations that the particular choice of words used to frame the problem has an important effect upon the form of the reply. Perhaps the best illustration of the way our verbal habits lead us astray is to be found in what Woodworth and Sells (1935; Sells, 1936) have called the *atmosphere effect*. To exemplify this notion they point to careless constructions like 'The laboratory equipment in these situations were in many instances . . . .' The plural 'were' appears incorrectly because of the atmosphere of plurality created by the surrounding words. Atmosphere effect is still another name for the intraverbal connections, determining tendencies, or dependent probabilities of occurrence of verbal units.

More specifically, Woodworth and Sells argue that the words 'all,' 'no,' and 'some' in the premises of a syllogism give a verbal atmosphere that calls for a corresponding conclusion. Their experimental data support this argument. The atmosphere effect is, if anything, more pronounced for bright subjects than for dull ones. Almost anyone can be trapped into this kind of error. For instance, *Polk* is pronounced *poke*, with the *l* silent, and *folk* is pronounced *foke*, also with a silent *l*, and the white of an egg is pronounced . . . ? It is a rare subject who remembers that the white of the egg is not the yolk, but the albumen.

In these examples verbal habits operate as a substitute for thought. Habits that function faithfully for the illogical events of daily life are tricked and betrayed by a syllogism. In the realm of logic the most improbable sequences of words are acceptable: 'If two is smaller than three, then snow is white.' Most nonlogicians regard this sentence as a strange use of 'if-then.' The fact is that logic is a formal system, just as arithmetic is a formal system. To expect untrained subjects to think logically is much the same as to expect preschool children to know the multiplication table.

Scientists find that ordinary language is a poor system to symbolize the precise relations and distinctions with which they work. To avoid the traps of linguistic habits they make up languages that have explicitly defined symbols and relations among symbols. Then there is no temptation to fall back upon what sounds all right or what seems like common sense. To quote Whitehead, "When the initial statements are vague and slipshod, at every subsequent stage of thought, common sense has to step in to limit applications and to explain meanings. Now in creative thought common sense is a bad master. Its sole criterion for judgment is that the new ideas shall look like old ones. In other words it can act only by suppressing originality." A reliance on familiar patterns of words may save us from thinking about many routine chores and get us by in polite conversation, but in more exacting situations it can point our whole endeavor in the wrong direction and blind us to the answer that sits in plain sight.

Problem Solving

The search for the conscious elements of thought was a confusing failure. More and more psychologists came to feel that they had been asking the wrong questions. The functions, not the structure, of the mind seemed the more reasonable quest. Before a mind can be observed, it must function; the person who belongs to it must act or speak. Then it is possible to say something scientific about his acting and speaking. Questions about his mind can be left to others, for they are beyond the domain of science. Science must be a public, communicable affair, and minds are notoriously private.

The most radical form of this functional approach became known as *behaviorism* because its proponents insisted that the only scientific data available to psychologists are data about behavior. This brand of psychology had its roots in the study of animals. Darwin turned attention to evolution, and his work influenced many psychologists to compare man and animal. Morgan, Thorndike, Hobhouse, Yerkes, Washburn, Watson, and many others had for years been asking psychological questions about animals. These workers were accustomed to getting along without the aid of their subjects' introspections. If human introspections were unreliable, they had other methods.

Because the early behaviorists rejected introspective reports of the structure of the mind and worked predominantly with animals, it was sometimes assumed that they rejected all forms of language and refused to speak to their subjects. This assumption was quite wrong. Language was recognized as a form of behavior. They did not prefer the actions of the leg muscles to the actions of the speech muscles. Verbal behavior played a crucial role in their scheme of things. For Watson, at least, verbal behavior and thinking were identified (J. B. Watson, 1920).

The emphasis shifted, therefore, from the analysis of the thinker's mind to an analysis of his behavior, verbal or otherwise. The new interest was in the methods animals and people used to solve problems. What conditions lead to mistakes, and what conditions are necessary for success? Give people puzzles or practical problems and see what they do with them. The object is to study "the reasonably well specified behavior which occurs when an individual—human or infrahuman—engaged in active commerce with the environment meets an obstacle and his activity is impeded. One straightforward line of action is no longer apparent; the individual is faced with alternatives, must pause and choose" (D. M. Johnson, 1944).

The Pendulum Problem. To illustrate the kind of work that has been done with problem-solving behavior we shall discuss an experiment conducted by Maier (1930). The subjects were provided with four poles, two lengths of wire, eight pieces of lead tubing, a C-clamp, two burette clamps, and several pieces of chalk. They were told, "Your problem is to construct two pendulums, one of which will swing over this point (indicates cross on floor) and one that will swing over this other point (indicates other cross). These pendulums should be so constructed that they will have a piece of chalk fastened which will make a mark on the points on the floor just indicated." The solution to the pendulum problem is shown in Fig. 49.

The problem was used to determine the importance of preliminary instructions in problem solving. One group of subjects was given the problem with no additional instructions. Another group was shown several of the component parts of the solution: how to make a plumb line out of a cord, clamp, and pencil, how to make a long rod out of two short rods and a clamp, and how to hold a bar against the vertical edge of a doorway by wedging against it another bar that reached to the opposite vertical side of the doorway. Another group was given a hint, "I should like to have you appreciate how simple the problem would be if we could just hang the pendulums from a nail in the ceiling. Of course, that is not a possible solution, but I just want you to appreciate how simple the problem would be if that were possible." A final group was given both the component parts *and* the hint.

Only one subject out of the 62 used in the first three groups succeeded in solving the problem. Eight out of 22 subjects in the fourth group solved the problem. From these results Maier argues that the mere knowledge of the component parts of a solution is not enough. Some other factor, which he calls *direction*, is necessary to integrate the parts into a solution. On the other hand, direction alone is insufficient if the thinker is not familiar with the component parts of the solution. Both the correct direction and a knowledge of the components are necessary.

When the thinking starts off with false assumptions, it is very difficult to abandon them.   Some subjects attempted to build a tripod to support a pole from which the pendulums could be hung, but the structure invariably collapsed.   The direction had to shift to include the ceiling of the room.

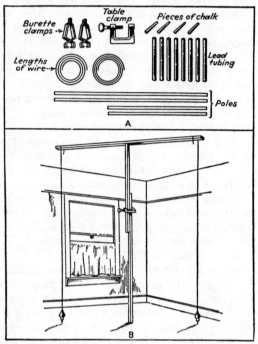

FIG. 49.   Materials available to the subject (*A*), and the correct solution of the pendulum (*B*).   (*From Crafts et al.*, 1950.)

The concept of direction is similar to the older concept of determining tendencies.   The situation and the subject's past experience produce a certain set toward the problem.   If his set does not lead to a solution, he has difficulty changing it.   On the other hand, something new is added in the solution of Maier's problem.   It is not merely a matter of selecting one from a number of familiar alternatives.   A new configuration of the alternatives is discovered. Maier makes the discovery of a new configuration the basis for a distinction between *productive* and *reproductive* thinking (Maier, 1940).   Something new is added as a result of productive thinking.

Recognizing the Solution.   Maier's study is only one of many that show the importance of the configuration of the component parts of a solution.   It is difficult to account for these configurational aspects of problem solving by association theory as it is usually put forward. It is not sufficient to say that the subject flounders about blindly in a trial-and-error manner until he accidentally hits upon the solution and that he remembers the associations among the component parts of his accidental solution. Solutions do not appear in a haphazard manner.

The usual way of stating the problem is to ask, *Where does the correct solution come from?* This question requires us to discover under what conditions a solution will appear. Thus Maier's experiment explores the thinker's knowledge and orientation as conditions governing the solution of a particular problem. Where the solution comes from is a difficult question. Things are simpler if we break it down into two questions: (1) *How do we generate possible solutions*, regardless of whether they are right or wrong? (2) *How is a correct solution recognized when it does occur?* We can assume for the moment that the thinker generates numerous solutions to a problem and that most of them are wrong. The wrong solutions are rejected, and eventually a solution appears that is accepted. Or if the solution is reached after a series of steps, choices must be made at each step between the wrong direction and the right. The problem is to discover how the choice is made. Introspection is no great help. Some possibilities are rejected unconsciously—they simply do not rise above the threshold for verbalization.

The importance of recognizing the answer when it occurs can be shown in terms of Huxley's typewriting monkeys. Six monkeys type at random for millions and millions of years. Eventually they produce every book in the British Museum just by the blind operation of chance. We know that thinking does not proceed by such stupid, trial-and-error methods. The thinker has his previous experience to draw upon, and this enables him to avoid many pitfalls. This previous experience is described by association theory as a network of verbal connections of great complexity and fluctuating strengths. Suppose we build these connections into the monkeys; we teach them to type letters in sequences corresponding to a fiftieth-order approximation to the statistical structure of English letters. Now the monkeys are constrained by contextual associations in much the same way the original authors were constrained. These associations enable the monkeys to reduce the time required by many millions of years. The point is, however, that even with these verbal habits established the monkeys would not know when they had produced a sonnet or a book or an answer to a problem. They would simply keep typing away, for one sequence of words would be no more useful than any other. The additional factor that the monkeys need in order to act like men is the ability to reject the trivial sequences and to preserve the important ones. Not only must a thinker generate possible solutions; he must recognize the correct one when it occurs to him. Just how the answer is recognized is a crucial problem for the student of thinking.

FIELD THEORIES AND THE RECODING PROCESS

We have come a long way with the association theorists. They offer us a detailed account of the acquisition of verbal behavior, of intraverbal associations, of information storage, and of the early thought experiments. On these problems they have very little competition from the field theorists. The field theorist is not concerned with choices of specific verbal responses. He prefers to talk about the over-all pattern or configuration. The specific responses may change while the configuration remains the same. Now that we have encountered what seems to be a purely configurational problem, therefore, we can turn to the field theorist for an explanation.

Field Theories of Thinking. The fullest accounts of thinking by the field theorists seem to be those of Duncker (1935) and Wertheimer (1945). These

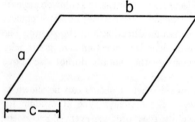

men speak of the pattern in which the component parts of the problem are arranged, the reorganizing principles imposed upon the components, and the eventual restructuring of the components in a form that coincides with the form of the desired solution.

FIG. 50.   The parallelogram problem.

Consider an example. In the course of teaching children to determine the area of a parallelogram

Wertheimer manages to introduce most of the puzzles that a theory of thinking must contend with. What, he asks, is the best way to teach school children to determine the area of a parallelogram? One way, an ugly but quite correct way, is to give the children the drawing shown in Fig. 50 and the following rules for manipulating the distances *a*, *b*, and *c*:

1. Subtract *c* from *a*.
2. Add *c* and *a*.
3. Multiply the sum and difference.
4. Take the square root of the product.
5. Multiply the root by *b*.

The result of these five steps is the area of the parallelogram. Children can memorize these five steps. They can generalize them to other parallelograms of different dimensions. Their answers are correct. And yet, Wertheimer protests, the method is ugly, and the teaching is terrible.

What is wrong with this method of teaching? The trouble is that the students are given no opportunity to grasp the inner structure of the situation. If you ask them, "Could you show that the answer obtained in this way is really right?" they have no way to answer.

If the area of the parallelogram is posed as a problem to children who have just learned to find the area of a rectangle, some do not respond, some try to remember, some start making speeches, some begin to think. For those who think, the trouble soon focuses on the two lopsided ends. Resolution comes when they see that one end needs just what is too much at the other end. If one end is cut off and fitted into the other end, the strange parallelogram becomes a familiar rectangle. The problem is solved.

Wertheimer's example draws a sharp distinction between blind connections and a structural grasp. If thinking is nothing more than behaving in accordance with conditioned reflexes or habits, there is little choice between these two methods of teaching. Associative bonds are associative bonds, and one bond is as good as another. In the simpler forms of association theory there is nothing to say that one set of connections is better to learn than another. A configurational theory, on the other hand, recognizes troublesome regions that must be manipulated and transposed according to the structural requirements of the solution.

Is this an explanation? Have the field theorists answered the question, or have they merely posed it more clearly? Suppose we grant that there are two ways to tackle a problem, one that involves the blind memorizing of associative bonds and the other that involves a more intelligent manipulation and organization of the component parts. What do we know about this more intelligent form of solution?

Restructuring and Recoding. To begin the analysis of what field theorists mean when they talk about restructuring the problem situation, take a very simple example. One field theorist (Katona, 1940) told people that the Federal expenditures in a certain year amounted to 5812151922.26, and they memorized the figure. A week later he asked them if they remembered the number. They remembered that the expenditures were about 5.81 billions, but the rest of the number had been forgotten. Another group of subjects was instructed simply to "try to learn the following series." These subjects discovered that if the numbers were grouped 5–8–12–15–19–22–26, the difference between successive numbers is 3, 4, 3, 4, 3, and 4. When they discovered this principle, most of the subjects were able to remember the answer a week later.

In this simple task the difference between memorizing and organizing is again illustrated. The subjects who discover an organizing principle are superior to those who do not. The task also illustrates something we can call *recoding*, and in many problems it can be shown that the restructuring process is, in whole or in part, a matter of coding the information in a new form. The amount of information in a sequence of symbols is a simple function of the number of symbols only so long as the symbols are independent and equally likely (cf. Chap. 5). If a particular symbol can be predicted from the symbols surrounding it, then successive symbols are not independent and the sequence does not carry the maximum amount of information. Only the unpredictable symbols can carry information; the symbol that is known in advance can tell us nothing new. When symbols are not independent, when some sequences are more probable than others, it is possible to recode the information into a form that uses fewer symbols. This recoding simply reduces or eliminates the redundancy and makes each new symbol carry a greater portion of the load.

In the light of these remarks consider once again the sequence of numbers used in the example. When these numbers are presented as the Federal expenditures there is no reason to suspect dependencies among them. Any sequence of 12 digits seems reasonable, and the subject assumes there are 12 independent items of information. The second group of subjects discovered that this is not true. The sequence is redundant. Once this discovery is made, the sequence can be recoded in a more efficient way, in a way more easily remembered. In the recoded form it is necessary to remember only that the sequence starts with 5, that you add first 3 and then 4 and 3, etc., and that there are 7 members of the sequence. The essential information consists of the numbers 5, 3, 4, and 7. Now compare the two groups of subjects again. The first group remembered 3 digits, and the second group remembered the equivalent of 4 digits.

The recoding principle is one of the most powerful tools of science. To take a familiar illustration, consider the law of falling bodies. Suppose that we want to know how far a body falls through space when it has been falling freely for a given number of seconds. One way to tackle this problem is to make measurements, summarize the measurements in a table, and then memorize the table. At the end of 1 sec the body has fallen 16 ft, at the end of 2 sec it has fallen 64, at the end of 3 it has fallen 144, after 4 it has fallen 256, etc. Then we memorize: 16, 64, 144, 256, 400, etc. This is a very stupid way to proceed because we memorize each number as if it were unrelated to all the other numbers. There is a relation, successive symbols are not independent, and all the measurements can be recoded into a simple rule that says the distance fallen at the end of t sec is $gt^2/2$. The value of g is about 32. All we need remember is $16t^2$. Now we store all the measurements away in memory by storing this simple formula.

Scientists are constantly looking for dependencies of this sort. When they discover one, it becomes possible to summarize large masses of recorded data in a short, simple sequence of symbols. The relations, if they are significant enough, get themselves dignified as laws or basic principles of the science. The law and the original data contain the same information, but it is packaged in a rememberable form by the law.

Recoding operates in our daily experience, though less precisely than it does in science. We witness a complex event that we want to remember. We cannot recall all the details, and so we select that information which seems critical, encode it in words, and remember the words. Our choice of what is worth recoding and remembering is not always a wise one, and we are seldom able to reconstruct the original event exactly.

It would seem, therefore, that when the field theorist talks about 'restructuring' we can often substitute the word 'recoding.' The fact that the field theorists tend to use visual problems that can be presented only in the form of a picture or diagram tends to make them use words like 'see' the solution, the 'form' or 'structure' of the problem, 'look for' missing relations, 'focus' on a trouble area, etc. These visual terms should not mislead us, for there are other kinds of patterns than visual patterns. The thinker who relies upon visual pictures of his problem will have many a hard day before he discovers why it is impossible to square the circle. The problem can be recoded in other ways than by a perceptual restructuring.

Recoding a Solution in Words. The importance of the recoding procedure makes itself felt when we try to translate a solution into words. Getting the solution into symbols is necessary for several reasons: (1) to verify it, (2) to make it precise, (3) to use it in further thinking, and (4) to communicate it to others. It is possible to solve a problem and still not be able to communicate it to others. The thinking process is not complete until the solution has become communicable. It is a common experience to have a sudden stroke of insight that resolves an entire problem, only to find when the insight is put into words that there are many things wrong with it. Indeed, it is often difficult to talk intelligibly about just those matters we have thought about most.

We can borrow another problem from Wertheimer to illustrate the difficulty. Suppose we are asked to prove that the opposite angles formed by the intersection of two straight lines are equal. In pictures, the problem is to prove that angles a and b in Fig. 51A are equal. Most of us would have to struggle

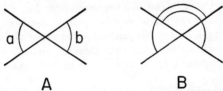

A   **B**

Fig. 51. The problem as posed in A is to prove that angle a equals angle b. Most subjects find the problem simpler if the angles are indicated as in B.

a bit with this problem, but if the experimenter draws the angles as in Fig. 51B, we have an almost immediate insight. The solution seems crystal clear. "This is equal to . . . and that . . . yes, yes, of course."

If we let the problem drop at this point, however, there is a good chance that we did not see the solution at all. Call the common angle c. Then we must write:

$$a + c = 180°,$$
$$b + c = 180°,$$
$$a + b + 2c = 360°,$$

and then . . . . But something has gone wrong! Just how do we state the solution? Try again:

$$a = 180° - c,$$
$$b = 180° - c,$$
$$\therefore a = b.$$

Ah, now we have it. But there's many a slip between the insight and the full, communicable statement.

In commenting on this problem, Wertheimer writes:

> The line of thinking, the direction, is in this case not *one* succession of items; there is a symmetrical two-directedness, each critical angle being dealt with as a part in its whole, formed by the introduction of the third angle, which subsequently can drop out again through the symmetry of the operations . . . . The successive habit— and so the widespread theory that thinking is by nature so—is due to its adequacy in summative situations in which the performance of one operation is merely additively connected with others. It is due further to the fact that we cannot write down two propositions simultaneously, that in reports we have to proceed with one thing after the other. That is one of the reasons why diagrams are often useful.

If a solution comes because several processes go on simultaneously, the problem is not solved until the simultaneous pattern of symbols is recoded in a successive pattern of symbols. Here is another instance where information in one pattern must be converted into another pattern. This kind of translation from one pattern to another runs through most of the thinking we do.

In overt speech we must use sequential forms. The speech mechanism can make only one sound at a time; only the dominant reaction tendency of the moment can use the final common path to the speech muscles. On the other hand, inner speech may be cast in a sequential form, but it is not necessarily so. Subvocal speech can consist of many reaction tendencies that compete and interact. At this level we compare and edit and search for words. Several directions of association may run simultaneously, and it may take minutes of introspective reporting to describe in sequential language a few seconds of inner speech.

We can conclude that thinking is not all done with words. If this were true, what need would there be for this final translation of the solution into communicable form? A man who did all his thinking verbally would not need this final process to restructure his thoughts in the sequential forms of language.

Anticipating the Solution. The field theorist describes the process of solving problems as a modification of the problem configuration that proceeds until the problem materials correspond to the configuration of the solution. The recognition of the solution when it occurs is the recognition that the problem configuration conforms to the solution configuration. This description makes it obvious that an understanding of what a solution might be like if we could find it is an important first step in thinking. In facing a problem it is often helpful to ask, Suppose I had solved this problem, what would the answer look like? This anticipation of the form of the solution enables us to narrow the range of alternatives and provides a goal toward which the problem materials can be manipulated. It may turn out that there are many different ways of recoding the problem materials to fit them into the schematic solution. This multiplicity of answers is characteristic of most of our daily decisions. Or there may be only one configuration, as is the case for most puzzles studied in the psychologist's laboratory. Or there may be no solution at all if we have asked a stupid question.

The psychologist's subjects have several advantages over thinkers outside the laboratory. They are usually assured that they have all the relevant information and that there is a single configuration of this information that fits the requirements of the solution. The practical case is less well defined. We encounter a situation where we have no appropriate response. We try those habit patterns which are easily available. If none works, we begin to realize we face a problem. Our verbal habits constrain us to familiar and perhaps unsuccessful formulations of an answer; our language forces our thought in certain directions. We struggle to reformulate the problem and to obtain the necessary information. We cannot even be sure there is an answer. Configurational aspects guide the process, but it is not always as clean and pretty as when an experimenter underwrites the happy ending.

The general procedure in thinking seems to be a search for new ways of encoding the information given by the problem. The search is guided by our conception of the form a solution must take or the form we want it to take. The contextual, or syntactic, patterns of the language impose constraints upon the configurations the answer can assume. The answer must come out in a sequence of words that seems probable against the background of our habitual intraverbal connections. Transformations of the problem materials that produce an improbable configuration are distrusted and are often discarded as opposed to common sense.

ABSTRACTION AND CONCEPT FORMATION

It is stupid to memorize a mass of details when the information they contain can be recoded into an easy-to-remember form. The question is how to discover that a new and simpler recoding is possible. What are the techniques for discovering dependencies?

The problem is how we find a general rule from an examination of several particular cases and what suggests to us that such a rule might exist. It is not the logical aspects of induction that concern us, but the psychological aspects. We hunt for similarities and try to discover a functional relation among them. The form this hunting takes varies as the nature of the problem varies. In the parallelogram we found a similarity between the two lopsided ends. In the sequence of numbers we found a similarity among the successive differences. Once the relation is found, the problem can be simplified.

The process of abstraction—finding similarities and discarding dissimilarities—has been studied in the laboratory. One technique (T. V. Moore, 1910) is demonstrated by the drawings in Fig. 52. These rows of designs were exposed to the subject by turning the disk behind a window. As the successive sets of designs appeared in the window, the subject searched for the common design that persisted in the successive sets. Another experimenter (Hull 1920) used groups of Chinese characters. Every character consisted of a basic

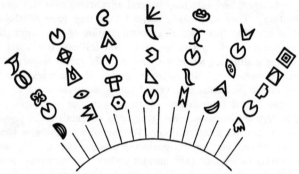

FIG. 52. Designs presented in a study of abstraction. The groups of five designs are exposed successively while the subject searches for the common design. (*From Moore*, 1910.)

radical embedded in complicating embellishments. There were 12 radicals, and each had a nonsense name. The question was how the subjects came to recognize correctly new members of a class by abstracting the common, radical aspects. Still another form of the abstraction experiment is illustrated in Fig. 53 (Smoke, 1932). A mib is a triangle with a line perpendicular to its shortest side. The subject sees the figures one at a time until he can give a definition of the nonsense name. Then he is asked to give the definition, draw some examples, or distinguish which is which in a test series.

These experiments show a gradual increase in correct responses. It often happens, however, that the subject is not able to express in words the rule he is using to make correct responses. Subjects may make consistently correct discriminations long before they are able to explain to someone else how they do it. After a brief inspection of Fig. 53, for example, you might be able to select mibs from non-mibs even though you could not give an accurate definition that some other person could use.

An abstraction is a response to one aspect of a complex situation regardless of the context in which the aspect occurs (cf. Chap. 8). The evidence indicates that new concepts and new abstractions are formed slowly and depend upon the gradual accumulation of knowledge about and experience with the kind of problem faced. When we ask how a new abstraction is formed, we are asking how the learning process operates to strengthen associations between certain invariant aspects of the materials and the particular response that symbolizes this aspect. Our verbal habits are a treasury of abstractions learned in just this way.

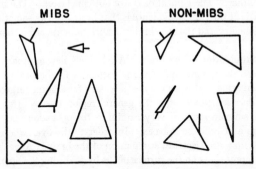

FIG. 53. The designs are exposed one at a time, and the subject attempts to form a definition of the word 'mib.'

APHASIA

We often gain valuable knowledge about a process when we see it break down. Thinking goes on in the brain. What happens to thinking when the brain is damaged? Since we are concerned primarily with the relation between thinking and talking, we shall confine this discussion to those cases where brain damage affects verbal behavior. These cases are known as *aphasia*. We shall ask, What happens to thinking when different verbal functions are damaged or destroyed?

Most of the medical history of aphasia (Head, 1926, Vol. I) is concerned with the problem, Is there a particular place in the brain that governs speech? In 1861 Paul Broca provided the first evidence that there might be a restricted region or center in the brain entrusted with the control of speech. This center was located in the left third frontal convolution. Broca's evidence consisted of anatomical studies of damage in the brains of patients who had suffered a loss of speech. Broca believed that linguistic disturbances could always be attributed to lesions in this center, which came to be called *Broca's area*.

There has been much controversy about the importance of Broca's area in aphasia and about the whole concept of localizing complex psychological processes in a restricted area of the brain (Morgan and Stellar, 1950, Chaps. 21–26). Those opposed to the concept argue that to locate the damage that destroys speech and to localize speech are two different things. Not all patients suffer the same defects. To many students of aphasia it seems more important to classify the kinds of functions that are impaired than to locate the spot on the brain that causes the trouble. Aphasic symptoms can arise from lesions in so many different places that the clinician is seldom able to advise the surgeon where to apply his knife. Among the modern investigators one can find almost every point of view, ranging from a belief in strict, detailed localization at one extreme to a belief in a generalized loss of abstract intelligence at the other. The clinical data are not conclusive. The most one can say on the basis of the clinical evidence is that brain injuries sometimes produce a linguistic difficulty and that the brains of such patients often show damage in Broca's area.

Electrical Stimulation of the Brain. A relatively new approach that can be used to explore the integration of verbal behavior in the brain makes use of electrical stimulation. It is sometimes necessary for a brain surgeon to remove damaged or diseased tissue from the general region that is often involved in speech. The surgeon must be very careful or the operation may damage the speech centers and produce aphasia. In order to discover where the speech centers are he may use electrical stimulation of the brain. A weak stimulus is applied at different spots on the surface of the brain during the operation. The patient's verbal behavior is observed as the stimulus is moved about. When the stimulus produces vocalization or interferes with speech, the surgeon tries to leave the area intact, for the chances are that removing this tissue will produce an aphasia.

The most extensive reports of such stimulation and its effects on verbal behavior are contained in the work of Penfield and Rasmussen (1950). They found that vocalization without words has a definite localization in the sensorimotor area of the human cerebral cortex on both sides. Arrest of speech, or the spontaneous statement on the part of the subject that he wanted to talk but could not, was also produced by stimulation in much the same sensorimotor areas. This arrest was instantaneous, as though some portion of the motor mechanism needed in speaking were inhibited or were preempted for some other movement. When a patient was asked for an explanation, he might say, 'I couldn't get my words out,' 'I felt like stuttering,' 'could not open mouth,' 'could not get breath.' Production of vocalization by stimulation always interrupted speaking.

Sometimes, stimulation of Broca's area on the dominant hemisphere also produced arrest of speech. In this case, however, the blocking occurred without associated movement or sensation. The patient was apt to explain afterward, for example, that 'I didn't know what I was counting' or 'I could not think.'

Motor elements required in speaking, such as vocalization and movements of lips, tongue, diaphragm, etc., have representation in the sensorimotor cortex on both sides of the brain. Speech could be interrupted by stimulating the facial area on either side of the brain, but speech was not abolished when those areas were removed. Stimulation of Broca's area did not produce either speech or vocalization, but it could interrupt speech because it interfered with what the patient called thinking.

The Clinical Picture. In order to appreciate the great complexity of aphasic symptoms it is necessary to consider some actual cases. Most clinicians recognize three general types of aphasia: (1) *expressive*, where the ability to talk is more impaired than the ability to perceive speech, (2) *receptive*, where spoken sounds are not correctly perceived although the ability to talk is relatively intact, (3) *amnesic*, where the patient forgets the names of common objects, although his ability to perceive speech and to produce it are otherwise unimpaired. We shall give two examples of each of these types of aphasia.

Cases of Expressive Aphasia. The first case is reported by K. Goldstein (1948, 190) to illustrate the simplest form of expressive aphasia. At the age of fifty the patient, a businessman, suffered a stroke that paralyzed his right arm and left him speechless. He remained well oriented in space and time, understood questions, followed directions. His intelligence did not seem changed after the stroke. He was in normal contact with his family and remained interested in his business. He responded normally in tests of abstraction that required him to respond to particular aspects of a situation regardless of the context in which the aspects occurred. His only trouble was that he could not speak. Only occasionally some words such as 'yes,' 'no,' or 'oh God,' might occur, but he could not repeat these on request. He was able to indicate what he wanted to say by knocking on the table with his fingers to tell how many letters or syllables were in the word he could not speak. Repetition and reading aloud were totally lacking. Since the right hand was paralyzed, he was forced to write with the left. With the left hand he was able to write spontaneously, to take dictation, and to copy. He could move his lips, jaw, and tongue correctly on request or in imitation of the doctor's movements.

A more interesting and ironic case has been reported by Weisenberg and McBride (1935, 160). It illustrates an expressive aphasia complicated by some receptive difficulties. The unlucky victim was a man forty-nine years old, a professor of Romance languages who had seven different languages at his command. This man was taking a train trip when he suffered a thrombosis of the left middle cerebral artery. He discovered his plight when he tried to talk to a porter. He was unable to utter a sound. A few minutes later paralysis of the right side of his body began, affecting both his arm and leg. In a few days he began to improve, but progress was slow, and 8 weeks after the attack he was speaking with considerable effort, often hesitating, and always having difficulty in the articulation of words. The following conversation is the most adequate speech he could manage during these early interviews:

(Do you sometimes think of words more easily in some other language besides English?) Yes . . . yes . . . constantly . . . the . . . I feel . . . the "family" . . . er, "members of the family" . . . I get in Spanish . . . and French rather . . .

rather . . . er rather than in English . . . an' English is not coming . . . . (Does the German come easily?) No! . . . (Or Italian?) No . . . . Except in "ausgegangen" . . . and so forth . . . . I study my German for eight and nine and ten and eleven . . . and so forth . . . an' humorously . . . "ausgegangen" . . . an' my German . . . I . . . er learn it at school for six years . . . an' Junior and Senior in college . . . I took it up again.

This man could count, name the days of the week and the months of the year, and run through the alphabet without much difficulty. He made some errors in naming objects, but most of his difficulties were expressive rather than perceptive. He could repeat words, understand conversation, and carry out fairly complex instructions. When reading aloud he proceeded slowly and made many mistakes in pronunciation, but he indicated his comprehension of the material by answering questions on it. In writing he formed simple sentences and complained that he had to use "schoolgirl English." The following letter is an illustration:

Dear Anne:

I like the flowers very much and I feel perfcetly wild about them. Send some up to-morrow. I feel a right to-day, but I am anxious to go out the next Saturday.

'The next Saturday' is more nearly French than English construction, a type of error that he made rather frequently. His writing in French or Spanish was equally simple. In writing to dictation, however, he was above the average normal performance.

When the examination was begun, during the third month after the attack, it was noted that names of objects, colors, or other words sometimes came to him first in French or Spanish. When he was questioned about his use of French or Spanish constructions with English words, he usually failed to recognize the error. The foreign languages, like the English, were disturbed in particular ways, and those performances which suffered most in English were also most severely affected in the foreign languages. In each foreign language, as in English, the patient understood far more than he could express. During the next 9 months there was a gradual and consistent improvement in all the languages. Fourteen months after the attack he was able to return to work and taught successfully about half his usual number of hours.

Cases of Receptive Aphasia. Almost as distressing as the linguist who could not express himself is the case of the lawyer who could not understand what was said to him (Weisenberg and McBride, 1935, 222). The lawyer's attack came shortly after the death of his wife. While attempting to telephone he found he could not make himself understood. The following record was taken from one of his conversations 2 weeks after the attack:

I just sat here last night by himself . . . wrote these things that I told myself . . . now they're things that I just made lying here in the night while I had no one to live . . . didn't want anyone . . . she really wasn't fit for it . . . she ought to have been in bed several months . . . several days . . . (Gestured to indicate behavior of nurse who had a bad cold in her head.) . . . like this all night . . . and I couldn't stay awake . . . I couldn't sleep, with all that thing to have her.

Although spontaneous speech was disturbed, it was nevertheless plentiful and freely articulated. This patient had less difficulty than the professor when he tried to talk. The lawyer's chief trouble came when he tried to understand speech. He had great difficulty understanding directions or questions that contained more than one word. A simple question answered correctly by the average four-year-old child, 'What must you do when you are cold?' was too difficult for this man who had been one of the outstanding attorneys in his state.

He improved during the first month but was still unable to respond to commands or questions that involved a twofold direction or two key words. His ability to read was also seriously impaired. Sometimes he would garble the words and confuse a whole sentence but still be able to indicate by checking an illustrative picture that he had understood the statement. At other times he would read the sentence correctly and mark the wrong picture. His failure to respond appropriately was more marked with the more complex sentences, and here he misread and misunderstood simple names that separately would not have confused him. His difficulty in grasping words was so great that he could not repeat four digits, three words, or sentences of six syllables. His short memory span is reflected in his speech, for he could not seem to remember how his sentences had started. On nonverbal material he was less handicapped than he was in understanding language.

In the 2 years following the attack the lawyer improved considerably, and he was able eventually to follow ordinary conversations. He had difficulty whenever he attempted to carry on two or more conversations at once and also failed to respond adequately to complex statements that had no direct reference to the particular, concrete situation.

The lawyer's case represents a predominantly receptive aphasia complicated by some expressive disturbances. A case that illustrates receptive difficulties in a purer form has been reported by K. Goldstein (1948, 223). The patient, a thirty-four-year-old seaman, had no disturbance of visual perception and was able to hear tones normally. Memory for previous and recent events was normal. He had poor mathematical abilities that were probably due to a poor education. His intelligence was average. He did not often speak spontaneously but answered in well-constructed sentences, sometimes hesitantly. He sometimes failed to name objects correctly, but this ability improved with time. His perception of speech was not grossly disturbed in normal conversation, although here and there he missed a sentence. Following directions was often impossible. He showed wrong objects or parts of his body when they were named. His ability to repeat spoken words was highly disturbed. If one began to recite the alphabet, he could repeat correctly, but he did not recognize the mistake if a letter was omitted or a wrong one was given. Counting showed similar difficulties. He was seldom able to repeat sentences, and nonsense syllables he refused to repeat. Reading was unimpaired. His poor writing may have been due to his poor education. Copying was accurate. He could write at dictation only those words he was able to repeat. When he tried to repeat spoken words, he did not often confuse words that sounded alike; he was more apt to confuse words belonging to the same associative cluster (*e.g.*, 'church' instead of 'God,' 'house' instead of 'village,' 'cat' instead of 'mouse').

Cases of Amnesic Aphasia. As a clear-cut example of amnesic aphasia, Weisenberg and McBride (1935, 302) give the following description of a thirty-five-year-old salesman. This man's spontaneous speech was hesitant but well articulated. His conversation was often delayed for several seconds while he tried to recall some particular word. During the delay he made frequent use of phrases such as 'in fact,' 'of course,' 'naturally.' He could count, name the days of the week and the months of the year, or recite the alphabet. It was always easier for him to produce these items in their serial order than it was to produce any item of the series of itself. On the perceptual side, the patient could repeat single words and short sentences with no difficulty in articulation, but sometimes he did not follow directions correctly. Silent reading was slightly better than reading aloud, but both were slow and inaccurate. He could write only simple words on dictation and his spelling was very poor. Simple arithmetic was fairly good, but two- or three-place numbers caused difficulty. He could not remember the result of one computation while he worked on the other. His memory span was adequate for only four digits, three letters, or sentences of five or six syllables. His memory of a short story showed that he remembered more of it than he was able to express in suitable words. He could reproduce learned material most readily when precise verbal formulation was least essential.

Although these difficulties in expressive and receptive functions seem severe, the core of this patient's trouble was his inability to remember words. When he could not name an object, he could usually recognize its name. For example, when he was asked to name a large pocketbook he could not, but he rejected the suggestions that it might be a map, a trunk, a purse, money, or a bag and accepted the exact name immediately. His word poverty did not seem as severe in concrete cases or when he could rely upon an automatic type of response. But in abstract thinking he was continually handicapped. When asked the difference between 'wood' and 'glass,' he talked about wood alone, then complained that he had forgotten the other word.

A rather striking case of amnesic aphasia has been studied by Gelb and Goldstein (K. Goldstein, 1948, 253). The patient was a German soldier who had been injured by a grenade. This patient talked a lot, had no motor difficulty, and showed normal sentence formation. His spontaneous speech showed a lack of nouns, adjectives, verbs, and particularly the names of concrete objects. His ability to repeat words, sounds, and short sentences was normal. He could select a named object out of a large collection of objects, but he could not name the object when it was presented to him. A knife was called 'for cutting,' scissors 'for cutting,' a tape measure 'to measure,' a penholder 'for writing,' etc. The response was usually accompanied by expressive pantomime. His inability to name colors was so marked that he seemed color-blind. He could not call a color simply 'red' but might suggest that it was 'cherry red' or 'strawberry red,' etc.

The patient was given a heap of colored woolen skeins. He was asked to pick out all the skeins of a given color and put them together. Or he was given one skein and asked to choose strands of the same or similar color. When he was asked to sort the skeins to find all similar colors, regardless of brightness, he proceeded slowly and hesitantly. He had great difficulty with this task. He made wrong selections, sometimes picked up the right one but rejected it, etc. He compared a sample again and again with the skeins until he chose some that were identical or very similar to the sample. Though urged to go on, he could choose only a small number. The task of choosing identical colors was done quickly and correctly. Sometimes he would match a very bright shade of red with a blue or green skein of equal brightness. Sometimes other aspects, softness, coldness, warmth, etc., determined his choice. The surprising thing, however, was that although he seemed to be choosing according to a certain attribute he was not able to choose in this way if he was asked to do so. He might, for example, arrange the skeins as if guided by an attempt to produce a scale of brightness. He would begin with a bright red, then add one less bright, and so on to a dull red one. But when later asked to place the skeins in succession according to brightness, he was incapable of doing it. These disturbances show that his amnesic aphasia had effects upon his ability to form abstractions, effects that extended far beyond the purely verbal difficulties.

Gelb and Goldstein were struck by the possibility that the basic difficulty in amnesic aphasia is the difficulty of forming abstractions. In order to remember that a certain object is called a chair, we must be able to use the abstraction that has been built up through experience with numerous chairs. The particular chair must be associated with an abstract category of objects. When the patient responds 'something to sit in,' he demonstrates that he is familiar with the object but has not performed the operation of associating this particular object with others to form the abstract class of chairs. Only when two things are nearly identical does the patient class them together. He does not forget the word 'chair,' but it does not occur to him as a category independent of some particular event (cf. K. Goldstein, 1940, Chap. 3).

Some Speculative Conclusions. The clinical picture of aphasia and its various manifestations does not permit a simple analysis. Nevertheless, there are some speculative conclusions we can draw about the importance of the different verbal functions in thinking.

Consider first the expressive aphasic. What seem to be lost here, to a more or less severe extent, are the sequential coordinations necessary for the production of connected speech. In some cases all sequential motor functions of speech seem lost. The patient must begin again by relearning the coordinations for the individual speech sounds, then learn how to combine these into syllables and words, then learn how to combine the words into sentences. Even after successful retraining, the expressive aphasic has much difficulty with grammatical forms. The little words—articles and prepositions—do not come easily and readily and must be searched out each time they are needed. The little words are often omitted, which makes his speech sound like a headline or a telegram. The contextual constraints of the sentence do not act automatically to reduce the range of alternatives that can be selected for each succeeding word.

Cases of expressive aphasia have been reported in which the patient's ability to think was described as unimpaired. It is often difficult to know what the clinician meant or what tests he used, but presumably the patient could still solve problems, form abstractions, and perform well on an intelligence test. So long as the task does not involve the production of speech, the patient behaves normally. From this we must conclude that thinking can be carried on without the aid of the sequential habits of normal speech. Normal subjects often *substitute* these sequential habits for thinking and so produce the answer with less effort. But it is clear that we cannot identify thinking with the running off of verbal sequences.

Consider next the receptive aphasic. This patient can be likened to the normal subject in an articulation test. The normal subject hears an acoustic pattern and then selects one out of a set of alternative words as the word he has just heard. As noise or distortion is introduced into the channel, the information content of the acoustic pattern is reduced. With a marginal amount of information coming through, the subject may not be able to narrow down the range of alternatives to the one correct response. If he gets only the vowel sound, he can narrow his search to the set of words containing that vowel. But then he must guess. The patient with receptive aphasia is in a similar situation, except that the distortion is introduced within his own nervous system. Not enough information gets through to enable him to narrow his search down to the one correct response. His private distortions do not lead him to confuse words that sound similar. The patient confuses words in the same associative cluster. Enough information may get through to narrow his search to a group of associated words, but exactly which word it was he cannot decide.

Like the subject in the articulation test, the receptive aphasic is often aided by context. It is not unusual to find that a word in isolation evokes the wrong response; yet when the word is used in a sentence he responds adequately. Or a subject may perceive a word correctly when he cannot repeat the individual vowels and consonants that make up the word.

Since receptive aphasia is known to exist in a relatively pure form without serious damage to other psychological functions, we conclude that these perceptual processes are not an indispensable element of the thinking process.

The perceptual processes involved in recognition and the motor processes involved in the production of spoken sequences are both peripheral to the thinking process. When we come to the amnesic aphasic, however, we find a close relation between the deterioration of verbal performance and ability to solve problems and form abstractions. These patients usually show a defect of categorical behavior. A group of similar objects cannot be associated in such a way as to form a category that includes them all. It is as if the associative clusters themselves had been damaged or destroyed. The patient with amnesic aphasia cannot handle two aspects of a situation simultaneously or shift from one attitude to another. Since he cannot form abstractions or move easily from one abstraction to another, the patient cannot deal with problems in the same way a normal person does. Still, he may be able to solve problems and deal with objects in a specific, concrete situation.

Expressive and receptive difficulties may modify the way the patient thinks, but a loss of categorical behavior provides a serious handicap for both talking and thinking. The normal individual is able to abstract a common property of a group of objects or events. This property receives a name. During thinking this abstraction is associated with other abstractions until a configuration occurs which is recognized as a solution to the problem. When the ability to abstract is impaired, speech shows a lack of nouns and verbs, the names of the abstractions. And thinking cannot proceed by the association of abstractions but is bound to the particular and the concrete.

DISCUSSION QUESTIONS

1. How could you determine experimentally whether or not the direction of thinking is a matter of trial and error?

2. What is a hunch?

3. Can you distinguish several levels of abstraction?

4. Why do the problems of the ancient Greek geometers appeal to field theorists as materials for the study of thinking?

5. What would happen if you gave subjects an unsolvable problem? Do you think they might become emotional about it?

6. Give some instances where verbal habits: (1) make things look like problems that really are not; (2) mislead the thinker in finding a simple solution; (3) are inadequate for phrasing the problem or its solution.

Selected References

Goldstein, K. *Language and Language Disturbances*. New York: Grune and Strattan, 1948. A summary of the author's observations and conclusions on aphasia over a period of more than forty years.

Hadamard, J. *The Psychology of Invention in the Mathematical Field*. Princeton, N.J.: Princeton University Press, 1945. A mathematician wonders how he does it.

Humphrey, B. *Directed Thinking*. New York: Dodd, Mead, 1948. A very readable account of the psychology of thinking.

Titchener, E. B. *Experimental Psychology of the Thought Processes*. New York: Macmillan, 1909. Reviews the early thought experiments, discusses at length the matter of imagery during thought.

Wertheimer, M. *Productive Thinking*. New York: Harper, 1945. A field theorist examines the problem of thinking.

Woodworth, R. S. *Experimental Psychology*. New York: Holt, 1938. Chapters 29 and 30 deal with problem solving and thinking.

Chapter 12

THE SOCIAL APPROACH

> The increase of communication may not only fail to give agreement in valuations and modes of conduct but may actually be used to increase conflict, competitiveness, and slavery. For sharing a language with other persons provides the subtlest and most powerful of all tools for controlling the behavior of these other persons to one's advantage—for stirring up rivalries, advancing one's own goals, exploiting others.
>
> —C. W. MORRIS

Social organization without communication is impossible. The influence of a group can extend only as far as the group has effective channels for communication. A person who does not talk to any of the members of a group is necessarily isolated from that group. A person who talks only to members of one group is necessarily dependent upon that group for all his information. The pattern of communication among members of various social groups is an important key to social structure. The relation between the pattern of communication and the eventual action of the group is quite complex. We can study it in detail only for small groups of people in rather artificial situations. When we want to study the circulation of information among thousands or millions of people, a statistical summary must be used. This chapter shows how the communication net can affect the behavior of small groups, examines statistically the factors controlling information flow in large groups, and considers the conditions under which propaganda and rumor are most effective.

COMMUNICATION NETS

Before we tackle the practical problems and experimental methods of the social approach, we must first develop a language for talking about relations among the members of a *social group*. A social group is two or more people held together by a *social relation*. The relation among the members can be any interpersonal relation that we are able to define and recognize. The relation that we are most interested in is 'talks to' or 'communicates with.' We can state the communicative organization of the group by a series of sentences of the form 'A talks to B' or 'A does not talk to B.' Such a sentence is given for every pair of members in the group. In the same way, other relations can be used to show other organizational aspects of the group. 'Is a friend of,'

249

'pays money to,' 'commands,' 'disagrees with,' etc., are all recognizable social relations. Any one or more of these relations may play an important role in the functions of the group.

The Pattern of Channels. The structure of the group under the relation 'talks to' forms a *communication net*. The communication net is described completely by the set of sentences that state whether the relation holds between every pair of members. These statements can be treated as a kind of algebra (Luce and Perry, 1949; Luce, 1950), but it is simpler to think of them in terms of diagrams. The different members of the group are designated in the diagram by letters. If the relation holds between any two, then an arrow is drawn from the first letter to the second. Two communication nets are diagramed in Fig. 54. The net on the left represents part of the net formed during a radio broadcast. The talker on the radio, A, can speak to all the other members,

Fig. 54. Diagrams illustrating different communication nets. Letters represent members of the group, and the arrows indicate the directions in which messages can pass.

but none of the others can speak to him. C and D can communicate, but all the rest are isolated. According to some definitions this broadcasting net does not organize the members into a group. The net permits action, but not interaction, among the members. The diagram on the right in Fig. 54 might represent the net formed by five people meeting face to face to discuss a topic. Every member can talk to every other member. This sort of organization in a face-to-face situation is sometimes called a *primary group*.

According to our definitions, all the telephone subscribers in the world form a social group. Telephonic channels of communication exist whereby any one can talk to any other one. Ordinarily we would not refer to this collection of people as a social group because the fact is that they do not communicate. Only a tiny fraction of all the possible telephone connections is ever used. This fact suggests that we should modify our statement of the communicative relation. Instead of saying who *can* communicate with whom, we are more interested in who *does* communicate with whom. So we introduce the notion of *traffic density*. If a particular channel is frequently used, we say it has a high traffic density. If another channel is never used, we say it has zero traffic density. All channels with zero traffic density can be discarded in our study of a social group because they cannot affect the way the group functions. Any channel that exists but is not used might as well not exist; it can be deleted from the diagram of the communication net.

The traffic density over each of the arrows in the diagram can be indicated by a number that tells how many messages pass over the channel per unit of time. A high traffic density indicates that the particular channel is important in the functioning of the group. Analysis of the traffic densities can reveal bottlenecks in group communication that may decrease the group's efficiency.

It is sometimes necessary to modify the statement of the relation 'talks to' still further. In primary groups any talker is necessarily heard by every other member, and yet his remarks may be addressed to a particular member of the group. If we wish to preserve this distinction in the description of a communication net, we can distinguish two nets. One net shows the traffic densities for *directed communications*, the other for *undirected communications*. The radio broadcast is almost necessarily undirected, whereas the telephone net carries nothing but directed communications.

The Pattern of Information. In addition to these qualifications of the basic relation, there are numerous qualifications that we may want to impose upon the description of the members. Suppose, for example, that the communication net exists for the sole purpose of spreading information to all members of the group. For any particular item of information, therefore, we would like to be able to say whether or not each member had received it. The statement of which members know which items is the *pattern of group information*. For example, in a three-member group all three may know the item, or only A and B, or A and C, or B and C, or only A, or B, or C, or none of the three members may know the item. In this example there are eight different patterns of information about a single item among the three members of the group. In general, there are 2^{mn} different patterns of information among m members with respect to n different items of information. Thus we see that the information patterns of the group are quite numerous and varied, even for relatively small groups.

The pattern of group information changes as the group communicates. One pattern exists if only A knows a particular item. As soon as A communicates this item to B, however, the pattern shifts. Therefore it is necessary to state the time at which any particular pattern of information existed. If we know the pattern at any particular time, and if we also know the order in which the different members communicated, we can reconstruct the pattern at any later point in time. A group continues to communicate until the pattern is one in which every member knows every item of information. When this uniform pattern is attained, there is no longer any need to communicate. Then the group activity stops until some new item of information is introduced.

This description raises the question, however, as to how the members of the group know when they are finished. How can one member know that all the other members know everything he has to say? Or, more generally, how do the members know the pattern of information at any time? If B knows a particular item, it is a waste of time for A to tell him that item again. What A knows that B knows must govern what A communicates to B. In other words, two kinds of information must be communicated. The *primary information* is the message that the group is attempting to circulate. The *secondary information* is knowledge about who knows what, knowledge of which pattern of information exists at the moment.

The particular primary information that the group is trying to communicate has little to do with the way the group operates. The secondary information, however, is determined by the structure of the net and can have a strong influence on the behavior of the members. Secondary information is given to the talker by the recipients' responses. If the talker says, 'John has a black coat,' he conveys primary information to the recipient. If a recipient then conveys this message to another person, the original talker can listen also to see that the message is relayed correctly. But he cannot check that his message got across if his recipient never repeats it or if it is repeated where he cannot hear it. The secondary information, that the recipient knows the item, must somehow return to the original talker. Thus in the functioning of the group the repetition of messages serves as a safeguard against mistakes. If the talker never hears his message repeated correctly, he must assume that a mistake was made somewhere. In that case he must try again. So he repeats his message until the recipients eventually show him that they have received his information correctly. Then he can proceed to the next item.

In normal conversation secondary information is conveyed by facial expressions, 'yes,' 'what,' etc., or the general relevance of subsequent behavior. These responses carry no primary information. They simply advise the talker about the recipient's state of information. In Chap. 8 the importance of the listener's response is discussed in terms of the reinforcement it provides for the talker's behavior. Such reinforcements are a kind of secondary information; the talker is rewarded by learning that he has communicated successfully. When the reinforcement is given, it reduces the talker's need to communicate. Thus every communication plays a double role, for it both lets the people know and also lets the people know that the people know.

Reasons for Social Communication. In the preceding example it is assumed that the purpose of the net is to provide information to the members. The group functions until the pattern of information is homogeneous over all members. The net may serve other purposes. If the group is organized for the purpose of taking some particular action, it may not be necessary to continue until everybody knows everything. It may be sufficient that a single person, the leader or the spokesman of the group, have all the information.

In many groups an important function of the net is to permit the members to reach a common opinion. In spontaneous groups, where members can join or resign freely, uniformity of opinion is often an important condition for the survival of the group. If the group is divided by a strong difference of opinion, members on the two sides of the argument communicate in order to change the opinions of the others. If the difference cannot be resolved, the group may split.

The analysis of the opinion-spreading group is not greatly different from the analysis of the information-spreading group. The question becomes, Who *believes* this item? instead of, Who *knows* this item? The primary information takes the form of arguments pro or con. The secondary information is carried by the recipient's reply. The reply tells the talker whether he has succeeded in changing the recipient's opinion. Instead of the pattern of information, we specify the *pattern of opinion* at successive instants in time. The group continues to function until it reaches unanimity or becomes exhausted.

The description of group communication can become still more complex if some additional relation is imposed upon the members. The most important additional relation is 'dominates' or 'is superior to.' In most groups some members have higher status than others. Such groups are called *hierarchies*. The hierarchy structure is described completely by listing, for each member, every member who is his superior. In these groups it is well to keep track, not only of who talks to whom, but of the status level of both members. Differences of status influence the traffic density over the different channels and play an important role in determining which way opinions change.

We have assumed that the members of a group are motivated to communicate with one another in order to attain uniformity of information or of opinion within the group. Another reason for communicating is to change one's position in the group or to move from one group to another. A member may wish to change his status in a hierarchy or may wish to join some subgroup within the larger group. When a member cannot move in the desired direction, he wants to talk about it.

Still another important reason for communication is the desire on the part of the members to express their emotions. Festinger (1950) has pointed out that expressive messages are consummatory rather than instrumental. *Instrumental communication* requires feedback from the recipient. The talker wants to know whether or not his message had an effect. *Consummatory communication* does not depend upon the effect it has on others. The talker is usually not interested in secondary information about the effects of his consummatory communication. The expression of the emotion reduces his need to communicate regardless of its effects.

We have, therefore, four basic reasons for social communication, (1) to increase uniformity of information, (2) to increase uniformity of opinion, (3) to change status in the group, and (4) to express emotions. All four types of messages may travel over a net, and a single message may fall into more than one class. For example, a member may give information in the hope that it will lead the group to adopt his opinion and so prepare the way for his own promotion.

So much for the logic of social communication.

COMMUNICATION IN SMALL GROUPS

We turn now to some of the attempts to observe and record what goes on in group situations. The simplest way to go about this is to put a couple of people together in a room and watch them. We can keep a record that tells when both are silent, when one talks, or when both talk. Such a record of the timing of their conversation will show that at first they are quite polite. Neither interrupts, both wait for the other to finish. As they get to know each other, the rate of interaction increases and interruptions become more frequent. The proportion of the time that each person spends talking usually settles down after several interviews to a relatively constant value. The two individuals eventually approach a stable conversational relation (Chapple, 1940).

Problem Solving in a Free Situation. A better structured situation can be created by giving the people some task to perform together or some problem to solve. The results obtained from the group can then be compared with the results obtained from individuals working alone. For example, subjects were required to make up words out of the letters contained in a given word (G. B. Watson, 1928). One subject, working alone, could make up about 32 words in the time provided, but groups of five or six persons cooperated to produce about 75 words in the same length of time. We should not conclude from this result that the group is more efficient at this task than is the individual. If the same individuals worked alone and their work was later combined, it was found that they produced about 87 different words. Another experimenter (Shaw, 1932) posed more difficult problems to be solved. The groups obtained a higher proportion of successes than did persons who worked alone on these difficult problems. The group's advantage could be attributed to the fact that incorrect suggestions and mistakes were more readily caught and rejected. The redundancy of the group effort provided a safeguard against errors.

In order for a group to catch its mistakes, some members of the group must correct others. This usually involves changing opinions about what the group should do next. Under what conditions can opinions be changed? One condition involves the *cohesiveness* of the group. This property of groups is the attraction that the group has for its members and the strength of their desire to remain members. If a difference of opinion arises in a highly cohesive group, there are more attempts made to influence the members and the influence is more often accepted without resistance. When there is a range of opinion in the group, most of the communications tend to be directed toward those members whose opinions are at the extremes. The greater the pressure toward uniformity, the greater is the tendency to communicate to these extreme positions and the greater is the actual change toward uniformity (Festinger *et al.*, 1950).

Problem Solving with Restricted Nets. Most of the studies of group communication do not try to control the arrangement of channels between the members. The conference or committee situation is of major practical interest, and most experiments adopt its face-to-face conditions. As soon as we begin to control the various channels, we must deprive some members of direct contact with others. The isolation so created tends to make the situation unnatural or artificial. The principal reason for imposing such restrictions is to gain better control over the group's operations and so permit a more careful exploration of the conditions necessary for efficient cooperation. Restricted nets are of more than purely theoretical interest, however. Such situations do arise occasionally in games, in telephone conversations, in military communications, etc.

In one experiment of this sort (Leavitt, 1951) five subjects were seated around a table, but separated from one another by vertical partitions. There were slots in the partitions through which written notes could be passed. By varying the slots that were open, the channels among the five could be manipulated into any desired pattern. Four patterns were tested: (1) in the *circle*

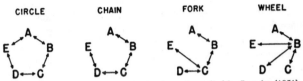

FIG. 55. Diagrams of four communication nets studied by Leavitt (1951).

each person could pass notes to the person to his right or left; (2) the *chain* was identical to the circle except that one more slot was closed, and so the subjects on either side of this closed slot found themselves at the two ends of the chain; (3) the *fork* was a four-member chain, and the fifth subject could exchange notes with one of the inner members of this chain; and (4) the *wheel* put one subject at the center of the net in such a way that he could exchange messages with all the other members, but the other four could not exchange information without passing it through the central member. These four nets are shown in Fig. 55.

Each subject was given five different symbols out of a possible set of six. The task was for the entire group to discover as rapidly as possible the one symbol held in common by all five members. Each group completed 15 such tasks during the experimental session. Records were kept of speed, errors, and number of messages. At the end of the experimental session the subjects were given a questionnaire before they talked to each other.

The peripheral men in the wheel always sent their information to the central man (B), who arrived at the answer and sent it out. This plan of operation usually evolved by the fourth or fifth trial and was not changed. The fork

also operated so that the most central man (C), got all the information and
sent out the answer, but this organization evolved more slowly than it did in
the wheel. The chain was not as stable as the wheel and the fork. Usually
the center man (C) sent out the answer, but this function was occasionally
performed by one of the men on either side of him (B or D). The organization
evolved more slowly in the chain than it did in the wheel and the fork. The
circle showed no consistent pattern of operation. Members of the circle simply
sent messages until they received or could work out the answer for themselves.

The circle made the greatest number of errors. The fork and the wheel
made the fewest errors. The different nets did not differ significantly, however, in the time it took them to finish the problem.

One of the questions asked at the end of the experimental session was 'Did
your group have a leader? If so, who?' In the circle there was no agreement
as to who had been the leader. In the chain the central man (C) was recognized as the leader by about two-thirds of the members who thought there had
been a leader, and no one recognized the most peripheral members (A and E)
as the leader. In the fork 85 per cent of those members who thought there was
a leader recognized C's leadership. In the wheel nearly everyone knew there
was a leader and everyone agreed that the leader was B. Thus the emergence
of recognized leadership (under the conditions of this experiment) was closely
related to the centrality of the member's position in the communication net.

The subjects were also asked how well they enjoyed their jobs. Members
of the circle liked the job better, on the average, than did the members of the
other nets. The lowest morale was found among the members of the wheel.
When the answers from the wheel, the fork, and the chain were analyzed, it
was found that subjects in the most central positions were the best satisfied
and subjects in the most peripheral positions were the most discontented.

If we contrast the circle with the wheel, we find that (1) the circle was unorganized, unstable, passed the greatest number of messages, was leaderless but
satisfying to its members, and got the job done about as rapidly as any other
net, whereas (2) the wheel was well organized, stable, passed relatively few
messages, and had a clearly recognized leader but did not satisfy four of the
five members.

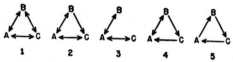

Fig. 56. Diagrams of five communication nets studied by Heise and Miller (1951).

Restricted Telephone Nets. Heise and Miller (1951) used telephonic channels in a three-member group. The subjects were located in different rooms.
Each had his own microphone and earphones over which he could speak and
hear messages. The five nets tested are shown in Fig. 56. If a talker was

connected to two listeners, he always talked simultaneously to both of them. The channels were arranged so that a known amount of white noise could be introduced. This noise masked the speech and produced errors that had to be corrected before the group could continue.

The first kind of problem given these groups was similar to the standard articulation test (Chap. 3). The problem was constructed as follows: First a test list of 25 monosyllabic words was assembled. Then pairs of consecutive words from the test list were collected in three sets to form three sublists, one for each subject. The pairs of words were given to the subjects in their correct order as they appeared in the original test list, but each subject had only one-third of the total number of word pairs. The problem was for all three subjects to reconstruct the original test list in its entirety and in its correct order. One subject starts the problem by pronouncing word *a*. This is passed about until it reaches the subject who has the pair of words *ab*. He then introduces *b*, which is passed on until it reaches the subject with the pair *bc*, etc. The subjects were prohibited from sending any message except the actual test words. Secondary information had to be conveyed by pauses or by repetitions of the test words and could not be given by explicit questions or confirmations. This restriction made it possible to specify the articulation score for the average message under the given noise conditions.

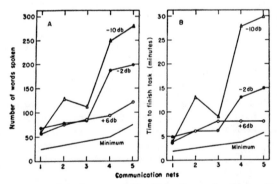

Fig. 57. Performance of the five nets of Fig. 56 for the word problem. Performance is measured in terms of (*A*) total words spoken and (*B*) time required to finish the task. The three functions were obtained for three different speech-to-noise ratios. (*From Heise and Miller*, 1951.)

The results summarized in Fig. 57 were obtained after the group had received considerable experience with this type of problem. In Fig. 57*A* the number of words spoken during the task is plotted for each of the five nets for three speech-to-noise ratios. The minimum curve represents the smallest number of words that the groups would have to say if there were no errors and no repetitions. When the speech-to-noise ratio was good (6 db), the results followed this minimum curve rather well and the differences among the five nets were relatively small. When the noise conditions became severe (-10 db), large differences appeared among the nets. Essentially the same result is obtained if, instead of number of words, we plot the time required to finish the task.

When noise is introduced, some nets fail badly, whereas others seem relatively unaffected. The noise introduces errors. The group's defense against error is to make good use of secondary information. The nets do not differ greatly in their distribution of the primary information, but they do differ widely in their distribution of secondary information. In net 1 everybody hears every repetition of his message and can catch any mistakes immediately. In net 5 a subject cannot hear his message repeated by the man he spoke to; if an error occurs, there is no way to tell who introduced it. When noise conditions are good, the secondary information is not important because there are few errors. When the noise is intense, secondary information becomes crucial. The noise-resistant nets are those which give the members the clearest picture of the group's pattern of information.

A second type of task required a little more initiative and imagination from the subjects. The test materials consisted of 25-word sentences, as simple in thought and expression as possible. The 25 words were distributed randomly into three lists. At the beginning of a test each subject received his portion of the words. His words were listed vertically in the order in which they occurred in the sentence. The task was, as before, for all of the members to reconstruct the original sequence of words in the correct order. Each word had to be fitted into place on the basis of the context of the sentence.

The results are summarized in Fig. 58. The results are similar to those shown in Fig. 57, with one noteworthy exception. With the more mechanical problem net 1 showed the greatest resistance to noise. With the sentence problem net 1 fell victim to noise, and net 3 showed the greatest resistance. The difference between these two nets is that 1 is leaderless, whereas 3 has a clearly central position that forces its occupant into leadership. If these data are correct, therefore, it means that on a mechanical problem leadership is unnecessary, but with a problem that demands more complex decisions a leader is able to increase the group's efficiency.

Both the word and the sentence problems demand communication by the members. No one subject can proceed until he receives information from the others. It is simple to devise tasks that do not require communication. For this purpose Heise and Miller adopted the anagram task used by G. B. Watson (1928). The group's goal was to get the largest number of words on all three papers. A word could count three times toward the group total if it appeared on all three papers. Thus communication could increase the group total, but it was not essential to the task. Only nets 1, 3, and 5 were tested.

With this problem the particular communication net did not affect the total number of words that the group was able to form. When intense noise was introduced into the channels, the group totals fell but no net was more noise-resistant than any other net. More words were spoken over net 5 than over net 1, but no other difference appeared among the nets.

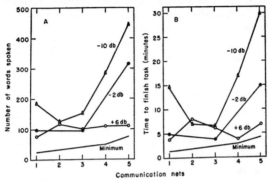

FIG. 58. Performance of the five nets of Fig. 56 for the sentence problem. Performance is measured in terms of (*A*) total words spoken and (*B*) time required to finish the task. Three functions were obtained for three different speech-to-noise ratios. (*From Heise and Miller,* 1951.)

The anagram problem does not involve secondary information to any great extent. When a new word is discovered, the discoverer speaks it over his microphone. If someone hears it, well and good. If no one hears it, the group does not have to suspend all other operations until everybody is sure that everybody has the word. When the importance of secondary information is eliminated in this way, the differences among the nets are also eliminated.

Comparison of these three types of problems makes it clear that the group's goal must be carefully specified before we can predict the effects of controlling the channels in the net. An arrangement that is optimal for reaching one goal may not have similar advantages when the goal is changed.

Bavelas (1950) has suggested that some communication nets may prevent the members from having insight into the group's problem. In order to explore this notion, he uses a problem that requires the formation of squares out of odd bits of cardboard. Five squares are cut up, and the pieces are distributed among the five members of the group. The members can pass pieces or messages over the communication channels. The task is to redistribute the pieces until all five members can form a square. There is only one distribution of the pieces that enables everybody to form a square, but there are many partial solutions where one member can form a square out of pieces the other members need so that the other members are completely blocked. When one member forms a square that blocks the group's progress, he must break up this square so that the pieces can be redistributed before the group effort can succeed. The member who has this false success is understandably reluctant to abandon it. The ease with which he can take this course of action away from his own goal depends to a large extent upon his knowledge of the total situation. Secondary information about the success or failure of the other members is absolutely essential for the group's success. When the communication among the members is restricted to any severe degree, the distribution of secondary information is usually more restricted than the distribution of primary information. Thus any severe restriction of the communication channels makes the solution almost impossible.

COMMUNICATION IN LARGE GROUPS

As long as the group is relatively small, it is possible to analyze the communication net in detail. When the group has as many as 10 members, however, the number of possible combinations is unwieldy. With 100 members a detailed analysis is practically impossible. When the problem gets this complex, we must search for short cuts.

A possible short cut when the number of members begins to get out of hand is to look for subgroups within the larger group. These subgroups can then be treated as if they were the individual members of a small group. An example is provided by a study of the visiting relations among the 61 families in a small German village (Loomis, 1946). The heads of these families were grouped according to political affiliation as Nazi (21 families), Social Democrat (23 families), Communist (6 families), and other (11 families). This classification gives four subgroups within the larger social unit of the village. The observed frequencies of visiting between families are shown in Fig. 59. The squares represent the four political groups, and the numbers in the squares represent the number of families. The numbers by the arrowheads represent the traffic densities for social visiting. Thus 49 visiting relations involve Nazis visiting Nazis, 32 involve Nazis visiting Social Democrats, 25 involve Social Democrats visiting Nazis, etc. All possible channels between the groups are used, but some are used more frequently than others. There is a

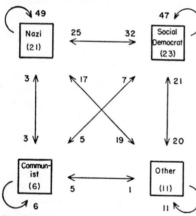

FIG. 59. Net of visiting relations among families in a small German town. Families are grouped by political affiliation. Numbers beside arrows indicate traffic densities. (*After Loomis*, 1946.)

tendency for visiting relations to be established between families of the same political affiliation, but the tendency is small.

The usual procedure with large groups is to use statistics. We may not be able to trace out the exact paths over which the information travels, but we can state certain average values. The averages are based on the assumption that channels exist more or less randomly and homogeneously throughout the group. Suppose we have a group of 1000 people who can exchange messages freely (so far as we know) in any direction. Since there are too many channels to consider each one in detail, we make a simplifying assumption. We assume that the frequencies with which messages originate or terminate at any member are distributed uniformly through the group. A given message is just as likely to go to one member as to any other; it is just as likely that the message originated with any one member as with any other; and a member is just as likely to send himself a message as he is to send a message to any other member. If there are 1000 members of this group who can send or receive the messages, then each person has one chance in 1000 of having sent or received any particular message. Now suppose we form subgroup A within the original group of 1000 members. There are, let's say, 100 members in subgroup A. What are the chances that a particular message will go to a member of this subgroup? Each member has 1 chance in 1000 of receiving it, and there are 100 members— thus there are 100 chances in 1000 that some member of A will receive the message. Similarly, the chances are 100 in 1000 that any particular message was sent by a member of A.

Consider now another subgroup, B, that has 10 members, none of them members of A. What is the chance that a message will both originate with subgroup A and terminate with subgroup B? Since we are asking for the probability of simultaneous events, the answer is obtained by multiplying the two probabilities together. The chance that A sent it is 100/1000, or 0.1, and the chance that B received it is 10/1000, or 0.01, so the chance that both A sent and B received the message is $(0.1)(0.01)$, or 0.001.

The subgroups A and B can be identified with two cities, and the number of people living in the cities is the size of the subgroups. The chance that any message will originate in city A and go to city B is then proportional to the product of the populations of the two cities. If P_1 is the population of the first and P_2 is the population of the second city, the traffic density between them should be proportional to P_1P_2. The larger the two cities are, the greater the chance that messages will pass between them.

We know a little more about the situation than this equation indicates. If two people in a group find it difficult to exchange messages, the probability that they will communicate should be reduced. With 1000 people in the group a member on the easternmost fringe may find it much easier to send messages to his neighbor than to send them all the way to a man on the western fringe of the group. When a large number of people belong to the group, it is reasonable to assume that the likelihood of messages passing from one person to another is inversely proportional to the distance between them (Zipf, 1949; Stewart, 1947; Miller, 1947). The greater the distance, the lower the traffic density.

When we combine the effects of the sizes of the subgroups and the distance between them, we obtain the equation

$$M = k \frac{P_1 P_2}{d}.$$

In this equation M is the number of messages, P_1 and P_2 are the populations of the two subgroups (cities), d is the distance between them, and k is a factor of proportionality.

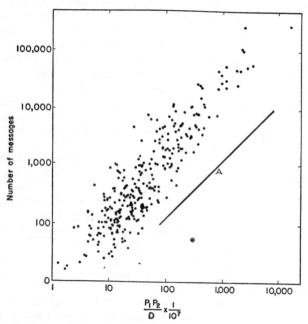

FIG. 60. Number of telephone messages exchanged between 311 pairs of cities, plotted against P_1P_2/d. Line *A* shows the slope predicted by the equation. (*From G. K. Zipf, Some determinants of the circulation of information, Amer. J. Psychol., 1946, Fig. 6. By permission of the publishers.*)

This equation can be tested with empirical data. Figure 60 shows the result obtained by Zipf (1946) for the number of long-distance telephone calls between cities. The number of calls between pairs of cities is plotted on the ordinate, and the value of P_1P_2/d is plotted on the abscissa. The points cluster about a straight line over a range of four logarithmic units. The only exception—the calls between Chicago and Grand Rapids—is indicated by a circle. (Zipf suggests this is a typing error in the data given him by the telephone company.) If the equation fitted precisely, the straight line would have a slope of 1.00; an increase of one logarithmic unit along the abscissa should produce an increase of one logarithmic unit along the ordinate. Line *A* is drawn with a slope of 1.00 to aid in the comparison of theory and data.

The data in Fig. 60 show a slightly steeper slope than theory predicts. The telephone messages were counted for the entire area that the cities served as toll centers. The populations were counted for only those people living within the city limits. If this discrepancy is proportionately larger for the larger cities, the deviation from the predicted slope is explained.

The equation has also been tested by Zipf for other kinds of messages: the number and length of out-of-town obituaries in the *New York Times*, the number of out-of-town news items in the *Chicago Tribune*, the out-of-town circulation of both the *Times* and the *Tribune*, the number of tons of goods moved by Railway Express, and the numbers of passengers on bus lines, railroads, and air lines. In all cases the data conform, more or less closely, to the predicted trend.

THE EFFECTIVENESS OF MASS MEDIA

When literacy was rare and radios and motion pictures were undreamed of, information reached the bulk of the people slowly, if at all, by word of mouth, by rumor, legend, or ballad. The distortion and error inherent in this method of communication is so great that those who heard the news probably knew as little of the truth as those who did not. Among the few advantages of this system of communication are a rich fund of legends to pass the winter nights and a resistance to deliberate manipulation by interested parties. A huge propaganda organization—an advertising agency, for example—would find no channels for its wares to travel. Whispering campaigns might be used, but who knows what form a rumor will take by the time it reaches the consumer?

General education and mass media of communication have changed entirely the relation between the people and their sources of information. Communication has become a major industry—several industries, in fact. Although the new channels of communication have enriched and strengthened our democratic way of life, many Americans view with alarm the power of these new channels and our dependence upon them. When every word goes to millions of people, the man who controls the words is in a position to direct the beliefs and actions of millions. Or so it seems.

Occasionally the power of mass media is pointed up in a dramatic fashion. Such an instance occurred on the evening of October 30, 1938, when thousands of American radio listeners were panic-stricken by a broadcast that described an invasion from Mars. The Martians set people all over the United States praying, crying, or fleeing frantically to escape death (Cantril, Gaudet, and Hertzog, 1940).

If the public consisted of a group of puppets who believed all they heard and did all they were told to do by their newspapers and radios, there would be a real danger in mass communication. Problems of control would be far more critical than they actually are. The truth seems to be that mass media can influence people, but only in the direction that the people want to go. The acceptance of propaganda depends upon the attitudes and beliefs of the acceptor (Coffin, 1941).

Questions about mass media of communication can be divided into (1) what is said, (2) who hears it, and (3) what is the effect. We consider each in turn.

What Is Said. How can the content of mass communication be described? We might use our intuitive impressions about the material; most of us would agree that the *Reader's Digest* does not follow slavishly the Communist party line. A more reliable approach is to make use of the methods of content analysis described in Chap. 4.

Take a specific application of the method to a practical problem. The following study made by Lasswell (1949, Chap. 9) was used in litigation that arose in connection with the McCormack Act. This act provided for the registration of foreign agents with the State Department and was intended to disclose the identities of those disseminating antidemocratic propaganda in this country. Content analysis was used to determine whether or not certain publications, which had failed to register, were in fact distributing such propaganda. The government asked Lasswell to analyze their publications and to be prepared to testify concerning what was said in them.

Lasswell used eight standards to define what he meant by propaganda.

The Avowal Test. The simplest test, but not the most reliable, is to look and see if the publication makes an out-and-out declaration that it is a propaganda channel for one side or another. Thus one publication said, "Soviet news that's straight from the USSR . . . . Outstanding Soviet writers and specialists in many fields give you an authoritative picture of life in the USSR."

The Parallel Test. Here the problem is to determine the degree to which the contents of the publication run parallel with the contents of channels known to be carrying antidemocratic propaganda. In one case Nazi propaganda was grouped into 14 themes, and a search was made for these themes in the publication being studied. In a period of 3 months, Lasswell found, there were 23 statements consistent with the Nazi themes for every statement that was contradictory. Such close agreement seldom occurs by chance.

The Consistency Test. Are the general aims of the periodical consistent with the avowed strategic aims of the foreign source? For example, one aim of Nazi propaganda was to show the war guilt of Germany's enemies and the peaceful aims of Germany herself. The percentages of articles and editorials consistent with this aim were: *Today's Challenge*, 46 per cent; *Forum Observer*, 15 per cent; *Reader's Digest*, 2.5 per cent; *Saturday Evening Post*, 0 per cent. The suspected publications, *Today's Challenge* and the *Forum Observer*, were far closer to Nazi aims than the other two magazines.

The Presentation Test. Here the question concerns the balance of favorable and unfavorable treatment given to a controversial symbol. For example, the number of favorable references to the USSR in the *Moscow News* outnumbered the unfavorable references by more than 600 to 1, while the favorable references to all other countries were outnumbered 5 to 1 by unfavorable references.

The Source Test. Another possible test of propaganda is the balance of sources relied on. For example, 20 per cent of the space in the *Moscow News* came from acknowledged governmental and party sources in Russia. No government other than the USSR was used as a source, nor was any party other than the Communist party relied upon.

The Concealed-source Test. This test requires a considerable amount of research in order to establish where unacknowledged items originated. Occasionally, however, plagiarism can be discovered.

The Distinctiveness Test. Propaganda can often be detected when parties to a controversy use distinctive vocabularies. In the *Moscow News* the use of 'the People,' 'the Workers,' 'Collective and State Farms,' 'Stalin' or 'Stalinist,' 'Soviets,' 'Lenin' or 'Leninist,' 'Revolution,' and 'Five-Year Plan' occurred far more frequently than in any major national newspaper in the United States. Even when isolated from context, most of these words are ideologically alien to Americans.

The Distortion Test. During the period of the Second World War when Germany was winning, realistic reporting would tilt the balance of favorable references to German strength in Germany's favor. Objective reporting will not automatically produce a fifty-fifty split between favorable and unfavorable references. The question is therefore a relative one, and differences in degrees of unbalance are significant. In one case the suspected periodical was compared with the *New York Times* in the way it handled the same news stories. The differences may be additions or omissions. It was found that 58 per cent of the additions in the suspected source (that were not carried in the *Times* account) favored foreign propaganda aims, while only 3 per cent of the additions contradicted them. Of the material omitted by the suspected account, 48 per cent was contradictory to foreign aims, and 16 per cent was consistent. Compared with the treatment provided by other newspapers, therefore, the suspected publication was carrying a larger proportion of proforeign items and suppressing a larger proportion of antiforeign items.

Who Listens. The communication net of mass media provides little secondary information. This lack is keenly felt by those responsible for the content of the communication, and much research has been done to let the source know what the recipients think of his verbal behavior. The communications industry serves two masters, the advertisers and the public. In order to satisfy the advertiser it is necessary to prove to him that there is a large audience of potential customers. Thus there is a demand for accurate statistics about how many and what kind of people are reached by the various media. This task may become very complex. A magazine may sell a known number of copies, but circulation figures do not say how many people read each copy. More detailed research is needed to count the number of readers. But what is a reader? Is the man who glances nervously through a magazine in a dentist's waiting room considered a reader? How many items must he read in order to qualify? With radios the task is somewhat simpler, for devices can be attached to record where the radio was tuned. Even these devices do not say whether anybody was listening. To specify with any exactness at all who is in the audience requires patient and skillful research.

Different audiences for certain kinds of communication derive from differences in the interests of men and women. Women make up the vast majority of the daytime radio audience. Women read the fiction in a magazine, while men prefer the nonfictional material. In general, women are less interested in public affairs.

The audience can also be analyzed according to age. About two-thirds of the radio listeners who are in their twenties say that popular music is their favorite type of radio program. Only one-fourth of the listeners over fifty agree with them. There is a similar age factor in movie attendance. Almost half the twenty-year-olds go to the movies at least once a week as compared with only a fifth of those over fifty. In magazines the younger readers favor light fiction, while their elders tackle heavier nonfiction.

The educational level of the audience is also of interest. About two-thirds of the nation reads magazines with some regularity. Among college graduates the proportion is about 9 out of 10, among high-school graduates about 7 out of 10, and among those with less than a high-school education about 5 out of 10. Radio programs presenting classical music or public affairs find the more highly educated listeners more interested than those with little education. What good is achieved by documentary films and serious radio programs when only educated people listen to them? The group that the educator would like most to reach is the group with the least interest in what he has to say.

An important fact to remember about audiences is that they select themselves. Democrats read Democratic newspapers. Sports enthusiasts read the sports page. People go to movies about subjects that they already have an interest in. If a radio program praises some minority group, the audience consists largely of members of the minority. People do not often seek out the things they ought to learn. They look for more information about things they already know or believe. The propagandist cannot select his audience. His audience, if he has one, selects him.

What Happens. The effects of mass media are largely a matter for speculation. Objective evidence is hard to get. Just how much influence did *Uncle Tom's Cabin* have, or to what extent does the Hearst press mold public opinion? Most of the available data come from interviews conducted shortly after the audience has received the communication. What the long-term effects may be is difficult to assess.

An example can be taken from the work of the Information and Education Division, U.S. War Department (Hovland, Lumsdaine, and Sheffield, 1949, Chap. 8). The question is, When the weight of evidence supports the main thesis being presented, is it more effective to present only the materials supporting the point being made, or is it better to introduce also the arguments of those opposed to the point being made?

In order to answer such questions it is necessary to have a quantitative measure of the effect of the communication. This measure was obtained by giving men a preliminary questionnaire to survey their opinions before they received the communication, then giving a second questionnaire after they had received it. The comparison of their answers before and after gave an indication of the effect.

When the experiment was planned early in 1945, during the Second World War, Army morale was suffering because the men expected an early end to the war. The Army wanted to impress the troops with the magnitude of the job still ahead, and this topic provided an opportunity for the experiment. Military experts believed the war might continue for some time, but arguments were available on both sides. Radio transcriptions were used to present the two kinds of argument, and they appeared in the form of a commentator's analysis of the war in the Pacific. The commentator's conclusion was, in both cases, that the job of finishing the war was a tough one that would take at least two years after victory in Europe.

Program A. The major topics included *only* the arguments that the war would be long. The arguments were: problems of distance and logistics, resources and stock piles of the Japanese, the quality of the main bulk of the Japanese army that we had not yet met in battle, and the determination of the Japanese people. 15 min.

Program B. The same topics were included as in program A, but 4 min. was devoted to considering the other side of the picture. The counterarguments were our naval superiority, our previous progress despite a two-front war, our ability to concentrate on Japan after victory in Europe, Japan's shipping losses, Japan's manufacturing inferiority, and the increasing effectiveness of our air war. These arguments were discussed at relevant points in the rest of the program. 19 min.

Considerable pains were taken to conceal from the men the fact that they were serving as subjects in an experiment. One group of men was used that did not hear either transcription. This group served as a control to determine the effects of other news upon opinions.

The results were different for men who had different initial opinions. The men who initially estimated a short war were more apt to change to a longer estimate after hearing program B (48 per cent) than they were after hearing program A (36 per cent). The men who initially estimated a long war were more apt to lengthen their estimate after hearing program A (52 per cent) than after program B (23 per cent). Presenting both sides of the argument is more effective with the men who are initially opposed to the point of view being presented. But if the men are already convinced, the inclusion of both sides of the argument is less effective than a one-sided presentation. It was also observed that the men with better education were more favorably affected if both sides were presented. Thus the least effect was observed when both sides were presented to poorly educated men who were already convinced of the point of view being advocated.

Many of the men who believed the war would be short and who heard the two-sided program B noted an important omission in the counterarguments. The possible effects of Russian aid against Japan had not been mentioned. This omission lowered noticeably the effectiveness of program B for those men who counted on Russian aid and noticed the omission. If a presentation supporting a particular conclusion attempts to take both sides of an issue into account, it must include *all* of the important negative arguments or the presentation may boomerang by failing to live up to the expectation of impartiality and completeness.

The boomerang effect has been noted in other studies. An example can be taken from a radio broadcast in which an officer of a county medical association tried to convince his listeners that they should never have x-ray pictures taken by unlicensed operators (H. B. Wilcox, quoted by Lazarsfeld, 1948). After a short introduction that stressed the importance of x-rays in diagnosis and therapy, the speaker gave a few sentences about their history. Then he discussed the dangers of x-rays and of the high voltages involved and gave a few examples to make the point more vivid. Because x-rays are dangerous, he continued, city and state governments have a system of licensing. This system was described for 3.5 min. Then he said that x-rays were not ordinary pictures and that sometimes special drugs are needed. Then the speaker listed some medical specialists and gave the names of institutions that recognized these specialists as competent x-ray technicians. Then he gave more information, especially on fluoroscopic examinations. Then he summarized the characteristics of x-rays and stressed once more the importance of not patronizing quacks. Total time, 14 min.

How effective was this program? Fully 60 per cent of the time was spent trying to impress listeners with the importance of specialists. Is there not a good chance that listeners would regard this 60 per cent as a commercial advertisement for the doctor's profession? This turned out to be the case. When listeners were interviewed, many negative effects were discovered. One listener said it was an attempt by the doctors to protect their business. It was saying, "Buy my product, it's better for you than somebody else's." Many listeners were not convinced of the dangers he stressed. "He never said what would happen to you if an unlicensed person did it." The listeners were not convinced that quacks were a real possibility. "General Electric probably wouldn't sell to anybody without a license." Some listeners rejected the medical specialists along with the quacks. "These people can get a license but that doesn't prove they are competent."

A perfectly well-intended talk thus went so far astray in its effects that many listeners resented it and resisted the talker's arguments. In order to avoid these boomerang effects, radio networks and motion-picture studios often hire social psychologists to organize tests on their material before it is released.

It is not easy for a propagandist to achieve the effect he desires. People select what they want to hear and show no reluctance to disagree with it if it contradicts their own opinions or observations. Mass media of communication succeed (1) if they urge people to do what the people already wanted to do, or (2) if, as in the case of advertisements, they try to direct into a particular channel action that people were sure to take in some form or other anyhow, or (3) if they are followed up by personal contacts and discussions held face to face, or (4) if all channels are under the complete control of the propagandist and no counterarguments are ever presented in any media. The power of a propaganda campaign is not so alarming as it might seem on first consideration. People seek out and believe what they want to believe, and they let themselves be pushed in the way they want to go. Thus the best counterpropaganda is a social and economic system that satisfies most of the people's needs most of the time.

RUMOR

When false information acquires wide acceptance and is passed along from person to person with no secure evidence offered, we call the phenomenon a rumor. In times of social crisis rumors can become dangerous to a community by spreading alarm or raising hopes needlessly. They may even be used deliberately by subversive groups to arouse hostility and dissension. Most of our rumors are idle gossip and serve little purpose but to pass the time of day or to avoid the embarrassment of dead silence. Most rumors reflect the motives of the people who spread them. Scandal appeals to sexual motives, malicious gossip and slander satisfy a dislike of some person or group, pipe dreams thrive where there is hope and desire.

Successive Reproductions. In Chap. 10 we mentioned the inaccuracies involved in simple testimony. Now suppose that this testimony is passed along through four or five people in succession. At each repetition there are new chances for error. Each participant imposes his own distortions on the account. After the story has passed through several hands, it may be completely unrecognizable as an account of the original event.

In order to study the successive distortions introduced along the rumor chain, Allport and Postman (1947) developed the following experimental procedure: Out of a college class or forum audience a group of six or seven people is selected. They are asked to leave the room. They are told only that when they return to the room they must listen carefully to what they hear and be able to repeat it as exactly as possible. A picture of some detailed situation is then shown, and some member of the audience is requested to describe it (while looking at it) to the first subject. He is asked to include about 20 details in his description. The members of the selected group are called back one at a time and placed where they cannot see the picture. The first subject hears the description. The second subject is called in, and the first subject repeats what he has heard. Then the third subject is called in, and the second repeats the account to him. So the account proceeds through several steps. The successive descriptions are recorded by the experimenter for more careful dissection later.

As an example of the kind of records obtained, examine the following sequence of reports. The picture used is shown in Fig. 61.

Description from the Screen. This is a picture of an elevated train stopping at Dyckman Street. Evidently an Avenue Express. It shows the interior of the train with five people seated and two standing. There are the usual advertising signs above the windows. One is about smoking a certain cigarette, one is a soap ad, another about some camp, another is a political ad for a certain McGinnis for Alderman. Seated is a man with a hat on and a newspaper. He is a funny, rounded man engrossed in his newspaper. Next to him is a woman with a shopping bag on her right arm, eyeglasses, and a funny hat. Then there is some empty space, and in front of it a Negro in a zoot suit, pork-pie hat and loud tie, talking with a defense worker wearing old clothes: overalls, high boots, sleeveless sweater, and cap. He seems to be a shipyard worker, has a razor in his left hand, and is evidently arguing with the Negro. Next person sitting is a woman with a small baby in her arms, watching the two men in their argument. She is commonly dressed and has long hair. Sitting next to her is a man in a cloak, a Jewish rabbi, reading a book, with a funny hat. He is wearing a long coat, not modern. Sitting next to him is a fat man, fast asleep, with his hands clasped.

First Reproduction. A picture of a subway train, stopping at Dyckman Street. It shows the interior of the subway car, about five people sitting, two standing. There are the usual ads, one for cigarettes; one for a political candidate, McGinnis. The people sitting are a fat man interested in his newspaper, next to him a woman, then an empty seat, then a Negro in a zoot suit having an argument with a defense worker carrying a razor. It seems to be a serious argument. Then a woman holding a baby, then a man who appears to be a Jewish rabbi; a fat man fast asleep. The two men are standing; a fat woman is watching the two men standing.

Second Reproduction. Scene is in a subway train at Dyckman Street. This is the interior of the car with five people sitting and two standing. There are the usual ads, one for cigarettes, one political for a candidate named McGinnis. People sitting are a fat man very interested in his newspaper, a woman, then an empty space, then a Negro and a defense worker. The Negro is wearing a zoot suit, and one of them is carrying a razor. They are having a serious argument standing. Then there is a woman and child and another man.

FIG. 61. Picture used to study the distortions introduced into rumors. (*From Allport and Postman*, 1947.)

Third Reproduction. This is a scene inside a car at Dyckman Street. There are seven people in the car, five sitting and two standing. Among the signs is a political one for a man named McGinnis. People standing are a fat man and a woman with a baby. Sitting down are two men, then a space, then a woman and two defense workers having an argument. One is a colored man with a zoot suit who has a razor in his hand. The argument must be pretty heated.

Fourth Reproduction. Scene is in a subway car. Five people are seated and two standing. Signs and ads are along the top of the car. One is for McGinnis for Congress. There are a man sitting and a woman, and two defense workers. One of them is a Negro in a zoot suit who is waving a razor. A woman is standing with a baby in her arms. There is a fat man standing.

Fifth Reproduction. The scene is in a subway car, with five people sitting and two standing. In the car there are advertisements; one of the ads is for McGinnis for Congress. In the front of the car there are a man, a woman, and two defense workers, one a Negro with a razor, which he is waving in anger. One person is standing, woman holding baby. The man standing is a fat man.

Sixth Reproduction. This is a picture of a typical subway scene. In the picture three people are standing. The subway has the usual characteristics. There are ads, one of McGinnis for Congress. Sitting down are a man and a woman. Two other men, one a Negro, are discussing the coming election. The Negro is waving a razor. In another part a woman is standing, holding a baby. You also see that in the subway.

The razor shifts, you will note, from the white hand to the Negro. The woman with the baby is soon standing. The number of people standing varies. And McGinnis grows in stature from a candidate for alderman to a candidate for Congress, while the other signs drop out.

Allport and Postman distinguish three types of distortion that occur. *Leveling* occurs when successive versions omit details, grow shorter and easier to grasp and remember. With *sharpening*, some detail that happens to be preserved gains in emphasis and importance. *Assimilation* occurs when the special interests, motives, expectations of the subject influence his interpretation of what he hears.

In most cases we receive information from several sources—newspapers, radios, conversations, magazines. We check one of these sources against the other and so perform, in a limited way, a kind of statistical comparison of the several versions. Because the network of communication channels in a social group permits each member to be connected with the source of information via several paths, the social situation provides its own kind of redundancy. By checking one path against another it is often possible to detect the errors and distortions. To illustrate how this might work, we can try to reconstruct the original from several distorted fragments. Allport and Postman give several protocols obtained from the same original picture. From their records we extract the following group of accounts. All of them are the third reproduction (fourth communicatee) in a series.

There are four colored men working, one holding a hand grenade. There is a church steeple with a cross on it. The time is ten minutes past two. There are also signs along the side of the road.

This is a battle scene. The scene is one of general ruin, evidently a village shot up pretty badly. In the left foreground is a lieutenant in charge. There is a soldier lying down and shooting over the stone wall of the ruins of a restaurant. There is a church steeple on which a clock says ten minutes to two. There is also an ambulance with a couple of fellows running away from it. In the distance is the enemy. Somewhere in the foreground there are a lot of fellows, one of them a lieutenant because you can see the bar on his shoulders. A Negro in the picture is apparently trying to urge the men on to fight.

The scene is in France. There are two soldiers in a trench and a wounded soldier. There is an ambulance in the picture, and a house in the background, also a church with a steeple; the time is . . . I don't remember. There is a signpost 'Cherbourg 21 miles, Paris 50 miles.' There is a Negro soldier in the picture.

The picture is a battle scene. There is a church in the background with a clock which shows ten minutes to two. There is an airplane and a bomb bursting. A road sign says 150 miles to Paris and 21 miles to Cherbourg.

Now catalogue the various items we have been told are in the picture. After a little work we construct a table that looks about like this:

Mentioned 4 times: Church, clock (or time)
Mentioned 3 times: Negro, several men, road signs, steeple
Mentioned 2 times: Soldiers, ambulance, ruins of battle, 'Cherbourg, 21 miles'
Mentioned 1 time: Hand grenade, restaurant, house, lieutenant, enemies, trench, airplane, bomb, stone wall, 'Paris 50 miles,' 'Paris 150 miles'

It is reasonable to assume that any item mentioned in two or more of the accounts can be accepted. If the item occurs in only one of the four accounts, we cannot be sure that it was not a mistake. With this crude criterion, therefore, we would expect to find in the picture: a church with a steeple and a clock that says ten minutes before two; at least one Negro and several other men, some or all of them soldiers; an ambulance; battle ruins; road sign that says the distance is 21 miles to Cherbourg and that also gives the distance to Paris.

When we check this account against the original picture, we find it correct in all respects but one—the distance to Cherbourg is 50 kilometers.

Notice, however, that we were able to get back to the original picture with some accuracy because we had four independent channels of information. If the channels are not independent but converge at some point and all pass through a single individual, we are not able to eliminate any distortions that this one individual may introduce. Accurate information cannot be restored once it is lost. If several independent channels are not open, we have no way of checking errors.

Attempts to Trace Rumors. One of the interesting questions to ask about rumor is how it travels. Who passes it on, who hears it? In a small group in the laboratory such questions are easily answered, but in real life situations it is much more difficult to follow the spread of a rumor through a group. One method is to interview all the members of the group at some time after a particular rumor has been circulating. The interviewer inquires whether or not the person has heard specific things, from whom did he hear them, to whom has he told them, and when and in what settings did these communications take place. The method seems reasonable in theory, but in practice there are difficulties. Most people cannot remember who told them the rumor or to whom they passed it on. In one study of this sort (Festinger, Cartwright, *et al.*, 1948) the interviews were conducted about 6 months after the rumor. The rumor was dramatic, and there was no difficulty in determining whether or not a member had heard it. Those who had heard it recalled it vividly. But there was much vagueness about whether or not they had told the rumor to anyone else.

In order to shorten the time between the rumor and the interviews, a further study planted two rumors in the group (Festinger, Schachter, and Back, 1950). All members were interviewed from 24 to 48 hr after the items had been planted. Even after such a short interval there was considerable vagueness about where they had heard the rumors or to whom they had told them. People do not seem to pay a great deal of attention to the sources of their information but remember only the content of the messages.

Another method enlists the cooperation of members of the group. This method was used to study rumors in an organization that had 5 levels in its hierarchy and employed about 55 members (Festinger, Back, Schachter, Kelley, and Thibaut, 1950). Seven participant observers were carefully selected from the organization. Before a rumor was planted these 7 members were told its content and the time it would start. If the rumor reached them or if they overheard it, they were instructed to ask questions about it. The participant observers were able to avoid detection, and during a 4-month period 9 different rumors were circulated. At the end of the study all 55 members were interviewed in an attempt to ascertain all of the persons who had heard each rumor. From these interviews it was estimated that almost 80 per cent of the rumor transmissions had been reported by the 7 spies.

Two of the 9 rumors concerned a small morale committee that existed in the organization. These rumors spread quickly within this subgroup but did not spread outside of it. The other seven rumors produced 17 transmissions, which the participant members recorded. Eleven of these were directed upward in the hierarchy, 4 were directed to someone on the same level, and only 2 were directed downward. This result illustrates the general rule that members who want to move upward in a hierarchy tend to communicate in that direction.

DISCUSSION QUESTIONS

1. Under what conditions will the central member of the information net be the leader of the group?

2. Can a leader maintain his central position in the net of command if he is not in a central position in the information network?

3. Secondary information represents the group's awareness of itself. Compare this with the notion that an individual's awareness depends upon his ability to react to his own reactions.

4. What similarities are there between propaganda and suggestion?

5. What contributions does the development of scientific polling techniques offer for the study of mass media of communication?

6. Why are educational programs on the radio generally so unpopular?

7. What rumors have you heard lately? Can you analyze them to discover what needs they satisfy and what sources of distortion they reflect? Who told them to you? Have you passed them on?

Selected References

ALLPORT, G. W., and L. POSTMAN. *The Psychology of Rumor*. New York: Holt, 1947. Reviews the relevant experimental information about rumor and supplements it with many actual instances.

DENNIS, W. (Ed.). *Current Trends in Social Psychology*. Pittsburgh: University of Pittsburgh Press, 1948. The paper by Lazarsfeld, pp. 218–273, is a good, short summary of the status of research on communication via mass media.

FESTINGER, L., K. BACK, S. SCHACHTER, H. H. KELLEY, and J. THIBAUT. *Theory and Experiment in Social Communication*. Ann Arbor, Mich.: Institute for Social Research, University of Michigan, 1950. Summarizes several laboratory and field studies, along with the ideas behind them. Chapter I is particularly valuable.

KRECH, D., and R. S. CRUTCHFIELD. *Theory and Problems of Social Psychology*. New York: McGraw-Hill, 1948. A thorough review of social psychology. Chapters IX–XI are background for this chapter.

LASSWELL, H. D., N. LEITES, *et al*. *Language of Politics*. New York: Stewart, 1949. A collection of articles by Lasswell and his co-workers on the techniques and applications of content analysis.

BIBLIOGRAPHY

ADAMS, D. K. Experimental studies of adaptive behavior in cats. *Comp. Psychol. Monogr.*, 1929, *6*, 1–166.

ALLPORT, F. H. *Social Psychology*. Boston: Houghton Mifflin, 1924.

———, L. WALKER, and E. LATHERS. Written composition and characteristics of personality. *Arch. Psychol., N.Y.*, 1934, *26*, No. 173.

ALLPORT, G. W. Attitudes. In C. Murchison (Ed.), *A Handbook of Social Psychology*. Worcester, Mass.: Clark University Press, 1935.

——— and L. POSTMAN. *The Psychology of Rumor*. New York: Holt, 1947.

ATHERTON, M. V., and M. F. WASHBURN. Mediate associations studied by the method of inhibiting associations. *Amer. J. Psychol.*, 1912, *23*, 101–109.

BAGLEY, W. C. The apperception of the spoken sentence: a study in the psychology of language. *Amer. J. Psychol.*, 1900, *12*, 80–130.

BAKER, S. J. The pattern of language. *J. gen. Psychol.*, 1950, *42*, 25–66.

BALDWIN, A. L. Personal structure analysis: a statistical method for investigating the single personality. *J. abnorm. soc. Psychol.*, 1942, *37*, 163–183.

BALDWIN, J. M. *Mental Development in the Child and the Race: Methods and Processes*. New York: Macmillan, 1895 (3d Ed., 1906).

BALKEN, E. R., and J. H. MASSERMAN. The language of phantasy: III. The language of the phantasies of patients with conversion hysteria, anxiety state, and obsessive-compulsive neuroses. *J. Psychol.*, 1940, *10*, 75–86.

BARTLETT, F. C. *Remembering*. London: Cambridge, 1932.

BAVELAS, A. Communication patterns in task-oriented groups. *J. acoust. Soc. Amer.*, 1950, *22*, 725–730.

BERELSON, B., and P. SALTER. Majority and minority Americans: An analysis of magazine fiction. *Publ. Opin. Quart.*, 1946, *10*, 168–190.

BETTS, E. A. An evaluation of certain techniques for the study of oral composition. *Res. Stud. Elem. Sch. Lang.*, No. 1, *Univ. Ia. Stud. Educ.*, 1934, *9*, No. 2, 7–35.

BLANKENSHIP, A. B. Memory span: A review of the literature. *Psychol. Bull.*, 1938, *35*, 1–25.

BLOCH, B., and G. L. TRAGER. *Outline of Linguistic Analysis*. Baltimore: Linguistic Society of America, Waverly Press, 1942.

BLOOMER, H., and H. H. SHOHARA. The study of respiratory movements by Roentgen kymography. *Speech Monogr.*, 1941, *8*, 91–101.

BLOOMFIELD, L. *Language*. New York: Holt, 1933.

BODER, D. P. The adjective-verb quotient; a contribution to the psychology of language. *Psychol. Rec.*, 1940, *3*, 309–343.

BODMER, F. *The Loom of Language*. New York: Norton, 1944.

BORING, E. G., H. S. LANGFELD, and H. P. WELD. *Foundations of Psychology*. New York: Wiley, 1948.

BRENER, R. An experimental investigation of memory span. *J. exp. Psychol.*, 1940, *26*, 467–482.

BUSEMANN, A. *Die Sprache der Jugend als Ausdruck der Entwicklungsrhythmic.* Jena: Fischer, 1925.

———. Über typische und phasische Unterschiede der Kategoricalen Sprachform. *Z. pädag. Psychol.*, 1926, *27*, 415–419.

BUSWELL, G. T. Fundamental reading habits: A study of their development. *Suppl. Educ. Monogr.*, University of Chicago Press, 1922, No. 21.

CANTRIL, H., H. GAUDET, and H. HERTZOG. *The Invasion from Mars.* Princeton, N.J.: Princeton University Press, 1940.

CARHART, R. Some aspects of model larynx function. *J. acoust. Soc. Amer.*, 1942, *14*, 36–40.

CARMICHAEL, L., H. P. HOGAN, and A. A. WALTER. An experimental study of the effect of language on the reproduction of visually perceived form. *J. exp. Psychol.*, 1932, *15*, 73–86.

CARROLL, J. B. Diversity of vocabulary and the harmonic series law of word-frequency distribution. *Psychol. Rec.*, 1938, *2*, 379–386.

CATTELL, J. M. Ueber die Zeit der Erkennung und Benennung von Schriftzeichen, Bildern und Farben. *Philos. Stud. (Wundt)*, 1885, *2*, 635–650.

———. Ueber die Trägheit der Netzhaut und des Sehcentrums. *Philos. Stud. (Wundt)*, 1886, *3*, 94–127.

———. Psychometrische Untersuchungen. *Philos. Stud. (Wundt)*, 1886, *3*, 452–492.

CHAPPLE, E. D. Measuring human relations: An introduction to the study of the interaction of individuals. *Genet. Psychol. Monogr.*, 1940, *22*, 3–147.

CHEN, H. P., and O. C. IRWIN. Infant speech: vowel and consonant types. *J. Speech Disorders*, 1946, *11*, 27–29.

——— and ———. The type-token ratio applied to infant speech sounds. *J. Speech Disorders*, 1946, *11*, 126–130.

CHOTLOS, J. W. Studies in language behavior: IV. A statistical and comparative analysis of individual written language samples. *Psychol. Monogr.*, 1944, *56*, 75–111.

COFER, C. N., and J. P. FOLEY. Mediated generalization and the interpretation of verbal behavior: I. Prolegomena. *Psychol. Rev.*, 1942, *49*, 513–540.

COFFIN, T. E. Some conditions of suggestion and suggestibility. *Psychol. Monogr.*, 1941, *53*, No. 4.

COLLARD, J. Calculation of the articulation of a telephone circuit from the circuit constants. *Elec. Commun.*, 1930, *8*, 141–163.

CONDON, E. V. Statistics of vocabulary. *Science*, 1928, *67*, 300.

CRAFTS, L. W., T. C. SCHNEIRLA, E. E. ROBINSON, and R. W. GILBERT. *Recent Experiments in Psychology* (2d Ed.). New York: McGraw-Hill, 1950.

CRANDALL, I. B. Dynamical study of the vowel sounds, II. *Bell Syst. Tech. J.*, 1927, *6*, 100–116.

CRINIS, M. DE. Die Entwicklung der Grosshirnrinde nach der Geburt in ihren Beziehungen zur intellektuellen Ausreifung des Kindes. *Wein. klin. Wschr.*, 1932, *45*, 1161–1165.

CURRY, R. O. *Mechanism of the Human Voice.* New York: Longmans, 1940.

DALE, E., and R. W. TYLER. A study of the factors influencing the difficulty of reading materials for adults of limited reading ability. *Library Quart.*, 1934, *4*, 384–412.

DAVIS, E. A. The development of linguistic skill in twins, singletons with siblings, and only children from age five to ten years. *Inst. Child Welfare Monogr. Ser.*, No. 14. Minneapolis: University of Minnesota Press, 1937.

DENNIS, W. (Ed.). *Current Trends in Social Psychology.* Pittsburgh: University of Pittsburgh Press, 1948.

DEWEY, E. *Behavior Development in Infants.* New York: Columbia University Press, 1935.

DEWEY, G. *Relative Frequency of English Speech Sounds.* Cambridge, Mass.: Harvard University Press, 1923.

DIVEN, K. Certain determinants in the conditioning of anxiety reactions. *J. Psychol.*, 1937, *3*, 291–308.

DODGE, R., and B. ERDMANN. *Psychologische Untersuchungen über das Lesen auf experimenteller Grundlage*. Halle: Niemeyer, 1898.

DREYER, G. The normal vital capacity in man and its relation to the size of the body. *Lancet*, 1919, *2*, 227–234.

DUNCKER, K. *Zur Psychologie des Produktiven Denkens*. Berlin: Springer, 1935. (Translated by Lynne S. Lees, On problem-solving, *Psychol. Monogr.*, 1945, *58*, No. 5.)

DUNN, H. K. The calculation of vowel resonances, and an electrical vocal tract. *J. acoust. Soc. Amer.*, 1950, *22*, 740–753.

EBBINGHAUS, H. Über eine neue Methode im Prüfung geistiger Rähigkeiten und ihre Awendung bei Schulkindern. *Z. Psychol.*, 1897, *13*, 401–457.

EGAN, J. P. Articulation testing methods. *Laryngoscope*, 1948, *58*, 955–991.

—— and F. M. WIENER. On the intelligibility of bands of speech in noise. *J. acoust. Soc. Amer.*, 1946, *18*, 435–441.

EIDENS, H. Experimentelle Untersuchungen über den Denkverlauf bei unmittelbarren Folgerungen. *Arch. ges. Psychol.*, 1929, *71*, 1–66.

ELDRIDGE, R. C. *Six Thousand Common English Words*. Buffalo: Clement Press, 1911.

ESPER, E. A. A technique for the experimental investigation of associative interference in artificial linguistic material. *Language Monogr.*, 1925, *1*, 1–47.

ESTOUP, J. B. *Gammes stenographiques* (5th Ed.). Paris, 1917.

FAIRBANKS, G. The relation between eye-movements and voice in the oral reading of good and poor silent readers. *Psychol. Monogr.*, 1937, *48*, 78–107.

FAIRBANKS, H. Studies in language behavior. II. The quantitative differentiation of samples of spoken language. *Psychol. Monogr.*, 1944, *56*, 17–38.

FARNSWORTH, D. W. High-speed motion pictures of the human vocal cords. *Bell Lab. Rec.*, 1940, *18*, 203–208.

FESTINGER, L. Informal social communication. In L. Festinger *et al.*, *Theory and Experiment in Social Communication*. Ann Arbor, Mich.: Institute for Social Research, University of Michigan, 1950.

——, K. BACK, S. SCHACHTER, H. H. KELLEY, and J. THIBAUT. *Theory and Experiment in Social Communication*. Ann Arbor, Mich.: Institute for Social Research, University of Michigan, 1950.

——, D. CARTWRIGHT, *et al.* A study of rumor: Its origin and spread. *Hum. Relations*, 1948, *1*, 464–486.

——, S. SCHACHTER, and K. BACK. *Social Pressures in Informal Groups: A Study of a Housing Project*. New York: Harper, 1950.

FISHER, M. S. Language patterns of preschool children. *Child Develpm. Monogr.*, Teachers College, Columbia University, 1934.

FLESCH, R. *The Art of Plain Talk*. New York: Harper, 1946.

——. A new readability yardstick. *J. appl. Psychol.*, 1948, *32*, 221–233.

FLETCHER, H. *Speech and Hearing*. New York: Van Nostrand, 1929.

FOLEY, J. P., and Z. L. MACMILLAN. Mediated generalization and the interpretation of verbal behavior: V. 'Free association' as related to differences in professional training. *J. exp. Psychol.*, 1943, *33*, 299–310.

FOSSLER, H. R. Disturbances in breathing during stuttering. *Psychol. Monogr.*, 1930, *4*, 1–32.

FRENCH, N. R., C. W. CARTER, and W. KOENIG. The words and sounds of telephone conversations. *Bell Syst. Tech. J.*, 1930, *9*, 290–324.

—— and J. C. STEINBERG. Factors governing the intelligibility of speech sounds. *J. acoust. Soc. Amer.*, 1947, *19*, 90–119.

FREUD, S., *Psycopathology of Everyday Life*. New York: Macmillan, 1914.

FRIES, C. C., and A. A. TRAVER. *English Word Lists*. Washington, D.C.: American Council on Education, 1940.

GALTON, F. Psychometric experiments. *Brain*, 1879, *2*, 149–162.

GATES, A. I. Recitation as a factor in memorizing. *Arch. Psychol., N.Y.*, 1917, *6*, No. 40.

GLAZE, J. A. The association value of nonsense syllables. *J. genet. Psychol.*, 1928, *35*, 255–267.

GOLDSTEIN, H. *Reading and Listening Comprehension at Various Controlled Rates.* New York: Bureau of Publications, Teachers College, Columbia University, 1940.

GOLDSTEIN, K. *Human Nature.* Cambridge, Mass.: Harvard University Press, 1940.

———. *Language and Language Disturbances.* New York: Grune and Stratton, 1948.

GRAY, G. W., and C. M. WISE. *The Bases of Speech* (Rev. Ed.). New York: Harper, 1946.

GRAY, W. S., and B. E. LEARY. *What Makes a Book Readable.* Chicago: University of Chicago Press, 1935.

GRIGSBY, O. J. An experimental study of the development of concepts of relationship in preschool children as evidenced by their expressive ability. *J. exp. Educ.*, 1932, *1*, 144–162.

GRINGS, W. W. The verbal summator technique and abnormal mental states. *J. abnorm. soc. Psychol.*, 1942, *37*, 529–545.

GUILFORD, J. P., and K. M. DALLENBACH. The determination of memory span by the method of constant stimuli. *Amer. J. Psychol.*, 1925, *36*, 621–628.

HADAMARD, J. *The Psychology of Invention in the Mathematical Field.* Princeton, N.J.: Princeton University Press, 1945.

HANLEY, M. L. *Word Index to James Joyce's Ulysses.* Madison, Wis., 1937. (Statistical tabulation by M. Joos.)

HARLOW, H. F. The formation of learning sets. *Psychol. Rev.*, 1949, *56*, 51–65.

HART, H. Changing social attitudes and interests. In President's Research Committee on Social Trends, *Recent Social Trends in the United States; Report.* New York: McGraw-Hill, 1933. Vol. I, 382–442.

HAWKINS, J. E., JR., and S. S. STEVENS. The masking of pure tones and of speech by white noise. *J. acoust. Soc. Amer.*, 1950, *22*, 6–13.

HEAD, H. *Aphasia and Kindred Disorders of Speech.* New York: Macmillan, 1926. Vols. I and II.

HEBB, D. O. *The Organization of Behavior, A Neuropsychological Theory.* New York: Wiley, 1949.

HEIDER, F. K., and G. M. HEIDER. A comparison of sentence structure of deaf and hearing children. *Psychol. Monogr.*, 1940, *52*, No. 1, 42–103.

HEISE, G. A., and G. A. MILLER. Problem solving by small groups using various communication nets. *J. abnorm. soc. Psychol.*, 1951, *46*, 327–335.

HENLE, M., and M. B. HUBBELL. "Egocentricity" in adult conversation. *J. soc. Psychol.*, 1938, *9*, 227–234.

HILGARD, E. R. *Theories of Learning.* New York: Appleton-Century-Crofts, 1948.

HOVLAND, C. I. Human learning and retention. In S. S. Stevens (Ed.), *Handbook of Experimental Psychology.* New York: Wiley, 1951.

———, A. A. LUMSDAINE, and F. D. SHEFFIELD. *Experiments on Mass Communication.* Princeton, N.J.: Princeton University Press, 1949.

HOWES, D. H. *The definition and measurement of word probability.* Ph.D. thesis, Harvard University, 1950.

——— and R. L. SOLOMON. Visual duration threshold as a function of word-probability. *J. exp. Psychol.*, 1951, *41*, 401–410.

HUDGINS, C. V., and F. C. NUMBERS. An investigation of the intelligibility of the speech of the deaf. *Genet. Psychol. Monogr.*, 1942, *25*, 289–392.

——— and R. H. STETSON. Relative speed of articulatory movements. *Arch. néerl. Phon. exp.*, 1937, *13*, 85–94.

HULL, C. L. Quantitative aspects of the evolution of concepts. *Psychol. Monogr.*, 1920, *38*, No. 123.

HULL, C. L. The meaningfulness of 320 selected nonsense syllables. *Amer. J. Psychol.*, 1933, *45*, 730–734.

———. The goal-gradient hypothesis applied to some 'field-force' problems in the behavior of young children. *Psychol. Rev.*, 1938, *45*, 271–299.

HUMPHREY, B. *Directed Thinking*. New York: Dodd, Mead, 1948.

IDOL, H. R. A statistical study of respiration in relation to speech characteristics. *Louisiana St. Univ. Stud.*, 1936, No. 27, 79–98.

IRWIN, O. C. The developmental status of speech sounds of ten feebleminded children. *Child Develpm.*, 1942, *13*, 29–39.

———. Infant speech: consonantal sounds according to place of articulation. *J. Speech Disorders*, 1947a, *12*, 397–404.

———. Infant speech: consonant sounds according to manner of articulation. *J. Speech Disorders*, 1947b, *12*, 402–404.

———. Infant speech: development of vowel sounds. *J. Speech Hearing Disorders*, 1948, *13*, 31–34.

——— and H. P. CHEN. Infant speech: vowel and consonant frequency. *J. Speech Disorders*, 1946, *11*, 123–125.

JAKOBSON, R. *Kindersprache, Aphasie und Allgemeine Lautgesetze*. Uppsala: Almqvist & Wiksell, 1941.

———. On the identification of phonemic entities. *Travaux du cercle linguistique de Copenhague*, 1949, *5*, 205–213.

JENKINS, J. G., and K. M. DALLENBACH. Oblivescence during sleep and waking. *Amer. J. Psychol.*, 1924, *35*, 605–612.

JESPERSEN, O. *Language, Its Nature, Development, and Origin*. New York: Macmillan, 1922.

———. *Growth and Structure of the English Language*. New York: Appleton-Century-Crofts, 1923.

JOHNSON, D. M. A modern account of problem solving. *Psychol. Bull.*, 1944, *41*, 201–229.

JOHNSON, W. Language and speech hygiene. *Gen. Semantics Monogr.* No. 1 (2d Ed.). Chicago: Institute of General Semantics, 1941.

———. Studies in language behavior. I. A program of research. *Psychol. Monogr.*, 1944, *56*, No. 2.

———. *People in Quandaries*. New York: Harper, 1946.

JOOS, M. Acoustic phonetics. Supplement to *Language*, 1948, *24*, 1–136.

JUNG, C. G. *Studies in Word-association* (translated by M. D. Eder). London: William Heinemann, 1918.

KAEDING, F. W. *Häufigkeitswörterbuch der deutsch Sprache*. Steglitz bei Berlin: Selbstverlag des Herausgebers, 1897–1898.

KAISER, L. Some properties of speech muscles and the influence thereof on language. *Arch. néerl. Phon. exp.*, 1934, *10*, 121–133.

KARWOSKI, T. F., and F. BERTHOLD. Psychological studies in semantics: II. Reliability of free association tests. *J. soc. Psychol.*, 1945, *22*, 87–102.

———, F. W. GRAMLICH, and P. ARNOTT. Psychological studies in semantics: I. Free association reactions to words, drawings and objects. *J. soc. Psychol.*, 1944, *20*, 233–247.

——— and J. SCHACHTER. Psychological studies in semantics: III. Reaction times for similarity and difference. *J. soc. Psychol.*, 1948, *28*, 103–120.

KATONA, G. *Organizing and Memorizing*. New York: Columbia University Press, 1940.

KELLEY, T. L. Individual testing with completion test exercises. *Teach. Coll. Rec.*, 1917, *18*, 371–382.

KENT, G. H., and A. J. ROSANOFF. A study of association in insanity. *Amer. J. Insanity*, 1910, *67*, 37–96, 317–390.

KENYON, J. S. *American Pronunciation: A Text-book of Phonetics for Students of English*. Ann Arbor, Mich.: Wahr, 1932.

KORZYBSKI, A. *Science and Sanity.* Lancaster, Pa.: Science Press, 1933.

KRECH, D., and R. S. CRUTCHFIELD. *Theory and Problems of Social Psychology.* New York: McGraw-Hill, 1948.

KRYTER, K. D. Effects of ear protective devices on the intelligibility of speech in noise. *J. acoust. Soc. Amer.*, 1946, *18*, 413–417.

LASSWELL, H. D. A provisional classification of symbol data. *Psychiatry*, 1938, *1*, 197–204.

———, N. C. LEITES, *et al. Language of Politics.* New York: Stewart, 1949.

LAZARSFELD, P. F. Communication research and the social psychologist. In W. Dennis (Ed.), *Current Trends in Social Psychology.* Pittsburgh: University of Pittsburgh Press, 1948.

LEAVITT, H. J. Some effects of certain communication patterns upon group performance. *J. abnorm. soc. Psychol.*, 1951, *46*, 38–50.

LEHMANN, A. Ueber Wiedererkennen. *Philos. Stud. (Wundt)*, 1889, *5*, 96–156.

LEMMON, V. W. The relation of reaction time to measures of intelligence, memory, and learning. *Arch. Psychol., N.Y.*, 1927, *15*, No. 94.

LEOPOLD, W. F. *Speech Development of a Bilingual Child*, Vols. I–IV. Evanston, Ill.: Northwestern University Press, 1937–1949.

LEWIS, M. M. *Infant Speech.* London: Kegan Paul, Trench, Trubner & Co., 1936.

LICKLIDER, J. C. R. Effects of amplitude distortion upon the intelligibility of speech. *J. acoust. Soc. Amer.*, 1946, *18*, 429–434.

———. The intelligibility of amplitude-dichotomized, time-quantized speech waves. *J. acoust. Soc. Amer.*, 1950, *22*, 820–823.

———, D. BINDRA, and I. POLLACK. The intelligibility of rectangular speech waves. *Amer. J. Psychol.*, 1948, *61*, 1–20.

——— and G. A. MILLER. The perception of speech. In S. S. Stevens (Ed.), *Handbook of Experimental Psychology.* New York: Wiley, 1951.

LIGHTOLLER, G. H. S. Facial muscles. *J. Anat.*, London, 1925, *60*, 1–85.

LOOMIS, C. P. Political and occupational cleavages in a Hanoverian village, Germany. *Sociometry* (New York: Beacon House, Inc.), 1946, *9*, 316–333.

LORGE, I. The English semantic count. *Teach. Coll. Rec.*, 1937, *39*, 65–77.

———. Predicting reading difficulty of selections for children. *Elem. English Rev.*, 1939, *16*, 229–233.

———. Predicting readability. *Teach. Coll. Rec.*, 1944, *45*, 404–419.

——— and E. L. THORNDIKE. The value of the responses in the free association test as indicators of personality traits. *J. appl. Psychol.*, 1941, *25*, 200–201.

LUCE, R. D. Connectivity and generalized cliques in sociometric group structure. *Psychometrika*, 1950, *15*, 169–190.

——— and A. D. PERRY. A method of matrix analysis of group structure. *Psychometrika*, 1949, *14*, 95–116.

LYON, D. O. The relation of length of material to time taken for learning and the optimum distribution of time. *J. educ. Psychol.*, 1914, *5*, 1–9, 85–91, 155–163.

MCCALL, W. A., and L. M. CRABBS. *Standard Test Lessons in Reading.* New York: Bureau of Publications, Teachers College, Columbia University, 1926.

MCCARTHY, D. The language development of the preschool child. *Inst. Child Welfare Monogr. Ser.*, No. 4. Minneapolis: University of Minnesota Press, 1930.

———. Language development in children. In L. Carmichael (Ed.), *Manual of Child Psychology.* New York: Wiley, 1946. Pp. 476–581.

MCGEOCH, J. A. The influence of associative value upon the difficulty of nonsense-syllable lists. *J. genet. Psychol.*, 1930, *37*, 421–426.

———. *The Psychology of Human Learning.* New York: Longmans, 1942.

——— and F. MCKINNEY. Retroactive inhibition in the learning of poetry. *Amer. J. Psychol.*, 1934a, *46*, 19–33.

McGeoch, J. A., and F. McKinney. The susceptibility of prose to retroactive inhibition. *Amer. J. Psychol.*, 1934b, 46, 429–436.

Maier, N. R. F. Reasoning in humans. I. On direction. *J. comp. Psychol.*, 1930, 10, 115–143.

——. The behavioral mechanisms concerned with problem solving. *Psychol. Rev.*, 1940, 47, 43–58.

Marbe, K. *Experimentell-psychologische Untersuchungen über das Urteil, eine Einleitung in die Logik.* Leipzig: Engelmann, 1901.

May, M. A. The mechanism of controlled association. *Arch. Psychol., N.Y.*, 1917, 5, No. 39, 1–74.

Mayer, A., and J. Orth. Zur qualitativen Untersuchung der Association. *Z. Psychol.*, 1901, 26, 1–13.

Mead, G. H. The genesis of the self and social control. *Int. J. Ethics*, 1925, 35, 251–277.

Meringer, R., and K. Mayer. *Versprechen und Verlessen.* Stuttgart: Göschen, 1895.

Merkel, J. Die Zeitlichen Verhältnisse der Willensthätigkeit. *Philos. Stud. (Wundt)*, 1885, 2, 73–127.

Miller, G. A. The masking of speech. *Psychol. Bull.*, 1947a, 44, 105–129.

——. Population, distance and the circulation of information. *Amer. J. Psychol.*, 1947b, 60, 276–284.

——. Language engineering. *J. acoust. Soc. Amer.*, 1950, 22, 720–725.

——. Speech and language. In S. S. Stevens (Ed.), *Handbook of Experimental Psychology.* New York: Wiley, 1951.

——, J. S. Bruner, and L. Postman. Familiarity of letter sequences and tachistoscopic identification. *J. gen. Psychol.*, 1954, 50, 129–139.

——, G. A. Heise, and W. Lichten. The intelligibility of speech as a function of the context of the test materials. *J. exp. Psychol.*, 1951, 41, 329–335.

—— and J. C. R. Licklider. The intelligibility of interrupted speech. *J. acoust. Soc. Amer.*, 1950, 22, 167–173.

—— and J. A. Selfridge. Verbal context and the recall of meaningful material. *Amer. J. Psychol.*, 1950, 63, 176–185.

Moore, P. Motion picture studies of the vocal folds and vocal attack. *J. Speech Disorders*, 1938, 3, 235–238.

Moore, T. V. The process of abstraction. *Univ. Calif. Publ. Psychol.*, 1910, 1, 73–197.

Morgan, C. T., and E. Stellar. *Physiological Psychology* (2d Ed.). New York: McGraw-Hill, 1950.

Morris, C. W. Foundations of the theory of signs. *International Encyclopedia of Unified Science*, Vol. I, No. 2. Chicago: University of Chicago Press, 1938.

——. *Signs, Language and Behavior.* New York: Prentice-Hall, 1946.

Moses, E. R. A brief history of palatography. *Quart. J. Speech*, 1940, 26, 615–625.

Mühl, A. M. *Automatic Writing.* Leipzig: T. Steinkopff, 1930.

Negus, V. E. *The Mechanism of the Larynx.* St. Louis: Mosby, 1929.

Newman, E. B. Forgetting of meaningful material during sleep and waking. *Amer. J. Psychol.*, 1939, 52, 65–71.

O'Connor, J. *Born That Way.* Baltimore: Williams & Wilkins, 1928.

Ogden, C. K. *The System of Basic English.* New York: Harcourt Brace, 1934.

—— and I. A. Richards. *The Meaning of Meaning* (Rev. Ed.). New York: Harcourt Brace, 1947.

Ohms, H. Untersuchung unterwertiger Assoziationen mittels des Worterkennungsvorganges. *Z. Psychol.*, 1910, 56, 1–84.

Osgood, C. E. The similarity paradox in human learning: a resolution. *Psychol. Rev.*, 1949, 56, 132–143.

PEAR, T. H. *Voice and Personality.* London: Chapman & Hall, 1931.

PENFIELD, W., and T. RASMUSSEN. *The Cerebral Cortex of Man; a Clinical Study of Localization of Function.* New York: Macmillan, 1950.

PIAGET, J. *Le Langage et la pensée chez l'enfant.* Neuchâtel and Paris: Belachaux et Niestle, 1924. (Translated by M. Warden, *The Language and Thought of the Child.* New York: Harcourt Brace, 1926.)

POTTER, R. K., G. A. KOPP, and H. C. GREEN. *Visible Speech.* New York: Van Nostrand, 1947.

_____ and G. E. PETERSON. The representation of vowels and their movements. *J. acoust. Soc. Amer.*, 1948, *20*, 528–535.

QUANTZ, J. O. Problems in the psychology of reading. *Psychol. Monogr.*, 1897, *2*, 1–51.

RAZRAN, G. A quantitative study of meaning by a conditioned salivary technique (semantic conditioning). *Science*, 1939, *90*, 89–90.

_____. Semantic and phonetographic generalizations of salivary conditioning to verbal stimuli. *J. exp. Psychol.*, 1949, *39*, 642–652.

REED, H. B. Repetition and association in learning. *Ped. Sem.*, 1924, *31*, 147–155.

RIESS, B. F. Semantic conditioning involving the galvanic skin reflex. *J. exp. Psychol.*, 1940, *26*, 238–240.

_____. Genetic changes in semantic conditioning. *J. exp. Psychol.*, 1946, *36*, 143–152.

RIESZ, R. R. Differential intensity sensitivity of the ear for pure tones. *Phys. Rev.*, 1928, *31*, 867–875.

RUDMOSE, H. W., *et al.* Voice measurements with an audio spectrometer. *J. acoust. Soc. Amer.*, 1948, *20*, 503–512.

RUSSELL, B. *Introduction to Mathematical Philosophy.* London: G. Allen, 1919.

RUSSELL, G. O. *The Vowel.* Columbus: Ohio State University Press, 1928.

SACIA, C. F., and C. J. BECK. The power of fundamental speech sounds. *Bell Syst. Tech. J.*, 1926, *5*, 393–403.

SANFORD, F. H. Speech and personality. *Psychol. Bull.*, 1942a, *39*, 811–845.

_____. Speech and personality: a comparative case study. *Character & Pers.*, 1942b, *10*, 169–198.

SCHLOSBERG, H., and C. HEINEMAN. The relationship between two measures of response strength. *J. exp. Psychol.*, 1950, *40*, 235–247.

SEASHORE, R. H., and L. D. ECKERSON. The measurement of individual differences in general English vocabularies. *J. educ. Psychol.*, 1940, *31*, 14–38.

SELFRIDGE, J. *Investigations into the Structure of Verbal Context.* Honors thesis, Harvard University, 1949.

SELLS, S. B. The atmosphere effect. *Arch. Psychol.*, *N.Y.*, 1936, *29*, No. 200.

SELZ, O. *Zur Psychologie des Produktivens Denkens und des Irrtums.* Bonn: Cohen, 1922.

SHAKOW, D., and S. ROSENZWEIG. The use of the tautophone ("verbal summator") as an auditory test for the study of personality. *Character & Pers.*, 1940, *8*, 216–226.

SHANNON, C. E. A mathematical theory of communication. *Bell Syst. Tech. J.*, 1948, *27*, 379–423, 623–656.

_____ and W. WEAVER. *The Mathematical Theory of Communication.* Urbana: University of Illinois Press, 1949.

SHAW, M. E. A comparison of individuals and small groups in the rational solution of complex problems. *Amer. J. Psychol.*, 1932, *44*, 491–504.

SHERMAN, M. The differentiation of emotional responses in infants: II. *J. comp. Psychol.*, 1927, *7*, 335–351.

SHOWER, E. G., and R. BIDDULPH. Differential pitch sensitivity of the ear. *J. acoust. Soc. Amer.*, 1931, *3*, 275–287.

SILVERMAN, S. R. Tolerance for pure tones and speech in normal and defective hearing. *Ann. Otol., etc., St. Louis*, 1947, *56*, 658–677.

SIVIAN, L. J., and S. D. WHITE. On minimum audible sound fields. *J. acoust. Soc. Amer.*, 1933, *4*, 288–321.

SKINNER, B. F. Has Gertrude Stein a secret? *Atlantic Monthly*, January, 1934, *153*, 50–57.

———. The verbal summator and a method for the study of latent speech. *J. Psychol.*, 1936, *2*, 71–107.

———. The distribution of associated words. *Psychol. Rec.*, 1937, *1*, 69–76.

———. *The Behavior of Organisms*. New York: Appleton-Century-Crofts, 1938.

———. The alliteration in Shakespeare's sonnets: a study in literary behavior. *Psychol. Rec.*, 1939, *3*, 186–192.

———. A quantitative estimate of certain types of sound-patterning in poetry. *Amer. J. Psychol.*, 1941, *54*, 64–79.

———. *Verbal Behavior*. William James Lectures, Harvard University, 1947. (To be published.)

SMITH, M. E. An investigation of the development of the sentence and the extent of vocabulary in young children. *Univ. Ia. Stud. Child Wel.*, 1926, *3*, No. 5.

SMITH, M. K. Measurement of the size of general English vocabulary through the elementary grades and high school. *Genet. Psychol. Monogr.*, 1941, *24*, 311–345.

SMOKE, K. L. An objective study of concept formation. *Psychol. Monogr.*, 1932, *42*, No. 191.

SNYGG, D. The relative difficulty of mechanically equivalent tasks: I. Human learning. *J. genet. Psychol.*, 1935, *47*, 299–320.

SOLOMONS, L. M., and G. STEIN. Studies from the Psychological Laboratory of Harvard University: II. Normal motor automatisms. *Psychol. Rev.*, 1896, *3*, 492–512.

STEINBERG, J. C. Effects of phase distortion on telephone quality. *Bell Syst. Tech. J.*, 1930, *9*, 550–566.

———. Effects of distortion on speech and music. In H. Pender and K. McIlwain (Eds.), *Electrical Engineer's Handbook* (3d Ed.). New York: Wiley, 1936.

STERN, W. *Zur Psychologie der Aussage*. Berlin: J. Guttentag, 1902.

——— and A. BUSEMANN. Die Sprache der Jugend. *Z. pädag. Psychol.*, 1925, *26*, 110–112.

STETSON, R. H. Motor phonetics. *Arch. néerl. Phon. exp.*, 1928, *3*, 1–216.

STEVENS, S. S. (Ed.). *Handbook of Experimental Psychology*. New York: Wiley, 1951.

———, and H. DAVIS. *Hearing: Its Psychology and Physiology*. New York: Wiley, 1938.

STEWART, J. Q. Empirical mathematical rules concerning the distribution and equilibrium of population. *Geograph. Rev.*, 1947, *37*, 461–485.

STÖRRING, G. Experimentelle Untersuchungen über einfache Schlussprozesse. *Arch. ges. Psychol.*, 1908, *11*, 1–127.

STRAYER, L. C. Language and growth: the relative efficacy of early and deferred vocabulary training studied by the method of co-twin control. *Genet. Psychol. Monogr.*, 1930, *8*, 209–319.

SUMMEY, G. *American Punctuation*. New York: Ronald, 1949.

SYMONDS, P. M. The sentence completion test as a projective technique. *J. abnorm. soc. Psychol.*, 1947, *42*, 320–329.

TENDLER, A. C. A preliminary report on a test for emotional insight. *J. appl. Psychol.*, 1930, *14*, 122–136.

THORNDIKE, E. L. *The Teacher's Word Book*. New York: Teachers College, Columbia University, 1921.

———. *The Fundamentals of Learning*. New York: Bureau of Publications, Teachers College, Columbia University, 1932.

———. Semantic changes. *Amer. J. Psychol.*, 1947, *60*, 588–597.

———. The psychology of punctuation. *Amer. J. Psychol.*, 1948, *61*, 222–228.

——— and I. LORGE. *The Teacher's Word Book of 30,000 Words*. New York: Bureau of Publications, Teachers College, Columbia University, 1944.

THURSTONE, L. L. The relation between learning time and length of task. *Psychol. Rev.*, 1930, *37*, 44–53.

TITCHENER, E. B. *Experimental Psychology of the Thought Processes.* New York: Macmillan, 1909.

TRABUE, M. W. Completion-test language scales. *Contr. Educ.*, No. 77. New York: Bureau of Publications, Teachers College, Columbia University, 1916.

TRUBETZKOY, N. S. Wie soll das Lautsystem einer künstlichen internationalen Hilfssprache beschaffen sein? *Travaux du cercle linguistique de Prague*, 1939, *8*, 5–21.

TRUSSELL, M. A. The diagnostic value of the verbal summator. *J. abnorm. soc. Psychol.*, 1939, *34*, 533–538.

TSAO, J. C. Studies in spaced and massed learning: II. Meaningfulness of material and distribution of practice. *Quart. J. exp. Psychol.*, 1948, *1*, 79–84.

UNDERWOOD, B. J., and R. H. HUGHES. Gradients of generalized verbal responses. *Amer. J. Psychol.*, 1950, *63*, 422–430.

VERNON, P. E. The matching method applied to investigations of personality. *Psychol. Bull.*, 1936, *33*, 149–177.

VOELKER, C. H. Technique for a phonetic frequency distribution count in formal American speech. *Arch. néerl. Phon. exp.*, 1935, *11*, 69–72.

VOGEL, M., and C. WASHBURNE. An objective method of determining grade placement of children's reading material. *Elem. Sch. J.*, 1928, *28*, 373–381.

WATSON, G. B. Do groups think more efficiently than individuals? *J. abnorm. soc. Psychol.*, 1928, *23*, 328–336.

WATSON, J. B. Is thinking merely the action of language mechanisms? *Brit. J. Psychol.*, 1920, *11*, 87–104.

———. *Psychology from the Standpoint of a Behaviorist* (2d Ed.). Philadelphia: Lippincott, 1924.

WATT, H. J. Experimentelle Beiträge zu einer Theorie des Denkens. *Arch. ges. Psychol.*, 1905, *4*, 289–436.

WEGEL, R. L., and C. E. LANE. The auditory masking of one pure tone by another and its probable relation to the dynamics of the inner ear. *Phys. Rev.*, 1924, *23*, 266–285.

WEISENBERG, T., and K. E. MCBRIDE. *Aphasia.* New York: Commonwealth Fund, 1935.

WELBORN, E. L., and H. ENGLISH. Logical learning and retention: a general review of experiments with meaningful verbal materials. *Psychol. Bull.*, 1937, *34*, 1–20.

WELLMAN, B. L., I. M. CASE, I. G. MENGERT, and D. E. BRADBURY. Speech sounds of young children. *Univ. Ia. Stud. Child Welf.*, 1931, *5*, No. 2.

WERNER, H., and E. KAPLAN. Development of word meaning through verbal context: An experimental study. *J. Psychol.*, 1950, *29*, 251–257.

WERTHEIMER, M. *Productive Thinking.* New York: Harper, 1945.

WEST, H. F. Clinical studies on respiration. VI. A comparison of various standards for normal vital capacity of the lungs. *Arch. intern. Med.*, 1920, *25*, 306–316.

WHORF, B. L. Languages and logic. *Technol. Rev.*, 1941, *43*, 250–272.

WILKINS, M. C. The effect of changed material on the ability to do formal syllogistic reasoning. *Arch. Psychol., N.Y.*, 1928, *16*, No. 102.

WILLIAMS, C. B. A note on the statistical analysis of sentence length as a criterion of literary style. *Biometrika*, 1940, *31*, 356–361.

WILLIAMS, H. M. An analytical study of language achievement in preschool children. *Univ. Ia. Stud. Child Welf.*, 1937, *13*, No. 2, 9–18.

——— and M. L. MCFARLAND. A revision of the Smith vocabulary test for preschool children. *Univ. Ia. Stud. Child Welf.*, 1937, *13*, No. 2, 35–46.

WOLFLE, D. L. The relation between linguistic structure and associative interference in artificial linguistic material. *Language Monogr.*, 1932, No. 11.

WOOD, A. *Acoustics.* New York: Interscience, 1941.

WOODROW, H., and F. LOWELL.　Children's association frequency tables.　*Psychol. Monogr.*, 1916, *22*, No. 97.

WOODWORTH, R. S.　*Experimental Psychology*.　New York: Holt, 1938.

———— and S. B. SELLS.　An atmospheric effect in formal syllogistic reasoning.　*J. exp. Psychol.*, 1935, *18*, 451–460.

YULE, G. U.　On sentence length as a statistical characteristic of style in prose; with application to two cases of disputed authorship.　*Biometrika*, 1938, *30*, 363–390.

————.　*The Statistical Study of Literary Vocabulary*.　London: Cambridge, 1944.

ZIPF, G. K.　*The Psycho-biology of Language*.　Boston: Houghton Mifflin, 1935.

————.　The meaning-frequency relationship of words.　*J. gen. Psychol.*, 1945, *33*, 251–256.

————.　Some determinants of the circulation of information.　*Amer. J. Psychol.*, 1946, *59*, 401–421.

————.　*Human Behavior and the Principle of Least Effort*.　Cambridge, Mass.: Addison-Wesley, 1949.

INDEX